Joseph
Thomas

THE WEST INDIES

IN 1837

Being

the Journal of a Visit to Antigua
Montserrat, Dominica
St. Lucia, Barbados, and Jamaica

Elibron Classics
www.elibron.com

Elibron Classics series.

© 2005 Adamant Media Corporation.

ISBN 1-4021-7749-6 (paperback)
ISBN 1-4021-1836-8 (hardcover)

This Elibron Classics Replica Edition is an unabridged facsimile of the edition published in 1838 by Hamilton, Adams, & Co., London.

Elibron and Elibron Classics are trademarks of Adamant Media Corporation. All rights reserved.

This book is an accurate reproduction of the original. Any marks, names, colophons, imprints, logos or other symbols or identifiers that appear on or in this book, except for those of Adamant Media Corporation and BookSurge, LLC, are used only for historical reference and accuracy and are not meant to designate origin or imply any sponsorship by or license from any third party.

CASS LIBRARY OF AFRICAN STUDIES

SLAVERY SERIES

No. 6

General Editor   C. DUNCAN RICE
Department of History, University of Aberdeen

Published by
FRANK CASS AND COMPANY LIMITED
67 Great Russell Street, London WC1

First edition 1838
New impression 1968

THE WEST INDIES

IN

1837;

BEING THE

JOURNAL OF A VISIT TO ANTIGUA,

MONTSERRAT, DOMINICA,

ST. LUCIA, BARBADOS, AND JAMAICA;

UNDERTAKEN FOR

THE PURPOSE OF ASCERTAINING THE ACTUAL CONDITION OF THE
NEGRO POPULATION OF THOSE ISLANDS.

BY

JOSEPH STURGE AND THOMAS HARVEY.

LONDON:
HAMILTON, ADAMS, & CO. PATERNOSTER-ROW.
PRINTED BY B. HUDSON, BIRMINGHAM.
MDCCCXXXVIII.

PREFACE.

In order to explain the circumstances under which the information, detailed in this volume was acquired, it is necessary to apprize the reader, that in the course of last year, one of the individuals, whose names appear on the title page, became anxious to ascertain, by personal inquiry, the results of the Imperial Abolition Act in the British West India Colonies. To such an investigation he was impelled, not merely by the inconsistent and contradictory statements received from the West Indies, but by observing the ambiguous character of the Report of the Parliamentary Committee; a document which bears strong indications of having emanated from a tribunal, in which the accused parties were themselves judges.

Having consulted several friends, on whose judgment he could depend, and having completed the arrangements for the proposed mission, he embarked for the West Indies, accompanied by JOHN SCOBLE and THOMAS HARVEY.*— WILLIAM LLOYD, M. D. was also of the party; not as directly connected with their object, though affording his co-

---

* It may be expedient to inform the general reader, that, with the exception of JOHN SCOBLE, the whole party consisted of members of the Society of Friends. It will not, it is trusted, be considered to be obtrusive on this occasion, to introduce the following extract from a volume entitled "Christianity and Slavery; in a course of Lectures preached at the Cathedral and Parish Church of St. Michael, Barbados, by EDWARD ELIOT, B. D. Archdeacon of Barbados."—(Hatchard, 1833.) The author writes, "While the first settlers and planters in this colony, were impressed with the importance of a religious establishment, ... they appear to have been altogether regardless of the duty which devolved more

operation in carrying it into effect. The undertaking, throughout, was entirely independent of any Anti-Slavery Society. The party were not, in any sense of the word agents; but private persons, yet engaged in what was properly a public object. The expenses of the individual with whom the design originated, were defrayed by himself; and those of two others, his professed associates, were liberally borne by a few friends, who felt a deep interest in the result of the inquiry.

Soon after their arrival at Barbados, Dr. LLOYD and JOHN SCOBLE sailed for British Guiana; and the latter subsequently returned to England, being the bearer of important information respecting the present state of Slavery in the colonies comprised in that province. The present volume relates principally to Antigua and Jamaica. The first of these important islands is now a scene of new and distinct interest; as affording practical evidence of the safety and rising prosperity, consequent on immediate and complete Emancipation. Jamaica was investigated with a solicitude due to the anomalous condition of the largest negro population in the British West Indies. To these islands the public attention is thus more emphatically invited.

Should it be objected, that in the following Narrative, details of a nature, tending, in certain instances, to the discredit of personal character, have been disclosed, it may be pleaded, that such information has a most important bearing upon the great question; and that it was legitimately ac-

immediately on their ministers, but which was imperative also on themselves, of preaching or publishing the gospel to the imported African slaves. . . . . In the few instances where the endeavour was made by proprietors to christianize their slaves, according to their own belief and form of worship, the opposition to the measure was so strong, that it led to repeated prohibitory laws, some of which possess the harshest features of persecution. I allude to the pious, though unsuccessful exertions of the early colonists, of the Society of Friends. Theirs is the praise of having first attempted, amidst obloquy and suffering, to preach the gospel in this island to the heathen African slave."—(pp. 11. 12.)

quired. The object of the visitors was perfectly understood in the islands; and it was known that the results would, or might be, unreservedly published on their return. No facts, however, are stated, which were originally related on any condition of secresy; and where confidence was even implied, it has not been consciously violated. Fidelity to their object has alone directed them, in placing any of the following details on record. They are not aware that any hostile feeling has mingled itself with their better motives. It would indeed, have been far more agreeable to their feelings, to have used the language of praise, rather than of reprehension; for they entertain a warm and grateful sense of the courtesy, kindness, and hospitality, with which they were treated in the colonies, by planters, public functionaries, and ministers of religion.

How far those, who thus offer the present volume to public examination have accomplished their proposed object, is left to the decision of competent judges. In this point of view alone, they invite, and indeed claim attention. To any practised skill in literary composition, they do not pretend. It is the *subject* to which they are desirous of attracting even a nation's regard. They are actuated by an anxiety deeper than can be expressed, to awaken the public mind to its importance; and to stimulate the benevolent, the christian patriot, to lively sympathy, and to animated exertion in behalf of the oppressed.

It may surprise many to be assured, that their subsequent details are stated with moderation; and that a vast mass of facts is yet in reserve, capable, not only of confirming what is now narrated, but of deepening the shades of their darkest representations. The reader's consideration is particularly directed to the Appendix, as containing information, collected with considerable labor, and carefully compiled. The writers much regret the circumstances of haste under which this publication has been prepared. But the case admits no delay; and they, therefore, cast the fruit of their investigation, like bread upon the waters, with the

PREFACE.

hope, that a blessing may accompany it; and, that it may promote, in however small a degree, the glory of God, and the happiness of that injured, oppressed, and still enslaved portion of their fellow men and fellow subjects, who have been the objects of their labors, anxieties, and prayers.

11th MONTH, 30th, (NOV.) 1837.

We embarked at Falmouth, on board the Skylark Packet, commanded by Lieutenant C. P. LADD, R. N., on the 17th of 10th Month (October) 1836; and after a pleasant voyage, came in sight of land on the 12th of 11th Month (November.) Land was announced from the mast-head about eight o'clock a. m., and in three or four hours the dark outline of the eastern shore of Barbados was visible from the deck. We cast anchor in Carlisle Bay before midnight. On the following morning most of the passengers were on deck at sunrise; some ready to greet the familiar appearance of a well known shore, and others to receive the novel impressions of a tropical clime and country. The view of the town and Bay is very beautiful. Bridgetown extends almost from point to point, along two or three miles of a curved shore. The white houses are interspersed with cocoa-nut and palmetto trees. After leaving the vessel, we realised in our first brief hour on land, our earliest and probably our deepest impressions of the characteristic features of the country. The vegetation is wholly different from that of Europe. The larger trees are chiefly palms, and the smaller beautiful flowering shrubs. Many of the fences are composed of a gigantic species of cactus, the prickly pear. It seemed extraordinary to see the sickly exotics of an English conservatory, growing in such luxuriant vigour. Our feelings also were deeply interested in finding ourselves in the midst of a dark population. There were all shades of color, from fair mulatto to black. We could not avoid being struck with the beautiful and intelligent countenances and European foreheads of many of the colored children.

CONTENTS.

CHAP. I.
	PAGE
BARBADOS	1

CHAP. II.
VOYAGE TO ANTIGUA 9

CHAP. III.
ANTIGUA 18

CHAP. IV.
RESULTS OF EMANCIPATION IN ANTIGUA 69

CHAP. V.
MONTSERRAT 80

CHAP. VI.
DOMINICA 90

CHAP. VII.
MARTINIQUE 108

CHAP. VIII.
ST. LUCIA 119

CHAP. IX.
BARBADOS 128

CHAP. X.
BARBADOS,—GENERAL REMARKS 150

CHAP. XI.
JAMAICA 156

CHAP. XII.
JAMAICA—JOURNAL OF WILLIAM LLOYD AND THOMAS HARVEY 287

CHAP. XIII.
RESULTS OF THE APPRENTICESHIP IN JAMAICA 344

CHAP. XIV.
CONCLUSION 373

CONTENTS OF APPENDIX.

[A] ANTIGUA.

	PAGE
SECTION I.—POPULATION	i.
II.—COMMERCE AND AGRICULTURE	ii.
III.—RELIGION, MORALS AND EDUCATION	v.
IV.—LOCAL GOVERNMENT	viii.
V.—LAWS OF ANTIGUA	xi.
VI.—THE ABOLITION ACT	xiv.
VII.—THE FOUR & HALF PER CENT DUTIES	xiv.
VIII.—WASTE LANDS	xv.

[B.] DOMINICA.

SECTION I.—TABLE OF INCREASE AND DECREASE OF THE NEGROS ON VARIOUS ESTATES	xvi.
II.—LOCAL GOVERNMENT	xviii.
III.—THE LATE GOVERNOR	xx.
IV.—COMPARATIVE CONDITION OF THE NEGROS	xx.

[C] MARTINIQUE.

SECTION I.—PETITIONS OF THE COLORED PROPRIETORS FOR IMMEDIATE ABOLITION	xxii.

[D]

II.—BARBUDA	xxiv.

[E] BARBADOS.

SECTION I.—PAUPER POPULATION	xxvi.
II.—STIPENDIARY ADMINISTRATION OF THE ABOLITION LAW	xxvi.

CONTENTS OF APPENDIX. xi.

SECTION III.—SCALE OF LABOR .... xxxii.
        IV.—THE LATE GOVERNOR............ xxxiii.
        V.—APPRENTICESHIP OF FREE CHILDREN xxxiv.

[F] JAMAICA.

SECTION I.—PRISCILLA TAYLOR................. xxxv.
        II.—HALFWAY TREE WORKHOUSE ...... xxxv.
        III.—NONREGISTERED SLAVES .... xxxvi.
        IV.—STATEMENTS OF THE APPRENTICES xxxvii.
        V.—JAMES WILLIAMS .... lxviii.
        VI.—ARCADIA ESTATE. .... lxxi.
        VII.—STATISTICAL TABLES. .... lxxvi.
        VIII.—THE BAPTIST MISSION .... lxxxii.
        IX.—WILLIAM HAMILTON .... lxxxiii.
        X.—RELIGIOUS INSTRUCTION AND EDUCATION .... lxxxv.
        XI.—VALUATIONS .... lxxxvi.
        XII.—MARRIAGES OF APPRENTICES .... lxxxviii.
        XIII.—A. L. PALMER................. lxxxix.
        XIV.—COMPUTED VALUE OF "EXTRA ALLOWANCES" IN EXTRA LABOR. xcii.

CHAPTER I.

BARBADOS.

11th Month, 13th, (November) 1836.

THE SABBATH.—We took up our quarters at Lewis's Hotel. An improved state of public opinion appears to have elevated this establishment to the level of European notions of propriety. The other principal hotels in Bridgetown are reported to be a standing reproach to the morals of the colony.

The first appearance of West India houses is striking to a European. We were ushered into a spacious room, without carpet or hangings for the walls; these and many other things necessary to comfort and cleanliness in England being here almost incompatible with both. The doors and windows are usually kept wide open, and the partitions between the rooms and passages are sometimes nothing more than jalousies, or framed Venetian blinds, so that the apartments are thoroughly ventilated by the constant current of air, which tempers the heat of the climate. Glass windows also are to a great extent superfluous; the jalousies being a sufficient protection from the weather. These arrangements are of course irreconcilable with that retirement which is so justly valued in our own country.

The last few months have been unusually hot. The thermometer stood this morning at 86° in our sitting room. One of our fellow passengers, a resident for many years in the West Indies, told us he never felt it so oppressive. In the evening we went to the Wesleyan chapel, a spacious and elegant building, which was completely filled by a respectable and well-dressed congregation. The white persons appeared to be in the proportion of one in fifteen. No distinction was observed in the seats. We were much struck with the silence and complete decorum which prevailed, and with the harmony of the singing, which was led by two or three black men, one of whom we were informed occasionally officiates as a local preacher. After the service, we had an interview with the excellent missionary who occupied the pulpit. His name is MOYSTER. He was formerly stationed on the African shore, near the post now ccupied by THOMAS DOVE among the Foulahs.

14th.—We made an excursion early this morning into the interior of the island. Barbados has rather a sterile aspect towards the coast, but our route was through a district in a high state of cultivation. The land was entirely occupied by cane grounds, fields of Guinea corn, plots of yams, &c. We saw several gangs of negros at work with their hoes, under the superintendence of a driver, who having been deprived of his whip, now carries a staff as a badge of authority. The number of women seemed to preponderate. They were sufficiently clothed. Their huts are wretched little thatched hovels, crowded irregularly together. The views from the rising ground of the estates' buildings, the houses with their avenues of cocoa palms, and the boiling houses with their windmills, are often very picturesque. We called on our return at a Moravian mission station, to the minister of which, Brother KLOSE, we had a letter of introduction. He informed us that about fifteen hundred apprentices attend his chapel, of whom about one thousand are considered to be in membership. An infant school has been established on the premises. We observed some little children sitting on the steps of the schoolhouse, although it was at least an hour too early. They often come, we were told, at six o'clock, when their parents go to the field. Another schoolhouse for the older children is about to be erected, partly with aid obtained from the government grant.

In the course of the day JOHN SCOBLE and JOSEPH STURGE met by appointment the superintendent of the Wesleyan mission, and another of their ministers. They professed themselves willing to aid our inquiries " as far as was consistent with their instructions from home." In effect, those instructions appeared to us to preclude their giving information as to the physical condition of the negros. They fully confirmed our previous information of the general desire of all classes of the apprentices to learn; and said that they made the best use of the opportunities within their reach. The cost of erecting schoolhouses of simple construction, capable of accommodating one hundred children, is about £25 sterling; besides land, which averages from £30 to £50 sterling per acre. There is no general disposition on the part of the planters to encourage education. The local legislature has not yet sanctioned the legality of dissenting marriages, so that difficulties in this respect have rather increased than decreased since 1834. Another individual whom we saw to-day, informed us that the mortality among the free children had been very great since 1834, particularly in the early part of the new era. This he attributed in part to the prevalence of measles and other epidemics.

The children however had not proper attendance when sick, as their parents were usually compelled to repay the time they devoted to them. The planters expected the parents would apprentice their children, and resorted to severe measures to compel them to do so; but the mothers resisted to extremity. It was at length found that it would not do to be so hard upon mothers. Some of the planters are now considerate, others severe. A great grievance to which negros are subjected, is the practice of fining gangs in *time* for bad work. If an overseer is, or pretends to be, dissatisfied, he calls in one or two persons to look at the work, and then summons his people before the magistrate; who mulcts the whole gang, idle and industrious together, in two, four, or even eight, of their Saturdays.

It may here be mentioned, that we met in this island a missionary from Berbice, who informed us that the apprentices in that colony were in a wretched state. He considered the apprenticeship to be a complete failure. There was not and could not be a medium between slavery and personal freedom. The magistrates were in the hands of the planters. The governor was well-meaning, but very much in the dark as to the actual working of the system; as he formed his opinion on the official reports which he received. Very little is to be seen of the true state of the predial population of the colonies in or near the towns. The negros are greatly defrauded of their time. Speaking of their desire for instruction, he said many of them would gladly fetch and bring back on their shoulders, boys from his school to their own huts, a distance of three miles, in order to take a lesson from them in reading; and that they were delighted when they could obtain his permission for their little teachers to remain all night with them.

Joseph Sturge and Thomas Harvey embarked this afternoon for Antigua in the mail-boat.

Dr. Lloyd and John Scoble remained a day or two longer in Barbados before proceeding to Demerara. The following account of their visit to the jail at Bridgetown, is given by the latter.

"From the council chamber we proceeded into the jail yard, where were collected a large number of negros employed in breaking stones. The male negros are required to break thirty baskets a day—the women twenty five baskets a day. The stones are very hard and the hammers very soft; the consequence is, that it is a most laborious operation. In failure of their appointed tasks, they are flogged both male and female! This I learned on the spot. Among the women thus employed was one very far advanced in pregnancy. I was very much pleased to learn that some of the more powerful negros would break a few more baskets than their required amount, and give their surplus to the weaker, to save them a flogging. From this part of the yard we proceeded to the back of the prison to inspect the tread-mill. It was going when we reached it—fifteen male negros of different ages, from boys to men, were on it, and the cat was in constant requisition on their sides, shoulders, and legs, to keep them up to their work; and even when the miserable creatures kept step properly, if they did not *tread down* they were flogged. On the top of the tread-mill were a number of negros who secured the arms of those that were too weak to hold on by the rail. The usual time for them to be on the tread-mill is ten minutes. From the mill we proceeded to the jail. The first room we entered was about thirty by thirty-five feet, in which one hundred and ten negros are at present obliged to herd together from four in the afternoon until next morning; how they can live in such an atmosphere as must be created by so large a number of persons being congregated together in a tropical climate, I cannot tell.— The next apartment visited was about half the size. There were confined in it thirty-five males, committed for various felonies. The jailer informed me that sometimes negros were incarcerated there twelve months previous to trial, and are then discharged without it. Often when it is inconvenient for the prosecutor to appear, or he does not choose to appear, cases are adjourned to the next Sessions, a period of six months. How iniquitous a system is this! We returned back to the tread-mill. The women were then on; such a sight I never saw before; they were dressed in coarse dowlas, descending from the hips like trowsers, below the knees, and upwards to the bosom, leaving the neck exposed, fitting close round the body. The arms from below the shoulders bare, the legs bare also. The heads shaved quite close, with a handkerchief tied round them. They were up for ten minutes, and had been up during the morning four times before, and were to be put up twice after we left. No difference whatever was made between them as to the amount of punishment. When we arrived, they had been up about three minutes, and the brutal driver was flogging them with the cat with as much severity as he had previously flogged the men; he cut them wherever he listed, and as often as he pleased. We were dreadfully shocked, but determined to witness the whole proceeding. On the mill there was a mulatto woman, perhaps about thirty, dreadfully exhausted—indeed she could not step any more, although she had been on only a few minutes.

The driver flogged her repeatedly, and she as often made the attempt to tread the mill, but nature was worn out. She was literally suspended by the bend of the elbow of one arm, a negro holding down the wrist at the top of the mill for some minutes; and her poor legs knocking against the revolving steps of the mill until her blood marked them. There she hung groaning, and anon receiving a cut from the driver, to which she appeared almost indifferent. When the ten minutes were up, the negro above released her arm, and she fell on the floor utterly unable to support herself, and at last managed to stagger out of the place. Her sufferings must have been terrible. But she was not the only one who suffered. A black girl, apparently about eighteen, was equally exhausted. When we arrived, she was moaning piteously. Her moans were answered by the cut of the whip. She endeavoured again and again to tread the mill, but was utterly unable. She had lost all power, and hung, in the same helpless way with the mulatto woman, suspended by the left arm, held on by the wrist by a negro above. The bend of the arm passed over the rail, and the wrist was held down tightly, so that she could not alter her position, or get the least ease by moving. It was most affecting to hear her appeals to the driver, 'Sweet massa, do pity me—do sweet massa, pity me—my arm is broke.' Her entreaties to be relieved were answered by cuts from the whip, and threats that did she not cease to make a noise, he would have her down and flog her. The fear that he would carry this threat into execution led her to suppress her feelings as well as she could. I then engaged the attention of the driver in a conversation, and managed to place him towards me in such a position that he could not see the mill, and by a multitude of questions, occupied about two minutes of the time, until the glass had run down; thus saving the poor creature any more flogging. When let go, she sunk on the ground exhausted, but managed shortly after to crawl away from the scene of her suffering. Dr. Lloyd and I went shortly after to that part of the mill where the women are kept; the whole of them were in a state of profuse perspiration, and scarcely able to speak. We examined the legs of the mulatto woman, and found them shockingly bruised, the skin in one part about the size of a dollar torn away. The poor black girl had lost the skin off the bend of her arm, and was suffering dreadfully from the cramp. In reference to the latter female, I observed the driver cut her across the naked ancles, leaving the mark of his cat visible. I spoke a few kind words, which greatly affected them. Thus then, it appears, that in Barbados women committed to the tread-mill are catted *ad libitum*—the driver's feelings alone being the rule which governs him in the use of his scourge. During the whole time these scenes were transacting, the Barbados Legislature were holding their Sessions within thirty yards of the tread-mill."

CHAPTER II.

VOYAGE TO ANTIGUA.

11th Month, 14th, (November) 1836.

ONE of our fellow passengers is from Demerara, and has with him two negros. He informs us that he is buying out, in different Colonies, the time of such apprentices as are disposed to emigrate to Demerara.

15th.—The first island at which we touch is St. Lucia. Early this morning we were in sight of it, and also of St. Vincent, and Martinique. St. Lucia is one cluster of mountains covered to their very summits with trees and brushwood. It is impassable except on foot or horseback. The cane and coffee grounds are situated in the fertile gorges and ravines. With a telescope we could discover many of the houses of the planters, their sugar works and negro villages. The outlines of the mountains are remarkably bold; an effect partly owing to the clearness of the atmosphere. Clouds are always floating about or resting on some of the summits; but rain and mist, although frequent, are of almost momentary duration. A peculiar feature of the island are its three conical hills called the *pitons* or sugar loaves, one of which is inaccessible. The mailboat stopped for an hour at the port of Castries, which gave us an opportunity of seeing the town. Like Bridgetown it is dirty, straggling, and disagreeable. The English West India towns, judging from these specimens, are very ill constructed for the purposes of health in such a climate.

Most of the vessels we have seen have been sloops bringing supplies of cattle and mules from Porto Rico to the French and English islands. Barbados is the only considerable English colony which raises provisions and stock enough for its own consumption and for export; and to this its superior prosperity is mainly owing. St. Lucia and most of the other islands, notwithstanding their boundless fertility, are dependent to a deplorable extent on imported supplies; so that one or two successive seasons of short crops and low prices of produce occasion a general depression; as the out-goings of the planters are large and constant.

16th.—Martinique is in sight of St. Lucia. We passed the celebrated Diamond rock about sunset. This morning when we came on deck, we were in full view of the beautiful bay and town of St. Pierre. Martinique is one of the finest of the lesser Antilles. Its mountains are higher than those of St. Lucia, and it possesses also a considerable extent of fine table land, which, with the sides of the ravines, and every accessible and many apparently inaccessible spots, is brought into cultivation. We could distinguish several very numerous gangs of negros at work in the cane fields. The town of St. Pierre has an aspect of comfort and opulence. A line of tamarind trees runs along the beach. The streets are built in two or three long ranges parallel with the shore. They are shaded by the height of the houses, and kept cool by a stream of water perpetually gurgling down a stone channel in the centre. The town is abundantly supplied with this luxurious element. It is built on a narrow strip of land, which is almost overhung by mountains rising immediately behind it. The black population were well dressed and seemed to share the general prosperity. A casual visitor of the ports of these islands, where slavery prevails in its unmitigated form, might be easily misled as to the character of the system by the appearance of the population.

We reached Dominica in about four hours from St. Pierre. It presents a still bolder and more precipitous wall of mountains to the sea than Martinique or St. Lucia; and, as in those islands, many spots are cultivated, from which it is difficult to conceive how the produce can be conveyed. It is the most subject to hurricanes of all the islands, and during the last few years has suffered from the prevalence of a coffee blight. Coffee, which used to be its staple, is now being fast supplanted by sugar. We landed at Roseau about sunset, in a canoe manned by free blacks, which shot through the water at the rate of six or seven miles an hour. There were crowds of black and colored people on the beach, jabbering in their French *patois*. The little knot of whites were very angry that the mails should be landed in such confusion; and displayed a bitter spirit towards the free blacks, whom they stigmatized as thieves, brutes, skulking drones, &c. &c. The aspect of the town of Roseau is very foreign.

17th.—We were all night becalmed under the lee of Dominica. The principal ports of these islands are situated on their western or south-western coasts to the leeward, which renders the navigation from one to another, in sailing vessels, very tedious and uncertain. A breeze this morning soon carried us to Guadaloupe, but left us again under the lee of that island; so that we were some hours toiling to Basseterre.

Guadaloupe is less beautiful than Martinique, and did not appear to us so highly cultivated. The town of Basseterre is situated near its south-western extremity on extensive lowlands, sloping gradually upwards to the bases of an amphitheatre of mountains. We availed ourselves as usual of the opportunity of landing for a few minutes. The principal street is wide and enlivened by fountains. An avenue of beautiful tamarind trees runs down its whole length, under which the inhabitants meet to spend their evenings. The number of military, officers of customs, *guarda costas*, &c. to be seen here and at Martinique, marks the difference between the French colonial system and our own. We saw few white people in Guadaloupe. The prejudice against color is probably not so strong as in our own islands, as we observed several persons, white, brown, and black, working together on a tailor's board; we witnessed, however, a specimen of barbarism which we had not expected to find—several copper-colored boys in a boat in an entire state of nudity; they were of Spanish-Indian and negro blood.

18th.—We were again yesterday becalmed under the lee of Guadaloupe. To a lover of the picturesque who had no stronger impulse to carry him onward, a detention amidst this beautiful archipelago of islands would be delightful. The hills of round, conical, and irregular figures, rising abruptly from the ocean, and cleft into the most romantic gorges and ravines, are covered with perennial verdure, and clothed to their summits with primeval forest: they are evidently of volcanic origin. In St. Vincent there is still an active volcano, and in several of the other islands are hot springs and *souffrieres*. This morning we passed near Montserrat, and several of the smaller islands,

ANTIGUA.

and saw the mountains of Nevis and St. Kitt's in the distance. We at length made Antigua, and after some hours spent in tacking and beating about with a contrary wind, succeeded in entering the harbor of St. John's; which, though of difficult access, is spacious and secure. Here, as elsewhere, the black and colored population find employment in great numbers in fishing and pilot boats. We bought a quantity of fish from one of their boats, of brilliant colors, such as we have little idea of in Europe. One of them was barred with a rainbow, covered with green spots, with fins and tail painted in green and red stripes. As we approached the island, we could hear at a distance of one or two miles, the shrill, constant, ringing noise of insects and reptiles. We landed at St. John's, late in the evening.

Our fellow passenger from Demerara, above mentioned, was engaged in a traffic which has not been inappropriately termed in these islands the Demerara slave-trade. He was a man of insinuating address, well informed and intelligent, and appeared to be on terms of intimacy with persons of respectability in the different islands. He spoke of the object he was pursuing without any reserve or concealment, and even furnished us with some documentary information respecting it. He informed us that the labor of unattached predials is worth from five-sixths of a dollar to a dollar per day in Demerara. The cost of their maintenance is less than half a dollar per week. They work seven and half hours per diem for six days in the week. In answer to our inquiries how the amount of labor was ascertained which a negro could perform in seven and half hours, he said they knew pretty well " what was the most that they could get out of them."

The apprentices may leave work after the seven and half hours are out, unless they choose to work in their extra time, which they frequently do at a low rate. The estates in Demerara are generally on a larger scale than in the other colonies. One with 250 negros will yield a revenue of about £4000 sterling annually. The negros are very fond of living near town, and on this account he thinks the distant estates will have to be abandoned after 1840. The Governor, Sir J. C. SMYTH, was determined to enforce the Abolition Law, and therefore, he said, "we don't like him." He spoke highly of the liberality of the British Government in the matter of compensation. "You may depend upon it," he said, "though few like to acknowledge it, it has been the salvation of nine-tenths of us." He knew thirty or forty planters whose mortgages would have been foreclosed ere this, had not the question been settled at the time and in the way it was. He informed us that he had imported into Demerara, three cargoes of laborers, consisting either of free persons from Antigua, or apprentices, whose time he had purchased from the other colonies. They were all indented to himself for a longer or shorter period, and were principally domestic servants or handicraft laborers. He would have preferred predials, but they were more difficult to obtain. His present object is to collect eighty predial laborers at Tortola, in order to take them to Demerara. The expense of transport and maintenance averages nearly twenty dollars per head. Of the two negros who were on board, one was his personal servant, and appeared to us to be employed in the respectable vocation of a *decoy;* the other was a young man about eighteen, whose time he had purchased at Barbados for the low price of forty-eight dollars. His former master did not like him, nor he his master; indeed the youth's wish to emigrate was so strong that he had indented himself for more than the four years, yet remaining of the apprenticeship. Of the previous importations, fourteen had been obtained from Nevis, who had cost him on the average eighty dollars each; a few also from St. Kitts, where the disposition to emigrate is very great; and though at present it is successfully resisted by the planters, he thinks the island will be nearly depopulated after 1840. Besides these he had obtained laborers from Montserrat and Antigua. From two lists, with which he furnished us, of names and other particulars, it appeared that he had bought at Montserrat the term of apprenticeship of thirty field laborers and one domestic, at various rates of from fifty to one hundred dollars each. Small sums of from one to four dollars were paid to them in advance as presents, and they were indented till August 1st, 1840, under an agreement to receive two dollars per month wages. In Antigua he had induced thirty-two negros of both sexes, carpenters, sailors, house-servants, and a few field-laborers, to indent themselves for various periods of one to four years, at a rate of wages of three to seven dollars per month, and generally on higher terms after the first year. The various amounts advanced to them were to be deducted from their earnings. The indenture stipulated that the servant "shall perform all lawful hours of assiduous labor for the full term of ———years; all sick and absent days to be made good;" and that the master, besides the specified amount of wages, shall supply "food, clothing, and medical attendance, according to the usages of the colony of British Guiana." In order to obviate the inconvenience of this singularly vague document being disputed, the local authorities of Demerara have passed an ordinance declaring such agreements valid, whether executed in that or in any other British or Foreign Colony, in the presence of a magistrate or otherwise, and by any negro of the age of fifteen years or upwards. A statement of the cost of negros thus conveyed to Demerara, deducted from the profit of their labor as apprenticed field-laborers, and allowing one-fourth for casualties, shews a profit upon each of upwards of £100 sterling; an inducement sufficiently strong to give a great impulse to this revived form of the slave-trade. Our informant complained bitterly of the opposition of the authorities of Antigua. He said that the laborers of that colony were in a wretched condition; and yet those who wished to emigrate, were impeded by fictitious charges of breach of contract, and other obstacles thrown in their way by the planters.

The following occurrence, as we were entering the Harbor of St. John's, threw a little light on the sentiments of some of the colored people of that island, on this kind of emigration. A fine intelligent young man came on board, to offer us the use of his boat. Our fellow passenger, who seemed to know every body, immediately addressed him; "Do yo know * * * ?" "Yes Sir." "Where is she now?" "I dont know, sir." "Well, I can tell you; she is in Demerara." "I hope so, sir." "Now do you believe she is in Demerara, or on the Spanish Main?" "I dont know, sir; that's a delicate question, sir." In the course of the preceding dialogue, he turned to us and said, that an idea was entertained, that the emigrants were taken to the Spanish Main and sold as slaves. We do not perceive that that they have any security against being carried to

New Orleans, Cuba, Porto Rico, or some part of the Spanish Main, and there sold as slaves, other than the enormous profit which is made by the safer speculation of carrying them to Demerara, and selling them there to the highest bidder as apprentices.

CHAPTER III.

ANTIGUA.

11th Month, 20th, (November) 1836.

THE SABBATH.—We went this morning to the Moravian Chapel. The congregation consisted of from six to eight hundred black and colored persons; a large proportion of whom appeared to belong to the predial class. Their attention and silence were striking, and their dresses remarkable for neatness and simplicity. The singing and chaunting were very harmonious. In looking over a congregation of blacks, it is not difficult to lose the impression of their color. There is among them the same diversity of countenance and complexion as among Europeans; and it is doing violence to one's own feelings, to suppose for a moment that they are not made of the same blood as ourselves. There is only one white person, besides the ministers and their families, who is a member of the Moravian Church in Antigua,—JOSEPH PHILLIPS; who is known in England in connexion with the Anti-Slavery cause. There were however present several other whites; besides some who bear very slight traces, either in complexion or feature, of their African descent. After the service we were introduced to the minister, BENNET HARVEY, and to several other persons. The mission premises are rather extensive. The buildings are of wood, very complete, and nicely arranged. The grave-yard, which is undistinguished by mounds, tombstones, or monuments, is planted with cocoa nut trees, and enclosed with palings and a fence of the great American aloe. We noticed a considerable number of negros, men and women, near one of the doors of the chapel, waiting their examination as candidates for communion. Another body of them was collected about a large round building, used as a rain-water cistern, drinking the pure element from a calabash.

Antigua is dependent on the heavens for its supplies of water. There are only two or three wells in the island which are not brackish. We looked into the Sunday school. The attendance was not numerous, as the morning had been rainy. A class of little girls were called out to read to us, which they did very nicely, and answered their teacher's questions with vivacity and intelligence. In the course of the afternoon and evening, one of us attended the parish church and Wesleyan chapel. In each case, the congregation was nearly as numerous as the Moravian. They exhibited much more gaiety of dress, especially at the former; but the distinction in seats seemed to be regulated at least as much by the aristocracy of wealth as color.

22nd.—We waited this morning upon the Governor, Lieutenant Colonel LIGHT, who received us very courteously, and kindly offered his assistance in the prosecution of our inquiries. He spoke very favorably of the working of the new system, observing that the expense of cultivating estates was less than formerly, and that the laborers were more industrious. He did not however, consider that the improvement in the morals of the people was co-extensive with their opportunities of instruction. He stated that much good had been done by the Benefit Societies, formed in connexion with the different religious communities. The Governor's secretary, (pro. tem.) who introduced us, is an agreeable, intelligent, young man of color.

We afterwards visited the day school of the Moravians. There were about one hundred and sixty children present, an attendance rather smaller than the average. Part of them belonged to the infant school, which is held in a detached building, from ten o'clock till twelve, daily. They were now sitting round the room, waiting for their elder brothers and sisters, who attend school two hours later. We were disappointed to find that not more than one eighth of the children could read in the Testament. Their teacher informed us that they were very backward also in arithmetic. We saw some of their copy books, a few of which were nicely written. In conclusion, a number of the scholars recited some passages of scripture, and the whole school sung a hymn before breaking up, exercises which they performed very well. Dreadful evils are occasioned to some of these scholars, from the lax morals of *a part* of the white inhabitants of the colony. Within the last three months, three girls have left the school in consequence of having formed improper connexions with white men. The last instance was one of their most promising scholars, a girl about seventeen, who it is believed, was sacrificed by her mother for gain. The authority of parents is much greater among the negros than in Europe, and it is sometimes thus horribly abused.

On our return, we visited the cells in which criminal slaves were formerly confined. They appeared sufficiently spacious and airy, and are now occupied by offenders against the police laws. In one of them was a little colored boy, about eight years old, who had been put in for the night by one of the police; solely at the request of his mother, whom he had displeased. We learn that considerable distress prevails among the aged and infirm part of the population. When the Abolition Bill was passed, a number of these were superannuated and pensioned on the different estates; but the provision made for them is too often totally inadequate to their maintenance. We heard to-day, of a poor woman who was allowed only a *dog*, which is about three farthings sterling, per day, from the estate on which she had spent her youth and strength as a slave.

23rd.—In the course of a morning's ride, we saw many estates, and gangs of negros at work. The usual employment was digging cane-holes with the hoe, which is very severe labor. The overlookers, as the *ci devant* drivers are now called, had no sticks of office; except such of them as carried a staff, to denote that they were rural constables. One of the most intelligent negros on each estate is usually invested with this authority. Our guide, an intelligent black, told us that the people worked as well as formerly; but that many of the women did not now come into the field before breakfast, as they staid at home to prepare the morning meal for their husbands and children. In these cases they receive wages only for three quarters of a day. The huts we saw looked larger and more comfortable than in Barbados, but they are clustered together in a way that must impede ventilation, and be injurious to health. The sites of the villages are often badly chosen.

The last fifteen months in Antigua, have been a time of extreme drought, a visitation to which the island is periodically subject. The coming crop therefore will fall considerably short of an average. Many fields of canes have *arrowed,* as the flowering of the plant is technically termed; which shews that they have reached a too rapid maturity. We called in the course of the day upon JAMES COX, the Superintendent of the Wesleyan Mission, who kindly promised to give us information respecting the state of education, &c. among the members. In the course of a general conversation, he told us that he thought the most sanguine expectations of abolitionists, had been realised in Antigua. He did not think there was a man in the island who would be willing to return to Slavery. He presented us with a catechism on civil, moral, and social duties, drawn up by their missionaries, and printed by the legislature, for general circulation. On looking it over, we find that what it contains is very excellent, and largely supported by scripture quotations. Fifteen pages, however, are devoted to the inculcation of subordination, and other duties of the lower classes, and one page only to the duties of the upper classes; an inequality which we hope will disappear in future editions; as ignorance and the imperfect performance of relative duties are quite as prevalent among the latter as the former. A minister from another part of the island, who was present, informed us, in reply to our inquiries, that the old and infirm people were not supported on all the estates, and on some received but a miserable pittance. We called upon several other persons in the course of the morning. One of them gave us some interesting information respecting the passing of the Abolition Bill, by the local legislature. It appears that the proprietors of Antigua deserve less credit than they claim for this beneficent measure. It was first proposed at a meeting of proprietors, by a planter, who produced statements to shew, that under a free system he would have to pay wages to one third only of the negros whom he should be required to support as apprentices; and that he could work his estates equally well by free labor, at a less expense. The proposition excited some commotion at first. The cry was raised that he was betraying the secrets of the planters, and that if this came to the ears of government, they would get no compensation. A persuasion, however, of the superiority of the free system, gained ground in future discussions, and now the most bigoted adherents of slavery acknowledge that free labor is best and cheapest.

24th.—We called this morning upon a gentleman who had kindly introduced himself, and offered to give us information on the cultivation of the island. He is the Town Agent for a large number of estates, and a resident of thirty years standing. His intelligence, experience, and piety, give great weight to his statements. He furnished us with calculations and comparative statements, to which we shall have hereafter occasion to allude. We called subsequently at the mission station of the brethren; where we found brother MORRISH from the interior. While we were sitting with them, an old man came for relief. He was a member of their church; and appeared to be upwards of eighty years of age, and quite blind. He said that he was allowed only six pints of corn-meal a week from the estate, and that last week he did not get even that. These poor and destitute persons are relieved in part, out of a sum annually supplied by some charitable persons in London, who are unconnected with the island, and of whom Bennet Harvey is the almoner; and in part also out of the funds of two Benefit Societies in St. John's, existing in connection with the Moravian Church. These institutions, one of which is composed of town and the other of country members, are formed like the English Friendly Societies, for the purpose of securing a fund available for the members in sickness and old age. The setting aside a portion of the fund for the benefit of those who do not contribute to it, is however, a feature of benevolence peculiar to the subscribers. Besides administering casual relief, the committee of the Town Benefit Society have established a hospital on the mission premises, consisting of a number of small, moveable, wooden houses, in which are supported twelve persons who are unable to work, from age or disease. We went to see this interesting establishment. Several of its inmates are afflicted with the dreadful diseases of leprosy and elephantiasis; their loathsome condition cannot shut them out from the active and benevolent sympathies of a society, whose members were nearly all slaves three years ago. On our return we visited the Jail, and House of Correction, which consist of contiguous buildings and premises; twenty eight are now waiting their trial, of whom twelve are for sheep-stealing which is felony. Of minor offences, cane stealing or breaking, constitutes a very large proportion. Of the prisoners who are undergoing punishment, about eighty are employed in a penal gang on the public roads. They do not work in chains, with the exception of five or six whose sentences of death have been commuted; and require only a very slight superintendence. The refractory are punished by being put upon the tread-mill on their return at night. Some petty offenders were breaking stones in the court yard. We observed a little boy of eight years old, who was committed, as we afterwards learned, for stealing a single cane, whilst passing through the fields on his way to town on an errand. For this he was sentenced to pay a fine of seven dollars, and in default of payment, to imprisonment and hard labor. Not to speak of the impolicy of making a criminal of such a child as this, the fine imposed is equivalent to his earnings for about three months, and is about a hundred and twenty times more than the value of the property stolen. The situation of these buildings is very cool and airy, and the rooms are spacious and clean. The prisoners are usually allowed nine-pence currency per diem for their support, which in consideration of the present scarcity has been increased to ten-pence, which is laid out for them by the superintendent. A chapel has recently been fitted up in one of the upper rooms, in which service is performed by the Rector of St. John's, early in the morning of the Sabbath.

We had a conversation in the evening with two of the Moravian missionaries; to whose society nearly half the laboring population of the island belongs. About nine-tenths of their people are negros. They are members by birthright, unless they forfeit their privileges by misconduct; but all are actually under the superintendence and religious care of the missionaries. The chapels are not sufficiently numerous to hold all their members; who are therefore compelled to attend, as it were, on alternate Sabbaths. Not more than two or three of their people are qualified to assist them in their schools. Infant schools, in their opinion, are much better calculated than any other institutions to raise the character of the next generation;

as well as, by bringing them up together from childhood under the same course of discipline, to extinguish the prejudice of caste, which exists between the colored and black population. The disposition of the negros is decidedly pacific; yet the Christmas following the 1st of August, 1834, was the first for thirty years that had been celebrated without the proclamation of martial law. Since emancipation ten or twelve *riotous fellows*, as they were termed, have been known to be carried to jail by a single constable. The 1st of August, 1834, was a day of deep and solemn religious observance. The Moravians are the only body who have thrown open their chapels on the subsequent anniversaries of that glorious day, many of the proprietors having set their faces against its celebration.

25th.—Our attention has been called to the mischief resulting from the non-recognition of the validity of marriages by Dissenting Ministers. An obsolete local Act, of the date of 1692, imposes a penalty upon any minister, not qualified according to the regulations of the Church of England, who shall celebrate the marriage ceremony. Other Acts also exist, which forbid the intermarriage of slaves and free persons; and discourage the marriages of slaves with each other. About twenty years ago, these acts began to be generally disregarded by the missionaries. From 1804 to 1834, the number of marriages of slaves registered at the Moravian Mission in St. John's, was nine hundred and four, and the number of divorces ten. Their example and that of the Wesleyans, were followed by the present Rector of St. John's, and subsequently by the other established clergy. The Emancipation Act having given the Establishment the power of receiving fees for the marriage of negros, and the ceremony having acquired a *civil* character, affecting the legal union of the parties, and the rights of inheritance of their children, the dissenting ministers received an intimation that they must discontinue marrying; which they have done accordingly. One evil consequence resulting from this state of things, is to discourage marriage ; as the fees of the clergy are heavier than the negros can always afford to pay. It is right however to add, that the excellent incumbent of the Metropolitan parish has made both marriage and burial fees, a free will offering, and his example has been followed by at least one other clergyman. The following relation forcibly illustrates the glaring evils which result from the nonvalidity of what are called sectarian marriages ; a question which the Act of Emancipation has raised into importance. Many years ago, a free black woman purchased a colored slave, gave him his freedom, and was married to him by a Wesleyan minister. The 1st of August, 1834, was in his estimation a day of *general release,* even from the connubial bond; and he proceeded to take another and younger wife of his own complexion. A license was obtained ; but the clergyman, being timely apprised of the facts, refused to perform the ceremony ; legal proceedings were threatened; but at length the parties paid a visit to a neighbouring foreign colony, and after a short absence, returned to Antigua—*married.* It is said, that other persons, similarly circumstanced, were waiting the result ; whose wishes were only defeated by the firmness of the established clergy. In other instances, we are informed, the parents of numerous families have taken advantage of the law, to dissolve their unions of many years duration. In some of the colonies also, and even in Antigua, proprietors have been found capable of taking advantage of the non-recognition of marriages, to forbid husbands and wives, resident, as is generally the case, on different estates, from visiting each other in their hours of rest and recreation.

We visited this morning the Methodist infant school. There were one hundred and thirty children present, of from two to seven years of age, and of every color; three or four white, twenty or thirty black, and the rest of every intermediate shade of complexion. Some of them repeated to us their usual rhythmical exercises, and a class of them read very nicely in the 5th Chapter of Matthew; the whole sung a hymn at the conclusion; the faces of the children were expressive of happiness and intelligence. The school appeared to be in an efficient state, and we thought it would bear comparison with the average of infant schools in England. The teachers were two colored young women.

26th.—We went this morning through the market, which was largely attended. Almost every sort of eatable commodity was exposed for sale; fruit, fish, meal, besides bundles of sticks and grass, cotton prints, &c. &c. The scene was a highly animated one, but the proceedings were conducted with great order. Previously to the Abolition of Slavery, the market was principally supplied by the agricultural peasantry, with articles of their own raising; but now this class are more generally buyers than sellers; and a large proportion of the merchandise is of foreign growth or manufacture. The increase of trade thus created, is one consequence of the payment of labor in wages. A Police Act came into operation about a fortnight ago, which affords an illustration of the new forms in which oppression will learn to exhibit itself in the

West Indies; one of its clauses prohibits country people from bringing their goods to market without a pass from the manager of the estate on which they reside. Unless they are provided with this pass, the police seize and confiscate their property, whether it be produce, poultry, or other stock of their own raising, or grass and wood collected on the estate, by the manager's permission. We had a long talk to-day with a negro, introduced to us by a friend as one on whose veracity we might depend. He appeared to be a serious, respectable man. The substance of his statement was, that their wages of one shilling currency, a day, (about five-pence halfpenny sterling,) were not sufficient to maintain them. He had a wife and six children, and an old mother to support; of whom, two of the children only were able to earn any thing. They could not manage without "minding" their little stock. He said that if a laborer was five minutes after time in the morning, the manager stopped his pay for the day. He complained also that he had just received thirty days notice to quit, because he refused to allow one of his children whom he wished to put to a trade, to go to the field, although he promised that all his other children should be brought up to estate labor. Men are sometimes taken before the magistrate and fined for trespass, for visiting their wives, living on different properties. In conclusion, however, as the laborers could not now be locked up in the dungeon and flogged, the change in their circumstances was yet as he emphatically expressed it, "Thank God, a great deliverance from bondage."

27th.—We went this morning to the Moravian Chapel. Several of the brethren reside at the station in St. John's. The one who occupied the pulpit to-day was a German; and his discourse was nearly unintelligible to us. The propriety of sending any but English missionaries to labor in our West India Colonies may well be doubted, unless the German brethren possess the faculty of easily acquiring a new language, in addition to the evangelical zeal and piety, which doubtless many of them do possess. A gentleman of great intelligence, and long resident here, remarked to us to-day, that the people have improved much in dress and general appearance, since Emancipation. The very features of the negros have altered within his memory, in consequence, as he believes, of their elevation by education, and religious instruction. Their countenances express much more intelligence, and much less of the malignant passions. A belief in the Obeah, and other superstitions, is not quite worn out even among the members of churches. Fears of poisoning used to be common among cruel masters and managers. Such would lock up the filtering apparatus which supplied them with water, and commit the key to a favorite slave. Others, would employ none but hired servants in their houses, not daring to trust their slaves. We visited the Wesleyan Sunday school in the course of the day. There were upwards of three hundred children present, of various ages, and of all shades of color. The school appeared to be in an efficient state, and was conducted in its various classes by a large number of teachers; all of whom were black or colored young men and women. The children as usual, looked happy and animated. Their bodily and mental faculties, certainly appear to be more rapidly developed, than in our colder climate; a circumstance which renders the extensive introduction of the infant system, into the West Indies a matter of the most urgent importance.

28th.—We left St. John's this morning, on a little journey into the interior, being kindly invited to Newfield, one of the stations of the Brethren. We called on our way on a planter, residing on his own estate, who is also a clergyman of the established church, and has built a little chapel of ease over his boiling house, in which he preaches to his people on the Sabbath. He informed us, that he had formerly two hundred slaves, of whom about one hundred and fifty of all ages were employed. He has now one hundred on his pay list, including children; and the cultivation of his estate is kept up as well as before, the deficiency being supplied by the introduction of the plough. It was not unfrequent formerly to have twenty or thirty at a time in the sick-house. Sham sickness has now entirely disappeared; as the laborers suffer by the loss of time themselves. One of the chief disadvantages of the new system, resulted from the idea of degradation attached to field labor. On this account he never took his domestics, as formerly from the field; because if they did not please him in their new capacity, they invariably refused to return to their agricultural labor. Speaking of the general question of Emancipation, he said, that he preferred the free system for himself, because he could employ many or few hands as he pleased. The expense of working estates was, he believed, about the same as before. On the whole perhaps, there had been an improvement in the moral condition of the people. There were no such outbreaks now, of the malignant passions as were frequent formerly. Things were managed with much less discomfort to the proprietor on this account. He observed that Antigua presented the only instance of a body of agricultural slaves, being emancipated without being made to pass through a transition state. It was in the power of the proprietors to revert to such a state, and it might be desirable to do so by giving the people their houses and grounds *on lease,* on condition of their paying a rent of so many days labor in the year. *This would attach them to the soil.* We proceeded from thence to Newfield. In the course of the day, our kind host, Brother Morrish, accompanied us to several of the neighbouring plantations. The first gentleman to whom he introduced us, who had always been esteemed an indulgent master, carried us to see his negro village, part of which has been rebuilt, and otherwise improved, since 1834. The houses are now very comfortable; consisting of one, and sometimes two rooms, of from ten to fourteen feet square, and kept very clean, a few of which are furnished with a four-post bed, and other household goods. Each kitchen is a little detached shed, thatched, and without chimney, apparently so ill adapted to culinary processes, that it is difficult to imagine how the villages escape an occasional conflagration. The huts are also thatched with cane-trash, thrown on in a very slovenly manner, but the interior roof is constructed of strips of palm leaves neatly plaited. In one which we entered, a young woman was sitting on the ground, with a very young child in her lap, which had on an obi necklace of horsehair, because its neck was "limber," as she expressed it. The minister took off the necklace, and spoke to her very appropriately on her sinful habits and superstition. She was not married.

We made inquiries of this gentleman respecting the comparative cost of cultivation under the present and former system, and subsequently received two letters from him on that subject. He was unable to furnish us with a statement in figures; but he believed the cost of working his two estates under the new system was greater than before, as they had always been full handed, and used to raise annually a supply of provisions sufficient for six or ten months' consumption. On the average of estates he did not think that the free system was dearer than slavery. He observed that there had not been even " moderately good weather" since emancipation, so as to give it a fair trial in other respects; but he fears that it will be found difficult to take off an abundant crop within the usual time.* Another planter whom we called upon told us that the people gave him much less trouble than before emancipation. He mentioned one estate in the island which had netted £5000 sterling this year; he thought, therefore, the free system must answer for some parties. In the evening, we had an interesting opportunity of observing the manner of exercising the discipline of the church amongst the Brethren, which convinced us that a real oversight is maintained over their large body of members. Certain evenings in the week are set apart for the members to come to have "a speaking" with the minister; and the arrangements are such that the whole pass before him once in six or eight weeks, and receive advice suitable to their condition. There is also, on each estate, a religious negro called a "helper," who watches over the members, and brings all delinquencies and disputes before the minister. Several cases were thus brought before him this evening. Two were of a serious character; the individuals being ac-

* We have found that many planters participate in this belief; but we are happy to add, that, on the few estates which were favored last year with good weather and a large crop, these fears have not been realized.

cused of living with women to whom they were not married:—their sentences were, to be put out of the church. Another case was that of a husband charged with beating his wife:—sentence, suspension. These decisions are taken to the monthly conference of the missionaries for confirmation. The addresses of the minister to the offenders were affectionately solemn and appropriate; and appeared to produce a deep impression. The people are more in fear of the church discipline than of legal punishment; and some planters employ the authority of the minister, rather than that of the magistrate, in enforcing due discipline and subordination on their estates.

29th—We went after breakfast to see a part of the Mission property; which has been let off in little plots to laborers on adjoining estates, who esteem it a privilege to tenant them; though they receive no equivalent increase of wages, in lieu of the hut and ground which they would otherwise occupy on the estate. The rent is six shillings currency, (two shillings and eight-pence sterling) per month for a cottage, and a quarter of an acre of land. One boy of fifteen, who has an aged mother to support, applied for a piece of land; and, when the minister hesitated, said "O massa, I can manage to pay the rent." He immediately set about clearing it with great spirit; and has now got it into nice order, and part of it planted with yams. The free cottage system has been tried to a small extent in one or two other places; and hitherto with complete success. At present, however, excepting in the towns, there are perhaps, not fifty independent cottages in the island. A part of the mission land has been also appropriated to the children of Brother MORRISH's infant school, who have little gardens to cultivate in their spare time. They are thus brought up to associate pleasurable instead of painful ideas with agricultural employments. We called in the course of this morning upon the Rector of the parish, (St. Philip's) with whom we had an interesting conversation on the state of education. His statements confirmed our own observation, that the island possesses schools in abundance, but that many of the teachers are inefficient, and that a normal school is greatly needed. Speaking of the state of agriculture, he observed that he had always understood from the conversation of proprietors and attorneys that the free system was less expensive than slavery, and that property was increased in value. A grazing estate of one hundred and ninety-six acres, the half of which was offered two years ago to a gentleman of his acquaintance for four hundred pounds, was then about to be sold by auction, and was expected to fetch not less than two thousand pounds. This estate we subsequently ascertained was sold for two thousand six hundred pounds. He related an anecdote to us of a negro, who was employed to bring some wine from St. John's, to a house eleven miles distant. The price agreed upon was one dollar and a half, for the whole quantity of fifteen dozen; which he earned by making two journies a day, equal to forty-four miles; bringing one dozen and a half upon his head each time. We afterwards paid our respects to Dr. NUGENT, the speaker of the House of Assembly; who resides in this neighbourhood. He received us very courteously; and, with characteristic liberality and candor, consented to give us information on the various subjects in which we expressed an interest. Another planter, whom we called upon on our way to Willoughby Bay, gave us a most encouraging account indeed of the success of freedom. Before 1834, there were one hundred and ten slaves on the property, of whom he could sometimes scarcely muster seventeen or twenty in the field. Their average weekly expense of clothing and allowances was twenty-seven pounds. He has now double the amount of effective labor; namely fifty-seven persons whose wages amount only to fifteen pounds weekly.* The estate derives a considerable profit also from the sale of ground provisions to the laborers. He observed to us that the other colonies would have done well to have followed the example of Antigua; but complained bitterly of the small thanks they had received from the Home Government. It appears to be a general sentiment here that Antigua is in disgrace at the colonial office in consequence of the rejection of the apprenticeship. We called at Willoughby Bay upon Charles Thwaites, the venerable father of education in Antigua. He has lived thirty-nine years in the island, the last twenty of which have been devoted to this work. We visited with him a large school of one hundred and twenty children; of whom only twenty are in the alphabet class. The rest can read in one or two syllables; and some of them in any part of the Bible. The principal teacher, a negro young man, governed the school, we were told, successfully, and in the spirit of love: yet it appeared to us that he taught the children rather by rote than intelligently. The children spelt correctly; and were quick in reply to scripture questions proposed by ourselves, or C. Thwaites. In the evening we proceeded to Grace Hill, another Moravian station, where, though entire strangers, we were kindly received by

---

* See Appendix A. Sec. II.

the Brethren BAYNES and MILLER. We esteem it a privilege to be permitted to witness the good which the missionaries are doing. Harmony, simplicity, and love, appear to reign in their households, and shine forth in their conduct and conversation. We heard to day a distressing account of a poor man, who was starved to death. He was unable to work; and had been detected stealing canes, to which he was probably impelled by hunger; as he had no allowance from the estate on which he lived. He ran away for fear of punishment, and was found dead in the open country at some distance from home. The most painful feature in the state of Antigua at the present moment is the destitute condition of the old and infirm, owing to the absence of a legal provision for them, and to the present distress from the long period of drought.

30th.—At Grace Hill the missionaries are about to let off a part of the mission property on the cottage system, as at Newfield. A considerable portion also of a neighbouring estate has been sold in acres, and half-acres, to the laborers; who have built cottages thereon for themselves, and still continue to work on the adjoining properties. The price paid has been thirty-five dollars per acre, and six dollars for the conveyance. We left early this morning for English Harbor. One of the Brethren kindly accompanied us as far as Falmouth; where he introduced us to Dr. MURRAY, whose lady has established an interesting infant school of about thirty children. They read and spelt pretty well, and were neatly dressed. The Doctor confirmed a statement we have frequently heard; that there has been a great decrease of sickness on the estates since Emancipation. On our way to English Harbor, we were overtaken by a gentleman who invited us to accompany him to the police office, where he was going to preside as a magistrate. We staid there several hours. The cases disposed of were nearly as follows:—1. A young woman, with an infant in arms, charged with going to town to market on Monday, after having been refused leave. Sentenced to pay one dollar to the estate. A fee of half a dollar is due to the treasury on each complaint; which is paid by the complainant, where the charge is not sustained; otherwise by the defendant, in addition to any other fine which may be imposed. Until very recently the magistrate was entitled to receive a fee of six shillings currency, (two shillings and eight pence) from complainants who did not sustain their charge; or twelve shillings from defendants on conviction. This gave rise to great abuses and oppressions till the fees were happily abolished by a recent act of the legislature. The defendant in the above instance paid the money in court, and immediately gave her manager thirty days notice to quit.—2. A young man charged with breaking forty-eight canes—fined three dollars to the treasury, and four to the estate. The amount was paid by his mother.—3. A man charged with stealing canes and corn, on an estate different to the one on which he lived; the watchman of that estate with connivance; and a girl with receiving part as a gift. The case against the watchman was dismissed; the girl admonished and directed to pay the treasury fee; and the principal offender sentenced to pay seven dollars as in the preceding case. There was no one to advance the money for him, and he was therefore sent to hard labor in the House of Correction for three months. He burst into tears on hearing the sentence. 4. An old man charged with stealing yams and cane-trash. He

was in the weeding gang at nine-pence per diem (fourpence sterling.) He had been sick for a week, during which he received no pay, and was compelled by hunger to take the yams to eat, and the cane-trash to boil them—fined one dollar to the estate. The manager advanced the treasury fee for him, and is to stop the amount from his wages. He acknowledged the defendant was very attentive to his work. It appears evident to us, that, in this deplorable case, want was the exciting cause of the offence. The penalty, if exacted, will be wrung from his bare means of existence.—
5. Two girls charged with trespass—The case against one of them was not sustained, as she had not been warned off the property. The other was admonished and dismissed, on payment of the usual fee to the treasury. The complainant was directed to pay the same fee for the other case; but this was not finally insisted on. He appeared surprised and dissatisfied, and said in an under tone, to the magistrate, that Mr.———(his employer) expected the girl would have been fined five pounds.—6. Several other cases of cane breaking were disposed of in a similar manner to the preceding. One woman, with an infant in arms, was fined a dollar for having a single cane in her possession. The Superintendent of Police, who acted as clerk, told us that taking canes was a temptation the negros could scarcely resist. They had been accustomed to do so from childhood; and little notice was taken of it during slavery The preceding cases, besides others not affecting the predial class, were disposed of summarily, without cross examination. The culprits had no adviser, and often could scarcely make themselves understood. The fines in most cases appeared to us excessive, bearing no proportion to the value of the pro-

perty destroyed. No allowance was made on account of the high price of provisions, and the low rate of wages; and none for the ancient custom and almost recognised right of the negro to take canes for their own consumption. No moral admonition was bestowed upon them—no remark on the sin of stealing. The penalty was the only motive held out to them, to act differently in future. The complaining overseers displayed a bitter and overbearing spirit towards the people. The fines appeared, when paid, to be raised by general contribution, amongst the friends of the defendants, and must be a heavy drain upon their resources. We were shewn, at the Police Office, the orderly book of the parish. The vestry are chosen by the freeholders, with power to tax the parish for the payment of the clergy, repairs and expenses of the church, relief of the poor, &c. They do not appear to extend relief to worn-out field-laborers. Subsequently we visited a large school under the care of the Established Church, which did not seem to be efficiently conducted. We went also to see the "Refuge for Female Orphans;" an interesting and most useful institution, which is dependent on the English "Ladies Society." It was declining for want of attention, its chief support had been Mrs. GILBERT, an excellent lady of color, now dead. Falmouth and English Harbor, though called towns, are scarcely worthy of the name. Each of them is situated on a small but very beautiful bay. On our way back to St. John's, we met several negros of whom we inquired respecting the change in their condition. They acknowledged that it was much improved. "Thank God," said one, "we are a hundred times better off than before." The particular amelioration which they chiefly dwelt upon was, that they could not be flogged. They complained, however, that it was hard for a man who had a family, to live on one shilling a day. They were all members of churches. It is not difficult to tell by a negro's countenance, whether he is in Christian communion. Those at the Police Office were evidently of the "baser sort," and one of the magistrates acknowledged to us, that it was not common for a Moravian to be brought before them.

12th Month, 1st, *(December.)*—One of us went this morning to attend the sitting of the House of Assembly. In the lobby he was introduced to the Chief Justice of the island, who said, in the course of a few minutes' conversation, that it was not to be supposed, that crime had really increased because there were now heavy calendars. Cases came before the magistrate, which were formerly decided by the masters. The peaceable and orderly conduct of the people had exceeded his anticipations; and there was no one he believed, who would deny, that the general result of Emancipation had more than equalled his expectations. From twelve to eighteen members were present at the assembly to-day. One of the most animated debates, was on the state of a piece of road. The way-wardens had requested the visiting magistrate to employ the criminal gang to repair it, which they refused, on the ground that it would be injurious to the health of the prisoners. A petition was presented against the decision by an hon. member, himself the chief party interested. He acknowledged that the place was malarious, but said that to employ voluntary labor at a high rate upon the improvement of it, " would be detrimental to the whole planting interest." It was a work of necessity, and the health of prisoners ought not to be considered, before that of the peaceable and orderly peasantry. To this it was replied, that the prisoners were condemned to imprisonment and hard labor, and not to sickness and death. They had no change of clothes, and would have to be shut up together at night to resist the influences of the malaria, under the most unfavorable circumstances. As, however, it was a work of necessity, it would be perfectly justifiable to employ voluntary labor upon it; and it was well known *that men would undertake any thing for money.* Though a good deal was said on the inconveniences likely to result from the employment of laborers at a higher rate than one shilling a day, the discussion on the whole was highly creditable to the House; and the question was finally decided in favor of the prisoners. It was stated in the course of the debate, that the negros are much more careful of their health than formerly. They did not use to mind working in the rain, but now a shower sends them flying in all directions for shelter. A letter was read to the House, from their agent in London, on the subject of a severe despatch of Lord GLENELG, against the late House of Assembly, in the matter of a recent quarrel with the Government.

The Agent said, that the despatch in question could not have proceeded from the amiable mind of his Lordship, but "appeared to emanate from the invariable atmosphere of the colonial office." He quoted the parody of the Morning Post, on Lord GLENELG, "*nul lem quod tetigit non damnavit;*" and said, he did not believe his Lordship had written, or even that he had ever read the dispatch in question; and he exhorted the House not to rest satisfied with having made out such a clear case in their reply to it; but to cause Lord GLENELG "to wince," by publishing to the world, a series of stringent resolutions on his conduct.

A petition was presented for the cleansing of a pond which supplied the town of English Harbor with water. The hon. member stated, that the old act had become obsolete, which provided that these ponds should be kept in order by contribution from the different estates of slave labor, which "had now happily ceased to exist." Another gentleman proposed, that as these ponds were equally for the benefit of rich and poor, that the laboring classes should be taxed to contribute their quota towards this object, either in labor or money. He complained that they required higher wages for such labor, than the regular rate of one shilling a day. A letter of thanks was read from JAMES COX, on behalf of the Wesleyan missionaries, for the grant of a piece of ground, in St. John's, for the erection of a new chapel and school. The proceedings were concluded by the reading of several bills, not of general interest.

2nd.—To-day was the commencement of the Grand Sessions of the Court of King's Bench. The business was begun amidst some disorder and confusion; the witnesses, prisoner, prosecutor, jurors and judges, speaking and asking questions indiscriminately. In one of the indictments were several mistakes of dates and places, which would probably have quashed the proceedings in an English Court. The witnesses usually gave their testimony in a clear, straightforward manner, without being prompted by interrogatories. The sentences were lenient; in which respect they differed much from the decisions of the magistrates at the police court of English Harbor. We called in the evening upon R. HOLBERTON, the Rector of St. John's, who is deeply interested in the condition of the negro population, and a most active and zealous supporter of schools and other institutions for their benefit. He told us that when he came from St. Vincent's, eight years ago, he was much struck with the superiority of the Antigua negros, in aspect, dress, and manners.

3rd.—We attended this morning the Police Office in St. John's. The cases were principally for assault and battery, and breach of contract; with recriminatory complaints of abuse, disorderly conduct, &c. The decisions of the magistrates were just and impartial, and the penalties lenient. Some of the cases were serious; others of a very trifling character. The appeal to the magistrate, is a privilege, of which perhaps the emancipated portion of the community avail themselves on too trifling occasions. This remark does not however, apply to the agricultural population; in their case a counterpart observation may be made on their superiors.

We called in the afternoon at the mission station of the Brethren. The minister was engaged in receiving and paying money, on account of his Benefit Societies. In addition to the sums disbursed for sickness, one man received a dollar for a sheep, which had died, and another, half a dollar for a pig; a new example of the modes in which the principle of mutual assistance is carried out in these generous institutions. We went afterwards to the school-room, where we found the teacher engaged with three or four negros, whom he teaches to write on the Saturday. They were fine intelligent men. One of them told us, that notwithstanding the hard times, and dearness of provisions, "he praised God every day for freedom." On the estate on which he lived, the people were never taken before the magistrate, or their wages checked, unless there was cause for it. The old people, however, were not supported; he and his brother had to maintain their aged mother. He complained too, that they could not take their property to market without a pass, which was never required from them during slavery. He acknowledged they did not work quite so hard as before, unless they received some extra indulgence or gratuity. Another of the men gave us similar testimony. We explained to them the principle of Savings' Banks, of which they appeared perfectly to comprehend, and appreciate the advantages. These institutions would be an invaluable auxiliary to the Friendly Societies. We had an opportunity in the course of the evening, of conversing with several other negros. The first was formerly on an estate of Sir C. B. CODRINGTON, and left it when freedom came, because he used to be flogged when a slave. On that estate the first gang, which then numbered one hundred and fifty, now musters only fifty. He complained of the low rate of wages. Another negro, an intelligent man upwards of sixty years old, told us that on the estate on which he lived, the manager broke up the provision grounds of the people, the week before August, 1834. He was a driver on the estate, but since they became free, he had been compelled to sell his stock, and quit the estate with his family, on account of the harsh treatment which he received from the manager; he has since been employed in tending the cattle on another property, at ninepence currency, (four-pence) per day. Although this old man had suffered in his circumstances by the change, yet even he laughed at the idea of preferring slavery to freedom. He gave us a graphic description of the severe labor of the boiling house in times past,*

* An intelligent manager observes, "As regards the mode of remuneration for night work, however the manager's sense of justice

continued through the night to the second crowing, or even till day-break. If there was not enough syrup produced, he used to be flogged for not flogging the firemen, and other negros, in the boiling-house ; or if the supply of canes slackened at the mill, the field driver was flogged for not flogging the cane cutters. On being asked if he would prefer slavery if the King gave orders that they should have their former allowances, and be in other respects on their former footing, without being liable to be flogged : he said " the King might order, but the King no know what they do." He seemed fully sensible of the advantage of being able to change masters. A female whom we saw was one of Lord CRAWFORD's slaves, emancipated under his will in 1832. After being made free, she continued to work in the field at the rate of seven shillings and sixpence currency, (three shillings and four-pence,) for five days labor per week, besides all the slave allowances of food and clothing. After August 1834, her wages were reduced to one shilling a day; when she left the plantation and came to get her living in town. Most of Lord CRAWFORD's people continued to work in the field after they became free.*

and right might have operated in favor of the laborer, the principle of *claim* to remuneration was not admitted. In general, however, I think it was afforded in a greater or less degree. An extra quart of meal, or yams, &c. and a *"little syrup,"* (i. e. three or four pints) was the most that was desired, and not unfrequently obtained by the persons immediately about the mill. The poor field workers used to fare much worse on those estates, where, want of means and mismanagement, rendered their attendance necessary to procure fuel, so long as the boiling continued. They seldom received more than as much hot liquor as they pleased to drink, for their extra work."

* It has always been asserted by the advocates of slavery, that emancipated negros invariably forsook estate labor. This is a fact in contradiction to that statement. Undoubtedly the greater num-

ANTIGUA.

4th.—THE SABBATH.—We went in the morning to the parish church, which is a spacious and elegant building, and on this occasion, filled with a congregation of about fifteen hundred persons. We are informed that distinctions of color are manifestly less observed within its walls than they were a year ago. It appears to be the custom of the upper classes to attend public worship; and the general observance of the Sabbath in the island is very exemplary.

5th.—We spent the greater part of the day with Dr. NUGENT, who very kindly gave up his time to us. The subjoined memoranda are a correct, though incomplete representation of the valuable information he communicated. We assure ourselves that he will not object to be cited as a witness to the favourable results of that great measure, of which he was one of the ablest and most earnest supporters. He is of opinion that under the free system the saving is great in those cases where the slaves were supported entirely on imported supplies, and less where they were fed on rations of ground provisions grown upon the estate. Different estates grew provisions for various periods of two, four, eight or ten months; the average being about five months. In the latter instances, the annual cash outlay would be greater than before; but on the average of the whole island, he believes the saving under the

ber used to seek out some other employment, upon which the stigma of degradation was less deeply impressed. In but few instances, even when willing, would they have been allowed to continue on the estates as field laborers. In all slave countries, however, freedom is a kind of patent of nobility; and hence the lowest order of free persons, both white and black, being too proud to labor, are usually more wretched and degraded than the slaves themselves. It is an error to suppose that the baleful influences of slavery are limited to the unfortunate class who are its immediate victims.

present system, to be considerable. One important economical reform was introduced the year before emancipation, by the repeal of the "Deficiency Law," which required a white man to be maintained on each estate for every forty slaves, under a penalty of thirty pounds a year. Two white women were considered equivalent, for the purposes of this Act, to one man. Many estates paid two, four, or more *deficiencies*. This partial and oppressive tax also prevented the employment of colored overseers, who are now gradually re-placing the whites, at a reduction of salary of about twenty pounds a year each. A purchasing and consuming population is beginning to be formed within the island itself. The sale of ground provisions to their laborers is already become a source of profit to estates. A negro will sometimes go the store-keeper to buy a gallon of molasses, and though this retail sale is at present more troublesome than profitable to proprietors, it will eventually become a source of revenue to them. The reduction of medical expenses is considerable. The estate hospitals have become useless. On a Monday morning, during slavery, the doctor would find eight, ten, or even twenty in the sick-house. Now, he has comparatively nothing to do. He is paid one-third less per head than before; but his duties have diminished in a much greater ratio. Before emancipation some estates were eaten up by their overpopulation. On one belonging to a relative of his, with three hundred and twenty negros, the saving effected by reducing the number of negros had been immense. In such cases there was generally some impediment to the transfer, or sale of the superfluous negros; either the estate was mortgaged, or had several owners, or was in trust, or in chancery, or entailed.

Several properties in this situation were on the point of being abandoned. Nothing could have saved them but a legislative measure of Emancipation. A property was instanced, possessing four hundred of the finest negros in the island, which appeared to be inextricably involved. The proprietor, residing in England, had turned his back upon it, and refused to receive or answer, the letters of his agent, who was thereby placed in a most painful situation. He had no means of carrying on the cultivation; he could get no help from home; and though a man of humanity, was embarrassed by prosecutions for not furnishing the people with the legal supplies. On the passing of the Emancipation Bill, the compensation money enabled the mortgagees to make some settlement of the affairs; superfluous hands, or rather mouths, were dismissed; the cultivation resumed with a fair prospect of success; and "the agent has been a happy man ever since." With regard to the general welfare of the colony, he told us that the proprietary body are more prosperous than before. Some estates have thrown off their load of debt, others have passed into the possession of capitalists, by whom their cultivation can be more effectively carried on. An estate was mentioned which cost, ten years ago, forty thousand pounds. He would give as much for this very estate now without the slaves, and consider it a safer and better investment. Another small estate was instanced, belonging to three equal proprietors. Just before Emancipation two of them sold their shares for one thousand five hundred pounds currency each; the third now stands out for more, one proof amongst many, that property has risen in value. Every one acquainted with the town of St. John's will acknowledge, that it is much more bustling and prosperous. Persons, returning to it after a year or two's absence, have been astonished at the change. The credit of planters is improved, and confidence restored. A few years ago, a gentleman offered to consign his produce to a mercantile house, on condition, that it would make him an advance to discharge a debt, due to his present merchants. The answer was negative. He has lately received a letter from the same party, offering advances. Another English firm, who, before Emancipation, were seeking to reduce their securities on estates as much as possible, have since sent out an agent to Antigua, to see if there were any openings to extend them. During the last fifteen or twenty years, many estates, chiefly in the mountains, or poorer lands, have gone out of cultivation. Some of these doubtless will again come under culture. One has already been resumed; the proprietor of which is paying his negros two shillings a day, greatly to the disturbance of his neighbours.

But there are *important exceptions*. A few estates have been disorganised, if not ruined, by the change; but in most instances, if not in all, this can be traced to the harsh and injudicious conduct of the owners or their agents. With regard to changes, present and prospective, our informant said, that the cane cultivation has been somewhat lessened, from several causes: 1st. An anticipation, well or ill founded, that it would be necessary to lessen it. 2nd. Because too many canes were cultivated before, the land not having been sufficiently cleaned and manured; and lastly, because a few laborers have forsaken the field, whose deficiency is not yet supplied by agricultural improvements. There has also been in the last year or two, an "invasion" of couch grass, which gives immense trouble. There are much fewer ground provisions grown than before; for, as it is not now the proprietor's duty to subsist his negros, he turns his attention to the most profitable article, sugar; and also because the negros at first manifested a good deal of caprice, in refusing to purchase provisions from the estate stores—preferring corn-meal, rice, &c. from the town. The planters have ceased to cultivate, perhaps to too great an extent; but these things will find their own level. There are as yet no non-resident laborers. All have a hut, piece of ground, and medical attendance, as before. No extra labor, therefore, is in the market, except that the planters occasionally hire the Saturdays of the people from neighbouring properties. Every estate maintains its full complement of laborers, both in and out of crop. There are no independent villages whatever, and though the people have the strongest desire to acquire what they call "a pot of land," meaning about an acre, yet great obstacles exist, because there are no suitable spots, except parts of actual estates, which the proprietors are unwilling, or unable to dispose of. The island can never realise the full benefits of the new system, till there *are* such villages, which would be to the planters as "reservoirs of surplus labor," enabling them to employ many or few hands, according to their actual wants. The economical advantages of free labor are indeed only beginning to be felt. Laborers and servants will become more *efficient*. A family requires at present three times as many domestics as in England. In the field, two or three men are required to manage a team in a plough, cart, or waggon. Agricultural implements, cane mills, and other machinery, will be improved. The plough has long been used in the island; but on many estates its judicious use is still a novelty. These and many other improvements, will be stimulated by a diminished supply of human labor.

The comparative improvements in the condition of the rural population are not to be enumerated. They are not flogged,* or locked up. They are their own masters, free to go or stay. They receive money wages, whilst they retain all their old privileges, except their allowances of food and clothing. A common source of dissatisfaction formerly was their food. They became tired of yams and Indian corn. Eddoes, (another farinaceous root,) would almost create mutiny. The law too did not prescribe how their rations should be distributed; so that corn was sometimes given them in the ear; and thereby a vast increase of their labor occasioned, perhaps in crop, by their having to parch and pound it. Now, they provide themselves with what they like; and are therefore better, if less abundantly fed. They are also much better dressed. Many make themselves ridiculously fine on Sundays. It is not uncommon, on that day, to see *ladies*, who toil under a burning sun during six days of the week, attired on the seventh, in silk stockings, and straw bonnet, with parasol, and gloves; and the *gentlemen* in black coats and fancy waistcoats. This extravagance is partly owing to the absence of an intermediate class, for them to imitate. They are probably possessed of more money than during slavery, but have less live stock; as immediately before August 1834 they con-

---

* It is due to Dr. N. to state, that the whip was disused on the estate on which he resides during the last fifteen years of slavery; one consequence of which humane system is seen in the fact, that only one of the negros has left the estate since they became free.

verted much of their property into coin, as is customary in every anticipation of extensive changes and revolutions. If they cultivate their grounds less than before, it is to be attributed to the drought, which has rendered it unprofitable to expend labor upon them. They do not work so well on the estates except when they are on task work; but though task work has not yet been extensively introduced, the cane cultivation is well adapted to it. Drunkenness is not a vice of the negro. His temptations are stealing and lying. Dances are a great source of demoralization. They sometimes aspire to suppers and even champagne, so called; and most absurdly give sums of four or five dollars for the honor of opening the ball, besides money to their partners. This tempts to robbery. If any change for the worse has taken place in their morals, it is in the case of domestic servants. Housebreaking, stealing money, &c. are sometimes heard of, which were before unknown: the offenders are usually dissolute free people, or former domestics.

The people are much more easily and pleasantly governed than during slavery. The proprietor has less "cark" and care; less bodily and mental fatigue, and infinitely less annoyance of all descriptions. Every difficulty used to be referred to him; constant disputes were to be settled, as to the work to be done by females, &c.; now he has no need to interfere. The disputes are carried to the magistrate. No one can conceive the irritation engendered by the old system; in addition to which, the obloquy thrown upon the planters was become almost insupportable. All this was swept away by Emancipation. "He did not believe there was a man in the colony who could lay his hand upon his heart and say, he would wish to return to the old state of things." Were there no other consideration, it gave him great pleasure to see men working in the fields, as free agents as himself. He sometimes pointed to a well dressed gang of laborers, and asked his friends whether it was not an exhilarating sight. Some would reply to him, that it was all very well if it did but last; but that now, every child was being educated; and that the next generation would be too much of gentlemen and ladies to work in the field. He however maintained, that there was more danger in partial than general education.

6th.—We went this morning to see the national schools in St. John's, where we were joined by the Rector, who kindly devoted the morning to us. Both the boys' and girls' schools were in a more efficient state than others which we have visited. A large proportion of the children were emancipated in August, 1834, viz. seventy-eight of one hundred and seventeen boys, and seventy-five of one hundred and twenty two girls. Some of these were very fair. We noticed one little girl in particular; and were much astonished, when she held up her hand with the rest that were made free. Her complexion was fair and clear; her hair flaxen, and with features perfectly European. The schoolmistress, an energetic old lady, appeared to take the most lively interest in her scholars, and seemed to be intimately acquainted with their individual histories, &c. Straw plaiting has been carried on in both schools; and in the boys', the making of shoes and trowsers, but the latter is at present suspended. We were next taken to see the Rector's infant school; a most interesting little establishment. Here the children were nearly all of the emancipated class. A little regiment of them come every morning from a neighbouring estate, under the guidance of an old woman, who carries their provisions in a basket on her head, and waits to take them home at night. The teacher, a young negress, is the most efficient native instructor we have seen, and the results are very perceptible in the superior forwardness of the scholars. She was very intelligent, and clever in her questions to the children. The Rector has five schools under his care in this parish. We next visited with him, the hospital of the "Daily Meal Society." This is the only public institution the destitute and diseased can resort to; and it is quite insufficient for the wants of the island. It is supported by voluntary contributions. A meal of soup and bread is served once a day, to about eighty persons; and there are fourteen or sixteen in-door patients. A new, large building is erecting for their accommodation. At present, they live in the moveable wooden houses of the country; an arrangement, which appeared to us to possess some peculiar advantages over the large wards of a hospital, for which it is about to be exchanged. Most of the inmates are pitiable objects, afflicted with leprosy and elephantiasis, which dreadful disorders are nearly, if not quite, confined to the black and colored races. We called in the evening upon JAMES COX. He gave us some pleasing details of the introduction and progress of the Temperance reformation. Teetotalism appears to adapt itself as readily to this, as to a colder climate. The Wesleyans have several little Temperance Societies on estates. JAMES COX is deeply interested in this cause, and is himself a fine, florid specimen of water drinking. A gentleman, whom we accidentally met with to-day, read to us part of a letter which he had just received from the neighbouring island of Nevis. It gave a deplorable account of the condition of the apprentices there. Many of them were in a state bordering on starvation, because the proprietors had given them larger provision grounds, and a day in the week to cultivate them, in lieu of their former allowances, and the dry weather had rendered their grounds unproductive. From the same cause, there had been a great falling off in the attendance of the schools, the parents not having food to give their children to take with them. The letter concluded by wishing "this system of apprenticeship at the bottom of the sea."

7th.—We went this morning to breakfast with the manager of an estate, which furnishes a striking proof of what may be done under a free system, liberally administered. He kindly furnished us with some valuable statistical information, and practical remarks. This estate, comprising about two hundred and fifty acres of cane ground, produced last year, two hundred and twelve heavy hogsheads of sugar, being sixty hogsheads more than its average for the last twenty years. Amidst the general drought, this and two or three adjoining properties, were favored with seasonable rains. The result completely falsifies the fears expressed to us by many planters, that a large crop could not be taken off without loss, by free labor.* This gentleman, on the contrary says, "Give me a supply of cash, and I will take off the largest crop it may please Providence to send." The number of efficient laborers is rather

* A note received since the commencement of the present year, from this gentleman, speaking of the crop about to be taken off, when we left Antigua, observes, "In five weeks we have cut seventy-seven acres of canes, made fifty hogsheads, and more than half done crop. So far from our people not being willing to labor, I believe they wish they had two hundred instead of forty more to make. *We only want such a year as* 1834, *for free labor to tell.*"

less than during slavery, but their loss has been supplied by the more extensive introduction of the plough and task-work, both which are employed to a greater extent than on any estate we have yet visited. Task-work has also been made the means of obviating the inconveniences which result from the present high price of provisions; the people earning from fifty to one hundred per cent. more than the customary rate of wages. Our host assured us, that his people worked *more regularly* than during slavery; a fact which was evident also from an inspection, which we were permitted to make of the pay list of the estate, during the earliest period of the free system in 1834, and the corresponding months of 1836. The increased amounts earned by the same number of laborers in the latter period, shewed an increase of industrious exertion. The negro houses on this estate, are large and comfortable. Some are about to be rebuilt at the expence of the proprietor. The attention of the people to the cultivation of their own grounds, is a striking proof of their industry and settled habits. We saw a piece of rocky ground, which had been taken in by permission, and converted into a garden, at an immense expense of labor, both in carrying mould and manure to it from a considerable distance, and in enclosing it by a stone wall. Their cottages have been also generally enclosed by neat fences, since 1834; and the whole conduct of the people exhibits as much stability, as though their leaving the estate was as unlikely to happen as during slavery, when it was nearly an impossible event. There is a nice little chapel on the estate, constructed out of one of the largest negro houses, in which service is frequently performed on the Sabbath, by one of the Wesleyan missionaries; and in which also is kept a school for the children, during the long noon interval of labor, by a woman remunerated by a trifling sum weekly, in addition to the privileges of her house and ground rent free. Besides this school, an adult class has been voluntarily formed and taught, by a negro domestic servant of the manager; and a third school has been instituted by the Archdeacon in one of the negro houses, chiefly for the adults and elder children of this and adjoining estates. On this estate there are fourteen mothers of families, who work, on the average, only half their time; and two who have withdrawn altogether from estate labor. The cash outlay on this estate, has been upwards of six hundred pounds currency, (about two hundred and fifty pounds sterling,) per annum more than during slavery. The crop however has averaged considerably more; and though this may be attributed to favorable seasons, yet the manager observes, that " as we plant only half the quantity of provisions, the greater part of our cane-land may be prepared out of crop, and the canes planted in better time. They will also, I am confident, be more productive after the land has been in fallow, than after provisions. The cattle also get a little more feeding."

Before returning to town we visited another estate in the same neighbourhood; the circumstances of which, in all important particulars, corresponded with the preceding; and from whose intelligent manager we received accounts equally satisfactory of the favorable effects of freedom.* The proprietor of it is

---

* From a number of answers to some written questions, which we proposed to this gentleman, we extract the following. "1st.—The change in our system is nothing like what might have been imagined. As yet, the substitution of reward for punishment, *and some faint efforts to economize labor*, are all that indicate a change. 2nd.—The

erecting new works and thirty new houses for the people of a very superior class, at an expense of several thousand pounds sterling. The cottages are being built on three sides of a large square, in the centre of which we understood it was intended to erect a school. The proprietor already supports an infant school on the estate which is held in a large room that also serves on occasion as a chapel. The children were in the usual state of forwardness. It is almost needless to add that the managers of these two estates are men of serious character and really concerned to promote the welfare of their people. They were both friendly to Emancipation, yet they assured us in strong terms

difference of the cost of cultivation, varies according to the locality and former circumstances of the Estates. Some estates used to grow food sufficient for their own consumption, without prejudice to their staple crop; a few more than sufficient, many for six or eight months; and the rest for three or four months. The first class, it is obvious lose by the change. The second I presume to be at par; whilst the third are decidedly gainers. It is however a question, whether the first class will be ultimately losers; presuming they continue to fallow such lands as were formerly appropriated to the growth of provisions. 3rd.—None, unacquainted with the negro character and habits, could easily comprehend the way in which, with an income in money of five-pence halfpenny sterling per day. they manage to exhibit such finery and extravagance in their dress, To us it is painfully manifest, that this weakness is indulged at the expense of all domestic enjoyments and comforts. Ordinarily, a mere fraction of their earnings is appropriated to their support; the cheapest and coarsest food, with the addition of herbs, &c. gathered on the estate will suffice. They take no thought for the future, anticipate no evil, provide nothing for sickness and old age, but spend all they can obtain in articles of dress, the most extravagant and unsuitable to their condition in life. They are yet slaves in habit and feeling, and *we must not be surprised if it be left for succeeding generations, to develope the entire blessedness of the change that has passed upon us.* 4th.—Some attention is paid, to avoid that waste of labor, which was but little regarded formerly; so that manual labor is lessened, though the substitutes for it are not yet extensively employed. Our that the measure had succeeded far beyond their utmost expectations.

In the afternoon we drove over to Parham, a little village interesting to us, both as a missionary and police station. The Wesleyan minister* is a man of color, and was born a slave in Bermuda. His history is remarkable. He is not, we believe, inferior either in education, qualifications, or usefulness, to any of his brethren in the ministry. The school under his care is in good order, and very numerously attended. The children are all emancipated but two; a circumstance which is employed to instil into their breasts sentiments of fervent loyalty. They were told we came from England; and asked "Who lives in England?" — "The

agricultural labors, during the manufacturing months, can only be performed by hand. The planting and weeding of canes, to which I chiefly allude, have both been attempted by the plough, but unsuccessfully. The consequence of this untoward coincidence is, that a greater number of hands must be kept on, than we should know well how to employ, in combination with an extensive use of the plough and other machinery; and there is such a tenacity respecting our laborers, that, on no account will we trust them from under our control; hence some estates are burdened with many more than they will employ, yet permit them to remain resident, in reserve for future contingencies, whilst neighbouring estates are suffering from present want of laborers. 5th.—The cultivation of cane has not, so far as I know, either increased or lessened. On this estate, a portion of the land formerly appropriated to provisions, is being brought into the routine of the sugar crop, suppose from ten to fifteen acres annually. 6th.—The proprietary body, must with some exceptions, be bettered by the change, allowing the rise in sugar its proper influence. Their credit is better, their capital at stake less; their personal responsibility also less; their properties are increased in value; their management and appropriation more free and uncontrolled. Bankruptcy was written on us in legible characters as an island; and most of the estates must have inevitably passed into the possession of the merchants."

* Edward Frazer, who has since visited England.

King." "What has the King done for you?"—"He make us free," was responded by upwards of one hundred little voices, with the greatest enthusiasm.

The police district of Parham comprises a circle of forty estates. The offences are chiefly breach of contract, trespass, absenting from work, and cane breaking. The officers mentioned to us several cases of distress, where the parties, becoming unable to work, had been compelled to quit the estates. In one instance, a woman with three children, left the estate on which she was formerly a slave, and went to reside with her husband on another. She became diseased in her feet, and unable to work, and her husband discarded her, although they had been regularly married by a Wesleyan minister. She and her children were turned off the estate. This is an illustration of the consequences of the non-recognition of Dissenters' marriages, and also of their being no public resource for the destitute poor.

9th.—With the Governor's permission we obtained some extracts from the police records. We also attended another sitting of the Court of King's Bench.—We have before noticed the character of the proceedings, and the leniency of the punishments. The last, we find, is partly owing to the expense of transportation and long imprisonments.

We visited this morning a planter who is the lessee of MACKINNON's estate, which has been alluded to in the British Parliament, as an illustration of the economical advantages of free labor.

He gave us much interesting information respecting tropical productions. Sugar, molasses and rum, besides a little arrow-root, raised by the negros, are the only articles of export from Antigua. Cotton, Indigo, and

Tobacco used to be its staples. The two former plants still grow wild in great abundance; and, as well as many others, might probably be made profitable articles of commerce. Among these is a species of acacia, which bears a great quantity of seed-pods, containing large proportions of gallic acid and tannin. The natives make ink and a black dye of them; and they have been exported to Europe, but for what purposes and with what results is unknown. Great inconveniences result from the exclusive cultivation of the cane; and but few of the planters, even since the compensation, are sufficiently independent to be able to turn their attention to any other article. He alluded in very strong terms to the annoyances of the old slave system to proprietors; of which he gave us some striking illustrations. It is apparent that the Abolition Act emancipated both planters and negros. One of the former on one occasion expressed their connection with slave property by an allusion to the Siamese Twins—a ligament of unnatural inconveniences. This gentleman complained of the great ingratitude which some of his negros, who had been very kindly treated, had displayed in leaving him. On the other hand, some had been stimulated to more industrious habits. One of the most worthless women on the property, once always pretending sickness and inability to work, had become as industrious a laborer as any on the estate. He asked her on one occasion the reason of the change in her habits. She replied significantly, " me get no money then, massa." Speaking of the apparent increase of crime, he told us that many not only minor offences but crimes were left to the summary judgment of the master, and that many culprits went entirely unpunished. The law took no cognizance of the offences of slaves, except such as were of a very heinous character or committed against the *public* peace. The crop had commenced on this estate; being from four to six weeks earlier than usual. We inspected, with much interest, the various processes at the mill, boiling house and distillery. The buildings were large, well ventilated, and cooler than we had expected to find them.

10th. We paid a second visit to the gaol. The condemned cells are small, exceedingly ill ventilated, and quite dark. There are at present two occupants of them, capitally convicted; one whose sentence has been changed to banishment; and another, waiting the result of an application to the authorities at home, on a point of law. We visited also the refuge for female orphans in St. John's; an institution similar to the one at English Harbour, but in more active operation. The little girls, seventeen in number, were engaged in making strawplait. They appeared to be very comfortable and kindly attended to. The President of the institution told us, that the number of applications for them, as servants, was four times greater than they could supply; and that those whom they had brought up had usually done credit to their care. They have been, of late years, limited in their funds; in consequence of the numerous demands made upon the benevolent portion of the public, by schools and other more recent institutions. In the present condition of Colonial Society, establishments like these are deserving the warmest encouragement; as they not only provide a maintenance and education for a particular class of orphans, but rescue them from a life of almost inevitable degradation and profligacy. One institution would suffice for this small island. We suggested a union of the two, at present existing; which we find had been proposed, but not effected. It would save the expense of two houses, two sets of instructors, servants, &c. There appear to be no material obstacles in the way. The junction might be readily brought about by the "Ladies Society," the chief patrons of the Refuge at English Harbour. We called in the course of the day upon Brother HARVEY, at the Moravian Institution. He informed us, that though the education of the young is now so general, he did not think that more than one-tenth of their adult members could read. We spent the evening with the gentleman mentioned in our journal of the 24th. ult. He attributes the advantages Antigua has possessed, to the early success which distinguished Missionary efforts. Sixty years ago the Speaker of the Assembly was a lay preacher of the Gospel; and there has always been, since, a succession of persons who have maintained the truth; till at length religion has become fashionable; and it is now no cross to become a Church member. Some interesting facts were mentioned relative to the former and present condition of the negros. During slavery the people declined in numbers; especially on the estates near town. This was partly, we were told, to be attributed to the fact, that women, in an advanced stage of pregnancy, after discontinuing estate labor, would employ themselves in bringing heavy loads of sticks and grass to market, for their own benefit. On certain estates, which were named, the slaves declined in numbers from twelve hundred to eight hundred; dating from the abolition of the slave trade. In such cases, it was often impossible to contract the cultivation proportionably; in consequence of the incumbrances of mortgages or settlements; so that the diminished number was compelled to perform an increased amount of labor, and thus the destructive ratio of decrease was accelerated. Some striking instances were mentioned to us of the extravagance of negro weddings. Some of them must absorb a year or two of the income of the parties; if they are not paid for, as they probably are, by general contribution amongst their friends. Many live together unmarried, because they cannot afford this foolish expenditure; but it is an evil which would be checked, in some degree, if Dissenters were allowed to perform the ceremony.

12th. We visited this morning an estate about twelve miles distant from St. John's, in the district called Bermudian Valley. It was purchased by two gentlemen, immediately after the 1st of August, 1834; and though a losing concern to its former proprietor, now yields, as we were informed by one of its present owners, a liberal profit per annum clear of expenses and interest. Our route was through the finest part of the island. We had little conception, that any part of Antigua was so beautiful as the quarter in which this estate is situated. The hills are of considerable elevation, and covered with forest. The climate is less arid; the natural vegetation far more luxuriant. The stiff soil does not, however, so well repay cultivation as the light calcareous mould of the other less interesting, but more profitable parts of the island. Another estate, and part of the one we visited, occupy an entire basin of great extent, and the surrounding amphitheatre of hills. On such properties the negros are allowed to cultivate any part of the woodland they please, for their own benefit. Their distance from town, however, prevents them from making much pecuniary profit of this privilege. They generally choose their ground on the sides of the mountains, as far out of sight as possible; a remnant, as was observed to us, of Slavery; when they were always afraid to let the Overseer know what they were doing. This is one of the estates that has derived advantage from the accession of laborers since Emancipation. The number on the pay list is exactly one hundred; and their attendance in the field is very regular. The manager complained that he had not yet been able to induce them to undertake task work. The habitual distrust of the negro, and his ignorance of calculation, frequently interpose obstacles to the substitution of task work, which managers have not always the patience and tact to remove.

We proceeded about noon to Grace Bay; a station of the United Brethren, very beautifully situated on the sea coast, opposite Mountserrat. We were kindly welcomed by the missionaries, Brother MOHNE and his wife. Their school is held in the church, and is attended by seventy children; there were but forty present this morning. Many come from a great distance, as this part of the island is much less thickly peopled than any other. About one-third of the children could read nicely in the New Testament; and their teacher, a young negress, questioned them in such a way as to shew that she might soon be qualified to conduct an infant school efficiently. We drove to town, through a very beautiful district, abounding with some of the most interesting tropical trees and shrubs; particularly with singular and gigantic varieties of the cactus tribe. The poisonous manchineal is in great abundance by the sea shore; and, like other large trees, frequently loaded with creepers, and parasitical plants. We called on our way, at Cedar Hall; thus completing our circuit of the Moravian stations in this island, which has been the scene of their most successful labors. Two of the Brethren are stationed here—one of them is seventy-four years of age, and has been thirty years resident. He is probably the oldest missionary in the West Indies. He told us, that when he came out, the missionaries dare not be known to keep a school; but taught a few by stealth on one evening in the week.

12th. One of us called this morning upon the Hon. SAMUEL WARNER, President of the Council, whose testimony, like that of the speaker, was decidedly favorable to the results of the Emancipation. There was not much difference, he thought, in the expense of cultivating his estate before and since 1834. The negros did less than before, when they worked by the day; but much more when they were on task work. Lately a field of cane-holes was opened on the latter plan, by a gang of his people, consisting of fewer than twenty to the acre, in the same space of time that would have been taken by forty to the acre under the slave system.

15th. We called this morning upon the Governor to take leave; and to thank him for his kindness in forwarding our views, by permitting us access to the records of the Police Offices, and Court of King's Bench, &c. He mentioned to us, that a gentleman, who was a proprietor, and also Attorney for sixteen estates, and who had been strongly opposed to Emancipation, had lately told him that he was at length satisfied with the change, and would be sorry to return to the slave system. In the course of the morning we were surprised and pleased by the arrival of two gentlemen, of the names of THOME and KIMBALL, from the United States, on a tour of inquiry like our own, into the results of Emancipation in these islands. We trust they will find the way opened to them, in some degree, by our previous investigation. Several gentlemen called upon us to take leave; and we made a number of calls with the same object. In the evening we went on board a little schooner, chartered to convey us through the islands to Barbados. In thus concluding the journal of our visit to Antigua, we acknowledge with thankfulness, that amidst many discouragements we have been enabled to pursue our inquiries with a good degree of success; and we trust, we shall yet be assisted by a strength, not of ourselves, in the much more arduous undertaking we have immediately in prospect in the islands where the apprenticeship is in operation. We should not do justice to our own feelings, if we did not record here our grateful sense of the readiness displayed by all classes in the colony, to afford us facilities of inquiry.

CHAPTER IV.

RESULTS OF EMANCIPATION IN ANTIGUA.

Antigua, being the only one of our intertropical colonies which has substituted for the apprenticeship complete emancipation, a careful and even minute examination of the results of that great measure, after more than two years of trial, is confessedly of the very highest importance. In the preceding pages* we have recorded our observations during a stay of four weeks; and though we have already incurred the risk of wearying the reader by detail, a large additional amount has been omitted of evidence in our possession, illustrative of the various points embraced in the investigation. Our opportunities of personal observation were extensive. We availed ourselves of the access publicly afforded to the Legislative Assembly, the Chief Criminal Court, the Police Offices, the places of worship, and the different schools. We had also the privilege of free communication with the most intelligent and influential persons in the colony; with the Governor, and others high in office; with members of the council and assembly; judges, barristers and medical men, ministers of religion, and schoolmasters, proprietors and managers of estates, persons of color, and lastly, the negros themselves. There is one subject upon which

* And also in Appendix A.

all are agreed—that the great experiment of abolition has succeeded beyond the expectations of its most sanguine advocates. Some indeed affect to regard the *future* with apprehension; but none will deny that the new system has hitherto worked well; or will hazard a declaration of preference for slavery. Many speak in emphatic terms, of the annoyances they have escaped by the change, and of the comparative comfort with which they now manage their estates. The measure has been felt to be one of emancipation of masters, as well as slaves, from a most oppressive bondage, except by such as clung to their authority with a tenacious avarice of power, and are not yet weaned from a love of dominion.

It may be asserted also, without fear of contradiction, that the proprietors are, in a pecuniary sense, far more prosperous than before Emancipation, notwithstanding the occurrence, subsequently, of two successive unfavorable seasons, and independently of the compensation they have received. The annual cost of cultivation is believed, by the most intelligent resident planters, to be on the average, one-fifth or one-sixth less than formerly; so that free labor is manifestly advantageous, taking even the narrowest view of the subject.* The *general* advantages however, of the change, imperfectly as they have been yet developed, would have more than compensated for a considerably increased expenditure. There has been an augmentation of the import trade of the island. Houses and land have risen in value. Estates are now worth as much as they were, with the slaves attached to them, before the alleged depreciation in their value,

* See appendix A, Sec. II.

in consequence of the agitation of the abolition question. The cultivation of one estate, which had been thrown up for twenty years, and of others which were on the point of being abandoned, has been resumed. The few sold since 1834 have been eagerly bought up at very high prices. The estates which were over populated have largely benefited by the dismission of their superfluous numbers: whilst the under peopled properties have profited by availing themselves of the labor thus thrown into the market. The credit of planters with their merchants is much improved. A purchasing as well as consuming population has been formed within the island itself. The negros buy considerable quantities of provisions from the plantation stores, and occasionally other agricultural produce. The success of emancipation on the different estates has been to a great extent determined by the character of the managers. It has been most distinguished, when an enlightened and indulged course has been pursued towards the people. There are indeed some striking exceptions to the general prosperity, of which several fine estates, belonging to a weathy English baronet, present the most painful example. These were under the care of an attorney* from Barbados, who adopted a system of such excessive severity, that the number of slaves was diminished by nearly one hundred in a few years. He was accustomed to complain that none of the children were reared; notwithstanding his great anxiety for their welfare, and frequent consultations of the faculty. He commenced the new era on the 1st of August, 1834, by turning the cattle of the estates into

---

* An attorney, in colonial phraseology, is one who holds a *power* of attorney, for managing the affairs of an absent proprietor.

the negro provision grounds, and endeavoured to reduce their wages to a minimum. In consequence of which conduct, the majority of his effective laborers forsook the estate to seek a subsistence elsewhere. The lands are now overrun with destructive weeds; and though this attorney is since dead, and his successor has adopted a different policy, it will be many years before what has been thus mismanaged can be recovered.

The prospective advantages of freedom are however far greater than any thing hitherto accomplished. No one will venture to compare slave laborers, in point of efficiency, with the agricultural population of a free country. The negros although free by law, are still necessarily located on the estates; and therefore prevented by circumstances from rapidly becoming a body of independent peasantry. They evince, however, a disposition to elevate themselves in the social scale, by their anxiety to purchase or lease small lots of land: few indeed have thus succeeded, in consequence of a groundless fear of their forsaking estate labor; yet, doubtless, the true interests of the Proprietary body will at length prevail over prejudice; and two great classes of landlords and yeomen, at present unknown in the Colonies, will be gradually formed.* Under present arrangements, the estates are burdened, during the whole year, with the support of the full complement of laborers, required during the crop; which is a great check to the introduction of animal labor and machinery. The manufacturing processes, occurring at a season when labor is never in excess, are many years in advance of the methods of agriculture which continue to be carried on by two or three times the

* See Appendix, Sect. VII.

immediate amount of human labor which would be required under a more perfect system. Great improvements in farming, and particularly the extensive introduction of, and best mode of working, the plough; together with a change of the present unvarying routine of cultivation by the alternation of green and cereal crops with the cane, have long ago been demonstrated to be necessary and practicable; and particularly by Dr. Nugent, in an able paper, drawn up several years ago, and adopted as their Report by the Antigua Agricultural Association. Slavery, however, interposed insuperable obstacles to change. Free labor, on the contrary will give an energetic impulse to improvement. In cases of insolvency or mismanagement, the weekly amounts for laborers' wages, though less in the aggregate than the cost of their former allowances, will bring about a crisis before the estates become so inextricably involved, as was frequent during slavery. The embarrassed Planter will no longer have the opportunity of purchasing his annual supplies of food and clothing for his negros, at usurious prices. His estates will pass in time into other hands, which can carry on the cultivation efficiently. It is anticipated that the present expensive and absurd system of agency and management will be gradually changed, by absentee proprietors, *leasing* their estates to tenants, or other representatives; who will thus acquire, as a resident proprietary, a direct interest in the improvement of the island. The planters will gradually release themselves from their servile dependance on the merchants. Under the present system, with a few exceptions, they are obliged to consign their produce to one mercantile house, instead of being able to choose the best market. They pay commissions more numerous and exorbitant than are known in any other branch of commerce. They are compelled to purchase plantation stores from their merchant at a high rate. They pay compound interest on the advances required, and finally, they are most injuriously controlled in the management of their property, as they are limited to the cultivation of such articles, as bring profitable freights to the ship-owners, and commissions to the merchants.

The advantages which the laborers have derived from Emancipation are numerous and complete enough to call for devout gratitude, on their behalf, from all who are interested in the progress of human happiness. The *exuviæ* of slavery still hang about them, as well as their masters, but they possess now the capacity of elevating themselves in the scale of being; and they have means in their own power of escaping from oppression, by the choice of masters. A cursory observer might suppose there was little to distinguish the agricultural districts from a slave community, seen under favorable circumstances, except the absence of the vulgar symbols of coercive power; but inquiry would convince him, that the one was a degraded condition, which could at best, by the most painful efforts, scarcely maintain the *status quo*, while the other contained active elements of prosperity. When the change took place, the masters were as little acquainted with the respect due to the rights of their free peasantry as the latter with the exercise of their newborn prerogatives. A combination was entered into to destroy competition for labor by enforcing a low and uniform tariff of wages. This succeeded for a time, but it was soon perceived, that though the planters might agree to pay able-bodied laborers a shilling a day, (five-pence halfpenny sterling,) they no longer possessed the power of compelling them to perform more than a fair equivalent of labor. This agreement, therefore, is now evaded in a variety of ways, some openly disregard it, others bid higher for the Saturday holidays of the laborers, and others supersede day labor by contract or taskwork. In the first year caprice was frequently manifested on the one hand, and a love of oppression on the other; but in this, the third year of freedom, the records of the Police Courts shew that both have materially decreased. The planters have little cause now to complain of love of change, want of industry, or irregular attendance on the part of their laborers; and the latter are less frequently annoyed by frivolous complaints before the magistrate. Freedom is "an ever-germinating principle," its gradual and progressive operation rather than the amount of good, considerable as it is, which has hitherto been effected, marks the contrast in Antigua between the present and the past.

To appreciate fully the results of Emancipation, it is necessary to revert to the evils of the state it succeeded. At a distance, the physical sufferings of slaves from direct cruelty and from the exaction of oppressive labor, are the most vividly realised by the imagination; but, in the presence of an enslaved people, the consideration of *these* is almost superseded by that of their moral degradation. As a citizen, a slave has no existence; and therefore neither rights nor duties. As a private individual, he has no responsibilities, no cares for the present or the future; nothing to stimulate his dormant intellectual energies into life. He has no filial or parental duties. His wife and children depend not on his exertions or his love for their comfort or subsistence; they belong not to him but to their owner, whose care it is to provide for their animal wants. A slave has no power of self-protection, but his skill in lying and deception. He has no property but by sufferance, and is therefore feebly impressed with a sense of the rights of property in others. He is exposed to a continual system of selfish fraud; no one keeps faith with him, and he is therefore filled with suspicion and distrust. Labor, a great blessing in disguise to man, brings him no wealth, comfort, or honor. It is degraded in his eyes by associations of coercion and punishment. Domestic comfort is unknown. Husbands and wives are not helpmeets to one another; they rarely reside in the same hut, or even on the same estate; for a slave does not, more than an European, choose his partner from the females of his own village. They work in the field without distinction of sex. The decencies of civilized life are to a most revolting and guilty extent unobserved. Wives and daughters are subject to the brutal caprice and absolute will of their owners. The sacred character of the marriage tie is therefore little understood, or lightly esteemed. Such is an imperfect catalogue of the evils of slavery. As far as a system can degrade man to the level of the lower creation, he is so animalised by slavery, that the most successful efforts of missionaries and teachers, and even of humane proprietors, can only palliate its inherent malignity. The Antigua negros, as a body, are not elevated above the stage of moral and intellectual childhood. Their character is distinguished by shrewdness, by petty vice, great want of reflection, and above all by distrust. They are, however, in a rapid course of improvement. They are gaining prudence and foresight from the influence of newly acquired responsibilities. They feel the security of their property.

They are acquiring domestic habits. Marriages are more frequent. Husbands and wives begin to dwell together, and mothers of families to withdraw from field labor to their household affairs,—germs of rising character, which contain most encouraging promises of advancement.

There is, probably at the present moment, a larger proportion of persons under the pastoral care of ministers of religion, and also of children receiving education in the schools, than in any part of the Parent country. A mere perusal of the religious and educational statistics of the island, unaccompanied by explanation, would however convey incorrect ideas of its state in both these respects. The children in the schools are very docile, and give abundant proofs of natural quickness and capacity. They easily acquire the more mechanical parts of learning, as reciting, singing, reading, and writing. Opportunity is rarely afforded them of advancing beyond a certain point, as they enjoy only the benefits of the routine of the English infant and Lancastrian systems. Their native instructors as a body, are inefficient, though many of them display talent, and a capacity of becoming, with the usual advantages of normal instruction, both able and intelligent teachers. At present, the *intelligent* instruction which the children receive, is chiefly communicated by their ministers and others, whose attendance, from the pressure of their more immediate duties, is necessarily irregular. This subject is the more important, on account of the interesting position which Antigua maintains among the leeward islands. The neighbouring colonies, whence the sons of respectable persons of color are frequently sent to this island for education, are now looking to her for a supply of teachers for the offspring of their apprentice population, and a few, such as they are, have already been sent to Montserrat and elsewhere.

The state of Antigua, as regards the public peace, would also be erroneously inferred from an unexplained statistical comparison of criminal calendars and police records. There has been an apparent increase of offences, owing to the fact, that Emancipation gave nearly thirty thousand citizens to the state; and that the magistrate now takes formal cognizance of offences which previously were summarily punished by the master. A large proportion of the middle class in the towns, are people of color, many of whom are persons of intelligence, education, and true respectability. The standard of morals is far more elevated among them, as well as the whites, than in the other colonies, though still in some respects lamentably below that of the mother country. The Sabbath is however more strictly observed than in England, and the attendance on public worship very exemplary. Although the island suffers from absenteeism, it has proportionably a more numerous resident proprietary than any other colony, except Barbados. To this circumstance has been attributed, with apparent justice, its adoption of the complete abolition of slavery, in preference to the Apprenticeship; the legislatures of the other islands being filled with attorneys, who form themselves a part of existing abuses, and whose interests are wholly identified with the maintenance of the present order of things.

We cannot conclude without observing, that though it is impossible to convey upon paper, the strong impression on our own minds, of the benefits which have resulted to all classes, from immediate Emancipation; yet, that those benefits would be greatly increased by such reforms as the Government at home might effect in the legislative and administrative departments of the colony.* It is not however our intention to reflect with undue severity on the local authorities. Their enlightened policy, in substituting a real Emancipation for the delusive measure of the Imperial Parliament, will claim for them the praise of future ages, and the gratitude of the African race in every part of the world.

---

* See Appendix A. *passim.*

CHAPTER V.

MONTSERRAT.

12th Month, 16th, (December.) 1836.

WE made the short passage from Antigua to Montserrat in the night, and landed early this morning at Plymouth, the town and port of the island. We met here HENRY LOVING, Esq., who was filling temporarily the office of Island Secretary. He is known in England as the delegate of the people of color in Antigua, and the able and successful advocate of their claims. We were also introduced to FRANCIS BURKE, a gentleman of uncommon intelligence and enterprize; he has been the importer of the Acasee seeds into England, which we have before mentioned as possessing the quality of Aleppo galls. The speculation failed, in consequence, as he believes, of the mismanagement of the party to whose care they were consigned. He has also been concerned in working the Souffrieres in Montserrat and Dominica. The ore in the latter contains seventy-two per cent of sulphur; in the former it is less pure. It has been shipped to America at a cost, on board, of four dollars per ton. The expense of freight forbids its being sent to England. His attention is at present occupied with the introduction of mulberry trees and silkworms. These succeed well in the neighbouring French colony of Guadaloupe, where several thousand pounds weight of silk of the first quality, were last year produced. It promises to be a valuable colonial product, as its introduction would supply work of a light description for the population of the towns, and for young and infirm persons, who are quite unfit for severe field labor. Our informant took us to see his mulberry trees, which, though raised within the last ten months from seed, are already large flourishing bushes, they are the white variety. Whilst we were examining them, the President of the island, HENRY HAMILTON, Esq., and ——— POLHILL, Collector of Customs passed, with whom we were made acquainted, and who kindly gave us some information in addition to what we had already learned in Antigua, respecting the measure introduced last year into the legislature of this colony, for the abolition of the remaining term of Apprenticeship. The Bill passed the Council, but was lost in the Assembly by a majority of *one*, in consequence of some of the representatives being proprietors of jobbing or task gangs. Their profit from their laborers would have entirely ceased by Emancipation, instead of being increased, like those of the owners of estates, by the change of apprentices into free laborers. On the rejection of the Bill, three of the members of the Council, and two other proprietors adopted it individually, by releasing their apprentices from further servitude. The policy which originated the measure, was of a selfish character. The planters had made an agreement with their negros, to allow them provision grounds and two entire days, besides the Sabbath, in lieu of all allowances; the latter performing the legal amount of forty hours labor per week, in four days of ten hours each. This arrangement is, under ordinary circumstances, as compared with other colonies, a very advantageous one for the apprentices; but about a year ago, a hurricane, followed by a severe drought, so completely destroyed their grounds, that the planters feared they would be obliged to support them by rations according to the provisions of the Leeward Islands' Amelioration Act. They therefore proposed to surrender the Apprenticeship. The five estates on which the apprentices were liberated, are quite as efficiently cultivated by free labor, as they were before.

The Collector informed us, that the imports of the island had greatly increased since 1834, which was owing he said, to the payment of wages to the laborers on these five estates, and on four others on which the apprentices receive wages, but remain attached to the soil, and under the authority of the Stipendiary. The rate is a bitt a day, (four-pence sterling,) and two bitts for the Saturday. The other apprentices in the island, frequently work on the estates on the Friday and Saturday, which are their own days. They prefer working for wages, although they have fine provision grounds. F. Burke says he finds no difficulty, by offering a trifle more than the customary rate, in procuring laborers to pick the pods of the thorny acasee, and to work the Souffriere; one of them a most disagreeable, and the other a most laborious employment. Although there are extensive, unoccupied lands, which they might obtain at a very cheap rate, the apprehension, so general in the colonies similarly situated, that the negros will quit the estates when free, does not exist in Montserrat.

We called in the course of the morning upon J. Collins, Rector of the principal parish, who is zealous in his endeavours to promote the good of the people;

and also upon the resident Wesleyan minister, —— WALTON, an intelligent and energetic missionary. The moral state of the apprentices is very degraded, in consequence of the dreadful example of the white and colored classes. Some improvement, however, has taken place within these few years. Marriage is becoming more general among the apprentices, though a great majority still live in concubinage. Many of those who are church members afford indisputable evidences of piety. They display a lively gratitude to their spiritual teachers, of which the following is an affecting instance. A rumour prevailed in the island that the Rector was going to leave it; a number of his apprentice congregation came to him, to entreat him to stay, and offering as an inducement to provide him a house free of expense from their scanty means. Happily their alarm was groundless. Nominal education is general in the colony, but the want of teachers and of school-houses is severely felt; the native instructors are very inefficient and irregular in their attendance. The legislature has passed an Act authorising the Wesleyans to perform the marriage ceremony, and legalizing those heretofore celebrated by them. The missionary informed us that he had lately visited Guadaloupe, where he had been courteously received by many planters, to whom he had introduced himself as a protestant missionary. He describes them as tremblingly alive to the progress of Emancipation in our colonies. They appeared to have given up the idea of preventing the abolition of slavery, and were only fearful that their government would grant them no compensation. A commission was lately sent to Antigua, which to the surprise of the French colonists, reported favorably on their return of the working of the free system.

The head of it was immediately dispatched to France with his Report.

We attended the sitting of the House of Assembly and Council. The latter usually meets with closed doors; but through the politeness of the Collector, who is a member of it, one of us was permitted to be present, and in the intervals of business received various interesting statements from the gentlemen present. Several of them expressed their willingness to abandon the Apprenticeship, if the four and a half per cent duties were remitted, or any equivalent encouragement held out to them by government. One, who had introduced on his estate a system of remuneration and taskwork observed, that the negros now did more work in six days than formerly in eighteen. Another, the owner and attorney of several estates, observed that his people did more work in the last two days in the week for which they received wages, than in the other four; and a third, who had conferred complete freedom on his apprentices, said that they were more industrious than before, and that his property suffered less from pilfering. In reply to an inquiry whether the emancipated negros shewed any gratitude for the boon of freedom, it was observed by one of the non-emancipationists that they well knew it was self-interest that dictated the measure. The Assembly was composed of a majority of persons of color. The business of the House to day was of little interest or importance, being chiefly the petty details of the Poor Law expences of the island. We were told that it was liberal in its general policy, and transacted affairs in a business-like manner. After the breaking up of the legislature, we were introduced to Dr. Dyett, the Speaker of the Assembly; he is one of the few of his class, who lends his support to the cause of religion and morality in the colony. He kindly gave his company to us for half an hour, though the prevalence of an epidemic, creates pressing calls upon his time. Montserrat has always hitherto been numbered among the healthy islands, being free from marshes and swamps; but during the last three years fever has prevailed, which Dr. Dyett attributes to the introduction of a prepared compost from England by a large absentee proprietor. This practice would seem a very useless and unprofitable way of manuring land, in a country abounding with pasturage and rank vegetation, and which would apparently afford means of forming compost in any quantity by the keeping of stock. The fever this year attacked six hundred persons, and has been fatal in about one case in thirty. It was prevailing in three of the families we visited this morning. Dr. Dyett gave us a deplorable account of the prevalence of intemperate habits. The free negros and apprentices are much addicted to rum, which is the greatest bar to their moral advancement. He confirmed a singular fact, which came under our notice in Antigua, by stating, that on the emancipated estates in this colony, and on those where wages are paid, the necessity for his professional attendance had very much diminished. We next called at the office of the stipendiary magistrate. He had just disposed of the cases brought before him. He informed us, that his duties were becoming less onerous by the decrease of offences. He observed also, that the apprentices displayed a love of dress, and that money was become quite a necessary to them; and that though they could easily maintain themselves by working during their own two days in their ample grounds, yet they usually preferred to be employed on the estates for wages.

Their own time was however, sometimes borrowed by their masters; in which case they were often greatly defrauded in the repayment of it. He shewed us in his rough journal, an instance where the complaints from one estate in one month, extended over two pages and a half; and where next month they were nearly comprised in as many lines. The estate was under the attorneyship of a member of the Council, who put it under the care of a brutal manager. Such representations were accordingly made, through Sir EVAN MAC GREGOR, to the Colonial Office, as brought directions from thence, to remove his employer from the Council, unless he were dismissed. His consequent dismissal explained the striking decrease of complaints above noticed. Some managers had endeavoured to make women, in an advanced stage of pregnancy, perform their full quota of work; but the Stipendiary had insisted upon allowing them six weeks before, and six weeks after confinement, as was usual during slavery. In one case a woman was brought before him late at night; not aware of her situation, he directed her to be locked up, intending to investigate her case in the morning. She was seized with the pains of labor, and delivered in the course of the night. The complaint against her was *refusing to work*. Both the magistrate and another gentleman who was present, agreed that there had been a large proportion of deaths among the free children; but as no registers were kept, there was no means of ascertaining the exact truth. If the payment of the compensation had been deferred till the end of the Apprenticeship, they believed that many lives would have been saved, as the greatest care would have been taken of the children and old people. The slave population of Montserrat, when the Apprenticeship Act came into operation, was six thousand four hundred and one; of whom one thousand one hundred and thirty were freed on the first of August, being under six years of age; of the others two thousand nine hundred and twenty-eight are females, and two thousand one hundred and sixty-three males. The remaining one hundred and eighty includes those who have been since manumitted, as well as a considerable number who have been sold to Demerara. This disgraceful traffic has been successfully carried on in this little and poverty-stricken colony; the ignorant apprentices having been induced by presents of a few dollars, and delusive representations, to have themselves appraised. The money is advanced by the apprentice trader, who immediately takes them on board his ship, where they receive a mock form of manumission, and then indent themselves to servitude in British Guiana. Many of the proprietors have set their faces against these proceedings; but others, of whom a few are in high station, have countenanced them, and have themselves driven a lucrative trade in the sinews of their apprentices. As we had reason to believe that in many of the colonies the apprentices had been fraudulently classified, we inquired of various persons, and find that all the plantation negros were returned by the valuers as *predial attached* laborers, by which this island, on the supposition that the other colonies were more honest, obtained a disproportionate share of the Compensation. There is also every reason to fear, that when the 1st of August, 1838, arrives, the domestics, and tradesmen or mechanics on the plantations, will be detained in servitude, or obtain their freedom according as their owners are conscientious or otherwise. This will assuredly occur if the Government do not take into their own hands this important subject. The apprentices have no voice to plead their own wrongs, and we ear the Stipendiary will fail them, when they most need his protection, as he is in some degree under planter influence, in consequence of his holding the appointment conferred by the President, of Serjeant of Police, at a salary of one hundred and ten pounds currency, (forty-eight sterling,) per annum, from the Island Treasury. By this reconciliation of obviously incompatible functions in his own person, he receives, as Serjeant, orders from himself as Magistrate; and is responsible also to himself as Magistrate, for his good behaviour as Serjeant. Again, as Serjeant of Police, he apprehends an offending apprentice; as Magistrate decides the case; and as Serjeant executes his own sentence.

The President administering the Government of Montserrat is himself a planter and apprentice-holder. The Constitution of the Assembly is more liberal than in Antigua, as the elective franchise is a forty-shilling freehold. The Courts of Law, however, are of the same character as in that island, but still more objectionable on account of the smallness of the community.

We were fortunate during our brief stay in having the opportunity of attending a sitting of the legislature, and also in meeting nearly every person in the colony, official or otherwise, who could afford us information. Many of the persons we conversed with, freely expressed to us their opinion, that the Apprenticeship was the only bar to a revival of the prosperity of the island. The ministers of religion are looking forward to 1840 for a great extension of their usefulness. We fear there is little hope of the measure of complete abolition before referred to, being re-introduced, in consequence of the *money value* of the apprentices having been so much increased by the speculations of the Demerara traders. When we re-embarked in the evening, ROBERT DYETT, our landlord, and a man of color, refused any compensation for our entertainment, in consequence of his considering us associated with those in England, who have always manifested a sympathy with his class, (when loaded with disabilities) as well as with the slaves.

CHAPTER VI.

DOMINICA.

12th Month, 19*th, (December.)* 1836.

THE voyage from Montserrat to this island is frequently performed in less than twenty-four hours, but we encountered such boisterous weather, that we did not arrive at Roseau till this morning. Sailing in a small vessel, with contrary winds, in a heavy sea, is not the smallest of the miseries of human life, so at least one is apt to think while it endures. We were too sea-sick to be sensible of danger, but our Captain told us he never before experienced such weather in these seas, and our little schooner lost a jib, and sustained some injury in her sails.

In the course of the morning we visited the prison. The treadmill was under repair. The keeper of the jail admitted that the man who superintended it, when in use, carried a cat; but he would not acknowledge that it was used, except to a trifling extent. The prisoners are put upon it fourteen times a day, for fifteen minutes each time. The upper rooms of the prison are airy and large, but too many persons are confined in each; the lower range are equally large but close, crowded, and ill-ventilated. The present number of prisoners is thirty five. We next called on the Rector, GEORGE CLARKE. He is much impressed with the importance of education. Nearly the whole population are Roman Catholic, and speak the French language, yet the desire for education, and the wish to learn English are so general, that he has no doubt he would be able to fill eight or ten schools, if the means were supplied to build them and to pay teachers. Much of the good he has been able to effect has been by education. The natural obstacles which the mountainous character of the island, and the isolation of the estates present to his extended efforts, are very great, but they are not insuperable. He believes also that the negros would come to learn notwithstanding their different language and religion; they would choose the best school, as they choose the cheapest store. The Rector took us to see an infant school, and also two schools for boys and girls. In the former, the children learn little besides the very first elements, and the usual recitations and motions; but they acquire, what are very important, habits of order and attention, and the English language. They are then removed into the upper schools. The children in these, read surprisingly well, considering that most of them have had to surmount the difficulty of learning a foreign language. They are also proficient in spelling and the tables, and the specimens of their writing shewn to us were very neat. In point of intelligence and general proficiency, they would bear a favorable comparison with the children in the best schools we visited in Antigua. A large proportion of them, however, are children of parents in the middle class, who ought to pay for their instruction. The attendance in the three schools was about one hundred; but nearly as many, we were told, had been kept away by the stormy weather this morning. There is another school at St. Joseph's, under the Rector's care, also attended by about one hundred. From a memorandum furnished us by C. A. Fillan, an intelligent young man of color, it appears, that the Wesleyan Society, of which he is a member, have one large Sunday school in Roseau, a day school at Prince Rupert's, seven or eight noon and night schools on estates, in which children are taught by the negro who can read best; and also " at Layou, a competent free man has lately been sent to instruct seven or eight, in order to qualify them to teach. He also gives lessons to the children, but he cannot be supported long."

We introduced ourselves in the course of the day, to William Lynch, Esq. one of the stipendiary magistrates. He is a man of color, and justly valued by those who have the pleasure of his friendship, both in England and the West Indies, for his intelligence and piety. He told us, that the duties of the stipendiaries have become less onerous from the decrease of complaints. The apprentices understand better than they did, what is expected of them. Little is being done, however, to fit them for the change in 1840. We cannot perhaps give a better idea of the religious and educational wants of the island, than is conveyed in the following remark of this gentleman, on the state of his own district, which comprises a population of two thousand apprentices and their free children, and includes several large English estates, on which the negros are considered to be more intelligent than elsewhere. " My official intercourse with the laboring classes, enables me to discover their ignorance of letters, and too general disregard of the Sabbath; as well as the other moral obligations of civil and religious society. I fear there are not eight of them to be found in my district, who can read in any book. The pastoral visits of ministers of religion are exceedingly infrequent, and instruction of any kind, rarely within their reach." We met at his dinner table, ten other gentlemen and three ladies, all of the colored class; three of the former were members of Assembly. They are relatives, and are just come into joint possession of an estate. They have commenced paying wages for the day and a half, of their apprentices' own time, at the rate of three bitts a day, (eleven pence sterling.) We have learned from several sources, that the proprietors and attornies of the island generally, compensate their apprentices for their own time, either by payments of fish, or by returning the time at their own convenience. They studiously avoid paying wages — a short-sighted policy, which originates in prejudice and interest; the attornies being also merchants, and receiving a profit on the fish supplied to the estates. We were informed that the refugees from Martinique, of whom there are from three to four hundred in the island, are as a body, peaceable, well-disposed and industrious. The gentlemen above mentioned have twelve of them on their estate, who work satisfactorily for wages. They are rarely employed, or in any way encouraged by the other planters. In some instances, even where negros who have bought their time, have been willing to remain as free laborers, they have been discharged from the estates. One of us called in the afternoon on JOSEPH FADELLE, Esq., known in England for his fearless exposure of colonial wickedness in high places.* He observed, that though there was less oppression than at the commencement of the Apprenticeship, he did not consider the condition of the people even now, better than during sla-

---

* Vide Appendix B. Sec. iii.

very. Had this visit been paid him twelve or eighteen months ago, four or five would probably have been publicly flogged within sight during the interview. There was a vessel to-day in the harbor, freighted with emigrants to Demerara. One of us went on board, and ascertained by conversation with the people, that they were going of their own free will. They were chiefly mechanics, free persons of color, from the Swedish and Danish islands of St. Barts. and St. Thomas. Some of them appeared very intelligent. They gave as a reason for indenting themselves, that they could not set up in their respective trades in Demerara, without serving at least one year. Not a single apprentice has been hitherto induced to leave Dominica.

20th.—We left at seven this morning in a canoe with WM. LYNCH, to visit one or two estates in his district, on the North West side of the island. The ocean is the high-way from Roseau to most of the estates. The island is, however, encompassed, and also intersected in various directions by roads, which are impassable except on mules or horses. The negros are expert rowers, and their long narrow boats, formed out of a single tree, cut through the water at the rate of five or six miles an hour. We had an opportunity of observing the mode of fishing among them. Three or four canoes, loaded with stones, take a large net about ten feet deep, and from sixty to one hundred yards in length, to some distance from the shore, which they let down; the lower edge being weighted with lead, and the upper supported by pieces of cork. The stones in the canoes are then thrown with great violence into the sea in such a direction as to frighten the fish towards the shore, when a canoe at each extremity drags the net rapidly to the beach, and the fish is secured. The near view, from the sea, of the hills and ravines is extremely grand. They are covered with luxuriant tropical verdure, and trees loaded with fruit and flowering shrubs, to the water's edge; except where the cliff, sometimes for considerable distances, presents a perpendicular face of rock. Dominica is truly a highland country, a land of mist, and rainbows, and mountain torrents. The beds of the valleys are the sites of the principal estates, and the light green of the cane fields is in beautiful contrast with the deep, rich verdure of the hills, which enclose them on either side. We arrived in about two hours at our destination,—a free village at the mouth of a considerable stream. We proceeded to the cottage of a respectable old negro woman, who keeps a shop for the sale of bread and provisions, the only one, we believe, in the island, except in the towns. The Stipendiary has taken a room in her house, which has been fitted up for his accommodation, when unavoidably compelled to be more than a day from home. His landlady has been ten years free. She is now upwards of eighty years of age, has never been married, but has always borne an irreproachable character. She appears to be a person of very cheerful piety, and exercises, we are told, the happiest influence over her neighbours. She is a class leader amongst the Wesleyans, who have a chapel in the village, where service is usually performed every Sabbath, by one of the missionaries or a local preacher. She is a bright example of usefulness and true respectability in a very humble sphere. Her house was in nice order and very clean, and the adjoining gardens neatly fenced. We met here a young man from Sierra Leone, who had been brought all the way from his native country, by a letter from an uncle in Dominica.

He is now anxious to return. He is an intelligent, well-disposed negro, and a tolerable scholar, and is employed by W. LYNCH, to teach a few of the children in the village and from the neighbouring estates.

Having sent a message to the manager of Hillsborough, the adjoining estate, he kindly sent his boat for us to cross the river, which for half a mile from the sea, is three hundred yards broad, and of considerable depth, beyond which it is obstructed by rapids. It abounds in fish. Its banks are covered with the bamboo, guava, &c. Coming from Antigua, the rank luxuriance of this more humid climate, struck us with astonishment. The orange, shaddock, lime, guava and other fruit trees grow wild in great profusion; the soil throws up natural rank grasses; creepers and shrubs hang about the steep sides of the cliffs, while the summits and more gentle declivities are covered with thick forest and brushwood. The cane grows too rank and luxuriant for the full secretion and maturation of its saccharine juices, so that it is less productive than in the dry, exhausted soils of Antigua and Barbados. The estate we visited is one of the finest in the island. It occupies a perfectly level plain of considerable extent, limited on one side by the line of bamboo, which marks the course of the river, and shut in on the other, in the form of a half circle, by a hill, apparently almost perpendicular, except on one sloping side, which is occupied by the negro gardens and huts. On the height above them is the manager's house, which is again overtopped by mountains, but which is still lofty enough to command a view of the works and cane fields, spread out like a map, with the sea front in the distance. A large stone vault, at some distance from the house, is used as the burying place of the white residents; and near the same spot also is a handsome tomb erected over the remains of a former attorney of the estate, at each end of which is a magnificent palmetto, or cabbage-tree, with trunks as straight and columnar as if chiselled out of marble. This is a much more beautiful palm than the cocoa nut tree, though at first sight they would usually be confounded by an European. The cabbage is the upper part of the trunk, which has a green appearance, and is of a pulpy, vegetable consistence. From the summit of this, branches out a graceful crown of gigantic leaves. The cabbage is described as very palatable, but unfortunately the tree must be destroyed to obtain it. The manager kindly provided us with horses and mules to make a little excursion up the valley. Our path was just wide enough for the animals to pass, with the river below us on one side, and a wall of rock many hundred feet high on the other, sometimes so absolutely perpendicular as to be free from vegetation, but usually covered with shrubs and creepers. One beautiful spot in this valley was marked by the tomb of an overseer of a neighbouring estate, who had died from fever produced by the fatigue of a three days' hunt of wild hogs in the woods.

The day was so showery, that we were soon compelled to return, but as far as we could see, all seemed to possess the same features of grandeur, and the same wild character of unsophisticated nature. Little of Dominica, except the river levels and the fertile sides of the ravines, has been brought into cultivation. Not a hundredth part of its resources has yet been drawn upon; for the traces of man's dominion over it are slight indeed. Almost all tropical productions may be cultivated here, and many grow wild, as the cotton tree; the varieties of the citron tribe, some of the spices, the plaintain, banana and several farinaceous roots, the palma christi, medicinal aloe, and many others, which produce valuable articles for consumption or export; and some of which, even in the West Indies, are freqnently the objects of difficult and costly culture. The island imports great quantities of timber, and numbers of cattle and horses, though valuable trees grow on every estate, and there is pasturage sufficient, without cultivation, to support uncounted herds. If it be asked, why man does not put forth his hand and gather the good things which nature provides with such spontaneous bounty, the reply is, that there is no surplus labor to devote to such minor matters; the sugar and coffee cultivation absorb all the resources of the island. Nothing would be easier than to turn its natural wealth to most profitable account, if the two great desiderata of capital and labor, were but supplied. Fourteen thousand laborers are lost in such a fertile wilderness. When the sin and stain of slavery is wholly removed, we may indulge the hope that the tide of emigration will set in to this, and other of these beautiful and almost uninhabited islands.

Many parts of the island have never been explored, except by the Maroons or runaway negros, and the rangers who were employed about twenty years ago, in the war of extermination against them. They were at that time about one thousand five hundred in number, but were entirely destroyed. Many were brought to Roseau and butchered in cold blood; and there is a well there, which though of sweet water, and in the centre of the market place, remains unused to this day, from a belief that it is defiled with the blood of these unfortunate people. The governor who sanctioned these atrocities was recalled. There are many wild hogs in the woods, and a small species of boa constrictor, the guana is not uncommon; and there is a large edible frog, which is caught in great numbers, and esteemed a delicacy. There are also two species of parroquets. The negros are a hardy, muscular race, but far beneath those of Antigua in appearance and intelligence. They have a downcast, distrustful look. Such at least was our observation on Hillsborough estate, where they speak chiefly English, and are considered superior to most in the island. Complaints have almost ceased on this estate, in consequence of a change of system on the part of the manager and his attorney; the latter having lately adopted liberal views. The number of negros is one hundred and three, including old people and children; the females being nearly as two to one. Nine infants have been born since the Apprenticeship, of whom six have died. The manager attributes this great mortality to the negligence and ignorance of mothers, who think that the estate will have a claim upon their children, if they take them to the hospital when sick, or if they allow the older ones to pick grass, tend goats, and do other work suitable to their years. The same want of confidence prevents the people from undertaking task-work, and from working willingly for remuneration in their own time. In the former case we were told by one who had good opportunity of knowing their dispositions, that they thought that task-work was offered them as a bait to see how much they could do in a given time, in order to increase their daily quota. While we were on this estate, a woman with an infant a few weeks old, in her arms, came to complain to the Stipendiary that the father of her child would not contribute to its support. He, it appeared, denied the paternity of it, being regularly married to another woman, by whom he has a family. The magistrate spoke to her on her sinful habits, but she seemed dead to all sense of shame, and went away in a sullen temper. She was very slightly dressed, and her back was marked with the weals of former flaggellations when a slave. The most deplorable consequences have resulted from the promiscuous intercourse and profligacy, which slavery has created. The fertility of the people has been impaired, and their natural affection for their offspring weakened. The whites have incurred a fearful responsibility by the example they have set the other classes. Deplorable, however, as is the present state of things, all agree that in this respect it is improving. Marriages are increasing among the negros, and the character of the married people, is manifestly better than that of the others. We asked to see the hospital, but after waiting some time, were told, that the woman who had the key was on her provision ground at a distance. As we had learned in Antigua that sham-sickness, or what was reputed such, was a marked feature of slavery, we were surprised to learn that this estate was free from it, till the circumstance was explained by the fact, that the negros thought the hospital was haunted by a jumboe, who made noises at night, a superstition which the manager took no pains to remove. We were shewn the cachot or lock-up, a building suitable for solitary confinement. The manager told us that he knew one estate where the cachot was so constructed, that a prisoner could neither stand erect nor lie down. The negros in this island are addicted to rum, an appetite created and fostered by their being rewarded with drams of spirits for extra labor, and as an encouragement in damp weather. They receive no allowances at all except of clothing, and presents of pork, flour and fish at Christmas. They support themselves by cultivating their grounds on the steep sides of the mountains, and by catching sea and river fish. We expressed to the manager our conviction, that it would be good policy to begin paying money wages instead of salt fish; thereby encouraging a desire for those comforts which money only can procure. He agreed with us and said that he had some time before attempted to act upon such views, but that "he had brought the neighbouring planters down upon him." At present all the money which the negros acquire, is earned by taking the surplus produce of their grounds to Roseau, and the other markets. Sometimes they offer the salt fish, which is so injudiciously forced upon them, for sale or barter at the shops. Of their privilege of attending market they are so jealous, that they will scarcely sell their poultry or other produce on their own estate or on the road, even at a higher price.

We had enquired of one of the negros who had rowed us down the river, what difference he found between Slavery and Apprenticeship. He said that he had not yet discovered any. He had once received *thirty-nine* by order of a former magistrate, while he never was flogged when a slave. On that occasion, he acknowledged he had been guilty of tipsy and riotous conduct. In reply to the same enquiry, the manager observed, that he did not think the apprentices were better off than during Slavery,* and that total emancipation would be advantageous for all parties. He did not fear being able to carry on the cultivation under a sys-

* See Appendix B. iv.

tem of freedom. Very few apprentices on this or the other plantations, have been registered as *non-predials*, of those who are immediately employed as domestics. The manager said they preferred to be predials, with the privilege of their large grounds, and related an instance to us, where a non-predial had been made a predial at his own request, giving as a reason, that when his mistress was not at home, " he did not get fed."— It appears to us that the domestics and mechanics of Dominica, as of some other colonies, have been extensively defrauded in the classification, by being registered as predials. The temptation to cane stealing is not so great here as in Antigua, as the negros can grow canes in their own grounds. In one instance on this estate, a considerable quantity were raised by some apprentices, which the attorney directed to be converted into sugar for them, receiving one third of the produce for the use of the mill. This *meteyer* system will probably extend in some of the colonies. We returned to Roseau in the afternoon in our canoe. The day was so continually showery, that we were prevented visiting an adjoining estate. The climate of Dominica is considered unhealthy, but will doubtless become more salubrious and less humid, as it is more extensively cleared and cultivated. We have found it quite bracing, and very different to the dry, relaxing air of Antigua, which is usually numbered among the healthiest islands. It is probable that each island might be beneficially resorted to, by invalids from the other. One of the great recommendations of Dominica, are its delicious rivers, which supply a beverage, the luxury of which, can only be appreciated in a tropical climate, and by those who have been recently restricted to the cistern rain water of Antigua. The last hurricane in Dominica, did much mischief to the estates' buildings, and negro houses. A loan was obtained from Government to rebuild them, which some of the planters openly declare their intention of never repaying. It is secured upon the estates. We heard of one estate where the negro houses and other buildings had been destroyed, on which the loan, instead of being applied to its specific object, was laid out in the general improvement of the property, and after considerable delay, the negros were compelled to rebuild their dwellings themselves, *in their own time.* The manager in this case, was fined in a trifling sum by the Stipendiary, but the poor negros received no compensation.

21st.—The coffee estates in this island, are nearly destroyed by the blight and hurricane. They are mostly small properties, in the hands of the old French residents. Such is their depreciation, that the negros on many of them might be purchased for ten pounds sterling each; but happily they cannot be sold without their own consent, and will not emigrate, or suffer themselves to be transferred to sugar estates. The coffee trees are fast being displaced by canes. On some of these properties the cane juice is manufactured into syrup in a rude way, by the simplest machinery, and sold in Roseau by the bottle. It is often made and sold on the same day.

We left Roseau this afternoon in a canoe, for the Souffriere, distant about eight miles, near the south west extremity of the island, leaving directions for our schooner to follow us in the evening. J. FADELLE and LEWIS BELLOT kindly accompanied us. The coast is of a somewhat different character, from what we surveyed yesterday. The mountains are higher and bolder, but the climate is less moist, and the vegetation less luxuriant. The Souffriere Bay is formed by two projecting reefs. The valley is extremely beautiful, and occupied by a very fine estate, the manager of which, kindly lent us horses and mules to proceed to the Souffriere, which is about two miles from the sea, on the first breast of a mountain. It appears at a distance, like a large white or yellow field on the side of a hill. The whole neighbourhood is filled with sulphureous vapors. A boiling spring issues from the hill, and forms a considerable stream. After crossing it, the fragments of wood and roots of trees appear converted into charcoal; the ground is perceptibly warm, and covered with fragments of almost pure sulphur. We ascended with some difficulty, striding over the hot rivulet, wading through the bushes, and in fear of dipping our feet into fissures filled with boiling mud, to the principal sulphur field, where the side of the hill seemed to consist almost entirely of sulphur. Immediately above it, three springs of boiling water gush out of the rock, from circular orifices, one or two inches in diameter. They fall into a natural caldron below, which was nearly hidden by the steam of the falling water. The bed of the rivulet, which they form, for the first one or two hundred yards, is stained so black as to give it the appearance of a river of ink. There is no crater, and no other evidence of volcanic action, except the boiling springs and this formation of sulphur; but we were told that earthquakes are often sensibly felt, and are sometimes even accompanied by a rumbling noise at certain seasons of the year. A description of the scenery in the neighbourhood of the Souffriere, would seem the language of hyperbole. The bed of the valley is in a high state of cultivation. We proceeded from hence across the island, which is here not more than

.three or four miles in breadth, to visit several properties. The first we called at, was that of a French proprietor, an agreeable middle aged man of liberal principles, and modest, retiring character. We saw on his estate, sad evidences of the ruinous effects of the blight. Coffee is generally grown on the precipitous sides of the hills, where the rain speedily drains off. A plantation of it in these smaller islands may be distinguished at a great distance, as it is cultivated in small diamond shaped fields, fenced in by a stronger and taller shrub, to shield it from the sea breeze. We next visited an estate, formerly belonging to a French proprietor, now dead, and still under the management of his nephew. He instructed his negros himself, with a view to emancipate them, but died before his property was sufficiently unincumbered to enable him to carry his intentions into effect. We saw numbers of the people, who bore witness by their appearance and manners, to the advantages they had enjoyed. A group of happy looking children ran away at our approach, but curiosity overcoming fear, soon brought them back again. We prevailed upon a little boy and girl to read to us, in a book of moral lessons in French, which they had with them. The boy read fluently, the girl was too timid. We gave each of them a small silver piece, when it suddenly appeared that many others could read. The proprietor of this estate, used to present mothers with the freedom of their first child, born in lawful wedlock, a measure attended with the happiest results. Several of the people have bought their apprentices since 1834. They are allowed to occupy their former houses and grounds, and to cultivate coffee, paying half the produce of the latter to the estate. The manager did not seem to be satisfied with this arrangement, but he thought they would not consent to work regularly for wages, though he acknowledged he had never put them to the test. We proceeded from hence to an estate belonging to the grandfather of one of our companions. It is situated immediately above the sea, and there is a parapet wall to prevent children and animals from falling down a precipice of several hundred feet into the water. This like the two preceding, was a coffee plantation, in a state of transition into a sugar estate. The proprietor is eighty-five years old, and of most venerable appearance; his long, white hair flowing down upon his shoulders. He is believed to be the oldest white person in the island. He is very infirm, but retains his mental powers, and much of his French vivacity. His wife is slightly colored, and still older than himself. He seemed delighted to see and to converse with us. His reminiscences extended over nearly three quarters of a century. Forty years ago he remembered expressing to an Irish Catholic priest, his conviction that the negros would some time or other be emancipated. He mentioned also some great lady having told him, that the nineteenth century would be distinguished by great earthquakes and commotions, which he considered to be a metaphor prophetic of Abolition. He was very much amused by one of us telling him, when asked to take wine, that he had drank only water for the last eight years. He said "the frogs drink water," "you are a frog," &c. Though, however, the idea of total abstinence from distilled and fermented drinks, appeared both to amuse and astonish him, yet he acknowledged he owed his advanced age to his temperance. He drank a glass of wine himself, "to the success of our good cause." This benevolent old gentleman, seemed to live in patriarchial style in the midst of his people. Some of the young children almost lived in his house, and served to amuse him with their play; one who was present, received his supper from the table. The negros on this property, we were told, have doubled their numbers within the last twenty years. Nothing can be a greater contrast, than the condition, appearance, and manners, of the people on some of these properties of the old French residents, and of those, on even the well managed English estates. On the former, there has generally been an increase, and on the latter a striking decrease of numbers.* The population of the island has been nearly stationary. The great discrepancy of the sexes, in favor of the females, will operate unfavorably for a series of years. After supper we took leave of this venerable couple, and by the light of a full moon, returned to the Souffriere Bay, where we found our vessel awaiting us, and embarked at ten p. m. The mountain roads of Dominica appear dangerous, but the horses and mules of the country are very sure-footed. The island was named by Columbus from its being discovered on a Sunday. When asked by the King of Spain for a description of it, he is said to have crushed a sheet of paper in his hand and presented it as a representation of the extreme irregularity of its surface. It would be difficult, perhaps, to describe it better.—Notwithstanding the apparent fertility of the island, the cultivation of the cane is described as very laborious. The yearly amount of sugar produced does not exceed three thousand hogsheads. Coffee was formerly its staple, but nearly all the properties on which it was cultivated have been ruined by the prevalence of "the white fly," during the last six years, by which many of the smaller proprietors have been reduced to poverty.

* See Appendix B. Sec. i.

CHAPTER VII.

MARTINIQUE.

12th Month, 22nd, (December) 1836.

Some of our friends in Dominica put into our hands copies of several petitions to the French Chambers, the last of which is dated only a month ago,* from the colored inhabitants of Martinique, (many of whom are themselves slaveholders,) for the immediate abolition of slavery. The views of the petitioners are just and admirably expressed, and coming from persons living in immediate contact with slavery, possess a peculiar value. As we must pass by Martinique, on our way to St. Lucia, we concluded to spend a day or two in St. Pierre and Fort Royal, in the hope of obtaining additional information respecting this anti-slavery movement. We reached St. Pierre, about ten o'clock a. m. A colored gentleman, to whom we had an introduction, came to us immediately on learning our arrival, and staid with us during the few hours we remained. He was a decided abolitionist, but was not one of those principally concerned in the petitions, though his signature was attached to them. Our short stay and the disadvantage we were under in not being able to converse fluently in French, prevented

* See Appendix C.

our seeking the acquaintance of the parties principally concerned in the affair. Our informant stated that there was a general belief in the colony, that the Government would abolish slavery within the next two years. There was also an impression among the slaves, that they would be emancipated. The hours of labor on the estates are from five a. m. to six p. m., with intervals of one hour for breakfast, and two for dinner. They receive no allowances, but have the Saturday for cultivating their own grounds, and Sunday for market day. He mentioned an instance of a slave, who had a free wife and children, and who possessed slaves and other property himself; but who could never induce his master to sell him his own freedom. The trade of the island is now considerably depressed, in consequence of the uncertain aspect of the future. The value of slaves has been much affected by the fear that they will speedily be emancipated without compensation. Fine, strong, young men, recently worth three to four hundred dollars, will now only realise from sixty to one hundred, when sold at public *vente*. The number of soldiers in the colony has been increased, and they are stationed in small bodies all over the island, to prevent the escape of the slaves to Dominica and St. Lucia. About one hundred planters are wealthy, but the majority of estates are encumbered to a greater amount than they are worth. There has been no clandestine importation of slaves into Martinique, since the accession of LOUIS PHILIPPE. We were informed it was generally reported and believed, that the British West Indies were ruined; that England was obliged to import sugar from France, and that some of the Antigua negros, not liking the new *régime*, had made their escape to

Guadaloupe!! Our companion introduced us to his father, who is a planter, and of different sentiments to himself. He confirmed what his son had said respecting the depressed condition of the colony, and the low price to which slaves had fallen, and also repeated some of the current rumours about the British islands. He observed that the slaves in our colonies were "perfectly happy" before Emancipation, because they had legal protection. In Martinique, however, a master could do any thing with his slave, short of putting him to death; and even in that case, if prosecuted, he would be sure to escape conviction. Since the change in the British colonies, the discipline on the estates had much relaxed; the slaves worked less and were less harshly treated. A strong proof, he thought, that the French Government contemplated the early and entire abolition of slavery, was, that it passed no ameliorating laws. No doubts were entertained, that the slaves would continue on the estates and work if made free, but he feared that the cultivation could not be carried on *profitably*. During our stay at this gentleman's house, we drank some eau sucrè, made of an inferior refined sugar; which on enquiring we found was French *beet-root* sugar.

We went afterwards to the Botanic Garden of St. Pierre, a scene of extraordinary luxuriance and beauty. It is situated in the basin, and on the sides of a circle of mountains, and is a complete labarynth of walks with fish-ponds, cascades, &c. It is devoted chiefly to tropical trees and shrubs of the Eastern hemisphere, with which it is supplied in great profusion and variety.

St. Pierre has from twenty-five to thirty thousand inhabitants. It is a place of great trade, and the principal port in the island, though the harbor is much exposed. We left St. Pierre about four p. m. in a canoe to Fort Royal, leaving directions for our schooner to follow us. It was rowed by five men, one steering with a paddle. They were all naked, except pantaloons, and had rather a savage appearance. One or two of them spoke a little English, but we could not understand a word of their French *patois*. The chest, shoulders, and trunk of the negro are usually a model of anatomical symmetry, and remind us of the antique bronzes. His head and limbs do not harmonize with European ideas of beauty. Two of our rowers were mulattos, the difference of their form was strongly marked. Our canoe was lined at the bottom, and on the sides, with a mat of soft reeds, on which we lay, with a roof over our heads supported on wooden pillars. We were obliged to follow the inlets and outlets of the shore, which made our voyage tedious, and we did not arrive till two hours after sunset. We met two vessels of considerable burthen, employed as droghero, for the shipment of produce, immediately from the estates on the coast. They were each rowed by ten or twelve slaves, who were some of them quite naked, and all nearly so. They stood on benches, placed at intervals across the vessel, and took a stroke with their long oars till they almost reached in a reclining position, the planks or benches behind them. They had then to step with one foot on the deck below, before they could recover their position on the benches to renew the effort. Nothing could be more wretched in appearance than the slaves engaged in this painful and laborious employment.

We reached Fort Royal about nine p. m., and with one of our men as guide, proceeded in search of the *cafè*, to which we had been recommended. We could not find it, and after enquiring at several hotels which were full, we were taken at length to one of rather an inferior description, which was undergoing a complete whitewashing. We found, however, the accommodations tolerable, after divesting our minds of all English ideas of comfort. We met here a gentleman, who spoke English well, and who gave us information precisely corresponding with what we had heard in St. Pierre, of the depreciation in the value of slaves, and of the large military force maintained to preserve the peace of the colony, and to prevent their escape to the British islands. Our landlady mentioned, that a gentleman of her acquaintance, had lately bought twelve slaves, at a very low price, on the speculation that the Government would abolish slavery and grant compensation. The same individual advised her not to sell one of her women that she wished to part with, for the same reason. Her own opinion, however, was that no compensation would be given.

23rd.—Though the seat of Government, and possessing the advantages of a spacious and secure harbor and a more central situation, Fort Royal has not half the commerce or population of St. Pierre, and it is daily declining. It is built with great regularity, and is capable of being rendered a beautiful town. On the South are two sides of a large square, enclosing a lawn called the Savanna, with promenades, shaded by tamarind trees. Near this square is the *Hotel du Governement*. The present Governor is *le Baron de Mackau*, formerly Admiral on this station, and the Officer who executed on the part of France, the treaty recognising the independence of the Haytian Republic. About a year ago he visited Antigua, for the purpose of ascertaining the result of Emancipation, and the impressions he received there, were thought to be favorable to abolition. We paid our respects to him about noon to day, and were received with much kindness. The Baron is past middle-age, stout, and of very benevolent aspect; he is familiar with the colloquial use of the English language. We told him, that having been informed of the interest he had expressed in Antigua, we thought he might be pleased to receive some recent information from thence. We then stated as briefly as we could, the result of our inquiries. He listened to us attentively and made several observations which shewed, that he was closely watching the progress of affairs in the British colonies. He quoted Sir LIONEL SMITH's recent speech to the Assembly of Jamaica, from which he concluded, that things must be progressing unfavorably in that island. The subject was one, he said, in which he felt a deep interest, and it was closely occupying the attention of the Government. It was intended to enlighten the slaves by education, and by increasing the number of priests. On our enquiring whether the planters were favorable to education, he said, some of them were not, but the Government was "positive." The negros themselves were much addicted to religious ceremonies, but shewed no great desire to learn to read and write. He observed that the negros of Antigua were much more enlightened than in their islands. During his visit there, he was delighted to witness their attendance at church, and the attention with which they listened " to the speech of the Doctor." Antigua, he observed, had been in a state of preparation for twenty years. We remarked that it would have made more progress in five years of freedom, than in twenty of slavery, to which he replied with a smile—" I see you would lose no time;"

adding after a pause, "my opinion is the same as yours." We made some remarks on the prospects of the British colonies, and on the Apprenticeship; but fearing we might be imperfectly understood, we offered to forward to him a short memoir on the subject from Barbados, which he said he should be happy to receive. We staid about three quarters of an hour, and left much pleased with our reception.

We went on board about two p. m. and set sail for St. Lucia. The black and colored people whom we have seen in St. Pierre and Fort Royal, are very superior in outward polish of manners to those of the English islands. The field negros, we were told by one party, were more, and by another, that they were less enlightened than in the English islands. They are less educated perhaps, but their faculties are sharpened by coming in contact on the market days with so large a body of white and free colored persons, as is to be found in the French towns. The situation of the French colonies, appears to be approaching a crisis, and we believe it depends upon the Parent Government, whether it shall issue in peace, prosperity and safety, or in general ruin and bankruptcy, if not in bloodshed. The present time is favorable for a great change, because the minds of all classes are in a state of preparation for it, whilst the uncertainty of the future is exercising a ruinous and depressing influence on trade and property. It is more than probable, that the colonies owe their present tranquillity, to the persuasion on the minds of the negros, that they will shortly be made free; and there appears to be no obstacle whatever to their emancipation, except the fears of the planters, that free labor will be too expensive. The question is become a purely economical one. In Martinique great annoyance and irritation exist respecting the escape of slaves to the British Islands, which has been checked for a time, by a large military force picquetted in parties of five or six men all over the island; but take away the hope of freedom from the slaves, and they will make their escape in spite of every precaution; and whether they drown in the attempt, or reach the opposite shore, the loss is the same to their masters and the colony. The distance from land to land, to Dominica on the one side, and St. Lucia on the other, is only twenty miles, and several of the parties who have recently escaped, have ventured across on mere rafts. Of three thousand slaves who have thus disappeared from Martinique, only twelve hundred are accounted for, as having reached the British islands; so that it would appear, that nearly two thirds perish in the desperate attempt. When it is considered that these slaves are chiefly men, and of the most robust of the people; and that the depopulation of the colony in a still more rapid ratio, is prevented only by bringing out from Europe, and maintaining, a body of two thousand soldiers, the oppressive burdens entailed upon this small colony by slavery, may be faintly appreciated.

CHAPTER VIII.

ST. LUCIA.

12th Month, 24th, (December.) 1836.

On coming on deck this morning, we found ourselves lying securely at anchor in the Bay of Castries, having had during the night a favorable wind. This is one of the finest harbors in the Leeward islands, being spacious and secure, free from shoals, and possessing good anchorage, though somewhat difficult of access, as it is almost land-locked. We called soon after our arrival on the Chief Justice, the Hon. JOHN REDDIE, whose acquaintance we had had the pleasure of making in England. We also addressed a note to the Governor, Sir DUDLEY HILL, to enquire when it would be convenient to him to see us; and in the interim, attended the Court where the Chief Justice was disposing of cases of misdemeanour, &c. Two prisoners, were successively indicted for petty thefts, both of whom pleaded guilty. The proceedings were entirely in French. The Governor whose cabinet was adjoining, sent his secretary to say he was ready to receive us. He gave us a courteous welcome to St. Lucia, and expressed a desire to faciliate our inquiries. He spoke favorably of the state of the colony, and of the condition of the negros. He had himself in his recent annual circuit of the island, asked them in the presence of their masters, whether they had any complaints; but with one or two exceptions, the answer had always been in the negative. Great improvements had been effected in the colony since his arrival. Its large debt was nearly liquidated, the port had been much improved by the construction of a wharf, and a road had been made across the island. Estates, he observed, had risen in value since Emancipation. The Martinique refugees, were on the whole, a peaceable, industrious set of laborers. The apprentices who bought out their time, usually continued to work for wages on the estates. He thought the appraisements were in some instances too high. He had endeavoured to dissuade some of them from purchasing their freedom, by telling them, that if they would wait till 1840, they would have their money to commence the world with; but they argued in reply, that wages were now very high, and would fall when all became free. We also called upon the Rector, who is the only Protestant minister in the island. There are but four hundred protestant inhabitants, of whom all are English but two. The Rector has three schools under his care, of which the one in town is attended by about forty children. They learn rapidly, though the lessons are in English; but as soon as they can read, their parents think they know enough, and remove them. The want of qualified teachers, is a great obstacle to more extended education. We were introduced in the course of the day, to WILLIAM MUTER, a proprietor of several estates, and an extensive merchant and ship-owner; and also to DR. ROBINSON, both of whom are members of Council, and actively concerned in promoting the welfare of the colony. The former invited us to visit his estates. He has no fears of his negros leaving him after 1840. He told us that he found it difficult to induce them to work for him on the Saturday, as they are entirely dependent for support on their labor in their provision grounds. One woman, on his offering her wages for her Saturday, asked him if he did not go to church on the Sunday; observing, that if she worked on the estate on Saturday, she must cultivate her ground on the Sunday; reasoning which admitted no reply. Dr. Robinson observed, that he did not think the condition of the negros in any respect improved under the new system, except that they work one hour per day less; and that unless different measures are adopted by the Government, they will be in no better state of preparation for freedom in 1840, than they were in 1834. The mortality among the free children has been very great, both from the want of attention to them on the part of the proprietors, and from the ignorance of mothers, who were however, by no means deficient in affection for their children. The number of females considerably preponderates in this, as in the other islands, which we have visited. Dr. Robinson mentions the only probable explanation we have yet heard of this anomaly. He believes that an inspection of the registry of slaves, from 1815 to 1834, would shew that half the males died before attaining the age of twenty, while not a third of the females died within the same period; a disparity which he accounts for, by supposing, that the severe labor to which both sexes are subjected at the same age, is less destructive to the female constitution, in consequence of its being more early matured. The population of the island, has however increased within the last few years.

25th.—Christmas Day.—A military band paraded the town early this morning, and serenaded the public functionaries in honor of the day. Among other tunes, they played one composed by the negros, and called "President Jeremie," a name much revered by the blacks. They found in JEREMIE, for the first time, a protector, and a dispenser of impartial justice; and we are assured that this single circumstance has contributed to elevate their national character. The benefits of his residence, were not, however, limited to the negros; as first President of the Royal Court, he possessed, under the old French Constitution, a civil as well as judicial power, which he exercised in a variety of ways, for the general good. Many important public works, and among others the church,—the sole protestant place of worship, were begun and perfected through his exertions and influence. His efforts were often frustrated by the continual local opposition, which he encountered, and he was left almost unsupported by the Home Government; but his chief opponents are now dead, and their sons, and those of them who remain, do not hesitate to say, that he was the greatest man who ever came to St. Lucia. Through his exertions, the obstacles raised by the proprietors to good government, have disappeared, and many of them are now willing to aid in the work of education, while those who are opposed to improvement are powerless.

26th.—We left Castries early this morning, on a visit to two of the estates of W. MUTER. The distance by land is about eight miles, and the road dangerous, fatiguing, and almost impassable, but through scenery of indescribable beauty. Our path was over a succession of lofty ridges, and through the estates which occupied the intervening valleys. From the heights, we had extensive prospects of mountains clothed with primitive forest, above and around us; and of ravines and valleys beneath us, in the same wild and uncultivated state, occasionally diversified by extensive gardens of the plaintain and banana, fields of canes, negro villages, and sugar works. St. Lucia is to a greater extent even than Dominica, an unoccupied wilderness. The character of the two islands is very similar; both possess a feature of singular beauty, in their large and perfectly level savannas, enclosed by precipitous hills, with a stream running through them to the sea. The two estates we came to visit, occupy one of these valleys. They are very fine properties, and in a high state of cultivation. There were on them both, about four hundred and fifty negros in 1834, of whom eleven have since purchased their time. Three of these remain working for wages, of whom one is a field laborer, receiving fourteen-pence sterling per day, besides house and ground rent free. We noticed a fine young ox dead in the pen, which was supposed to have killed itself by sticking its horns in the soft earth. The occurrence did not excite much attention. The loss of stock from the unskilfulness of the apprentices, is very great, and ought to be noted among the disadvantages of uncompensated labor. The crop has commenced on these estates, and is expected to yield about four hundred hogsheads of sugar. We went over the two boiling houses, at each of which there is a steam engine. In the colonies which we have visited, the night-work in the boiling house, has been of late years much curtailed, or altogether dispensed with, and so far as we can learn, without any disadvantage. We also went into one of the cane pieces, where a gang of about fifty negros, chiefly women were employed in cutting the canes. We spoke to the proprietor, who accompanied us, of the desirableness of married women, ceasing to be employed regularly in the field, and merely rendering assistance in the busy season. He expressed his full concurrence in our views. Here as in Dominica the cane is of more luxuriant growth than in Antigua or Barbados. It is reaped by two strokes of a sort of cutlass; the one taking it off about the middle, and the other close to the ground. The negro then cuts off the leaves, and the plant, which consists of the one or two incipient joints at the top of the cane. The cane, the plant, and the leaves are thrown into separate heaps, to be carried away on the backs of mules. In the cultivation of the cane, the season for planting and reaping is the same, and lasts from one third to half of the year. The cane is not indigenous, and though of such vigorous growth, it does not go to seed in the West Indies. It is propagated by the plants before mentioned, which of course can only be obtained during crop. On this estate, the piece which was being planted, was not holed in the usual manner, but hoed into ridges, in which the plants were inserted about twelve inches asunder, in rows running east and west, that they might sustain the least injury from the wind. The rows are five feet apart, so as to admit of the growing plants being weeded with the plough or horse hoe. This we believe is the mode in use in Mexico. It has been partially tried on this estate, and with success. The saving of human labor, as compared with the customary plan, is obviously very great. The proprietor intends on his next visit to England, to endeavour to bring out some Scotch peasantry, young married persons, to enable him to introduce the plough in an efficient manner. Even on these well managed properties many changes might be advantageously made. Among others the fields might be intersected by tram-roads, on which all the canes could be conveyed to the principal boiling house, which is large enough to manufacture sugar for both estates. The persons employed to feed the mill, and carry away the magass or pressed cane-trash, were chiefly women and young persons. There were six men and one woman employed as criminals, in the severer labor of carrying the bundles of canes from the place where they had been deposited by the mules, up to the mill. These had been condemned to six months' imprisonment and hard labor, for attempting to escape to Martinique, at the instigation of a refugee, who had persuaded them, that the French, by way of reprisal, had determined to set all British apprentices free, who came over to them. At the request of the proprietor, they were allowed to remain on the estate, working under the superintendence of the rural police, and being locked up at night. We visited the hospitals on both estates, which are roomy and well ventilated buildings. There were eight or ten patients in each, chiefly with sore legs. In this moist climate a slight scratch is liable to become an obstinate ulcer, unless it receives medical attention. It is singular, that elephantiasis and black scurvy, are rare here and in Dominica. They are diseases of the dry islands. The loss of infants also, by convulsions and locked jaw, so common in Antigua, is almost unknown. Dr. ROBINSON informs us, that the greatest number of deaths occur between the ages of eighteen months and five or six years; which he attributes to the unripe guavas and other indigestible fruits, which they gather and eat when their parents are at the field. He believes that infant schools would have an important, though indirect advantage in this respect.* On these two estates

---

*A striking confirmation of this observation of Dr. ROBINSON is contained in the following memorandum, dated 1832, furnished us among other valuable remarks by H. M. SCOTT, the benevolent proprietor

the free children have had the same attention as before, and consequently there has been no diminution of numbers, by excess of deaths over births. The proprietor took us to see his estate school, the only one in the island. The children are taught by a respectable colored man, who was formerly a carpenter on the plantation. There were about thirty present, from four to twelve years of age, who had been learning about eight months. Some of them read easy lessons of one and two syllables, and spell very correctly. Their pronunciation is extremely good, but we found they were ignorant of the meanings of many of the words. As soon as a few become familiar with English, they will be of great use in bringing the rest forward. We were taken to see a little girl in one of the cottages, who was an albino. Her skin was originally quite white, but is now sun-burnt to a light brown shade; her head was covered with white wool. The parents, who were both black, have had two other children distinguished by the same peculiarity.

On our return, we noticed on the hill sides, the cottages and gardens of some of the Martinique refugees. One of them has a little plantation of canes, which he manufactures into sugar, in a small, rudely constructed mill, and sells in Castries. This display of industry and enterprise, excited the jealousy of a neighbouring planter, who prosecuted the men for stealing two trees from his estate, to make a boat. The

of Hopeton and Lennox estates, Jamaica. "Previous to the establishment of a school at Hopeton in 1824, the greatest degree of mortality prevailed among the children of tender years, that is to say, from the time of weaning to eight years; it is remarkable that from the commencement of the school, (a period of nine years) only seven children, from two to fifteen years, have died, three of whom fell victims to the malignant dysentery of 1831.

refugee proved that he felled them on the bit of ground which had been given him to clear and cultivate for himself. There are six hundred refugees in this island, and it is allowed that they contribute to the prosperity of the colony. They have introduced at Castries, the manufacture of tiles, and the porous water jars, so extensively used in the West Indies. One gentleman, whom we visited, has one of them in his service as a groom, and spoke highly of his industry and good behaviour. The young man himself told us he did not love his own country, "it was no good." The majority of the refugees, it is said, bear an indifferent character, but it is only surprising that they are not totally demoralised and discouraged by the conduct of the government and proprietary body towards them. We passed to-day through a sugar estate, which, though possessing every advantage of situation, was in a state verging on ruin, from carelessness and neglect. Whole fields of canes were so choked with long grass and weeds, as to be fit for nothing but to be ploughed or hoed in. We set out on our return about an hour before sun-set. A shower had rendered the air still more clear than in the morning, and the scenery was if possible more beautiful. After sun-set the air was lighted up by fire flies, floating about like sparks, one moment extinguished and the next re-appearing. They seemed to be governed by a consentaneous impulse; sometimes the valley below us appeared like an abyss of darkness, suddenly it would become an inverted firmament, studded with stars; and then as suddenly relapse into darkness. The loud croaking of frogs, and the chirping of grasshoppers, filled the air with a singular night music. St. Lucia abounds with serpents, the most remarkable of which, are the boa constrictor, and a mahogany colored snake, of a very venomous nature, which is peculiar to some parts of North America, to this island, and to Martinique. It is frequently causing loss of life. Here also, and at Martinique, they have a bird of song called the "*rossignol*," which is believed to be identical with the mock-bird.

St. Lucia produces chiefly sugar and coffee. The average yearly produce of the former has declined from ten thousand to three thousand hogsheads since it became a British possession. The prospects of the coming crop are favorable; it is expected to reach four thousand hogsheads. The coffee plantations have also declined, in consequence, as is supposed, of an alteration of climate; but the injury is less extensive and severe than in Dominica. We passed to day through an abandoned plantation of cacoa, which was once extensively grown, but has declined in consequence of the low price to which it has fallen. St. Lucia is a crown colony and governed by Royal Orders in Council. It has, however, a colonial Council appointed by the crown, and consisting of an equal number of unofficial members, and of members holding important offices under Government. It possesses legislative powers, but is entirely under the control of the Colonial Office. The ancient constitution and laws of the colony are not yet abrogated, though they appear to be gradually disappearing. The French language is almost exclusively spoken by all classes. The lady of the Chief Justice, informed us that there were only two ladies in the colony who spoke English till the arrival, a few days since, of the wife and daughters of one of the Stipendiary magistrates.

St. Lucia has been more completely neglected, both by the government and people of England, than any other colony; and its black population is therefore more degraded and ignorant. It was observed to us by an enlightened and influential resident, that " not a ray of light has yet reached the island, from any of the religious or benevolent Societies of the mother country. Another gentleman assured us, that it has not received twenty pounds a year, for educational purposes from Government, out of the large sums which have been granted; nor any assistance fr omany of the Societies. The numbers at present under instruction, out of a laboring population of fourteen thousand, does not probably exceed one hundred children; yet there is a field open to teachers and missionaries, which appears to possess peculiar advantages to compensate for its peculiar difficulties. Many of the proprietors, we are assured, are ready to assist in furnishing suitable buildings for schools. The Council are anxious to speed the work, and have more than once brought the subject under the consideration of Government, but without effect. Several gentlemen have given us their opinion, that the obstacles to the education of the negros created by the French language and Roman Catholic religion, would be obviated by sending out natives of Guernsey, or others possessing a familiar acquaintance with French, and by the use of the books and scripture lessons prepared by the Irish Education Board.* It is generally agreed that the English language only should be taught in the schools, and that its diffusion is essential to the permanent improvement of the colony.

* These sentiments are recorded, as shewing the anxiety of some of the principal colonists to second any efforts that may be made to promote education. We would not be understood as expressing any opinion of our own on the propriety of establishing a particular system.

The resident proprietors are chiefly French; many of them are moral and respectable. A pleasing instance was mentioned to us, of judicious liberality on the part of one of them, the proprietor of a coffee estate. He gave two of his head negros a piece of ground to cultivate in canes, and lent them money to erect a little mill. They made the first year a profit of sixty pounds, and he reasonably anticipates, that they will be glad to continue as his tenants when they become free. This gentleman is actuated by native liberality and benevolence; like many of the French colonists, he has never been further from home than Martinique, where they are usually sent in early life for education. The dissolute morals of a part of the white and colored inhabitants of this colony, as well as of those which we have previously visited, with the exception of Antigua, cannot be described in a work intended for general perusal. The only redeeming feature in the existing state of things, is the general testimony, that marriages are increasing, and that there has been a visible improvement in recent years, in the morals of the colored people and apprentices.*

---

* Several circumstances were mentioned to us in St. Lucia, which it would have been our duty to have alluded to here, but they have subsequently been brought under the notice of the Government, and we therefore await the result of an authorised investigation.

CHAPTER IX.

BARBADOS.

12th Month, 27th, (December,) 1836.

We left St. Lucia last night. Our little schooner, we find, belongs to the Superintendent of Barbuda; three of the sailors are natives of that island, and our Captain is a colored man from Antigua.*

28th.—We arrived at Carlisle Bay this morning after a fine passage. We saw several small whales in the channel between Martinique and St. Lucia; and a few days ago, the sailors caught a dolphin, which gave us the painful opportunity of witnessing in its dying agonies, the changes of color, for which it is so celebrated. We thought them more extraordinary than beautiful.

Bridgetown, Barbados, 12th Mo. 29th, 1836.—We called to-day upon A. Stronnach, the agent of the Mico Trustees, who has recently arrived in this colony. He is busily engaged in raising a building, in a densely populated neighbourhood, for an Infant school. He has before him a prospect of extensive usefulness.

12th Month, 31st.—We paid a visit to W. Moyster, at Providence, in Christ Church Parish, a distance of seven miles from Bridgetown. Our road, for upwards of a mile, was through the principal suburb of the town, which is a place of great bustle and importance, com-

---

* See Appendix D.

pared with the other towns we have yet seen in the British islands. He related to us an instance of a Wesleyan minister, formerly resident in this island, who though a good man and an excellent preacher, lost the confidence of the negros; and with it his usefulness among them in the country districts, by marrying into a planter's family. The negros said of him, "He eat with manager, and drink with manager, and manager tell him what to say to us." We made many inquiries of him on the subject of education, and it appears from his statements, that the schools are totally inadequate to the wants of this dense population. About two hundred children attend the Sunday school at Providence Chapel, and he had also established at his own expense a day school, which was attended by seventy children; but he was about removing immediately to St. Vincent, and it would depend upon his successor whether it was continued. The Wesleyan chapel here was built at the sole cost of a neighbouring planter, now deceased, who has also left the society a considerable reversionary interest in the estates. This gentleman attached himself to the Wesleyans from their first arrival in the island, and shared in their early persecutions. He manifested a real concern to promote the physical comfort and moral elevation of his negros, and in his will bequeathed to each of them half an acre of ground. We subsequently passed through a part of the estate which is now in the possession of his widow. The negro houses are large and commodious, and each of them surrounded by a garden filled with cotton trees.

We were introduced to an individual in this neighbourhood, who is a man of color, and one of a class of small, independent freeholders, which is scarcely known in our other West India Colonies. He cultivates his patrimony of seven and a half acres of land, upon which he has erected a small mill and boiling house, where he grinds and manufactures into sugar, his own canes, and those of his brothers, who reside near him. He receives a fair proportion of the produce for the use of his works. He is the owner of two or three apprentices, and also employs, on the Saturday, laborers from the neighbouring estates, at one shilling sterling per day; a price, which he thinks cannot be given, when the cultivation is entirely carried on by free labor. The allowance of provisions to the apprentices is thirty pounds of yams or sweet potatoes, or ten pints of Guinea corn per week; two pounds of salt fish per week, and two suits of clothes per annum. Half an acre of land and twenty-six days in the year, i. e. every alternate Friday, are sometimes substituted for these allowances. Taskwork was extensively introduced some time ago, but has been generally abandoned; because, as he thinks, the " scale of labor " was too high.*

We called at the nearest parish school. The parishes are thirteen in number, and in most of them the Bishop has established a school. Being vacation week, we could not see the children, but we had some conversation with the master and two colored men, who were also schoolmasters. At this school there are more than one hundred on the list, of whom ninety is the average attendance. From the statement of the masters it appeared, that their schools had been injured by the sudden introduction of the pay system, instead of the gratuitous plan on which they were

---

*See Appendix E. Sec. iii.

commenced. They complained also that no uniform plan of instruction had been adopted; and that the clergy seldom visited their schools, or otherwise manifested any interest in them.

We returned to town by a different route. In the morning we had seen many negros going to market with their trays on their heads, and now met numbers returning, having disposed of the produce of their grounds, and supplied themselves with articles from the town in exchange. Barbados is very highly cultivated. The weather during the last year has been favorable, and there is a prospect of a large crop; the canes appear strong and heavy, and very few of them have arrowed. They present a great contrast to those of Antigua.

1*st. Month* 1*st., (January,)* 1837.—THE SABBATH. —We went this morning to the Moravian Chapel, in a part of the town called the Roebuck. There were about one hundred persons present at the service. This is a new station of the Brethren, and one in which they have the prospect of extensive and most useful labors; being situated at the edge of the town, with a dense and neglected population on one side, and a district of estates on the other.

2nd.—We called to-day upon several persons intimately acquainted with the state of the colony, and regret to state that all the information we received, is of an unsatisfactory nature; with the single exception, that the proprietors are prosperous, and that the island was never in a higher state of cultivation. One gentleman, who is in the interests of the planters, informs us that the small estates are worth double what they were five years ago, and that estates then valued at twenty thousand pounds, would now fetch thirty-five thousand.

Our informant said, he came out to Barbados with English feelings on the subject of slavery; but his residence in the colonies, and the acquisition of slaves, appeared to have given him a most unfavorable impression of the negro character. He complained particularly of his domestics. Though most anxious to be rid of them, he said they were such wretches, that for the sake of society, he could not conscientiously emancipate them. He was obliged to have three grooms to look after one horse, &c. Without at all concurring in a general extension of these sentiments to the non-predials, it is generally allowed in the colonies, that the Apprenticeship has had a more unfavorable effect on their character, than on that of the field laborers. Other disinterested persons speak unfavorably of the condition of the apprentices. The Stipendiaries are, perhaps, with a single exception, accustomed to share the hospitalities of the planters. Many of the apprentices complain, that they have fewer privileges than before; they are not allowed to raise and keep poultry and other small stock to the same extent; and in consequence, a rise of prices has taken place in Bridgetown market. The free children are much neglected. After 1834 many of the planters turned them off the estates, provoked by the disappointment of their expectation, that the parents would consent to apprentice them; an expectation which was baffled by the perseverance of the mothers, acting under the advice of the Governor, Sir LIONEL SMITH. This extreme measure against the free children, was happily not persevered in; but cases have recently occurred, where it has again been resorted to. On the estates of a once humane resident proprietor, the children are taken care of in the estates' nurseries as before; but in the vast majority of instances, they are neglected. If there is an Infant School in the neighbourhood, they resort to it several hours before the instruction commences, simply because they know not where else to pass the time; as their parents lock their doors when they go to the field, and the children are not allowed to be about the estates. The mortality amongst them has been very great since 1834. The boon of freedom granted, as if in mockery to their helpless infants, has proved a source of misery and bitter persecution to the negro mothers. In some cases where the planters have changed the allowances of the negros for half an acre of ground, and the alternate Fridays, the latter have suffered great distress, in consequence of being left without the means of support till their land was brought into cultivation.

3rd.—We visited this morning the infant school, under the care of Brother KLOSE, the Moravian missionary at Sharon. There were from sixty to seventy children present, of two to eight years of age. Two only of the older ones were apprentices, and their parents paid a consideration to their masters, for the privilege of sending them. A few of the children evinced a fair proficiency in reading, spelling, and the multiplication tables. Some of them wrote on slates. Speaking of the destitute whites, of whom there is a large number in the island, Brother KLOSE mentioned an instance of a lady, whose property was entirely destroyed by the hurricane of 1831,* and who was taken in and supported by one of her former slaves, who had previously purchased her freedom.

From Sharon we proceeded to Government House.

---

* See Appendix E. Sec. vi.

The Governor, Sir Evan Mac Gregor, received us politely. He expressed himself decidedly in favor of immediate Emancipation, as adopted by the legislature of Antigua; but with regard to the Apprenticeship, he thought the time was now come for conciliation. The remaining term being comparatively short, he thought it of great importance, that there should be no unnecessary irritation of the planters, respecting defects in the provisions of the local Abolition Bill, or abuses which will expire with the Apprenticeship. He would rather endeavour to convince them, that it is their interest to be on good terms with their laborers, and to induce them, if possible, to anticipate the period of ultimate Emancipation.

We had some conversation with the Governor, respecting the jail discipline of the island. We had previously heard of a case which occurred recently, of a woman who was sent by one of the Stipendiaries to the tread-mill. She had an infant in arms, which the jailer refused to receive, and which was therefore left on the road. The circumstance was reported to the Governor, who immediately ordered her to be released, and gave instructions to the Stipendiaries, not to send women with young children to the tread-mill. He has since directed, that pregnant women should not be put upon it. We mentioned the details which had been sent to us, by our fellow travellers Scoble and Lloyd, of the scenes they witnessed in the jail. Sir Evan had then very recently assumed the government. He had already turned his attention to the state of the jail, and had discovered and rectified some of the abuses. He had directed that the superintendent of the tread-mill should no longer carry a cat, but that if the prisoners were refractory, a magistrate should be sent for, and they should be summarily punished by his authority. We requested to be allowed to inspect the monthly journals of the Stipendiaries, which he kindly granted.

After leaving Government House, we called upon the Bishop, who gave us some valuable information on the state of education. There are about eight thousand children in the diocese, receiving instruction in schools under the care of the clergy. The number has declined within the last year, in consequence of an attempt made to introduce the pay system, which has failed except in Demerara. No opposition is now encountered on the part of the proprietors, but many of them manifest much apathy, and render no assistance. The teachers are black and colored persons. The greatest difficulty experienced in this island, is not the want of qualification on the part of colored teachers, but their preference for more lucrative employments. Besides the children actually attending school, many others receive instruction from other children, and improve themselves by attending the Sunday schools.

4th.—One of the Stipendiary Magistrates, has kindly furnished us with a tabular statement of particulars respecting the free children, which he has collected with considerable labor. From this document it appears, that out of eleven hundred and fifty free children, on the forty-nine estates, in the smallest district in the island; sixty-two receive food, fifty-one clothing, one hundred and eighty-nine medical care, twenty-seven some kind of education, and the remainder nothing, from the proprietors of the estates to which their parents are attached. Of those who receive food, clothing, and medical attendance, forty-nine belong to the estate of one humane proprietor.

We visited to-day Mount Tabor, the third Moravian station in Barbados, where we inspected the infant school, in which there were about seventy scholars. About ten or twelve read in the Testament, and spelt very creditably. A few also had begun to write. They were free children, and the master told us their parents were endeavouring to have all of them brought up to trades, and not to agriculture. This is one of the baneful effects of the Apprenticeship, which continues and increases the character of degradation, which is attached to field labor; and creates an injurious distinction between children of the same parents, who were above, and those who were under six years of age in 1834.

5th.—We availed ourselves this morning, of the permission of the Governor, to look over the journals of the Stipendiary magistrates, which occupied us for several hours.* We have made many inquiries respecting the manner in which the Stipendiaries discharge their duties, but neither the information we receive, nor the *primâ facie* evidence of their own records, tends to give us a favorable impression. The departure of one of the early magistrates, Col. BUSHE, is much regretted by the friends of the apprentices. He was removed by military promotion. Another of the present magistrates has the presumptive evidence in his favor, of having been persecuted by the planters, and of having been removed by Sir LIONEL SMITH, from the largest to the smallest district in the island. Were the magistrates disposed, however, to protect the apprentices, the master possesses such powers of annoyance and persecution, that the apprentice can have no effective remedy, in the exercise of his right of appeal. In many instan-

---

* See Appendix E. Sec. ii.

ces complaining negros have had their goats and poultry killed; in others, their houses have been pulled down, and sheds erected instead, six feet by seven, just wide enough to come within the letter of the law, which requires that they shall be provided with "lodging." The turning the free children off the estates; and changing their mode of subsistence by giving them half an acre of rocky, unproductive ground, and twenty-six days in the year, in lieu of allowances, have been already alluded to. We regret to state that the medical men are sometimes made parties to oppression. Three women were recently brought by a manager before a special magistrate, on a charge of refusing to work, two of whom had each a very young infant in arms, and the third twins. The manager produced a medical certificate of their capability. In this instance, however, the Stipendiary dismissed the cases.

6th.—We went this morning to the jail, and by permission of the Provost Marshal were shewn over the whole of it. The wards are kept very clean, and some attention is paid to classification. We were told, that the prison was always healthy, and that during the prevalence of the fever last autumn, not a single case occurred within its walls. So far in its praise. The number of prisoners is two hundred and four; the accommodations are much too small, and at night the rooms are excessively crowded. In one room there are ten men waiting their trial at the next sessions; and among them, some whose cases remain over from the last sessions, at the request of the prosecutor, to the Attorney General. As the sessions or assizes are held only once in six months, these men may endure a twelve months' imprisonment; at the end of which, they may be declared innocent, or if it should still not suit their prosecutor's convenience to appear against them, they may be discharged without any trial at all. It appears extraordinary, seeing the inconveniences experienced, by the insufficient accommodation in the jail, for so large a number of prisoners, and that all the judges and officers of the Court reside within the island, that there should be a jail delivery only once in six months; but that the oppressive consequences of this arrangement, should to some unfortunate prisoners who ought to be presumed innocent, till proved guilty, be aggravated by their cases being remanded over to the next Court, at the wish of their prosecutors, is an intolerable abuse. In another room of the jail, there are twenty men who have been tried and found "not guilty," who are detained till they have each paid twelve and a half dollars for the fees of prosecution. In another small room, were twenty-eight prisoners under sentence of transportation. We saw also the two sick wards, in which there were but few cases. Those who are sentenced to the tread-mill, have to work out afterwards any time they may lose by sickness.

We next went to see the treadmill. Several women and two or three weakly men were upon it. When they did not keep step, the superintendent struck them with his flat hand. There was a cat suspended on a nail in the room, but we did not see it used. The punishment did not appear too severe for the physical strength of the robust, but one of the men seemed quite unequal to the exertion. He was from the first slower than the rest, and soon suffered the mill to revolve against his knees, being held on by the arms from above, and occasionally making ineffectual attempts to resume the step. He was suffered to hang till the time expired. The superintendent told us, that this was the man's constant practice, and that it proceeded from sulkiness; but from an inquiry made by the Provost Marshal, who was with us, it appeared he had been sick. He was old and infirm, and we find it difficult to believe that he would endure torture rather than submit to punishment. Pursuant to an order of the late Governor, Sir LIONEL SMITH, the heads of all prisoners sentenced to the treadmill, are shaved. By the females this is considered the most degrading part of the punishment. It is put in force, whether they are committed for a few days or for three months; whether their crimes are such as imply a moral degradation of character, as stealing, or whether they are those nominal and constructive offences, which form the great mass of complaints against them under the Apprenticeship law; as alleged insolence, insufficiency or inequality of work, &c. Surely for such offences of women, as "linen badly washed, and impertinence;" "doing only half as much in potatoe hoeing one day, as they did the day before;" "the punishment of seven days treadmill, first class,"* would be more than sufficiently severe, without this additional degradation. These barbarous punishments appear to be based upon the theory, that the negro female does not possess the deep feelings and delicate sensibilities of her sex; or if she does possess them, that they are incompatible with her servile condition, and ought to be obliterated. On comparing our observations at the jail, with those of our friend J. SCOBLE, when he visited it six weeks ago, it appears that some of the more glaring abuses, have already been corrected by the new Governor. J. SCOBLE observes, that during the whole time the scenes he wit-

* Journals of Stipendiaries.

nessed were transacting, "the Barbados Legislature were holding their sessions within thirty yards of the treadmill." We incidentally learned, that Sir EVAN MAC GREGOR first became acquainted with the manner in which the treadmill was worked, by observing it from the windows of the Council Chamber. It is impossible to avoid the presumption, that under the same circumstances, Sir LIONEL SMITH must often have witnessed the sufferings, or heard the cries of the unfortunate victims of torture; yet under his administration these things were permitted to continue.

On our return from the jail, we called at the office of the Stipendiary magistrate for the town dictrict. The business for the day was nearly concluded. One negro complained against his master for not giving him his allowance of clothes. The magistrate told him to bring his master before him, but by way of warning, read to him the clause of the Act, imposing a penalty on apprentices preferring false and malicious charges, with an intimation, that he would be punished, if he did not sustain his case. In another case an apprentice summoned her master for refusing to give her a pass to get employment. It appears that many of the nonpredial apprentices procure employment for themselves, and pay their masters the weekly hire of half a dollar, supporting themselves entirely except in sickness. In the present case, the apprentice was willing to pay her hire regularly, but insisted on choosing her own service, while her master insisted on choosing it for her. The magistrate, apparently anxious to make her understand the relation in which she stood, said to her, "You are the property of your master, and he can do what he likes with you. You must not think you can go and work where you please. You are his property; he can make you stay at home to do his work, or he can hire you out to any person he thinks proper." Such is the position of the nominally emancipated negro, and such are the doctrines maintained by a functionary, appointed to carry into effect an Act for " *The Abolition of Slavery.*" The magistrate told us, that the nonpredials were fast buying out their time; he sometimes registered thirty manumissions in a month.

We have heard to day, that a measure is in contemplation, for apprenticing the free children, without the consent of their parents. This report has occasioned great alarm to the friends of the negros.* A gentleman with whom we conversed on this subject, told us that some time ago, a woman came to him with twins in her arms, about three months old, whom her master had desired to apprentice; and when she refused, he insisted on sending them away from the estate. They were taken to a charitable institution where one of them subsequently died. He knew another case, where a master sent away a child about a month old, and refused to allow its mother to go to see it. In this instance the interference of the late Governor, procured redress. He observed to us, that he considered the negro character had been much misrepresented. In the course of a long experience he had found them patient, enduring, and by no means vindictive. They are honest in great matters, though addicted to taking trifling articles, which they do not consider stealing. They have the same natural affection for their children as Europeans, notwithstanding all assertions to the contrary. They are of quick tempers, and apt in their

* See Appendix E., Sec. v.

disputes to break out into violent language, but rarely fight or injure one another. They attach great importance to being addressed in respectful language, and always use it in their common intercourse with each other. They are suspicious of their masters, and can rarely be induced to believe, when he offers them any indulgence, that he has their benefit and not his own in view.

We went this evening to an adult school which is held for an hour twice a week, in a room provided for the purpose by W. M. HARTE, the Rector of St. Mary's. There were about one hundred present, who were nearly all apprentices. Many have no other education than what they receive here.

7th.—We called on the Rector of St. Mary's, who gave us some particulars of the useful results of the benefit societies, formed in connection with his church. One of their regulations that married persons only shall become members of them, has been found very beneficial. Concubinage is now considered discreditable, and marriages are fast increasing among the colored and black population.

An individual upon whom we called to day, mentioned to us a case, of which all the facts have not been ascertained, because the investigation was conducted by the special magistrate, (COULTHURST,) with *closed doors.* So far it is known, that some time ago a letter was sent to the Earl of HAREWOOD, purporting to come from several negros on one of his estates, complaining against their manager for short allowances and ill treatment. Lord HAREWOOD, desirous no doubt to have the complaint inquired into, and if found true, the abuses rectified, sent the letter to his attorney, who handed it to the manager. The manager summoned the negros before the magistrate. They denied having written the letter, or having authorised any one to write it for them; but they persisted that the facts stated in it were true. They were severely punished. One of the men was degraded to an inferior employment, and to escape further persecution, has since raised the means to purchase his freedom. The following circumstance was related to us to day, as illustrative of the advantages of immediate Emancipation. Our informant was some years ago in the colony of Berbice, not long after the emancipation of the Winkel negros, a body of slaves belonging to the Government. He inquired of a person high in office, how these people were conducting themselves. The reply was, that nothing could be more deplorable, than their condition; they were idle and dissolute, and the pest of society; the Government could not have done a greater injury to the colony, than by emancipating them. Shortly afterwards, he saw the Protector of slaves, to whom he expressed his regret, on hearing of the conduct of these liberated negros. The Protector assured him, he had received a prejudiced account; that their deportment was most satisfactory, and that not one of them, that he had heard of, had been taken before a magistrate. Our informant subsequently went to the village where the Winkel negros resided, in order to ascertain which of these contradictory statements was true. He went into twenty of their dwellings in succession, and found in every one, evidences of industry and domestic comfort. In every house there was a bible or testament, and in most of them some one of the inmates could read.

8th.—We went this morning to the adult Sunday school connected with St. Mary's church. Besides a large number of old people, who were under examination as candidates for baptism; there were present about sixty scholars learning to read, in three or four classes. They were from fourteen to upwards of sixty years of age; several very old people were even in the alphabet class, and came, we were told, a distance of eight or ten miles to the school; an affecting proof of the general desire among the negros for education. From the school we proceeded to church. Though the Rector is free from prejudice himself, distinctions of color are still kept up in his congregation. Formerly black and colored persons were confined to the gallery; now they are allowed to occupy the pews in the lower half of the body of the church. The space appropriated to them was much crowded. At the close of the service, a collection was made for paying off the debt on the building of a new church in a neighbouring parish. From a statement which was read, it appeared that one hundred pounds had been contributed to this object, from the "hurricane fund." The application of this fund, deserves to be made a subject of parliamentary enquiry. The distribution of it has been by no means satisfactory to many of the sufferers. It is complained that some persons of small property, who were entirely ruined by the hurricane, had no relief from it, while others of large fortune obtained considerable grants.

One of us visited in the afternoon, the Wesleyan Sunday School, where there were assembled about three hundred scholars and sixty or seventy teachers. The conductor of it was a negro, who made at the conclusion a very appropriate address to the children and teachers. Some prizes of little books were then distributed.

9th.—A gentleman shewed us to day, two old maps of Barbados, which threw some light on the manners and customs of the early colonists. The first was of the date of 1675. The island appeared to have been at that time but partially cleared of its native forest. Among the figures of the wild and domestic animals, was the camel, which was used then and long afterwards, as a beast of burden. There was also a figure of a planter pursuing runaway negros, and firing at them with his pistol. In another map of more recent date, five Quakers' meeting houses were marked.

Archdeacon ELIOT and the Rector of St. Mary's, kindly accompanied us to visit some of the principal schools in Bridgetown, under the care of the establishment. We went first to the infant school, which is attended by one hundred and fifty children; and from thence to the boys' school, where, though it was the first day after the christmas vacation, the attendance was about one hundred and fifty, out of one hundred and eighty on the list. We heard several classes read, and answer questions, in which they displayed considerable proficiency as well as in spelling and arithmetic. About fifty of the children were apprentices. We had not the opportunity of ascertaining on what terms they obtained leave to attend school, except that in one instance, the owner received a consideration from the boy's parent, for allowing him to come. The master is a negro; he was educated in the school himself, and is a well qualified teacher. In the girls' school which we next visited, the attendance was about seventy out of eighty-five. They were nearly in the same state of discipline and proficiency as the boys. In the first class were several apprentices whose mistresses voluntarily sent them for improvement. Barbados is far behind Antigua in the general spread of education, but is in advance of it, in the character of its schools. Besides those which we visited to day, which are in a satisfactory state of efficiency, there are many good private schools for all classes.

10th.—We went at noon to the House of Assembly. This body, like that of Antigua, meets by short adjournments, and is always in session. It is annually elected. The proceedings to day, were not of much interest. Several bills were read a first, second and third time; and, so far as the lower House is concerned, were pushed through their several stages in one sitting. The Solicitor General gave notice, in a speech of considerable length, of a Bill to adopt on the part of this colony, the Imperial Act for a change in the judicial system. The Solicitor General appears to possess great influence in the House, and is reported to possess great influence out of it, particularly in the councils of the Governor. He is a young man of agreeable manners, and a persuasive speaker. He politely introduced himself to us, in the lobby of the House, and conversed with us for a few minutes on the state of the jail, and the administration of criminal justice; and also on the condition of the free children. Their destination, he observed, had become a vital question to the colony. They were now being brought up in habits of idleness and petty stealing. He wished they could be apprenticed till their mothers became free, were it merely for the purposes of maintenance and education; but complained of the jealousy existing on this subject in England, where it was characterised as a perpetuation of slavery. He observed, that sending the children away from the estate, had only occurred in one or two instances, and he expressed much indignation at the conduct of those who had been guilty of it. The great desiderata in the colonies were schools combining agriculture with learning.

11th.—The population of Barbados is supposed to be above one hundred and twenty thousand. According to the ordinary ratio of increase, the colony, without injury to itself, might afford the other colonies several thousand emigrants annually; yet the legislature has passed an Act, the effect of which will be to prevent the laboring population leaving the island. This Act awaits the sanction of the Home Government to become law.

We went this morning to the jail with the Rector of St. Mary's, who is chaplain to the prison. There were about one hundred and fifty present at prayers, whose behaviour was attentive and decorous. One only, of the white prisoners attended—the prejudice of caste being preserved even among criminals. The minister addressed them, at the conclusion briefly and affectionately. We called in the course of the day at the Secretary's Office, and obtained permission to inspect the registry of apprentices. They are duly classified as predials or non-predials, but the return is made by the planters, and tradesmen on the plantations are included in the former class.

We met to day a gentleman of great intelligence and extensive information, who told us, that he knew at least one planter in the island, an attorney for several estates, who was preparing for Emancipation by increasing the comforts of his negros. Probably there are many, who adopt the same enlightened course. He said, that in some instances, the nett profits of the last two years were equal to more than half the value of the fee simple of the estates, and that the prosperity of the planters was unexampled. He feared there was little or no improvement in the morals of a certain class of the colonists. He had heard men, who were accounted respectable, boast of their immoralities, and complain of the change which had taken place in the sentiments of the colored people, and of the presumption of the colored females in aspiring to marriage.

13th.—We went to see the Wesleyan day school. It was commenced some years ago, by a colored man, who was a cabinet maker, in humble circumstances. He observed a number of children, accustomed to play in the street before his door, and conceived the idea of occupying their time and attention more profitably by teaching them to read. He succeeded, and his scholars soon became so numerous, that he was compelled to seek other means of having them instructed. His efforts resulted in the establishment of the present school, which is held in a small, dilapidated building, crowded with about one hundred and fifty children. A considerable proportion of them are apprentices. We heard the first classes, both of boys and girls read and spell, and examined them also in arithmetic. Their performance was very creditable to themselves and their teachers. They answered scripture questions with unusual readiness. Though the expenses of this school are very trifling, yet it is dependent from month to month, on casual assistance.

A local magistrate mentioned to a gentleman of our acquaintance, that he had sent a man to the treadmill, for fourteen days, on a charge of trespass. The man was found at the house of an apprentice on another property, to whom he asserted he was lawfully married. On the magistrate being asked why he inflicted such a penalty, he said the law was imperative.* When the apprentices commit offences against any individual who is not their owner, or against the public peace, they are taken out of the jurisdiction of the Stipendiary Magistrates. This is sometimes made an engine of oppression. One flagrant instance has been mentioned to us, where a negro was accused of some crime by his master, and the threat of prosecution was held *in terrorem* over his head for fourteen months, during which period, he was subjected to much oppression; and when at length he was wearied out and ready to complain to the Special Justice, the threat was carried into execution. He was taken before a local magistrate, who committed him to to take his trial for the offence.

We had to-day the pleasure of making the acquaintance of Joseph Wheeler, the agent of the Bible Society, who has just arrived from Trinidad. Some time ago, he spent several weeks in Hayti, and his observations on the appearance and condition of its population, gave him a favorable impression. We have heard several who have visited Hayti, speak of it in similar terms; but, usually, the inhabitants of the other West India islands, are as little acquainted with its condition, as if it were in the other hemisphere.

We embarked this evening for Jamaica, in the Echo Steamer, which came into port this morning, having left England four days before the packet, which has been long expected, and is not yet arrived.

---

* During our stay in Antigua, we met a gentleman from this island, who informed us that he had thus punished husbands and wives, residing on different estates, for visiting each other, observing that the law allowed the magistrate no discretion.

CHAPTER X.

GENERAL REMARKS.

BARBADOS.

In all the islands which we have yet visited, where the Apprenticeship has been introduced, the Apprenticed laborers are peaceable and industrious; in all of them, property has risen in value since 1834; and, independently of the seasons, the production and export are as large as they were during slavery. In Barbados, the cultivation was never in a better state than at this moment; the ensuing crop is expected considerably to exceed an average, and estates have risen very greatly in value. This prosperity is chiefly to be attributed to the measures of the Imperial Parliament. The colony has received an immense compensation, for losses which it has not yet incurred; and which it is by no means probable that it will ever have to sustain. The state of things may to this extent be considered satisfactory, but it cannot illustrate the effects of Emancipation, except that the price given for estates, proves that the planters are at length persuaded, that they will be able to carry on a profitable cultivation after the year 1840. We do not find that the most distant fears are entertained, that the negros will forsake estate labor when free, or will refuse to work for reasonable wages. On the other hand, so far as the negro is concerned, the Apprenticeship is a system of unmixed evil, and though it may appear in some colonies to be a source of temporary profit to the planter, yet his real and permanent interests would have been far better secured, by adopting the course which has been pursued in Antigua. The Apprenticeship is not Emancipation, but slavery under another name; and though it appears to be in some respects a modified and mitigated slavery; it has also its peculiar disadvantages, which more than counterbalance whatever good it contains. It is not in any sense a state of preparation for freedom. Its introduction was attended with danger, from the disappointment of the excited expectations of the negros; its progress is marked by continual irritation, and at its close, all the real difficulties attending the change of slaves into free laborers, remain to be encountered under the most unfavorable auspices.

Barbados being one of the most important of the British Colonies, and differing from the other islands in its physical character, state of agriculture, and amount of population, as well as in some of the general features of its social system, the following observations may not be deemed unimportant. Though an undulating island, its highest hills are not more than a few hundred feet above the sea. It is, in fact, a coralline formation, covered with a thin layer of soil, from six to eighteen inches deep, except in the valleys and lowlands, where the mould is of great depth and richness. On the higher ground, the rock is in many places exposed. The coasts are so little indented, that it has scarcely what can be called a harbor, but it possesses great advantages of situation, being, according to the regular course of the *trades*, the most windward of the islands, and consequently a station from which all the others are easily accessible. In one respect it is an exception among slave countries, being an extraordinary example of agricultural prosperity. One of the most limited in its natural resources, it is one of the most important of our colonies, in amount of produce, wealth, and commerce. In proportion to its size, it is more densely peopled than China, and is cultivated like a garden. Its soil, though it has long lost its natural fertility, is the source of far more wealth to its proprietors, than the virgin lands of more fertile islands. It has a large and busy capital and seaport, a numerous middle class, and a body of native resident proprietors, who have found it possible to forget that England is "home;" and who glory in the title of "Barbadians." They possess a real nationality, with characteristics, neither English, Irish, nor Scotch. Barbados is called "little England," by way of pre-eminence; a name which it deserves, from the prevalence of English comforts and refinements; though among other features of resemblance to the mother country, we regret to notice, a great body of white paupers,* and numerous licensed houses for the sale of spirits.

Paradoxical as it may seem, it is yet evident, that it owes its superior wealth to its exhausted soil and dense population. "By repeated croppings, the soil (of Barbados,) had become less than half a century since, so much worn, as to be almost unproductive in the sugar-cane; but by the substitution of other crops, particularly the Guinea corn, a system of soiling and tethering cattle was introduced, which has not only been the means of retrieving the lands, but has, perhaps, made them more productive than ever; adding at the

*See Appendix E. Sec. i.

same time to those numberless conveniences and resources, which never fail to proceed from a due attention to the brute animals."* It thus appears, that the wholesome pressure of circumstances, which, to the superficial observer, foreboded nothing less than the ruin of the colony, has occasioned the introduction of a more rational system of agriculture, and elevated the island to its present position. Both in the field and in the boiling-house, the system of the Barbadian planter is many degrees in advance of those of the colonists of the other islands. In the management of their slaves, *as slaves*, the Barbadians equally excelled. Like good farmers, they bestowed the same attention upon them as upon their cattle, and if the negros had been animals and not men, their success would have done honor even to their humanity. Their aim was to keep them in the highest working and breeding condition, in which they succeeded; and though ever reputed the severest disciplinarians, yet theirs was the only sugar colony where the population rapidly increased.

The Barbados legislature was the latest to pass an Act for the Abolition of Slavery, as required by the Imperial Government; and the planters have since succeeded in moulding the Apprenticeship into an almost perfect likeness of the system they so unwillingly relinquished. An equal, if not greater amount, of uncompensated labor, is now extorted from the negros; while, as their owners have no longer the same interest in their health and lives, their condition, and particularly that of mothers and young children, is in many respects worse than during slavery. For a complete exemplification of the character of the Appren-

* Dr. Nugent " Report of Antigua Agricultural Association."

ticeship, we refer to an analysis in the Appendix, of the record of complaints and decisions in the journal of a Stipendiary magistrate, with illustrative cases.* By these it appears that corporal punishments are almost laid aside; but the negros are deprived of their time, on which they are to a great extent dependent, for the maintenance of themselves and their offspring. The operation of the law which compels the apprentices to refund the time lost, when they are punished by imprisonment, (thus imposing a double penalty for the same offence), and the forfeiture of their Saturdays to the estates, have given the planters a direct interest in the punishment of their laborers. Nor must it be forgotten, that there are benevolent planters, who never have occasion to employ the authority of the Stipendiaries; and that this penal and oppressive law, with its costly and complicated administration, is upheld solely for the purposes of men, who know no other means of maintaining their authority, than *terror*, and who can comprehend no motive to induce their negros to labor, but *coercion*. The little that was wanting to make the Apprenticeship the heavy burden, that it now is, to the negros, has been supplied by Sir LIONEL SMITH's "scale of labor."†

The prejudice against color is stronger in Barbados, than in any other colony, although the colored class of its population, is numerous, wealthy, and respectable, and comprises some of the first merchants of the island. No colored student has yet been admitted within the walls of Codrington College. The public opinion of the colony is powerful, and exercises an unfavorable

---

* See Appendix E. Sec. ii.
† See Appendix E. Sec. iii.

influence. There are indeed, two kinds of public opinion, of unequal and opposite forces; first, that of the English public, feeble and indirect in its effects, but setting in a strong tide against slavery, and its accompanying abuses: secondly, the sentiments of the dominant party in the colony, in favour of existing institutions; the belief that the blacks are by nature of an inferior race, and born to a servile condition; and the spirit of caste cherished between the white, mixed, and black races. In none of the British Colonies is this local public opinion stronger than in Barbados; and the slavery of mind among the free classes, is scarcely less obvious than the outward bondage of the negros. Many who have a deep sense of existing wrongs, and some even, who are sufferers in their own persons, dare not express their sentiments; and an individual who refuses to think and speak with the multitude, must live a life of solitude in the midst of society. In all other respects, to one endowed with moral courage, "the spider's most attenuated thread" is not more weak, than this unseen but despotic power, which seals all lips, and fetters all minds.*

---

* The contrast between the state of society in this island and Jamaica, is in this respect remarkable. There the pro-slavery faction is louder and more violent; and persecution has within recent years, raged with all its fury; yet among those who presume to differ from the reigning opinion, there is a freedom of thought and expression, and an independence of action, which cannot be found among the same class in Barbados.

CHAPTER XI.

JAMAICA.

1st Month, 22nd, (January,) 1837.

We came to anchor at Port Royal early this morning, having had a fine voyage and very favorable weather since leaving Barbados. Being in the "trades," we did not employ the steam till within a day of our arrival. The distant view of Jamaica from the sea is of the same verdant and mountainous character as Dominica and Martinique but on a more stupendous scale. The lofty summits of the blue mountains are usually wrapped in clouds. Our only fellow passengers were Captain Belcher, and two of his officers, who were going to take the command of a surveying expedition on the Western coast of America. Their intention was to cross the Isthmus of Panama, proceeding in boats up the river Shagrees and thence across the mountains on mules. As we were entering the harbor, the fleet on this station were leaving it, to blockade the ports of the Republic of Granada, which includes the Isthmus. This intelligence threatened an unexpected obstruction to Captain Belcher's more peaceable operations, especially as he had many packages of valuable apparatus, which could not be conveyed across the mountains without the aid of the natives. We have met in our several voyages, three officers who have visited Pitcairn's island, in the South Seas, and each on different occasions. They all give the same account of the simple and amiable character of these islanders, but observe, that they are beginning to be corrupted by the vices of the Europeans and Americans, whose whaling vessels occasionally touch at Pitcairn's island for water and provisions. The distance from Port Royal across the harbour to Kingston, is about five miles. We went up in a boat with the mail-bags, a circumstance to which we owed the recovery of a number of our letters of introduction; a parcel of them having been stolen from us during our voyage from Barbados to Antigua. Those addressed to parties in Jamaica, had been loosely wrapped in a parcel, and forwarded by the very steamer in which we arrived. The Deputy Post-master General on opening the parcel, and discovering the nature of its contents, politely restored them to us, having learned our arrival from the young man in charge of the mails. As it was the Sabbath, we went in the evening to one of the Wesleyan chapels, a very large and substantial building, but not more than half filled. The congregation was composed of black or colored persons; the body of it being thrown open for the poorer class, and the galleries reserved for the more opulent. At the conclusion of the service, notice was given of sermons during every day in the ensuing week; and we found on inquiry, that the District meeting, or island Conference was about to be held, as well as the anniversaries of the various societies, having a religious or moral object. We subsequently called upon JOSHUA TINSON, the senior Baptist missionary, who gave us a kind welcome to Jamaica.

23rd.—We breakfasted with J. TINSON, at whose house we had the pleasure of meeting W. WEMYSS

Anderson. We were also introduced in the course of the day, to the Attorney General, Dowell O'Reilly, and to J. M. Trew, the Director of the Mico Institution. The Mico schools in Kingston are already established on a large scale; their advantages, however, so long as the Apprenticeship exists, will, with few exceptions, be limited to the free children. We attended in the evening the anniversary of the Jamaica Bible Society. There were five or six hundred persons present, of whom very few were whites. The addresses of the speakers were appropriate and excellent. J. M. Trew, who was in the chair, stated in the course of an animated speech, that at one of the Mico schools in the country, he had recently made a collection among the children for missionary objects. The little sums which they gave, exceeding what he expected from them, induced him to enquire how they obtained their money. They earned it by teaching their adult friends and neighbours to read, after the labors of the day were over. Nearly every one was occupied in teaching his parent, or uncle, or neighbour, and even in some instances, grandfather and grandmother; so highly do even the adult and the aged prize the opportunity of learning to read. The gift book of the Bible Society, comprising the New Testament and Psalms, has been very useful in encouraging the desire for instruction which is at present so general among the negros.

24th.—We have before alluded to the effect of the Apprenticeship on domestic servants. It has taken away to a great extent, the fear of punishment, without supplying any better motive for exertion, in the hope of reward. The landlord of the hotel to which we went on our arrival in Kingston, told us that he had twenty-five apprentices, of whose conduct he made the most grievous complaints. He did not take them before the Special Magistrate, because he knew they would then become totally unmanageable. But while describing the annoyances to which he was subjected, and expressing his desire for free servants, he complained, almost in the same breath, of government, because it did not send the captured slavers here, and apprentice the negros to the inhabitants. A person who has been in the colonies, ceases to wonder at the fact, that slave-masters of European birth and education, are usually more severe than those born in the West Indies. They are accustomed to the active energy of free servants, while the Creoles, though familiar from infancy with despotic power, are more easily satisfied with the indolent languor and comparative inefficiency of their slaves. Conversing on this subject with an estimable gentleman of this city, he observed to us, that, in this country, the heart and temper were often put to a severe trial; and that a man would learn more of his own character in a few months, than in England in as many years.

One of the Special magistrates, STEPHEN BOURNE,* called upon us this morning, and gave us an invitation to his house, which is situated in the mountains, about nine miles distant from town. We drove thither in the evening. The climate of the elevated portions

* This gentleman, to whom we are indebted for his hospitality, and for the opportunity of attending his Courts, has experienced much undeserved obloquy, in consequence of his being supposed to have made statements to us prejudicial to the Colonists. It is due to him to state, that he expressed great anxiety that we should see both sides of the question, and accompanied us to several estates in his district, which were likely to give us a favorable impression of the condition of the negros, and the character of their proprietors.

of Jamaica is temperate and salubrious. Our kind host and his wife, and their interesting family of seven children, of various ages, have enjoyed uninterrupted health, during their two years residence in the Colony. The property on which their house is situated, is a *ruinate* coffee plantation. Besides, orange trees in full bearing, mangoes, pines, and many tropical fruits, English apples, potatoes, peas, and other vegetables, are grown upon it. The latter, however, appear to degenerate.

25th.—This morning we accompanied our host to Silver-hill, an estate twelve miles distant, in the heart of this mountainous district, where he was going to hold a Court. Four cases of complaint were brought before him. They were all substantiated, and the offenders received suitable punishments and admonitions. They thanked the magistrate and appeared satisfied with his decisions, though some had been very earnest and ingenious in their defences. He had listened patiently to all they had to say, and by that means appeared to obtain their confidence. The overseer* of this estate is a man of color; he respects the law, though a strict disciplinarian. He has kept a registry of the births and deaths of infants as during slavery, from which it appears that the comparative number of deaths has not increased. The children have the same medical care, and the same treatment in other respects as before. Not a single free child works on the estate. The overseer asked a woman, in our presence, to let her eldest child, a boy of eight years, do light work for his clothing and allowance, but she

---

* In Jamaica an *overseer* is the person who is called *manager* in the other islands; and the overseers there are here called *bookkeepers*; an attorney, of numerous estates, is called a planting attorney.

replied, "that the child was free, and she did not wish to *bind* him." The effect of the apprenticeship on these children, is, in many respects, very injurious. The overseer treated us during our stay with great courtesy, and offered to accompany us to visit several neighbouring estates if our time had permitted. We returned in the afternoon. The sides of the mountains are devoted to coffee, which grows here without any protecting fence. All the original forest has disappeared, having been at one time cleared for cultivation. The estates are of great extent, and it is customary when the soil is worn out, or rather washed down by the heavy rains, to plant in new ground; as the steep mountain sides cannot be restored to fertility by tillage. The scenery of this part of the island, though often grand and beautiful, has not the freshness which characterises Dominica and St. Lucia. Other parts of Jamaica are yet uncultivated, and covered with primitive forest. The waste lands belong to the crown, but may be patented by any individual at a nominal rent. Many thousand acres have recently been taken up by various persons, which is a proof that the general confidence in the stability and increased value of real estates, is not diminished by the anticipation of complete freedom.

In the course of the evening, a negro came in great distress to the magistrate, to complain that his wife residing in this district had been taken to the court of a neighbouring magistrate, Captain BROWNSON, and sentenced to the treadmill for eight days. A letter was given her to the Governor. Though the Special magistrates are appointed each to a particular district, yet their commissions extend over the whole island; and one who has the reputation of impartiality with the apprentices, will frequently be applied to by many not in his district. Such applications are frequently made to S. BOURNE, who hears their cases, and is accustomed to refer them with a recommendation to their own magistrate. A line of conduct less offensive to his colleagues can scarcely be conceived; yet Captain BROWNSON, in a case of this kind, which lately occurred, sentenced four men to hard labor and to be flogged, whose offence was stated by himself in their warrant to be insubordination and " applying to Mr. BOURNE, instead of their own magistrate." In the present instance, he himself sends an apprentice to the treadmill, who is brought before him by her master out of another magistrate's jurisdiction. We subsequently took pains to learn the prrticulars of this case. The apprentice had obtained leave from her own magistrate to take a few days to arrange for the valuation of her daughter, who lived at a distance. Her owner summoned her before Captain BROWNSON, on a charge of absence from work. Notwithstanding her explanations, and her entreaties to be allowed to pay back the time or even double the time, she was sent to the treadmill, though far advanced in pregnancy. After making attempts on two different days to tread the mill, it became evident that she could not continue the exertion. She earnestly requested the gaoler not to put her on the mill again, and for the remainder of the time she was sent to work with the penal gang in the field, chained to another woman. Being unable to keep up with the rest, she was locked up in a cell on her return from the field at night, and the overseer threatened to lock her up the whole of Sunday; but, happily, the Governor's order for her release arrived the night before.

26th.—We visited another coffee plantation this morning. The overseer appeared to be a good tempered, frank, intelligent man, and made no complaints against his negros. A court was, however, held to determine a case affecting the lessee of a neighbouring property, which is a sad illustration of the heartlessness of a certain class of the colonists. A summons was issued requiring the defendant's presence, and warrants for two of his apprentices as witnesses; but as he sent a disrespectful message to the magistrate, refusing to attend, we had no opportunity of hearing any but the complainant's case, which she detailed in a long affidait. It was to the effect that she had lived with him for nine years, and was then discarded without any provision being made for herself, or her two children; and that when she went to his house to take away some of her property, she was repulsed and assaulted by him. Although the statement was *ex parte*, the principal facts were confirmed by other persons present. The affidavit related other particulars of a still darker shade, which as they refer to the state of things during slavery, we forbear to repeat. The overseer at whose house we were staying, observed that he had purchased the freedom of his colored children and their mother, and given them a home to live in. It was evident, however, that all his sympathies were enlisted on the side of the defendant, although we have no doubt he was himself incapable of similar conduct. He alluded to the subject without any apparent consciousness of immorality. It appears absolutely necessary, however repulsive, to detail some of the facts which come under our notice, illustrating the state of colonial morals; in order that it may be known, what obstacles really exist to the advancement of the negros, and how futile it would be, to expect that any good will be effected for them, through the agency of the generality of the present race of white residents. On our return to night, as well as on the preceding evening, a specimen of the opposition which an upright magistrate encounters in the discharge of his duty, came under our notice. Our host received two letters from a neighbouring Special Magistrate, and a planting attorney, both dated from the residence, and brought by the messenger of the latter. The purport of the first was to complain of BOURNE's *interference*, which, as before explained, consists in patiently listening to those who bring their complaints to him, and referring them, with a recommendation, to the justice or merciful consideration of their proper magistrates or owners. It was stated that this *interference* had "occasioned more punishment, than the misconduct of all the apprentices in the district." The letter of the attorney was to the same effect. Besides the insight which this incident gives into the gloomy despotism of this odious system, we cannot but remark the close alliance which is shewn to exist, between some of the magistrates and the planters.

28th.—We rode over to Spanish Town, which is thirteen miles from Kingston, and the seat of Government, in order to pay our respects to the Governor, Sir LIONEL SMITH, who gave us a courteous reception. The views he expressed during our interview were similar to those contained in his first speech to the Assembly and Council, and which appear to have characterised his whole course of policy since assuming the Government. He considered the negros of Jamaica far more degraded than those of Barbados or the other islands. During his predecessor's administration, no progress had been made in preparing them for freedom. The time had been lost in "squabbling" with the planters. It was necessary to adopt a conciliatory policy, and to endeavour to induce the proprietors to conform to the wishes of Government. He had already explained to some of them, that they could not otherwise expect that Government would sanction the Acts which might be necessary after 1840. Some restrictive measures, he thought would be required, both to secure the prosperity of the planters and the welfare of the apprentices. Both here and in Barbados, he stated that the resident large proprietors were humane men, and that all the oppression was caused by the owners of few negros, and the overseers of absentees. On his arrival in the island, he had found one of the parishes almost in a state of insurrection; he had appointed a Commission to inquire into the facts, and several of the overseers had been subsequently dismissed, and peace in consequence restored. We believe the Governor alluded to St. Thomas in the Vale but he did not mention the suspension of Dr. PALMER. On our leaving, he obligingly referred us to RICHARD HILL, the Assistant Secretary, for any information connected with the Stipendiary Magistrates' department.

We became acquainted in the course of the day with J. M. PHILLIPPO, the Baptist Misssionary, resident in Spanish Town, and with several Special Magistrates. An opportunity was unexpectedly afforded us to day, of learning the further particulars of the case of a woman being chained to a man, by order of a Special Magistrate; which J. STURGE had stated at a public meeting in England, on the authority of a private letter. The report reached Jamaica, where it was at once met by the newspapers with a confident denial: a convenient and summary mode of discrediting facts which is much resorted to in the colonies. We learned that the woman, PRISCILLA TAYLOR, resided not far from the Ferry Tavern, a well known halfway house between Spanish Town and Kingston. We therefore sent her a message to meet us on our return, which as it was the Saturday, her own day, she was able to do. We took down her own statement of facts, which she related with simplicity and precision, in the presence of S. BOURNE, who had been to Spanish Town, and accompanied us on our return. She appeared to be a decent, respectable woman, rather above her class. She said, "that B. (her master) had sent her to fetch a pail of water, and complained when she came back, that she had been too long. In the evening (Friday) she was put in the dark house, where she staid till Sunday afternoon. On the Monday she went to L. (the Special Magistrate) to complain, who said he would come next day to the property. He came, and sentenced her on the complaint of her master, to work in the field chained to a Mongola man, named JOE BUCKSTONE, who was standing by, and who had an iron collar round his neck, which he had had on some time. She was chained in the presence of the magistrate, by the overseer—the constable standing by. She said to L. "don't chain me to a man, I never had a chain round my neck in my life." She also told him that she was a married woman, and could not bear to be chained to a man. She was suckling a young child at the time. L. refused to listen to her. She and the man were ordered to the field, where she persuaded him to escape with her to Spanish Town. They went first to the Governor's house, and afterwards to C. a Special Magistrate, to whom she said " Massa and L. two friends, whatever

massa tell L. he will grant him the friendship to do it."
She begged C. to give her a paper to go into the workhouse; he did so, and there they unchained her from the man, and chained her to another woman, and the man to another man. She was punished two weeks in the workhouse at Spanish Town. B. then sent his overseer and the constable to fetch her home. She was then again chained to the man and sent to the field. She offered to work if the chain was taken off, but positively refused to work chained to the man. She was then taken to the dark house, where she was confined for two weeks. During the early part of the time the same man was locked up with her at night, when he came from the field. At the end of that time she was again taken before L. and sent to the workhouse at Halfway Tree, where she worked in the penal gang for a month."*

On our way home we called at Halfway Tree workhouse; our companion being the bearer of an order from the Governor for the release of the poor woman, mentioned a few days ago, who had been sentenced by Captain BROWNSON to the treadmill. We saw several of the same magistrate's commitments. In one of them part of the sentence was underlined, and ran thus :—"The twenty-five lashes not to be inflicted at present, but to remain suspended over his head for two months, and remitted if he behaves well during that time." We ascertained this mode of re-placing the lost power of the lash in the hands of the planters to be quite customary with him.

30th.—We came this evening to the Botanic Garden in the St. Andrews's Mountains, where we took

* See Appendix F. Sec. i.

lodgings for a short time, in order that we might attend some of the Courts of the Special Magistrates, BOURNE and HAMILTON. The garden was formed about forty years ago, in order to receive part of the collection of trees from the East Indies and South Sea Islands, brought hither by Captain BLIGH. It is now a coffee plantation and private property, having been long given up by the Legislature. There is still however a large collection of exotic trees.

31st.—We went this morning to breakfast with ROBERT OSBORN, one of the proprietors and editors of the Watchman newspaper, at whose house we met his estimable partner, EDWARD JORDAN. It was a high gratification to us to become acquainted with men, who have done and suffered so much in the cause of freedom. The former accompanied us to the Halfway Tree workhouse, as the St. Andrew's House of Correction is called. We noticed in the yard on entering, about a dozen negros, men and women, standing in a line near the door, who were heavily chained. On inquiring whether they were the penal gang, we were told they were apprentices from the estates, waiting* to be tried at the Court of Special Justice BROWNSON this morning. It was the practice, we were informed, to put them in chains before trial. In going over the buildings, we remarked that the solitary cells are excessively close, with scarcely any ventilation; and that the other rooms, though for the most part clean, afford very insufficient accommodation for the number of prisoners. There were many prisoners in the yard almost in a state of nudity. The supervisor, (as the principal officer of these institutions is called in Jamaica)

* See Appendix F., Sec. ii.

said he was out of clothing, and expecting a supply; but we attach little value to such explanations elicited by our inquiries or observations. One man had marks of blood on his shirt; and on inquiry we found he had been seriously injured by a blow from the driver, when on the treadmill. The supervisor inquired in a very harsh manner, why he had not mentioned it to him, when he asked the prisoners if they had any complaints. We spoke also to another negro, who was sick from the effects of a severe flogging; his back was a white mass of suppuration. Another pitiable object was lying about, whose body and limbs were swoln and ulcerated. He seemed a mass of disease, and was apparently of weak intellect. He was a watchman on Chester Vale estate, and had been sent there for suffering the cattle to trespass. So far from possessing activity enough to be a watchman, we do not think he could have walked across the yard. Even the supervisor said he ought not to have been sent. We next went to see the treadmill. There were two gangs of men and women, who, we were told, worked alternate spells of fifteen minutes each; an almost incredible amount of punishment. The men were put upon it during our stay; they were in the same state of exposure as before noticed. The women were standing near them waiting their turn. No regard was paid to decency in providing the latter with a suitable dress to work on the mill. We saw also in the workhouse, a young man of color named M'c VICAR, whose case has recently excited public attention. He is free, and in respectable circumstances, and was sent to the workhouse for twenty days, for an offence of a merely colorable character. The supervisor put him on the treadmill, which formed no part of his sentence; and which brought on a severe attack of hemorrhage. He appeared determined to seek redress by a suit at law. On looking over the visiting magistrates' journal, we observed, that no complaints were made by the prisoners, a circumstance which it is evident does not arise from the non-existence of abuses. There were many complaints of the supervisor, against the prisoners, and the written direction of the magistrate in each case was, " give him a few spells on the treadmill." As no extent of punishment is specified, the jailor on such authority may punish the prisoners *ad libitum*. We wereshe wn the corn meal and shads with which the prisoners are fed, which were of good quality. They receive one quart of the former, and one fish per diem. We afterwards heard a complaint that they were given with little preparation by cooking.

After leaving the workhouse, we proceeded to the court-house adjacent, and attended a meeting of the vestry, convened to address Sir LIONEL SMITH, on his assumption of the Government. At the close of the meeting, the Custos of the parish* detained the magistrates present, and in a very passionate speech, laid before them some charges brought against him by Lord SLIGO, who in a dispatch to Lord GLENELG, had stated some of the gross abuses in the Halfway Tree workhouse, and had implicated the Custos as cognizant of their existence.† Accusations of calumny and falsehood were unsparingly heaped on Lord SLIGO. The

---

* A parish in Jamaica, in proportion to the size of the island, is equivalent to a county in England. The Custodes of the several parishes have corresponding duties with the Lord Lieutenants, and Chairmen of Quarter Sessions in the Mother Country.

† See Appendix F. Sec. ii.

other magistrates expressed their indignation at Lord SLIGO's conduct, and their warm sympathy with the Custos, who, in reply, promised to send a triumphant refutation of the charges, which he observed affected all the magistrates of the parish as well as himself.

After these proceedings were concluded, we attended the Court of the Special Magistrate. Several negros were valued; one family of five persons for two hundred and ten pounds,* a weakly woman for fifty pounds, and a tradesman† on a plantation, for one hundred and twenty-two pounds ten shillings. The owner of this last was a local magistrate, who had been previously sitting at the table assisting in the other valuations. He enumerated all the good qualities of the man, his uncommon cleverness in his trade, his industry and honesty; adding that he was not buying his own freedom, but that some other planter, who wished to secure his services was going to advance the money for him. The present mode of valuations is a premium on worthlessness; and the honesty and faithfulness of a negro, are his greatest misfortunes, inasmuch as they frequently enhance his value beyond his means of purchase. After the valuations, several cases of complaint were disposed of by the magistrate, of which the most interesting, was one against two negros for refusing to work. They claimed to be free, and a man of color, an attorney's clerk, attended as their advocate. They had been slaves to a Spaniard in Carthagena, and had been brought from thence many years ago, to Jamaica

---

* Amounts hereafter will always be stated in Jamaica currency of which five pounds or shillings are equal to three sterling.

† The carpenters, coopers, smiths, &c. on estates, are called tradesmen.

by their master. They remained with him till his death, though they had never been registered as slaves according to law, either in 1817 or subsequently. The Special Magistrate, who ought either to have declared the men free, or to have at once declined exercising a jurisdiction in the case, sent for two *local* magistrates to advise him as to the proper course of proceeding. They declared without hesitation, that it had been decided both in the Colony, and in England, that non-registration did not confer freedom; and that there could be no doubt the men were apprentices. They concluded however, that the case ought to be referred to a superior tribunal. One of them turned to the adviser of the two negros, and rebuked him sharply for his interference, accusing him of disturbing their minds and making them uncomfortable, as they were "perfectly happy where they were, and must work somewhere;" it was, he said, "not doing as he would be done by, to interfere between a gentleman and his apprentices." The individual who was thus addressed, seemed quite abashed, he looked confused and guilty; such is the force of a vicious public opinion. He stammered out in excuse, that he should be sorry to interfere between master and apprentice, but that these negros "never had been even slaves in the eye of the law." There are a considerable number of non-registered slaves in this colony, who to this day, contrary to the plain letter of the Abolition law, have been detained in bondage.*

2nd. Month, 1st., (February.)—We went this morning by invitation, to breakfast with JOSEPH GORDON, one of the large planting attornies, and a member

---

* See Appendix F. Sec. iii.

of Assembly. He afterwards shewed us the works and hospital on his estate. The latter is a large, convenient building, and in a favorable situation; there were only three patients in it. We saw also a few of the negro houses, which were comfortable, consisting of two and sometimes three apartments. The best of them belonged to the hospital nurse and midwife, a very intelligent old woman, with whom we conversed for a short time. She told us that the number of deaths of infants was not greater than before 1834. There are about one hundred and forty negros on this estate, and twenty-six free children. The overseer observed that a greater insult could not be offered to a mother, than by asking her free child to work. He related an instance where he had made such a proposition, without success; it was evident even from his own account, that he had acted in a harsh manner, and did not offer money wages as an inducement. We passed twice to-day through the Hope estate belonging to the Duke of BUCKINGHAM, where we saw three white immigrants ploughing in the same field, in which a gang of negros were at work with the hoe. About fifty Europeans have been brought out to this estate, under an agreement which entails an enormous annual expense on its proprietor. No preparation was in the first instance made for their reception, and the hardships they endured, and their own intemperate habits, carried many of them off. Those who remain, are more comfortably circumstanced, and a few of them work steadily, but in this climate one negro is worth two or three Europeans.

2nd.—We attended a Court held by two Special Magistrates, BOURNE and HAMILTON, on a large coffee plantation in St. Andrews, called Dublin Castle, the property of Alderman Atkins. Many of the complaints brought by the overseer against the people were adjudged frivolous, and were dismissed. One was against four women in a late state of pregnancy, for the loss of a few minutes in coming late to work, and for insolence. The overseer's own witnesses proved that he had behaved towards them with great harshness and ill-temper; and also, that the women picked as much coffee as used to be exacted from them during slavery. The attorney for the estate, who was present, did not agree with the magistrates in their notions of government: he said in reference to the case of a man, who had been punished by a fine of time, that negros could not be managed without being occasionally flogged. He made heavy complaints against the people for idleness and general insubordination; and said they did not even cultivate their own grounds. A warm altercation occurred between him and one of the magistrates (Bourne); the former declaring, that these negros were a quiet, orderly, set of people, before the latter came into the district; to which the magistrate replied, by stating, that forty-nine cases were brought before him and Doctor Palmer, on the very first occasion of his holding a court on the property. Before leaving the estate, we were permitted to inspect the hospital, which is a sufficiently good building, but was in a most filthy condition.

3rd.—We accompanied the same magistrates to Craig-hill, a small coffee plantation, with fewer than forty apprentices; and one, therefore, which they are not required by law to visit. It is on the boundary of their respective districts, and so many complaints had been made by the apprentices, to each of the magistrates, that they concluded to visit it, and hold a joint court. Nearly the whole of the negros on the property attended the court, being concerned either as defendants, complainants, or witnesses. The first case was a charge made by the overseer against an apprentice, for stealing provisions. The offence was proved and punished. Next an old woman complained against one of her sons, that he had sold his provision ground in which she asserted a joint property. She was an African, and spoke very unintelligibly, but was eloquent in gesture and animation. She had had eight children, of whom, she said, "the best had gone before;" and those who were left, neglected, and illtreated her. Her son's offence was not, however, cognizable by the court. He in his turn complained that he had been compelled to sell his ground to another apprentice, in order to buy medicines and applications for an ulcerated foot. It appeared in evidence, that there was no hospital and no medical attendant for the estate. Another case of similar neglect was brought forward and fully substantiated against the estate, which was fined five pounds. The next case was the complaint of an apprentice against the overseer for locking her up for eighteen hours, without food or water, and sending his children, (two little colored boys, of the ages of twelve and five years,) to call her obscene names. Her statement was distinct and circumstantial, and was confirmed by the constable or head negro, by her husband and several other witnesses. The overseer acknowledged all the charges, and rested his defence on provocation and abusive language received first from the complainant. He failed, however, in the proof of his assertions, and was fined five pounds. He remonstrated against the highest penalty of the law being enforced against him; and said, that the whole gang were idle, worthless, and vagabond; that they were bought out of the workhouse, (as convict slaves,) for "an old song." He charged the witnesses with misrepresenting facts, and forgetting what would have made in his favor. The people warmly denied his imputation, and their conduct appeared to us to be marked by intelligence, consistency, and regard for truth. The above cases occupied so much time, that many other complaints of assault and ill-treatment, of a similar character, were deferred to another occasion. The negros on this property were, many of them, almost in a state of nudity. One boy, whom we asked, said he had been sent to the treadmill at Half-way Tree, for seven days, about three weeks ago; and that his clothes had been flogged to pieces there. His chest was sore from rubbing against the mill, and he is still scarcely able to walk from the effects of an injury in the knee, inflicted by the revolving wheel, when he lost the step. He declared that both men and women were flogged on the treadmill; the former with a cat, but the women with a strap. We fear, that the proceedings detailed above, are an example of the condition of the apprentices on many of the smaller properties. It is impossible for us to express the feelings of disgust which these scenes conveyed to our minds. During a short visit, which we paid in the evening to S. Bourne, a man came from Constitution-hill, another coffee estate, to complain, that his master had shot one of his fowls, which had a brood of chickens. He brought some of them dead in his basket. This is a species of persecution, against which the apprentice has no protection.

4th.—Yesterday and to-day, we have had striking proofs, from our own observation, of the industry of the negros, when working under a proper stimulus. As we went to our lodgings, which are nine miles from town, late in the evening, we met several parties of two or three men, women, and even children, coming down from the mountains with heavy loads of produce on their heads, from their own grounds for the Kingston market. Some of them had mules loaded, besides the burdens they carried themselves. We could hear other distant parties in the mountain passes and defiles, singing cheerful songs to beguile the tediousness of the way. Many come a distance of twenty, or even thirty miles, and pass the night in the open air on the road. English carrots, cabbages, and artichokes, besides yams, and other roots and fruits of the country, were among their supplies.

5th.—THE SABBATH.—We were kept close prisoners during the early part of the day by the rain. About one o'clock we were able to walk out, and paid a visit to the negro village on the Botanic Garden. The negros generally observe the Sabbath very strictly, so far as abstinence from work is concerned. In one house, however, we found them employed in shelling a quantity of palma christi seeds, preparatory to bruising and boiling them, in order to obtain the castor oil. Near one of the cottages was a little wooden frame, in which were set two small rollers, for pressing canes; of which a few were cultivated by the negros for their own consumption. There is little division of labor in a slave country; which is one means by which slaves, in every department, are so much excelled by free laborers. The negros construct their own houses, make their own clothes, cultivate their provisions with their own hands; they use oil of their own pressing for their lamps, and wicks prepared from cotton growing at their own doors. We enquired of two apprentices in one of the huts if they were married. They were not, though they had lived three years together, and appeared sensible that they ought to be. This large and extensive parish, though it is one of the longest settled in the island, is nearly destitute of opportunities of religious improvement. S. BOURNE, who resides near the Botanic Garden, has a Sunday school at his house, which we visited; it was attended by ten men, who were learning to read and write, and several boys in an alphabet class. One of the former was the head man on a neighbouring large estate. He was asked why so few children now attended the Sabbath school from that property, and replied, that the attorney disturbed and unsettled the people, or to use his own phrase, "made their minds chatter." He said, that many of the orange and mangoe trees growing on the property, had been cut down, in order to deprive the apprentices of the fruit. One of the boys present was the son of an overseer, who had gone to reside on another estate, and left him without any provision, and in bondage. The child was purchased and made free, and is now supported by his maternal uncle, who was present in the other class, and who is still himself an apprentice. Many of these calumniated people, shew themselves superior in moral worth to their haughty task-masters.

6th.—We accompanied S. BOURNE to visit several estates. Our route was entirely by mountain paths; and it would be impossible to do justice to the picturesque grandeur of the scenery. The hills abound with torrents and springs, and the vegetation, therefore, is very luxuriant. Sometimes we caught a distant glimpse of the sea. We crossed on our journey a lofty ridge, running directly across an immense valley. The pass was so narrow as not to admit of two riding abreast. We breakfasted at the house of an old gentleman of the name of WILES, who was the botanist on Captain BLIGH's expedition, and came with him to Jamaica, forty-four years ago. He was induced to remain by the Assembly, and to undertake the superintendence of the Botanic Garden, formed for the reception of the plants which they had brought. For many years past he has been a coffee planter, and though now upwards of seventy years old, is in full possession of the powers of an intelligent and well-stored mind. He told us, that the bread fruit tree, has not succeeded so well as had been anticipated. It thrives in moist situations, but never reaches the luxuriant growth of its native climate. The most valuable tree, he said, which has been introduced into Jamaica, in recent times, is the mangoe; a few plants of which were taken out of a French prize, captured about half a century ago, by Lord RODNEY. It has spread with great rapidity, and is now found in every part of the island; the fruit, which it produces in very great abundance, is dessert for the whites and food for the negros, as well as for cattle, horses, and hogs. Our host had no complaints against his apprentices. We next visited a small estate, on which there were about fifty apprentices, under the care of an overseer, who was himself a negro, and had formerly been a slave. He also governed the people with little aid from the magistrate. They had however their troubles, the estate being partly under the superintendence of a white-overseer, on a neighbouring plantation. One of the apprentices with an infant in arms, complained to the magistrate of a brutal assault committed on herself and child, by this man. The particulars are too gross for publication. Her child was evidently much injured by it. He was fined five pounds. In the hospital, there was a negro, who had been sent about a month ago to the treadmill, from the effects of which he is not yet sufficiently recovered to be able to work. The overseer told us, that he held him up as a warning to the other people, of what they might expect, if they were sent to the workhouse for punishment. The negros on this property, were a fine interesting set of people; they complained of their own accord, of one of their number, for not cultivating her grounds. She was admonished and threatened. They had on a former occasion, expressed a desire to have their children instructed, and were now asked by the magistrate if they were still in the same mind; they answered unanimously in the affirmative; adding, that they wished also to learn themselves. He accordingly held out to them some expectation, that he would endeavour to establish a school either on the estate, or in the neighbourhood. From hence, calling at another estate in our way, we proceeded to the residence of HINTON EAST, who had kindly engaged us to dine with him. His house is situated on the summit of a hill, with a climate ranging from $64°$ to $78°$ of Farhenheit. It is tempered by constant sea and land breezes. Captain EAST and his lady are surrounded by a young and interesting family. Their experience during the few years they have resided here, is in favor of the salubrity of the climate of the mountains.

7th.—We came to Spanish town this morning. The road from Kingston to the capital, crosses an immense fresh water swamp, into which one or two considerable streams empty their waters, and which extends for several miles to the sea. It abounds with rare specimens of aquatic plants, insects, and birds, and with eels, fresh-water turtle, &c. The road through it, which has been constructed at great expense, is liable to be frequently overflowed. The exhalations from the marsh are painfully obvious to the senses of the traveller, who is unavoidably compelled to cross it after sunset, or before sunrise. In any other than a slave country, it would long ago have been drained, and would now be teeming with exhaustless supplies of agricultural wealth. The capital is situated on the Rio Cobre, about seven miles from the sea, in a narrow plain, which extends in a curved direction, as far as Kingston on one side, and on the other a considerable distance into the interior of the island. This land is occupied by a few sugar estates, and pens or farms for raising cattle; but the greater part has been abandoned, and is now overgrown with brushwood, and the logwood, and acacia trees. As its climate is uncertain, and subject to frequent and severe droughts, the apprentices do not cultivate provision grounds; neither have they any allowances of food from their owners; they support themselves by cutting grass and firewood for the supply of the inhabitants of Spanish Town. They are sometimes reduced to extreme distress, when their time has been forfeited by sentence of the magistrate; and as they can neither collect their bundles of sticks and grass from the property of their masters, without permission, nor take them to market for sale, without a written pass, they are as completely under irresponsible control, as ever they were during slavery.

In the course of the morning, we visited the metropolitan girls' school, under the care of J. M. PHILLIPPO, which is supported chiefly at the expense of a society of ladies in England. There were ninety children present, many of whom were the colored offspring of overseers. There were at one time in this school, four or five children of a late Governor, the Duke of MAN-CHESTER; and one of its present teachers is the daughter of the Duke's *celebrated* secretary BULLOCK. Her freedom was purchased some years ago, by the English patronesses of the school. The dreadful state of social disorganization in Jamaica, is legibly written even on the surface of society. Its " bad eminence," is doubtless to be attributed, in part, to the corrupting influence of the long administration of the above-mentioned Governor. The matron of the school shewed us some nice specimens of plain and ornamental needlework. We also heard several classes read, and examined them in spelling and arithmetic. The children were neatly dressed and very clean. Many of them are apprentices; of whom fourteen colored girls are sent by their attorney from a single estate in the neighbourhood. They are intended to become teachers of estates' schools. There are five young women employed as teachers, two of whom conduct the school, and the others are qualifying themselves to fill the same station elsewhere. Several of them manifest great energy and ability, and their system of management is well adapted to ensure order and constant attention. At the word of command, the girls perform various mechanical exercises with their hands; and rise, turn, and resume their seats, or form classes, with instantaneous promptitude. J. M. PHILLIPO told us, that on the first establishment of the school, he had thought it impossible to conduct it without an European teacher; but that some of the colored teachers have proved themselves as useful and efficient, as an European could be expected to be. The principal teacher, a colored young woman, was purchased and made free by an old negro, her grandfather, who is still himself an apprentice. She did not know a letter at fourteen years of age. Besides the large number of children who receive in this school a scriptural education, we cannot but regard it as a valuable institution for qualifying teachers. It is worthy of even a more liberal support than it already receives; as the young persons who are at present training to conduct schools, are allowed only a dollar a week for their maintenance, which is less than they could earn by needlework and other employments. We had not time to visit the metropolitan boys' school, held in an adjoining room. It is on the same footing as the girls', except that it is dependent on casual funds, and thus entails a heavy burden and responsibility on the missionary, and is more limited in its usefulness as a normal school.

We attended in the course of the day a sitting of the House of Assembly, which has been summoned at this unusual period of the year, for a short session, to dispose of a great arrear of business, occasioned by the recent introduction of many new laws. It was occupied to day with a bill to regulate the medical faculty and register diplomas, which was warmly opposed by two of the members, who belonged to that profession.

We were introduced to ALEXANDRE BRAVO, one of the most extensive resident proprietors in the island, and a Custos and member of Assembly. He is esteemed liberal and humane; and in conversation with us, expressed the most enlightened views of political economy. He ridiculed the idea of independent cultivation, and the fears that are commonly expressed, that the people will refuse, when free, to labor "continuously" for wages. He finds no difficulty in purchasing all the labor that his own people have to sell, besides the spare time of many from adjoining estates. He considers slave labor, of all others, the most un-economical and expensive; and is persuaded that twenty free men are equal to one hundred slaves. Under a slave system too, agricultural operations must be carried on with immense masses of men, which he believes would not be required, even in West India cultivation, were it placed on a proper footing.

8th.—We visited to-day several estates, called the Caymanas, accompanied by G. O. HIGGINS, Special Magistrate, the ATTORNEY-GENERAL, and JOSEPH GORDON. The first of them Ellis's, is the property of Lord SEAFORD, and under the attorneyship of the last-named gentleman. The number of negros is one hundred and thirty-five, besides the free children who receive the same attention, as during slavery. The manager, who has introduced taskwork to a considerable extent, assured us, that the cultivation of the estate was kept up as effectively as at any former period. Complaints are rarely brought before the magistrate. We saw the hospital, in which were twelve slight cases: it was a good building but very dirty. We passed also through the negro village. As the people were at work, most of the houses were locked; such as we entered were comfortable, clean, and furnished. The village is situated in a grove of cocoa nut trees, which belong to the negros, who are dependent, in part, for their subsistence, on the sale of the fruit in Spanish Town and Kingston markets. On this estate, as well as on several others which we have visited, an attempt has been made to establish a school, but without success. The adjoining estate, Taylor's Caymanas, is a still finer property, and belongs to —— Ewing, of Glasgow. The resident attorney is arbitrary in his ideas of government, and finds ample employment for the Special Magistrate. The third Caymanas, Dawkins', is also a fine estate, under the attorneyship of T. J. Bernard. Like Ellis's, it is managed almost without the interference of the Stipendiary. Taskwork also has been introduced on it, by an arrangement with the apprentices. We enquired of the overseer, why he did not give the negros their taskwork by the week, so that they might save one or two whole days? He replied that in that case they would over work themselves. We were shewn a statement of wages paid for extra labor during crop, which amounted to one hundred and nine pounds for the season, or ten shillings a hogshead; which when distributed would be one shilling, for not less than two and a half days of severe extra labor per week, a remuneration so trifling as to prove, (if the arrangement is not compulsory,) how easily the apprentices are satisfied. We drove from hence to the Farm, a pen or cattle estate, belonging to Lord Carrington, and under the attorneyship of Joseph Gordon. The hospital is a large well ventilated building. Every hospital is furnished with that relic of former times, the stocks. The negro village of the Farm, is probably one of the best in the island. The houses are scattered over a considerable extent of ground, in groups of two or three, in separate neat inclosures. It is embosomed in a grove of cocoa nut trees, on which the negros are in part dependent for the means of support. Many of the cottages consist of two or three good rooms, in which are a little furniture, and in a few instances glasses and earthenware. They were remarkably clean, and the courts carefully swept. We were introduced to WHITEHALL ELLIS, the head negro, an intelligent man, who is still as active and as lively as a boy, though nearly seventy years of age. He has a numerous family of descendants, and is a man of considerable property, being possessed of a light tax cart, and a number of cattle and sheep. He owned before the 1st of August, nine slaves, twenty head of cattle, and seventy sheep, but like other prosperous men he has experienced occasional reverses. His speculations in slaves did not turn out well; he gave us a most amusing account of one of them, who stole some of his cattle, and sold them for himself in Kingston market, and then, pretending they were lost, almost killed his master, by leading him a wild goose chase in search of them, among the swamps and woods. As he, being himself a slave, could not hold slaves in his own right, he was likely also to lose the Compensation, through the faithlessness of the friend in whose name they had been registered. ELLIS invited us to his house, which is a large, comfortable, and furnished cottage, with *jalousies* in the casements. He produced a bottle of madeira, and wine glasses, and by so doing, according to West India notions, refuted the thousand and one statements of the Anti-slavery Society, of the physical sufferings of slaves. Among the negro houses, there is a small chapel, in which one of the apprentices occasionally preaches. The attorney asked the people whether they would send their children to school if he provided a teacher. They professed great anxiety to avail themselves of his offer. As we were leaving, a woman came forward to petition for assistance towards rebuilding or repairing her cottage. She manifested much distress. Old Ellis rebuked her sharply; " did she wish to bring massa's property into disgrace before the gentlemen?" "Where were her manners?" &c. The negros on this estate, are a fine, muscular race of people, and both their appearance and that of their dwellings, was one of comfort. It may be thought that they demonstrated the compatibility of slavery with happiness, but it must be borne in mind, that their privileges depended on the double accident of their belonging to a wealthy and humane proprietor, and being under the government of kind overseers. Many of the negros on Farm, are active, intelligent, and enterprising; why should such men be prevented from having free scope to increase their own wealth and that of the community? On the other hand, so far from complete emancipation being injurious to such estates as these, the people when free, will be too unwilling to leave their cottages and gardens, and fruit trees, the heirlooms handed down to them from their ancestors, to be likely to forsake the estates. Humane proprietors will have every advantage in procuring the labor of their free peasantry on the most advantageous terms.

9th.—The Rector of Spanish Town kindly accompanied us to the schools under the care of the establishment. Of these, there are three under one master and mistress, held in the same building. Two, Beckford's and Smith's, are charitable foundations with considerable funds, and the third is a school of industry, so named in consequence of an intention which has never been carried into effect, of associating some manual occupation with learning. The two former consist of thirty children each, and the latter of sixty. The children were principally colored, and apparently not of the lowest grade of society. We examined all but the alphabet class, which is a very numerous one. The proficiency of the children is below the average except in writing, in which they excelled.

We had the pleasure of making the acquaintance of CHARLES HARVEY, of Spanish Town, one of the few members of the legal profession, who will undertake the causes of oppressed negros. He has largely sacrificed his interests at the shrine of principle.

We again attended a sitting of the House of Assembly, and heard during the debate one of those violent attacks on Lord SLIGO, in which certain members of this notorious House, are accustomed to indulge. The Marquis was described as the calamity of Jamaica, and threatened with impeachment. One of the members told us, that the annual militia bill was about to be introduced, which he intended to oppose, though in a House composed of Colonels and Generals, he feared with little chance of success. The militia, he observed, was formerly necessary on account of the insecurity of slave property; now it is not only useless, but burdensome, and discourages persons from settling in the colonies. Throughout the islands, every free man of suitable age, is compelled to serve in this mock military force, except that a property qualification has been recently introduced to exclude the emancipated classes.

In the evening, we proceeded some distance into the interior. At the Rectory Tavern, in St. Thomas in the Vale, where we staid for the night, we unexpectedly met R. S. COOPER, S. M. to whom we had an introduction. He had just received a challenge to fight a duel from a planter in the district, because he had yesterday refused to punish an apprentice, whom the former accused of striking his child, a charge which was not sustained by the evidence. We subsequently learned, that this case was afterwards taken before local magistrates, who sentenced the woman for a month, to the House of Correction. It is therefore a double illustration of the degree of respect paid to the Special Magistrates, and of the facility with which the law is evaded.

11th.—Early this morning we drove over to Jericho, the residence of JOHN CLARKE, one of the Baptist Missionaries. He was absent from home, but we were kindly invited by his wife, to stay breakfast. Before we left, several apprentices called to be examined by the minister as candidates for Baptism. From their answers to our inquiries, it appeared, that the authority of the Stipendiary is employed to enforce a compulsory arrangement for extra labor during crop. Many of the negros are compelled to work by spells of eight hours in the field one day, and sixteen hours in and about the boiling house the next day, giving up their half Friday, for which amount of extra labor they receive an amount equal to two shillings and one penny per week. Soon after the commencement of the apprenticeship, four negros on the principal estate in this parish, were flogged because they refused to assent to this arrangement. Though they now submit to it quietly, the apprentices are not consenting parties; it is only agreed upon between the overseer and the magistrate. These people complained also, that the Special Magistrate, Captain REYNOLDS, would never hear what they had to say in their own defence, when brought before him. We next visited Rodney Hall workhouse, in which we found but two or three prisoners, besides life convicts. The penal gang was at work in the neighbourhood, and consisted chiefly of the latter, who were chained two and two. Most of them had been condemned under the old slave laws, as incorrigible runaways. In looking cursorily over the workhouse, the only observations of importance that we made, were that the insecure state of the building rendered it necessary to fasten the legs of the prisoners to an iron staple at night, on the inclined board, on which they slept. Two being chained together, and the leg of one of them secured to the staple. The treadmill also is a machine of dreadful construction. It is so great a height from the ground, that the prisoners ascend a rude ladder to a sort of platform, from which they step on the mill. They are then strapped to the beam above the mill, and the platform is removed. If they are unable to keep the step, they hang by the wrists and are liable to sustain the most serious injuries from the mill revolving against their breasts and legs. There was no machinery to regulate its speed. The supervisor acknowledged that it was so severe a punishment, that it could not safely be inflicted more than two or three times a day. The prisoners are usually put upon it morning and evening, for fifteen minutes each time. During our stay two Special Magistrates, REYNOLDS and COOPER, arrived to hold a court for disposing of some valuations. We took the opportunity of inquiring respecting the rate paid for extra labor during crop. They both confirmed the statements we had heard in the morning, of the amount of time required from the apprentices. One of them said it was a work of necessity, and in reply to our inquiry how the people were paid, said, the amount was very low, but that the negros appeared satisfied with it. The other contrasted the remuneration which the apprentices received during crop, with the extravagant price at which their labor was rated when they came to purchase their freedom. The time was so far spent in waiting for two local magistrates, that we could only stay to witness one valuation, that of a negro man and field laborer. His master and mistress, persons of color, were very angry with him for wishing to be valued, and even used insulting language to the Special Magistrate ; but amidst all their wrath did not forget to insist on the man's honesty and industry. The Special and Local Magistrates could not agree ; the latter rating him at two shillings and sixpence per day, and justifying their exorbitant valuation on the plea, *that a laborer could not be replaced.*

12th.—We went this morning to a church in Kingston, the minister of which is one of the most popular clergymen in the island. It was quite full, and we were pleased to observe, that there appeared to be no distinction of complexion observed in the arrangement of the seats.

15th.—We visited the Central Mico Schools. In the infant school, there were about one hundred and fifty children, from two to seven years of age; they were nearly all black ; the only white child being the son of a clergyman. They were in excellent order, and many of them shewed great quickness and intelligence, especially in asking and answering questions on scripture narratives, recited to them by their teacher. In each of the other schools for older boys and girls, there were from eighty to one hundred children. We examined most of the classes in the former, and found their proficiency such as did them great credit. Several of the monitors displayed great energy and talent, particularly a negro youth of fifteen or sixteen years of age, whom J. M. TREW, the agent of the Mico Trustees, is about to take with him to Trinidad, to assist in organising the schools there. The copy books were as usual, well written, and kept very clean. In the girls' school, besides going cursorily over the classes, we were shewn some specimens of needlework, which appeared to be very nicely executed. The Mico agents have already between three and four thousand children under their care, in different parts of the island, and the attendance at their schools is increasing. They have adopted the weekly pay system with success. They could not probably contribute more to the cause in which they are embarked, than by rendering their central establishment a series of model schools as perfect as possible, for the training of teachers.

16th.—We attended to-day the Assize Court at Spanish Town, and heard part of the proceedings in case of MACLEAN v. BOURNE. This is one of those actions pending against Special Magistrates, of which the public has recently heard so much. Its progress is a most unfavorable comment, not only on the feelings of the planters, but on the character of the Courts of Law, and the injudicious conduct of the Home Government.

We afterwards visited the workhouse and jail, accompanied by Major WILKIE, the Custos of the parish. In the workhouse, the apartments are clean and well ventilated. The treadmill appeared to be of the same construction as is usual in England, but there was no machinery to regulate its speed, which would therefore be slow or rapid, according to the number of prisoners upon it. The food of the prisoners, is the same in quality as at Halfway Tree. There were several white prisoners, who the Custos observed are kept quite distinct from the rest. They have a separate sleeping room, and are never chained or sent out with the penal gang to work in the streets. The latter have iron collars on their necks, and work chained in pairs, two men or two women. The premises forming the county jail, which we next visited, are divided by a wall; one side being occupied by debtors, and the other by criminals. The accommodations for the debtors are good, and a great contrast to the crowded, confined, miserable apartments and cells allotted to the prisoners. In the yard were many prisoners, tried and untried, each with a heavy iron bolt attached to one of his legs, which in walking he was compelled to lift up, by a string held in the hand. There was but one white prisoner, who had been tried for the murder of his wife, a colored woman, and to the great surprise of the court and the public, found guilty only of manslaughter. He was sentenced to three years imprisonment, the extreme punishment of the island law for that offence. He was living in a light and spacious upstairs room, unshackled by chains or iron collar, and enjoying the range of a gallery to walk in. Little precaution was taken to ensure his security, but the few inconveniences to which he was subjected, left him as little motive for attempting to escape. At the end of the gallery, in which this individual is domiciled, a permanent gallows has been erected since Lord Sligo's departure in front of the market-place. This is justly reprobated by many as a brutal and disgraceful exhibition. It is intended to strike terror into the minds of the lower orders, and is a singular exemplication of the prevailing notions respecting punishments and prison discipline.

We attended for a short time the sitting of the House of Assembly. A bill was announced to regulate the classification of the apprentices. The plan, which is likely to be adopted, is that of associating two magistrates nominated by the master with the Special Magistrate of the district, to adjudicate all doubtful cases. The rights of the apprentices, in that case, will be treated with as little ceremony as they are before a similar tribunal in valuations. We were introduced in the course of the day to S. M. BARRETT, a member of council, who kindly invited us to visit his estates.

17th. We accepted to day a polite invitation of ALEXANDRE BRAVO, to visit two of his estates, about ten miles from Spanish Town. Our route was through a district of level country, which was for the most part abandoned to trees and brushwood. It had formerly, we were told, been occupied by fine cattle estates, from whence the negros had been removed to cultivate sugar in the more mountainous parishes, which have a more fertile soil and moister climate. On the first estate which we visited, our host is erecting one of the most handsome and substantial mansions in the island. It is beautifully situated on a gentle acclivity commanding a view of the sea, from which it is distant three or four miles. It is built by the labor of his own apprentices, with materials supplied from his different estates. The work would do credit to English artificers. We could not but regard it is a monument of the confidence of a liberal and enlightened proprietor in the permanent prosperity of the country under a free system. On these estates, the most judicious means have been adopted, to habituate the people to work cheerfully for wages, and we are assured with complete success. The proprietor has introduced taskwork and remuneration, and has recently substituted money payments on a liberal scale, in lieu of all allowances of clothing, saltfish, sugar, rum, &c.; and in order to accustom his people to spend money, as well as earn it, he has established a shop on one or more of his estates. Many of his principal negros receive salaries varying from five to sixteen pounds per annum, besides liberal wages for their extra time, their house and grounds rent free, and the pasturage of a few hogs, cattle, or horses. We were requested to make our own inquiries of the negros, and accordingly entered into conversation with a number of them. One complained of the discontinuance of their allowances of salt-fish, &c. since Christmas. He was reckoning up, in the most perspicuous way, the value of each, according to the quantity allowed, when his master came in and listened very patiently to his charges, and then replied, by shewing, that the money which he gave them, was a full equivalent for those indulgences. A discussion of several other minor points followed, which terminated in the same manner. The principal orator, on the part of the negros, certainly exhibited an ingenious display of special pleading; but it was really pleasant to see the independent and free spirit of the negros, and the good feeling subsisting between them and their master; which, so far as our observation extends, is a rare exception to the general rule. The latter-related to us several anecdotes of similar disputes with his people, and said it was a mistake to suppose that the negro was not a reasonable being. On our return to town we called at the Whim sugar estate, on which there are two hundred and thirty apprentices. Its average production is one hundred and thirty hogsheads, but during the last two years, it has reached two hundred hogsheads per annum. The attorney, who is esteemed a good agriculturist, attributes the large crops to favorable seasons, though he acknowledged also, that the cultivation was kept up as efficiently as during slavery. He complained, however, that the people neglected their own grounds, and refused to work for wages in their extra time. He adheres to the eight-hour system, a circumstance which is sufficient to account for a large amount of disaffection. On our way home, we passed through Bushy Park estate, one of the largest and most populous in the island. We have been favored by the overseer of Bushy Park with a table of births and deaths on that estate, from which it appears, that the former, since eighteen hundred and thirty-four, have been forty-seven, and the latter eleven, from which it may be inferred, that the infants and pregnant women, and nursing mothers, have received the same indulgences, as during slavery, which we are sorry to say, is not generally the case.

19th.—THE SABBATH.—We attended this morning the various services at the station of the baptist mission in Spanish Town. The first of these was a prayer meeting, held very early in the morning, attended by about six hundred persons. At nine o'clock we visited the Sunday schools, in which were about one hundred children, chiefly in the alphabet class, who have no other means of instruction. At eleven the morning service commenced. The meeting-house, which holds about fifteen hundred, was densely crowded, chiefly by apprentices from the surrounding estates, who were very attentive and decorous in their deportment. At the conclusion, the minister married a young couple, who were apprentices on an estate some miles distant. The formula was that of the church of England abbreviated, to which was added a suitable exhortation and prayer. J. M. PHILLIPPO has married about three hundred of the apprentices within the last twelve months.

We were introduced afterwards to a number of the deacons and leaders of the church, who were assembled in a room adjoining the chapel. Some of them were free, but others were apprentices from the estates; many of them, fully equal in intelligence and information to English peasantry, of some of the agricultural districts. We enquired of them respecting the apprenticeship. One of them stood up and said, that he was a constable, and that he found it very difficult to act according to his oath, as he was expected to do all for his master, and nothing for the people; whereas he was frequently obliged to remonstrate with his overseer about the oppressions which he practised; that the apprentices now receive none of their former allowances of salt-fish, and only half their former quantity of clothing. It was very hard for them to subsist as their grounds were often burned up by drought; and that the overseer took their own time from them whenever he wanted it, and it was often a hard thing to get him to repay it. On our asking whether the people would be willing to work after eighteen hundred and forty, he said, "nothing was sweeter than for a man to labor for his own bread;" a sentiment to which all present responded. They told us that many had been flogged or sent to the treadmill, who had never been punished during slavery. Two of the individuals present had been sent to the treadmill, and sustained severe injury from its effects. The offences were merely nominal, and we were assured their characters were without reproach. Another poor woman present, who was the mother of eight children, and in declining years and health, had been sent to the treadmill because she could not work in the first gang, after having lived during the last years of slavery a life of comparative ease and indulgence. The overseer had also pulled down her house which was the best on the estate. All the apprentices complained that the magistrates did not give them a fair opportunity of speaking in their own behalf.

After this conference was concluded, we had an opportunity of witnessing the examination to which the candidates for baptism are subjected. A poor old woman was the first examined. She was closely questioned by the minister, but more especially by the deacons and leaders, respecting the time and cause of her "coming to religion;" her views in wishing to be baptized, and on the person and offices of Christ. She appeared to be a simple-hearted woman, anxious to forsake sin, and to join herself to a praying people; but her answers did not evince that clear acquaintance with the leading doctrines of Christianity, which was deemed essential; she was, therefore, deferred. The next probationer, a young man, was deemed suitable to be received. Before the decision is made, the candidate is requested to withdraw, and those present, who are acquainted with him, give their sentiments on the correctness of his outward conduct; what change is to be observed in it, and whether he is in their opinion a converted character. If it is concluded to receive him, he is called in, and after being exhorted by the minister, not to put his trust in the outward ordinance, is informed, that the church has unanimously concluded to admit him as a member; and on the first convenient occasion, he is baptized. We again attended chapel in the evening. It was as full as in the morning, with the exception of the space occupied by the Sunday school children; the congregation, however, was a different one, being principally composed of persons from the town.

20th.—On several occasions, we have seen the penal gang of men and women, in chains and collars in the streets of Spanish Town, and to day observed two pregnant women chained together in the gang. We set out this afternoon on a tour of the western part of the island, and arrived late in the evening at Jericho, in St. Thomas-in-the-Vale, where we were hospitably received by JOHN CLARKE, the baptist missionary of this station.

21st.—We had to day the opportunity of meeting several apprentices from estates in various parts of the parish, of which we gladly availed ourselves, being particularly desirous of obtaining the free and unbiassed testimony of the negros themselves, respecting the change which had taken place in their condition, since the introduction of the apprenticeship. We were careful to impress upon their minds, (on this as well as on all similar subsequent occasions,) that it was not probable they would derive the most distant benefit from our visit, and that our inquiries were made solely with a view to ascertain the truth, for the information of ourselves and other of our friends in England. The statements of these apprentices, who were all of them members of the church, and evidently persons both of intelligence and moral worth, are referred to the appendix.* The substance of them was as follows: they complained that they were compelled by a compulsory arrangement between their overseers and the Special Magistrates, to give their time during crop for scarcely any remuneration; and that out of crop, they were on many estates obliged to work a greater number of hours than is required by law. They have been gene-

* See Appendix F. Sec. iv.

rally deprived of the salt-fish which they used to receive, and have not nearly so large an allowance of clothing. Their field cooks, (the women who used to bring them water in the field, and to cook the dinners for the gang,) have been taken away. They do not receive the same attention when sick; less time is allowed to pregnant women before and after confinement, who, on some estates, are not allowed to leave field-work up to the time of their delivery. The only advantages which they enumerated, were that they were no longer liable to be flogged and put in the stocks at the caprice of their overseers and drivers. One of the men was a head-carpenter on a large estate, who had applied, about a year ago, to purchase his freedom, and was valued at three hundred and fifty-two pounds. This iniquitous proceeding excited attention both in the colony and at home; but the injured party has obtained no redress. He succeeded in obtaining a new valuation, when he was rated at two hundred and thirty pounds; but though he tendered half the money as an instalment, it was refused, and the valuation set aside. He has now almost given up the hope of freedom, and thinks it will not arrive in time to be of much benefit to him, as he is in weak health, and approaching sixty years of age. All these people spoke very affectionately of Doctor PALMER, and said he was the best magistrate that ever came into the parish. Before his time they never obtained their half Fridays, according to the law, and since he was removed, they have again been deprived of them. He encouraged them to clear and cultivate new provision grounds, and now they have "plenty of victual in them," while before they were so unsettled and afraid, that they neglected their grounds. One of the apprentices suggested as an effectual remedy for one of the greatest abuses to which they are exposed, that a cannon should be placed at Rodney Hall Workhouse with a soldier to fire it at the proper hours of shellblow. It would be heard on every estate in the vale. They said they should be perfectly satisfied if the law were but fairly administered; but that "the white people never dealt fairly by them, though they were always the first to cry out." Before we took leave of them, one of them was requested by the missionary to offer up a prayer, which he did, in appropriate and affecting terms, for the general extension of religion, for a blessing on the church, on their minister and his family, and on the friends of the negros in England, and lastly, that their minister might have given to him "a voice like a mighty shell, to make the word of life known."

There are connected with Jericho, four different stations, all supplied at intervals by one missionary. In these four churches, besides Creoles of Jamaica, and a few individuals born in Martinique and Georgia, U. S., there are native Africans of fourteen different tribes and nations.

22nd. We left Jericho very early this morning for St. Ann's Bay. Our road for the first eight or ten miles, was over mount Diabolo, which we presume derives its name from the length and steepness of the ascent. On looking back into the vale we had left, it appeared filled with a dense white fog, which, without a knowledge of the locality, might have been taken for the sea. Our first stage was a tavern called the Moneague, near the summit of the hill. St. Ann's is one of the most beautiful parishes in the island. It has no sugar estates in the interior, but is chiefly occupied in the cultivation of pimento, or coffee, or by large farms for the raising of horses, cattle, and mules. After leaving the mountains, the country opens into an undulating champaign partly covered with forest, but principally with pastures of guinea grass growing in tufts of such gigantic size, as almost to hide the horses and cattle feeding in the midst of them. Orange trees and other varieties of the citron tribe, loaded with their golden fruit, are thickly scattered over the landscape. The scenery is of a parklike character, the estates having no fences except the walls which bound them; while the gentle elevations are crowned by clumps of trees, and the lowlands occupied with herds of cattle.

We stayed several hours at the Moneague, and called upon a gentleman of the name of BRYDON, to whom we had an introductory letter. He had just sold his estate in this neighbourhood, as he was anxious to return home. He is still, however, attorney for several estates in an adjoining parish, where he told us all the people behaved well, but he allowed them their salt fish and other slave allowances. On one property they were at one time insubordinate, but he changed the overseer, and ordered that they should receive the salt fish, which had been discontinued, and their deportment has since been satisfactory. Near the Moneague, there is a parochial free school called Walton's, endowed with a house and estate, and two separate sums of twenty-five thousand and six thousand pounds, both on loan to the island treasury at eight per cent. The master is a clergyman, and M.A. and there is also a submaster. This wealthy charity educates and maintains *sixteen* parish scholars, between the ages of seven and sixteen years. The head master has also the privilege of taking private pupils.

In some parts of our journey, the trees on either

side of the road were covered with parasites, the abundance and variety of which is a peculiar feature of tropical vegetation. Some twine about the trunks of trees, like cords of all thicknesses, from cable to thread; others hang in green festoons, and sometimes they are so densely woven together as to form a curtain, excluding the interior from view. We drove to St. Ann's Bay in the evening. The little town on the Bay is beautifully situated, but so surrounded by sea swamp as to be very unhealthy. The neighbouring heights afford a pleasant and safe retreat for the more wealthy inhabitants. Near the coast are many fine sugar estates.

23rd. In the course of the morning we paid a visit to the workhouse and jail, which are contiguous premises, separated only by a party-wall. We were shown over them, in the supervisor's absence, by his deputy. In the jail there were three prisoners in chains, and with their feet in shackles, waiting their trial. We were told they had attempted to escape; the wall was sufficiently high, but it appeared the door was liable to be left open, so that they are compelled thus to suffer because the turnkey is careless. In the workhouse there were two prisoners in the solitary cells. One was a female apprentice, sentenced to that punishment and to the treadmill twice a day, for *deficiency of work*. She was evidently ill, and had been so, we were informed, from the time of her coming in, so that the second part of the sentence could not be carried into effect. In the women's sleeping room was a woman suffering from an injury sustained on the treadmill. She was in chains. A boy in the men's ward was ill from the same cause. The deputy told us that an old woman, now at work with the penal gang, had this morning sustained similar injury from the mill. There are about seventy prisoners in the jail and workhouse, for whom the sleeping accommodation is very insufficient. A large number of them are life convicts, principally "incorrigible runaways" from slavery. The treadmill at this workhouse is a cylinder about eight feet in diameter, with broad steps. The handrail above it has eight pair of straps fastened to it, with which the wrists of the prisoners are always secured. The board under the rail descends perpendicularly, and not in a sloping direction, towards the mill, and does not, therefore, afford them the slightest protection when they lose the step and hang by the wrists. In that case the sharp steps of the mill, which project twelve or fifteen inches from the cylinder, must revolve against the bodies and legs of the prisoners with torturing effect. Such are the faults in the construction of the mill, and the results are such as may have been anticipated. Every step is stained with blood both recent and old; the former being that of the poor old woman whom the deputy mentioned to us. It had been shed so profusely, that even the sand on the floor was thickly sprinkled with it. We asked him whether the prisoners on the treadwheel were flogged. He replied that it was necessary "to touch them up"— *women* as well as men. The latter, he said, were struck on the back, but the women on their feet. The whip, which we asked to see, is a cat composed of nine lashes of knotted small cords. The driver of the penal gang, superintendent of the treadmill, and other similar officers, in this, as well as in the other workhouses, are taken out of the gang of life convicts. It is fearful to contemplate the abuses committed by these petty tyrants, who, being already sentenced to imprisonment for life, are thus almost irresponsible, and beyond the reach of the law.

In a subsequent part of the day, while we were in the town, conversing with several persons, the Special Magistrate of the district passed by in his gig. He was quite intoxicated, and was being driven by the bookkeeper of a neighbouring estate, to which they appeared to be going to *administer* the Act for the *abolition* of slavery. This man's conduct and character are publicly and disgracefully notorious.

We called to-day upon the Baptist and Wesleyan missionaries. The former, T. F. ABBOTT, is engaged in building a new chapel to accommodate his large and increasing congregation. The latter also, — WILLIAMS, occupies a field of extensive usefulness. He informed us, that their churches have been increased by the addition of one thousand members in this parish alone, since 1834. We called also upon G. W. BRIDGES, the rector of the parish, who, though almost overwhelmed with grief by a most heavy domestic affliction, the harrowing details of which, have for some weeks past filled the public mind, received us kindly, and expressed a lively interest in the object of our journey.

24th.—We went this morning to see the treadmill at six o'clock, at which time the prisoners sentenced to this punishment, are put upon it previously to their being sent to the penal gang. Two mixed gangs of men and women were put upon it during our stay; the latter had no suitable dress, and were, therefore, liable to be indecently exposed. The lever, by which the speed of the wheel is regulated, was held the whole time by the driver, who sometimes relaxed his hold for a few seconds, which made it revolve with such rapidity, as to throw all the prisoners off. It is thus evident that the punishment may be increased beyond endurance at his caprice. Nearly all the prisoners were dreadfully exhausted at the end of fifteen minutes. One of the prisoners told us he was sent because a *cattle* (a steer) died under his charge. We observed this morning, that not only was the floor sprinkled, and the steps stained, but the very drum of the mill was spotted with blood. If the prisoners cannot keep step, they are suffered to hang, battered by the wheel, till the time expires. The old woman mentioned to us yesterday, hung the whole time, as she could not keep step from the commencement. She was so much injured, that she could not be put on the mill this morning; but that did not prevent her being sent to work in the penal gang in chains, and an iron collar.

We called at Drax-hall, one of the large sugar estates in the neighbourhood. The quantity of sugar produced has not diminished since 1834. The overseer told us, that he adopted the eight-hour system, giving direction to his bookkeeeper, "to draw the people off, when they have worked their time, according to the time they turn out in the morning." He gives them their salt-fish as he did during slavery, except when they behave ill. We were shewn the hospital, a wretched and filthy building, though, from its size, capable of being improved at a small expense. On going through the cane pieces, we met one of the apprentices, a constable or head man. We asked him what he thought of the apprenticeship, as compared with slavery; but, in the presence of Busha, (the overseer,) we could obtain no answer.

On our return, we rode to the place where the penal gang was at work, and saw the poor old woman who had suffered so much on the treadwheel yesterday.

She was a small weakly creature. Her legs were most severely bruised and lacerated. We subsequently learned from some negros from the same estate, that the late Special Magistrate had permitted her to *sit down* (discontinue labor) on account of her age, and that when he was removed, she was sent to mind sheep. One of them died, and she ran away two months, through fear of punishment. This was her offence. Several other women also shewed us the severe injuries which they had sustained on the tread-mill. Two of them had infants in arms, of two or three months old, and had been sent, as the driver expressed it, "for not being able to please their overseer." One old man was a pitiable object, both his body and limbs being swelled by dropsy, to a great size. He had been apprehended as a runaway. The strong men in the gang were employed in digging materials for the road out of a deep gully, which the women and weakly men brought up by a steep path in baskets on their heads; and this poor negro being too weak to carry a basket, was chained to two others, with whom he was compelled to climb up and down the difficult ascent. In the evening we had the opportunity of conversing with negros from seven different estates in this neighbourhood. Several of them were very intelligent; all were members of a Christian church, and appeared respectable, well-disposed people. As a proof that they did not complain, as a matter of course, those from one property, Carlton Pen, expressed themselves satisfied, and said, they had all the indulgences that were customary under the old system. Their statements are referred to the Appendix.*

* See Appendix F, Sec. iv.

Their complaints, which were almost uniform, included compulsory and unrequited labour during crop; frauds of time out of crop; being deprived of their old allowances; inattention to the sick; insufficiency of time allowed to pregnant women and nursing mothers; general ill-treatment by their overseers; and, partiality, injustice, and drunkenness of the Special Magistrate. They said, that all who were sent to the treadmill, returned sick and injured, some having to stay in the hospital afterwards for two, three, or even four months. They were not only daily defrauded of their time, but were frequently mulcted of their Saturdays. The whole of the people on Windsor estate, had been fined three Saturdays, for not turning out early in the morning, which, they said, was a false accusation. They were to begin paying these tomorrow. The whole of the apprentices on Cranbrook and Blenheim estates, had been mulcted five Saturdays, because a few canes had been stolen, and the thief could not be discovered. Watchmen are employed all night, but it is a compulsory service, for which they receive no remuneration. To such an extent are they thus deprived of their Saturdays, that they are obliged to work on the Sabbath for a subsistence. This statement of these negros was confirmed by one of the missionaries, T. F. Abbott, who mentioned to us in conversation yesterday, that the attendance at his chapel is affected by it; the people being compelled to go to their grounds on the Sabbath. The above-mentioned apprentices told us, that when they became free, they should be glad to remain on the estates, working for wages; but, that many of the overseers, told them what high rents they would have to pay for their cottages, and talked in such a way, that they thought they would be turned off, especially such as were getting old and weak.

25th.—We came this morning to Brown's Town, a small town in the interior of the parish of Saint Ann's. Our route, for the first ten miles, lay through a succession of cane-fields by the sea side; the view of the interior was bounded by beautiful green hills. On leaving the coast, the cultivation of the cane is discontinued, and our road over the hills lay through groves of pimento trees. Contrary to our expectation, we find the climate of the interior more tempered and salubrious, than that of the coast. In the course of the morning, we rode over to the Retreat Pen, belonging to S. M. BARRETT, an estate of great extent and beauty, being several miles in length and depth, and comprising both pasture and mountain woodland.— It is managed by a black overseer, named SAMUELS, who was born a slave on one of the estates of his present master. He is now free, and though he can neither read nor write, the property under his charge is in the finest order, and the people in the best discipline. With perhaps the single exception of the apprentices on Hopeton and Lenox estates, the Retreat negros possess, we believe, greater advantages than those on any property in the island. We walked with the overseer through the negro village. The houses are comfortable, and many of them of considerable size, and situated in the midst of neat gardens. They had shingled roofs, and cement or boarded floors. Most of the people were at their provision grounds, but SAMUELS introduced us to such as we found in the houses, as two friends of their master, who had come from England to see how they lived. They all appeared to be in prosperous condition. Most of the married people had large families. The number of apprentices, we understood, to be two hundred and twenty-eight, and of free children seventy-six. After leaving the village, we met many of the people returning from their provision grounds with heavy baskets, and sometimes mule-loads of provisions, which were either for sale in the market, or for their own use during the ensuing week. They appeared respectable, intelligent, and contented. We made many inquiries of them respecting the change in their condition since 1834, but found they had enjoyed the same privileges before, with the exception of their alternate Fridays. We asked them also, what they thought of being free in 1840; the men usually replied, "that they liked *free* well;" but the women seemed almost to dread the thoughts of change. SAMUELS observed, that very little alteration had occurred since 1834; the whip had been abolished ever since the proprietor first came to reside in the country. He said the apprentices continue to receive their saltfish and other accustomed allowances, and that the free children thrive "because Mr. BARRETT takes notice of them;" i. e., gives them the same allowances of clothing, and causes the same attention to be paid to them as during slavery. We saw about sixty or seventy hogs grazing in the open pasture, which were the property of the apprentices. They have also eight or ten horses among them, and feathered stock in abundance. We enquired if they cultivated their grounds industriously, and were told by the overseer that they did, and were even obliged to be restrained from taking in more new land. One man who had neglected his garden, had been punished by taking away two of his Saturdays, and sending him on two other days to work in his provision ground, under the superintendence of another apprentice. The culprit was so ashamed that he has behaved well ever since. SAMUELS assured us, that the apprentices worked well for the estate, and turned out early in the morning. A large proportion of them are Wesleyans and Baptists. Before the missionaries came among them, he observes, there used to be frequent broils; now, all is order and peace. A few years ago, none of them were married; he himself first set the example, and now there are only two mothers of families on the property, who are unmarried. He says, he finds it much better to govern by kindness, than by punishment, and that the people can be made ashamed of bad practices.

We met in the course of the day, in Brown's Town, Captain RAWLINSON, the Stipendiary Magistrate, of this district. He informed us, that the people on the whole, behaved well; and that the proprietors and managers, with scarcely an exception, are well-disposed; that the apprentices have their half Fridays, and that the pregnant women are allowed to discontinue work two months before confinement, and for several weeks after. There are only seven sugar estates in his district, the rest being coffee or pimento properties. He acknowledged that the Saint Ann's workhouse, which we visited yesterday, is a very severe place. We regret to observe, that his account of the treatment of the apprentices, does not at all correspond with what we subsequently heard from their own lips, nor with the testimony of impartial witnesses. We called on the resident baptist missionary, JOHN CLARK, at whose house we saw two apprentices from Penshurst, the property of G. W. SENIOR. One of them was JAMES WILLIAMS, a negro youth, about eighteen years of age, whose unpremeditated statements to us, correspond with the more detailed account which has since been made public in England.*

25th.—We breakfasted this morning at the mission house, with the teacher of the Mico school; JOHN CLARK being absent at a baptism by the sea-side, ten miles distant. There is a large Sunday school at the mission house, attended by from four to five hundred children and adults, which is superintended by the agent of the Mico trustees. The Mico school is the only day school, and it is attended by about sixty children, and the number is daily increasing. The teacher informed us, that those who can afford it, pay regularly a trifling weekly amount. He mentioned, that a short time ago, he was located on an estate, in the parish of Portland, where he was furnished with a house by the proprietor, on condition that the apprentices and their children should be taught free of expense. Those from neighbouring estates were required to pay fivepence per week. Such was the general desire to learn, that from several estates, whose population amounted to four hundred and seventy; three hundred and sixty-eight adults, and children were under his instruction. Many of them made considerable progress; but, after a short time, the school was given up, because the proprietor complained, that the master sympathized too much with the negros, and said, if any disturbance took place, he should attribute it to that cause. Our informant observed, that the work of education may be successfully promoted by any qualified person undertaking it with sincere intentions; but that in order to obtain the confidence of the people, it is necessary to avoid the intimacy of the overseers.

* See Appendix F, Sec. v.

The minister returned about ten o'clock, and an hour afterwards, the morning worship commenced. Though this is comparatively a new station, there were, at least, one thousand persons crowded into the chapel, and many could not obtain admittance. They listened attentively to an earnest and faithful discourse on regeneration, a subject which was so treated as to wean their minds from a dependance on the outward form of baptism, of which fifty-two of them had been that morning partakers. After the service, a marriage was celebrated with most appropriate simplicity, the form employed being a judicious selection of passages from the Old and New Testament. In the early part of the afternoon, the sacrament was administered; after which the people, many of whom came from estates at a considerable distance, generally dispersed to their homes. In the evening there was another service attended by about three hundred persons, chiefly from the town and its immediate vicinity.

During the day and in the evening, we availed ourselves of the opportunity of conversing with many of the members, who were apprentices on neighbouring properties. Their statements are referred to the Appendix.* It is impossible to do justice to them by any general summary; we will, therefore, observe that they include aggravated forms of every abuse, which we have yet heard complained of, and reiterated oppressions and cruelties of masters, overseers, and the Special Magistrate.

26th.—We left Brown's Town early this morning, and drove over to the Retreat Pen to breakfast. We afterwards saw the estate school, which is attended by

* See Appendix F, Sec. iv.

all the older free children, and a few of the apprentices. The classes read and spelt correctly, and a few of them wrote to dictation. The school does great credit to the teacher, a young woman, about nineteen, the daughter of SAMUELS, the overseer. We were afterwards shewn over the hospital, which is a good and airy building. We met there the medical attendant, who is a colored man, and an irregular practitioner, in considerable practice. He was formerly a slave on this property, but purchased himself because his wife was free and lived at a distance.

Our next stage was Stewart's Town, another small interior town in Saint Ann's, on the borders of the parish of Trelawney. We called on the Wesleyan and Baptist missionaries. At the house of the latter we met J. VINE, one of the six missionaries, sent out two years ago, by the London Missionary Society. He was stationed on Acadia, the estate of W. A. HANKEY, where his ministry had a very auspicious commencement, but was at length successfully obstructed by the attorney, and his longer residence rendered impossible, by the want of sympathy and positive discouragement he met with from the proprietor. His present residence, where we subsequently visited him, is about four miles from Stewart's Town, on the summit of a hill, where he has purchased a small spot of ground for a mission station. The house, which consists of two apartments and a porch or hall, is in a ruinous condition. In many places the sky can be seen through the roof. Two additional rooms are being built, which will make it barely tenantable. The missionary, his wife, and children, are surrounded by inconveniences, which nothing but a dedication to their work could enable them to endure. Their temporary chapel is a large canvass tent, which is crowded on the Sabbath by Negros from neighbouring and distant estates. When it ceased to be practicable for him to remain on Arcadia, J. VINE wished to obtain by purchase a small piece of ground separated from the rest of the estate by a public road. He would then have been situated in the centre of a circle, comprising a population of five thousand persons, the outer circumference of which would have been in every part, three or four miles, from any other mission station whatever. He shewed us a map of the locality, which he had traced, exhibiting its extent and population. After a tantalizing correspondence, his request was refused, because in the opinion of the attorney of Arcadia, the vicinity of chapels and schools, lessens the value of West India property. No similar situation could be obtained; all the land within the circle described, being attached to large sugar estates, and not to be purchased, because, in some instances, the estates were mortgaged, and, in others, worldly minded and hostile proprietors refused to wave an objection, which had such weight with one who was a professor of religion, and a patron of the mission. J. VINE obtained his present very inconvenient station with considerable difficulty and at an exorbitant price. A neighbouring proprietor told the person who sold it, that he would have given a still higher price, rather than a missionary should have had it. It is several miles from Arcadia.*

On our way to Falmouth, we called for a short time at Hyde Hall, an estate belonging to E. SHIRLEY, which has been mentioned with distinction in the first report of the apprenticeship committee of the House of

* See Appendix F, Sec. vi.

Commons. On this and two smaller adjoining estates of the same proprietor, about five thousand pounds per annum are paid in wages for the free labor of the apprentices in their own time. The overseer told us that they had nothing to fear from entire emancipation. He said he had often heard of troublesome negros, but though he had been on several estates, he had never met with any whom it was difficult to manage with kind treatment. We were shewn over the buildings. The hospital is one of the best we have seen. There were several patients; some with an eruptive complaint, said to have been imported by the German immigrants; and a poor man, whose hand was changed into a mass of fungous ulceration, proceeding from the prick of a bamboo. Ulcers and sores are much more obstinate in the negro, than in the European constitution. The works on Hyde Hall are extensive, and economy of labor is studied; the plough is much used, and tram-roads are beginning to be introduced at the works. There is a family of Sussex immigrants on the estate, consisting of a man, his wife, and four or five children, who landed three weeks ago, and seem hitherto highly delighted with their new country. The overseer shewed us some specimens of the lace bark. The tree which produces it is rare, and grows only on elevated situations in the interior. As every lover of specimens, of whatever kind, must be in this country, his own collector and curator, they are not easily obtained.

28th.—Falmouth, where we arrived late last night, is a town of increasing size and importance. It is one of the most beautiful in the island; but so surrounded by mangrove swamps that, were it all embayed, it would probably be uninhabitable from malaria. Being on a promontory, it is kept tolerably healthy by the constant sea and land breezes. We breakfasted with WILLIAM KNIBB, whom we found to be as ardent as ever in his advocacy of the rights of the negros. We afterwards accompanied him to see his new chapel, which is nearly finished, and is large enough to accommodate two thousand persons. It is erected in place of the building destroyed by the planters after the rebellion. Some of the individuals who distinguished themselves as chapel destroyers, are still in the magistracy, and one of them in this parish has been invested with the Special Commission.

In the course of the morning we visited the jail and workhouse, both which institutions are superior in cleanliness and arrangement, to any we have yet seen. The supervisor is said to be a humane man. The treadwheel is constructed as a machine for labor and not for torture. None but the contumacious are strapped on. No cat is used. There are in the workhouse no life convicts. The women, however, as well as the men, work in the penal gang, in chains and iron collars. There were in one of the rooms ten women from Lansquinet estate, each with an infant about a twelve months old in her arms. We saw two orders from the Special Justice connected with their case. One was for a strong body of police to be sent on the estate, where "a barrack was prepared for them," to quell, we presume, by their presence, a rebellion among the nursing mothers.* The other order was a

---

* The terms rebellion and insubordination have a different meaning in Jamaica, from that which belongs to them in England. One of the Special Magistrates, in a recent report, speaks of symptoms of rebellion appearing in his district, "particularly amongst the women." A few months since, a peaceable meeting of apprentices and others

warrant to lodge ten apprentices, (no names mentioned,) in the workhouse for three days. The supervisor acknowledged to us that their children had been allowed no food during a part of the day and night that they had been there, because they were not mentioned in the commitment, and the prison store contained nothing suitable for them. The statement of the woman was, that on Friday morning last, as it was very wet, and they were obliged to carry their children into the field with them, they did not turn out before breakfast. For this they were taken before the Special Magistrate, (PRYCE,) on Monday, who sentenced them to pay six Saturdays. They told them they could not, as their mountain grounds were six miles distant, as they were deprived of their half Friday's and of their salt-fish, and received now no sugar or flour for the children; that without their Saturdays, they had no means of obtaining subsistence. For their contumacy, they were sent to the workhouse for three days, and will still have to work the six Saturdays. We observed among the minutes of the visiting magistrates, an order dated some months ago, and signed by two magistrates, that women pregnant, or with children at the breast, should not be punished by imprisonment in the solitary cells; which here, as elsewhere, are dark and ill ventilated, and in which prisoners are always fed on low diet; also, that those who were confined in them, should be allowed a quarter of an hour per diem for air and exercise. This order was accompanied by a memorandum signed by the medical attendant, stating medical reasons for the necessity for such an order. A

---

in Spanish Town, was dispersed by reading the riot act, and calling out the military.

few weeks since, this order was rescinded by a minute signed by the Custos of the parish, WILLIAM FRATER, who merely remarks in general terms, that he has the sanction of the present medical man; the former having died in the interim.

We next visited W. KNIBB's school, which is under the care of T. E. WARD. It is a large and substantial building, built upon a site which has been converted within little more than a twelvemonth, from sea swamp into dry land. There were one hundred children present, among whom we heard eight little negros read in the Testament, who did not know a letter when the school was opened, eight months ago. We also examined a class in arithmetic and mental calculation. They answered difficult questions with great rapidity. We were presented with specimens of their writing, which exhibit the same rapid improvement in that art, for which almost all the negro and colored children are remarkable. We afterwards accompanied W. KNIBB, to Wilberforce, one of his mountain stations, six miles distant, where he has recently built a school and chapel. It is efficiently conducted, and is numerously attended, as there is no other nearer than Falmouth in any direction. In going to this station, we passed through Oxford estate, the property of EDWARD BARRETT, an absentee. There are on it three hundred negros, of whom nearly one-third are Baptists. We saw and conversed with one of the head negros, who had been offered his freedom for his good conduct during the rebellion, but had transferred the boon to his son, saying he could endure slavery better, as he was more accustomed to it. This estate is managed on a liberal plan; although few of the old allowances are continued. During crop the people are paid wages, *with good faith,* at the rate of one shilling for eight hours extra labor. There have been no punishments on the estate for two years past, and this old negro assured us, that the people did more work than ever, and that there was an annual increase in the crops.

3rd month.—1st *(March.)*—We paid a visit this morning, accompanied by — Kelly, a liberal magistrate, in the local commission, and by S. Pryce, the stipendiary of the district, to Goodhope, the centre of nine contiguous estates, belonging to one proprietor, and comprising a population of two thousand apprentices. The population on Goodhope is about three hundred and fifty. The great house and other buildings are on a very large scale. The hospital, which is almost large enough for a county penitentiary, was originally built for the joint purposes of a hospital and place of punishment for the nine estates; but is now appropriated as a hospital, school, and church. There is a salaried medical man resident on the estate, and also a clergyman, who, besides the duties of the Sabbath, takes charge of the school which is thrown open gratuitously to the neighbourhood, and numerously attended by the free children of the apprentices. The boiling-house and mill on Goodhope were in full operation, making about twelve hogsheads of sugar per week, of excellent quality. The overseer assured us that the negros worked as hard as during slavery. The range of workhouses is extensive; nearly every description of iron work, carpenter's and cooper's work, and masonry being executed by the apprentice tradesmen of the estate, who are very numerous, and many of them first-rate workmen.

On our return we made a short stay at the house of the Special Magistrate, who shewed us many of his reports, and gave us other information respecting his district. It includes a population of eight thousand apprentices and fifteen hundred free children; among whom there is a considerable preponderance of females. The reports frequently alluded to the steady and good conduct of the apprentices, and to the incapacity and obstinacy of the overseers. In one of them there was an order quoted, as entered by the medical attendant of one of the estates, in the Plantation Journal, that " the patients with sores should be kept in the stocks." This attempt to revive a brutal custom was fortunately defeated. The Special Magistrate mentioned that one of the largest proprietors in his district, a man too of liberal conduct, when he went into the neighbouring parishes of Westmoreland and Hanover, always returned much dissatisfied, declaring that the people there were taking off the crop without wages. We afterwards learned during our stay in those parishes that this was too true, and that the apprentices are deprived of an enormous amount of time, without any compensation whatever. On our return to Falmouth, we had an opportunity in the evening of conversing with a number of apprentices from Oxford and Cambridge, two estates belonging to a liberal proprietor in England. They are very favorable instances compared with other estates. Their statements will be found in the appendix.*

The parish of Trelawney is one of the largest and wealthiest in the island. It is almost exclusively planted with canes. The estates occupying plains and undulating lands near the coast, and the negroos' provision grounds being situated in the mountain woodlands of the interior, at distances varying from three to even

* See Appendix F, Sec. iv.

twenty miles from their homes. There are only three or four resident proprietors, although on almost every estate, there is a large and substantial "great house," furnished and kept in order, but only occupied by the planting attorneys on the occasion of their hasty and infrequent visits. The number of these expensive mansions would indicate that the parish once possessed a numerous resident proprietary. Although there are fewer abuses in this parish, than in many others, yet W. KNIBB, who has the most extensive opportunities of knowing the treatment of the apprentices, said, that during the last eighteen months, he had never heard of an oppressed apprentice having obtained effectual redress by making complaint; but that he was acquainted with numerous instances when their appeals to the magistrate had resulted in their being punished.

2nd.—We left Falmouth early this morning for Montego Bay, the chief town and port of the adjoining parish of St. James. We visited the workhouse and jail. The latter is a large, airy building, with spacious and convenient court and apartments. The workhouse is on a hill above the town, in a healthy situation, but the building is too small for its purposes, and in a state of dilapidation. The treadwheel was also a ricketty and miserable machine. Several of the solitary cells were perfectly dark and very insufficiently ventilated. There are at the present time thirty prisoners in the workhouse, including one life convict. Women as well as men work in the penal gang in chains and iron collars, in this as in other parts of the island. We called in the course of the day on THOMAS BURCHELL, the Baptist missionary, whose exertions and sufferings on behalf of the negros are well known in England, and also on his colleague S. OUGHTON. We had also the pleasure of making the acquaintance of J. L. LEWIN, a private individual residing in Montego Bay, who is one of the best friends of the negros, and has often advocated their rights.

3rd.—We visited Latium estate, which is situated in this parish, and is considered one of the best managed properties in the island. The number of slaves upon it in 1834 was four hundred and fifty. The Special Magistrate of the district, W. CARNABY, has obligingly furnished us with a memorandum of the Courts he has held upon it during the last fourteen months. Out of twenty-five official visits, complaints were brought before him on five occasions only, being in the whole thirteen cases, in eleven of which punishments were awarded, including one of flogging. From other information we learn that the apprentices are nearly all Baptists, attending Salter's Hill Chapel in the immediate neighbourhood; that there are eighty-three married couples among them, and that fifty of the free children attend the school at the mission station, which has been liberally encouraged by pecuniary aid from the attorney. The apprentices and their free children not only receive all their accustomed allowances, but are left in undisturbed enjoyment of their half Fridays and Saturdays. They are remunerated for the extra labor required from them during crop, as well as for as many of their own days, as they choose to employ in working on the estate. Under this management the crops are equally large, and the net revenue from the estate greater than at any former period. The Attorney, HENRY HUNTER, to whom we were introduced, gave us much valuable information. The minutest details of the management of the plantation for a series of years have been reduced by him to a tabular form at an incredible cost of labor. He kindly presented us with a copy of a series of calculations and statements, which show the immense superiority of free over slave labor, as well as the docility and industry of the negros, when encouraged by judicious and kind treatment. These are referred to the Appendix. Some extracts from these tables, exhibiting valuable and curious results, are given in the Appendix.* From 1817 to 1834, the population in Latium gradually decreased; since 1834, the births have been very numerous, and it has in consequence begun to increase. The number of patients in the hospital throughout the year has also decreased to a very great extent. On a large pen and coffee estate in another parish belonging to the same proprietor, the people have much increased in number since 1817.† We were shewn through the negro village and over the hospital, which presented an appearance of cleanliness and comfort. We conversed with a few of the people, though as it is their own half-day, they were most of them on their provision grounds. The head carpenter, a very intelligent negro, told us that when he became free, he would not leave Latium even if he could obtain higher wages elsewhere. The apprentices had been employed this morning in dividing a piece of fresh land contiguous to the fields where they worked, which had just been given them, in addition to their more extensive, distant gardens, "for shellblow grounds," in which they might employ the time between meals, and other short

---

* See Appendix F. Sec. vii.

† The proprietor of the Retreat Pen, which we visited a few days ago, informed us, that while the population has increased one hundred on that property, the numbers on a large sugar estate in his possession had declined to an equal extent within the same period.

intervals. A circumstance was mentioned to us which proves how great an amount of injustice may be perpetrated, by both masters and magistrates, in deciding against apprentices on those vague and general charges so commonly preferred by the overseers and book-keepers. On this estate the overseer became dissatisfied with the quantity of work performed, and took away the allowances of salt fish. When the amount of work came to be added up in the plantation book, it was found they had done more than at any former period. The arrears of allowance were therefore ordered to be paid up by the attorney.

4th.—We inspected the day school recently established in connection with the Baptist mission. There were about one hundred and fifty children present of all ages. They were in very good discipline, and their progress during the short time, satisfactory. An infant and sewing school are about to be formed on the same premises. These schools were opened by a public celebration of an extraordinary character. The missionaries requested their country congregations connected with the Montego Bay station, to send their children to be present. Many came from great distances, some nearly thirty miles, sleeping in little groups in the open road. The whole number was three thousand one hundred and seventy-two. There is also in Montego Bay a flourishing school on the Mico foundation, which we had not an opportunity of visiting.

We afterwards attended the Saturday court, which is held in the town by the Special Magistrates. A man and his wife, apprentices on adjoining properties, complained that an overseer's horse had trespassed in their ground, and entirely destroyed their provisions. This is an example of a frequent and very serious injury to which the apprentices are liable. The damage cannot be repaired sometimes for a whole season, and meantime they are destitute of food. In this case one of the Magistrates promised his interference. There were several valuations; one of a non-predial, a colored young woman who was very smartly dressed, and who no doubt filled the situation of "housekeeper" to an overseer, or book-keeper. The transaction appeared to be one of rivalry between two plantations underlings, one of whom became responsible for the amount of the valuation. Another case was that of a predial, a girl of seventeen. A witness valued her at ten pounds per annum. The magistrate, chosen by her owner, objected to the amount; when the pliant evidence immediately declared, he meant the nett amount, without the usual deduction of one-third for casualties. This deduction was however made. Another apprentice who wished to purchase his time was valued by his master, who described him as a mason and cabinet-maker, at sixty-nine pounds per annum. This case was adjourned. It appears to be common in valuations, not only to enumerate all the virtues of the apprentices, who are at other times so unscrupulously vilified, but to represent them as very proficient in a number of different and incompatible handicraft trades.

5th.—Thomas Burchell, like his brother missionary at Falmouth, is engaged in erecting his chapel, which was destroyed after the rebellion. The new building when completed will hold three thousand persons. The late persecution of the missionaries has given an astonishing impulse to their religious labors. The destroyed chapels are replaced by much larger buildings, which are yet inadequate for the accommodation of their hearers. The services of the Sabbath at this station are at present conducted in a large dwelling-house, from which most of the interior walls and partitions have been removed. According to the usual custom in Jamaica, a prayer meeting was held early in the morning. Three of the negros took part in it, one of whom was an old African; their expressions were often beautiful and eloquent. We afterwards visited the Sunday schools, in which there was five hundred and fourteen children assembled. The extensive diffusion of religious instruction and education by such an apparently limited agency is remarkable at all the stations of the Baptists which we have visited. The morning service commenced at ten, and was attended by at least three thousand persons, many of whom came from great distances. In the evening we came to Mount Carey, a mountain station of the baptist missionaries of Montego Bay. There is also a flourishing school here, attended on the Sabbath by five or six hundred children, and on other days by about one hundred. On our way the scenes of many of the principal events of the late rebellion were pointed out to us.

6th.—Mount Carey is in the heart of the districts involved in the rebellion. The works and buildings of every estate in its neighbourhood, were destroyed by the insurgents, and on many the effects of the recent desolation were still visible in the bare and unroofed walls of many of the buildings. In the course of the morning, we visited Eden, a well managed estate, and one which furnishes little employment for the Special Magistrate. Its population was on the average stationary from 1817 to 1834, and has since begun to increase. We next proceeded to Wiltshire estate, another well-conducted property. The resident Attorney, ——— FENTON, is the only manager at whose house Special Justice Norcott ever condescended to take refreshment. That individual, amidst some eccentricities, was distinguished by an inflexible love of justice. His name is held in grateful remembrance by the negro population of this parish. He was once overtaken on this property by a tropical shower, and after waiting in vain for its cessation, he at last consented to take a glass of punch, but on being asked to stay dinner, immediately took his flight in the rain. The Special Commission may be made almost a sinecure, by worthless magistrates, but the difficulties to which upright men are exposed, can only be appreciated by eye witnesses. Their districts are often twenty miles in extent in a country more mountainous than Wales or Scotland; frequently they cannot obtain houses within them; they are required to visit each estate twice a month, and in order to do this are obliged to keep from two to four horses, and to incur other charges, which their salaries in this expensive country are totally inadequate to sustain. When to these is added the incessant persecutions of the planters, and the harrassing pursuit of their duties, under a burning sun, it will cease to surprise, that so many of them have fallen victims to their labors, or have withdrawn in disgust. To avoid depending on the hospitalities of the overseers is nearly impossible, for it requires an inflexible resolution, and a capacity of enduring fatigue and hunger, which few possess, and still fewer have the principle to bring such qualities into action.

The population on Wiltshire has increased for many years past, ever since it has been under the management of its present attorney. He introduced the remedial provisions of the Apprenticeship, two months before the Bill came into operation. There has been only one punishment on the estate since, and that in a case of theft.

We met here two of the Special Magistrates, FACEY and ODELLE, in whose company we visited Montpelier, an estate belonging to Lord SEAFORD. This property is in the same situation as many others belonging to humane, well-intentioned proprietors, residing in England. The authority of the magistrate is in constant requisition. The overseer was absent on militia duty; one of the book-keepers shewed us the premises, though with some appearance of reluctance. A new substantial stone dungeon has just been erected. It consists, besides a narrow passage, of two arched cells, about twelve feet by nine, and eight or nine feet high, perfectly dark. The erection of such a building, at a time when penal confinement on estates ought to have wholly ceased, requires no comment; and it has not been built to remain untenanted. One of the attorneys without any magistrate's order, has twice directed to be locked up in it, thirteen old women, who refused to cut grass on their own days. They were kept during their confinement on a short allowance of bread and water. We saw also the hospital, which is the worst we have seen on a large estate, and is very dirty and offensive. It consists of three rooms and a passage, in which there are about twenty patients. There is a court before it, enclosed with a lofty fence of bamboos, pointed at the top, so as to exclude the inmates from all communication with their friends, at the pleasure of the overseer. We were shewn over the works and curing house. One of the hogsheads of sugar had been spoiled by the carelessness of the boilerman. The book-keeper told us, that they never interfered with the negros in the manufacture of the sugar, and that a book-keeper is stationed in the boiling-house, merely to see that the negros commit no depredations on the syrup or sugar. It appears then, that the science of sugar making is monopolised by the despised apprentices. One of the Special Magistrates intended to hold his Court on the estate to-day, but the overseer being absent, he could only take cognizance of complaints, and promise to decide them at his next visit. Several men said they had agreed to work a certain number of extra hours, but had not been fully paid the stipulated amount; a woman complained against the head book-keeper for abusive language; the estate against a man for stealing sugar; a cattle-boy against another apprentice for flogging him; and lastly, the thirteen old women before mentioned complained that they had again been deprived of their time. They were all apparently upwards of sixty years of age, and appeared quite unequal to any heavy employment. From Montpelier we proceeded to Belvidere. Before the rebellion this estate is said to have been most cruelly managed For a year past it has been under the care of a Scotch peasant, who came out as a ploughman, and has been promoted by a judicious attorney to the station of overseer. He is not only greatly improving the cultivation, but adding to the comforts of the negros. We have met with no one who has introduced the plough so extensively. We conversed with several of the negros in the boiling-house. They all said they were satisfied with their Busha, and would be glad when free, to remain as laborers on the estate. If the same question had been asked them a year before, they should have given a very different answer. They receive two-pence per hour for extra labor during crop, which is the most liberal arrangement we have yet heard of. There are eighteen persons on this estate past work, many of whom have been rendered so by former ill-treatment, which has induced premature old age. As we were leaving Belvidere, we met a number of the "King-free" children returning to it from the school at Mount Carey, which is five miles distant; so that these little creatures have to walk ten miles daily, to and from school. During our stay in Saint James's, we had several opportunities of hearing the narrations of the wrongs and oppressions of the apprentices from their own lips. Their statements are given in the Appendix,* as examples of the condition of the apprentices, and of the mode in which the abolition law is administered. They include flagrant instances of the frauds of time which are committed on the apprentices, of the enforcement of extra labor in and out of crop for little or no remuneration, of the neglect of the sick, oppression of nursing mothers, pregnant women, and mothers of six children who were exempt during slavery from field labor, together with instances of ill-treatment, of which no general description can be given. The worst cases are from the adjoining parish of Hanover. It may be proper to mention here the following circumstances :—One of the Special Magistrates in this part of the island, had occasion to fine an overseer for oppression. The man said, " he would have it out of the people's salt-fish," and sold two barrels of herrings, sent by the proprietor or attorney for the apprentices, and paid the fine out of the proceeds. The same magistrate imposed a fine recently in a flagrant case. The party appealed to the Governor, who desired him to *conciliate,* and directed

* See Appendix F, Sec. iv.

him to remit the fine. Another Special Magistrate applied to the Governor respecting the proper interpretation of a clause in the Act in Aid which was used to enforce nightwork, but received no answer. Similar instances of want o support and countenance are not infrequent.

Although Saint James's parish was the seat of the insurrection, and is still the hot-bed of colonial prejudice, yet in consequence of the exertions of one or two private individuals; the presence of several Special Magistrates of superior moderation and justice; of a few humane and enlightened managers of estates, and of one or two large planting attorneys, who appear desirous of acting in a liberal spirit; there are probably as many estates on which the apprentices enjoy some of the remedial provisions of the law, as in any other which is chiefly occupied in the cultivation of sugar. Saint James's is the only parish where the slaves, who were not duly registered, have succeeded in obtaining their freedom.* About three hundred have thus been emancipated, chiefly through the exertions of J. L. LEWIN. In this parish also, and the adjoining one of Trelawney, the pro-slavery feeling and influence are somewhat neutralized by the more liberal public opinion of the fine flourishing towns of Falmouth and Montego Bay.

7th.—We arrived this morning at Lucea, in Hanover, of which parish it is the port. It is a small but increasing town, situated near the north-west extremity of the island. In the course of the morning we visited the workhouse and jail, which are contiguous buildings on a promontory, immediately above the sea.

* See Appendix F, Sec. iii.

The jail consists of a court and four rooms, besides the jailor's house and two apartments in the upper story for debtors, which are at present unoccupied. The premises were very clean, but there appeared no attempt at classification, nor any space to carry that desirable object into effect. There were nine or ten men, and one woman in the yard, waiting to take their trial for misdemeanors or felonies, or in detention as witnesses. There were no chains, shackles, nor iron collars, which seem to be reserved for the apprentices. We afterwards inspected the workhouse, accompanied by ALEXANDER CAMPBELL, the senior magistrate, resident in Lucea. The prisoners are not secured at night by shackles, and though many of the women and men in the penal gang, wore chains and collars, yet this degrading livery was not universal in the case of females. The treadmill was of bad construction, and capable of being made an instrument of much torture. There were five women in the solitary cells; two of whom had been mentioned to us spontaneously by some negros at Montego Bay from the same estate, called Newmill. The account we had heard was as follows:—Two old women named LUCY ANN STEPHEN and JUDY EVANS, who had each of them eight children, of whom the youngest is now about thirteen, were allowed to sit down, (cease work,) from the time they had their youngest child until after the rebellion, when they were compelled to cut grass. They continued at this employment after the introduction of the apprenticeship, until they lately refused on account of their age and weakness. They were brought before the magistrate and sent to the workhouse. We enquired the names of the women in the cells, and found these two, and a third from Newmill, under the same circumstances. They were very old and infirm, and on our enquiring what they were sent for, replied, "too much piccaniny massa," i. e., they had so many children, that they were entitled to leave field work. We saw the magistrate's warrant, which directs them to be put in solitary confinement for ten days, and "fed on the usual prison fare without herrings." The case of another woman, who was in the yard, also excited our attention. She had been sent from Savanna la Mar in Westmoreland, in which town the workhouse of that parish is situated, to this workhouse, by two Special Magistrates, to be punished for fourteen days by penal labor, and put upon the treadmill every other day. Her alleged offence was running away and refusing to work. She was a domestic servant, and her absence from her mistress's house, she told us, was occasioned by illness. She was ill when she came, and was evidently so when we saw her. The supervisor and medical attendant of the workhouse, have more humanity than the stipendiaries, and treat her as an invalid. It is not uncommon to send apprentices out of their own parish to a distant workhouse; the motive being to send them away from any friend who might assist or sympathize with them; sometimes workhouses are resorted to, that have a reputation for cruel treatment. There are three life convicts at Lucea.

In this parish several non-registered slaves have succeeded in recovering their freedom. The first, who made the discovery and mooted the question, was flogged by the Special Magistrate as a refractory apprentice. He ran away to Spanish Town, a distance of eighty or ninety miles, to appeal to the Governor, and has not since been molested, except that his late master has made a claim upon the person employing him for wages at the rate of ten shillings a day, under what is called the *inveigling* clause in the Act in Aid. Those who have thus recovered their freedom, have succeeded only negatively by the refusal of the Special Magistrate to coerce them as apprentices. We have been informed of another case in the neighbourhood, in which a negro thus obtained his liberty, and hired himself to work on a plantation. When he applied for his wages, the overseer told him he should pay them over to his owner. The case was brought before the local magistrates; but the injured party could obtain no redress. The rights of these non-registered negros have been sacrificed by the supineness of the Home Government. We saw to-day an apprentice from a neighbouring estate, who gave us a striking account of the distress he and his fellow apprentices suffered, from the trespass of cattle on their provision grounds, which are quite unprotected and seven miles distant.

8th.—We attended this morning the weekly petty sessions, which are held by three or four local magistrates. The only case of interest was a charge against a negro for drunkenness and riotous conduct in the street. He said he was a sailor belonging to a Kingston vessel, which had left him behind. The presiding magistrate said, " We do not know that you are a free man; where is your free paper?" He said he had lost it. The same magistrate then suggested in an undertone, that he should be committed to the workhouse as a runaway apprentice; but his coadjutors decided in the negative, and the man was fined two dollars.* We afterwards, by permission, looked over

* Sir LIONEL SMITH, in his tour of the island, some weeks later than this, found a man in Lucea workhouse, who *had* been committed there merely for being without his free paper. The practice

the record of the proceedings of this court, which is kept by the clerk of the peace. Numerous cases against apprentices for petty theft, trespass, threatening language, and assault, were recorded in the decisions of the *local* magistrates. There were also numerous instances of complaints by European immigrants. These unfortunate, and too often dissipated people, have either died or left this neighbourhood. While they remained, they appear to have given much trouble to the magistrates. In the same book belonging to the clerk of the petty sessions, was an account of a coroner's inquest upon the body of an old man, who died about a year ago, in consequence of repeated cruel floggings by a former supervisor of the workhouse. This supervisor was subsequently tried for the wilful murder of this man, and narrowly escaped conviction; the jury having been locked up for three days before they could agree upon a verdict. At a subsequent meeting of the vestry there were found two magistrates, who are still in the commission of the peace, capable of proposing and seconding that he should be retained in his situation, " as it was a first offence."

During our stay in Lucea, we were hospitably entertained by JOHN STAINSBY, the rector of the parish. He is one of those who has ever manifested a sympathy with the oppressed, and is consequently, together with other estimable clergymen of the establishment, deemed " worse than a Baptist." We had also the pleasure during our stay of making the acquaintance of J. H. EVELYN, of the Customs, a gentleman who has likewise in times past interfered to his cost in the vain attempt

so abhorrent to every principle of justice of presuming a negro to be a slave, or according to the new nomenclature, an apprentice, unless he can prove his freedom, still continues.

to check or expose colonial abuses. In the afternoon we proceeded to Savanna la Mar, in the parish of Westmoreland. Hanover is a mountainous parish. The sides of the hills are yet, to a great extent, uncultivated; the plains and valleys are occupied by canefields. Westmoreland is of a different character, consisting chiefly of a plain of considerable extent, bounded on one side by the sea, and on the others by mountains. It is overgrown with thickets of the logwood and acacia, occasionally interspersed with sugar estates. We were overtaken in an early part of our journey to-day by the rain, which poured down in torrents for several hours. Many apprentices have mentioned their being compelled to work in the rain to the destruction of their health, as a grievance to which they were not subjected before the introduction of the present system. We had now an opportunity of verifying the fact by our own observation. We passed midway on our journey by Glasgow estate, belonging to R. WALLACE, M.P., for Greenock, and observed the gangs of negros still at work in the field. On another large estate, the name of which we did not learn, the apprentices were still remaining in the field, sheltering themselves as they best could under the canes.

9th.—We visited the workhouse this morning. The premises are small and confined. The supervisor, who appeared to be a humane man, informed us that there were seventy-six prisoners, of whom eight were life convicts, and the rest apprehended runaways or apprentices from estates. We arrived in time to see the penal gang collected previously to being sent out to their daily labor. The greater number of both sexes were in chains, and all had iron collars. Among them were three females with infants at the breast, who had each been committed to hard labor by the Special Magistrate; one for having three pints of sugar in her possession; another for quarrelling with her sister; and the third, who was a non-predial, hired out, for not paying her weekly hire. In the last case, it is more than probable, that the offence was unavoidably created by her situation as a nursing mother. A history of past sufferings was legibly inscribed on the backs of many of the prisoners, who were almost in a state of nudity, in the scars of severe floggings. The supervisor told us that prison dresses were being made for them. The majority of the prisoners sleep in two very small apartments, which we saw soon after the prisoners had left them for the day; they were almost insufferable on account of their closeness. We saw here two women, named SARAH NELSON and BESSEY GRANT, from Phœnix Estate, in the parish of Hanover, and who were sent to this instead of their own workhouse, for the offence of being unable to execute the compulsory task-work imposed upon them by the Special Magistrate. That functionary resides in the great house on Phœnix Estate, and the people complain that he coerces them without mercy.* This estate also belongs to a professedly liberal and religious proprietor. We were permitted to look over the files of the Special Magistrates' commitments, which frequently consist of nothing more than lists of eight or ten apprentices with their respective punishments affixed, without any mention whatever of complaints or offences. We saw two of the life convicts, both of whom were condemned after the rebellion. One of them, a very old man, as-

---

* See Appendix F, Sec. iv.

sured us, that the only charge against him, was his being a Baptist. The other was a fine young man, who is employed as a turnkey. The supervisor gave him an excellent character, and his countenance appeared to express both intelligence and integrity. The substance of his story, as related to us by himself, is as follows :—Before the rebellion, he and other negros agreed, that they would *sit down* after Christmas, and tell their masters they were free ; but that they would willingly continue to work "for any small salary." They did so, but afterwards, some of the ignorant negros, refusing to listen to the more "sensible," began to set fire to the buildings, and to make war against the white people. He tried in vain to check them, and when he heard they were searching for him to take his life, he ran away till the insurrection was over. He was then apprehended and condemned to the workhouse for life. This account is quite in accordance with what is known of the origin of the insurrection. The negros were encouraged to strike work, by the belief that the king had set them free, but that their masters were determined to retain them in bondage ; a delusion which was produced by the language, which some of the planters held to the negros, and by their conversations with each other in the presence of the negros on the progress of the anti-slavery cause ; at the same time, that the slaves on many estates, were exasperated by increased oppressions and cruelties. This conduct can scarcely be explained on any other supposition than that of a determination to create a disturbance, which should check any tendency in the Home Government unfavorable to the continuance of unmitigated slavery. The disturbance soon, however, rose to an alarming height ; a general panic spread among the whites, and the estates were abandoned to the insurgents, by whom property was destroyed to an immense extent. Very few of the free inhabitants lost their lives; but, at the courts' martial, which immediately succeeded the insurrection, hundreds of negros were sacrificed to the guilt, cowardice, and terror of the whites. Many were executed in parts of the island to which the disturbance never extended, and among the victims were some whose sole or principal offence, was that of their being Baptists or Methodists. The rebellion was charged upon the missionaries, and was made the pretext of that violent persecution in which many were driven from the island, and their chapels destroyed by men who held, and still retain, the King's Commission as Justices of the Peace. The sequel to these memorable events was transacted in England. Some of the accused missionaries have published a "Narrative" of the events connected with their mission during the progress of the rebellion, and of the proceedings which immediately followed it. Their statement was extensively circulated, and though it contains an exposure of the disgraceful means adopted to procure their crimination, and a great quantity of facts and evidence which fix the insurrection upon its real authors, yet the parties implicated, and their organs the island newspapers, have observed the most discreet silence respecting it, and still continue to designate the rebellion as "the Baptist war." The investigation of this subject is a matter of no slight interest at the present moment. Since the introduction of the present system, some leading persons in a certain district of the island, made representations through a high legal functionary to the Governor, that their parishes were in a disturbed state, and requested that troops might be sent. By private inquiries, Lord Sligo ascertained that the apprentices were industrious and peaceable. There can be no doubt, however, that goaded on by oppression, and alarmed by the presence of the military, they might easily have been driven to such a general desertion of the estates as would have been styled a rebellion, and suppressed with the rigorous severities of martial law.*

10th.—This morning we drove over to Paradise Pen, the residence of Thomas M'c Neel, the Custos of the parish, to whom we had several introductory letters. Although we found him very much occupied, he obligingly gave up a part of the day to us. He has under his care many estates, including an apprentice population of four thousand, of whom he observed that none give much trouble to the Special Magistrates. On all the estates, the old allowances are continued, to the extent even of clothing and medical attendance for the free children. He stated to us, that he believed that in the parish generally, things are going on as well as in any part of the island; a remark, however, which is not borne out by the crowded state of the workhouse at Savanna la Mar. The Custos spoke strongly against the revolting practice of working male and female prisoners in the streets and roads in

* More recently, on the occasion of Sir Lionel Smith's tour of the island, an anonymous letter was brought to him, which had been dropped in the parish of Saint Elizabeth. It purported to be written by an apprentice with the view of exciting insurrection; but was evidently the production of one but imperfectly acquainted with the dialect of the Creole negros, in which it affected to be written. Should any disturbances unfortunately occur before the termination of the present system, we venture to predict that the chief blame will not belong to the negros, who have shewn themselves unequalled in the patient endurance of fraud and oppression.

chains, and observed that he had done all he could to discountenance it. He shewed us several statements of the increase and decrease of negros, from which it appeared that on many of these estates, the births and deaths are as carefully registered as during slavery, and that in the last eight or ten years, there has been a slight increase of the population even on some of the sugar plantations. We saw also among the accounts of expenses, various annual donations of from two to ten pounds, to the head people for good conduct; also accounts of the purchase of cattle from the apprentices. The most striking remark which he made to us on his mode of management, was that the white people on the estates, required quite as much attention and oversight to keep them in their proper place as the negros. He accompanied us to visit the two estates of Lord HOLLAND. On the first, Sweet River Pen, the people were receiving the weekly distribution of salt-fish. About fifty of them came round the steps of the great house to converse with us, and enquired very eagerly whether we had seen Lord and Lady HOLLAND before we left England, and desired their best respects to be given to them, saying, they had always been very good to them. Their attorney wished them to explain what they intended to do after 1840. They replied that they could not make any agreement till the time came, as the attorney might die if they made a bargain with him. They expressed great anxiety to know what was to be done respecting their houses and grounds, and said, the uncertainty prevented their repairing or improving them. They said, that former times were bad enough; the apprenticeship was better, as they could not be flogged by the driver, but they wished they might be free immediately. One of their complaints was, that they had never seen their master, pointing, at the same time, to a very old negro, and intimating he had never seen his owner. They wished Lord HOLLAND would send out " his piccaninny or his cousin," with whom they might talk about the terms upon which they should remain when free. As we were leaving, they preferred a request to their attorney, to exchange their half Friday for every alternate Friday, as their grounds were six miles distant. From Sweet River we proceeded to Friendship, a sugar estate belonging to Lord HOLLAND. Here also we saw and conversed with at least fifty or sixty of the people in the presence of their attorney and the overseer. We did not find them very communicative. They said, however, that they had a kind master and mistress (Lord and Lady HOLLAND;) and, when free, which they wished might be to-morrow, they should be glad to remain on the estate and work for wages, rather than leave their houses and grounds to begin the world again. We asked them whether the Special Magistrate heard both sides fairly when they were brought before him. They replied that he would not let them speak; in confirmation of which the Custos strongly condemned the conduct of some of the stipendiaries. As we were leaving the estate, a number of women surrounded the attorney, and complained that their half Fridays had been taken away in crop, and not repaid them. He reminded them of the numerous indulgences they received, and said they must not reckon the time due to them with too much nicety. A noisy discussion ensued, the merits of which we could not understand; but the deportment of the people was rude and discreditable. We visited the hospital, which is a building on stone pillars, well contrived for its purposes, but dirty and out of repair

There was also near it a series of substantial, stone, penal cells, which we hope are now chiefly valued as building materials. The great house was untenanted. Its entrance, as well as that on Paradise Pen, was graced by a small cannon. We walked through a part of the negro village. The houses were of an inferior description, but there were some pleasing evidences of the industry of the people in their gardens and plaintain walks. The Custos, though himself a large attorney, candidly attributes the greatest evils to the prevailing absenteeism, and to the influence of the merchants. He appears fully aware of the importance of keeping the era of complete freedom in view in his dealings with the apprentices, and has encouraged those on his own estate by the expectation of being set free a year before the time fixed by law. He expressed a wish to see estate schools generally established. Speaking of the increased value of property, he mentioned an estate purchased eighteen months ago, for five thousand pounds, for which twelve thousand pounds have recently been offered; and that he had bought seventeen slaves in 1833 for nine pounds currency each, for every one of whom he had received at least twenty pounds sterling compensation.

11th.—We again visited the workhouse to see the treadmill in operation. Four men were first put upon it, whose wrists were as usual strapped to the handrail. The construction of this mill is so slight, and its cylinder of so small a diameter, that when the prisoners all stepped at once, their weight instantly increased its speed, so as to throw them all off. They were compelled to throw themselves into a sidelong posture, and take two or three steps at a time, in the most awkward and painful manner. The wheel then moved by jerks, quickly and slowly alternately. One young man of color, who was put on for the first time, after many ineffectual attempts to catch the step, hung suspended by the wrists during the greater part of the time, the wheel revolving against his legs. His cries were most piercing; "I don't know what they sent me here for; I have done nothing to be sent here." When he came off he appeared much exhausted. He told us that he was a carpenter on Grove Plain estate. The constable sent him to give an order to the gang, which he did, but they did not attend to it. The constable was sent by the overseer to repeat the order, with directions that if it were not complied with, the prisoner and the other people should be put in confinement. The constable, without repeating the order, locked him up at once. When released the next day, he asked the overseer what he had done to be locked up, for which he was taken before the Special Magistrate on a charge of insolence, and sent to the workhouse and treadmill for ten days. This account was subsequently confirmed to us by an apprentice from the same estate, with whom we had an opportunity of conversing. After the first spell was ended, the two women from Phœnix estate, whose case has been previously noticed, were put upon the mill. Being of lighter weight, the mill revolved more slowly, and they kept the step better, but were quite exhausted, and in a profuse perspiration when the time had expired. The supervisor told us that the prisoners nearly always suffered in the manner above-mentioned, when first put upon the mill.

We saw this morning a woman named MARY SAUNDERS, who had been sent to the workhouse under the following circumstances:—About a year ago, she was valued for nineteen pounds, and paid the money to

Special Justice PHELP, who told her, she was then free. Her master, however, dissatisfied with the amount, appealed to the Governor, and refused to receive the money. She therefore obtained no acknowledgment or "free paper," though she acted as her own mistress. Tired at length of a state of uncertainty, she also appealed to the Governor, on which the Special Magistrate issued his warrant, after she had been free for a year, and committed her to the workhouse as a runaway apprentice. She was at the time in daily expectation of her confinement, and had been delivered two days before we saw her of her tenth child. The supervisor appeared to have done all he could to palliate, by kind treatment, the inhumanity of the magistrate.

In the course of the morning we attended the Special Magistrates' court. There were three present of the names of PHELP, EMERY, and OLIVER, of whom the first took the most prominent part in the proceedings. The first case was that of a runaway apprentice complained of by his attorney, whose evidence was altogether hearsay, as he did not reside on the estate himself. It was supported by that of the head constable. The presiding magistrate, to remove all doubts, after first browbeating the prisoner, put leading questions to him, which made him criminate himself. He was then sentenced for one month to the house of correction. The same complainant next brought a charge against the head constable, for "disobedience of orders." He had been directed to bring to this court a woman, who had been a runaway from the estate for a year and a-half. The constable said he had never seen her, and did not know where she was. The attorney replied, that it was his duty to produce any of the gang when called for. The case was dismissed, the charge being too absurd even for a court like this to entertain. The brother of MARY SAUNDERS now stepped forward, and asked why his sister had been sent to the workhouse. He had witnesses to prove that the Special Magistrate, (PHELP,) told her she was free, and might go where she liked, at the time that he received the money. The same magistrate treated him very insolently, and said, that she had written a letter to the Governor full of lies about him, and that she was now committed as a runaway by the Governor's order.* He said he would not be called to account by everybody, and ordered the man out of court. Subsequently, the Custos entered the court, and spoke to the magistrates about this case. He had been one of the local justices concerned in the original valuation, and felt himself somewhat implicated in the case. From the explanations which followed, it was apparent that the facts were as we have already stated them, and that the conduct of the Special Magistrate had been most grossly arbitrary and illegal. There were several cases of valuation. A sickly colored child, about ten years old, was appraised at ten pounds, which was paid by her father, an overseer. A diminutive woman, valued as a predial apprentice, for thirty-

---

* Having the Governor's general permission to apply for information at the Stipendiary Magistrates' department in Spanish Town, we availed ourselves of it to obtain a sight of the official correspondence in this case; and can, therefore, state that this assertion of the magistrates, was a total misrepresentation of the Governor's instructions in the case, and that the act of committal was entirely his own. The poor woman subsequently memorialized the Governor, but obtained no redress, till she made a personal appeal to him, when he visited the workhouse on his tour round the island. He immediately ordered her release. The magistrate, we believe, escaped without censure.

four pounds; and, lastly, a tall, sickly, colored man, applied to be appraised, who was by trade a cooper. His overseer swore that he could make three puncheons a week, and that his weekly labor was worth twenty shillings to the estate. The magistrate, (PHELP,) put leading questions to the witness, as "He is a very valuable man, is he not?" "You say he is a good workman?" &c. The man pleaded that he was very sickly; that he could do little but overlook others; and that if he worked himself for a few weeks, he was sometimes laid by for months afterwards. An overseer was brought forward by him as a witness, who had formerly lived on the property for seven years, and who confirmed all these statements. The doctor, who had attended the estate during the last six months, was then called, who stated that the man had been under his care the whole time for ulcerated legs; but he did not consider the sores habitual. The Special Magistrate, who is supposed to be especially entrusted in valuations with the interests of the apprentice, said to the two local magistrates associated with him, "whatever you say, gentlemen, I shall be satisfied with." One of them appraised the man at seventy pounds, the other at forty-four pounds. The stipendiary wrote the two sums on paper, and added sixty pounds as his own estimate; the average of which amounts, fixed the value of the apprentice at fifty-eight pounds. We heard, subsequently, that this man had been severely flogged last week, by order of the Special Magistrate, which determined him to obtain at any price his release from bondage. Several cases of runaways, and of apprentices charged with petty thefts of canes or sugar, were subsequently disposed of. The business of this court was conducted in a manner and spirit, than which it is difficult to conceive any thing more objectionable. The Custos, who was present during the subsequent part of the proceedings, felt called upon, though himself a planter, to reprove the Special Magistrate for omitting to enquire of the prisoners what they had to say in defence, and for inveigling them by his questions into self-crimination.

We had the pleasure during our stay at Savanna la Mar, of seeing nearly all the Baptist missionaries in the island, who were assembled at the meeting of their annual association. It was truly a pleasure to us to meet again some of these estimable men, and to make the acquaintance of others, whom we had not previously known. We availed ourselves of the opportunity to obtain from them some statistical information relative to the state of education in connection with their congregations.* They also addressed to us the following letter on the subject of the apprenticeship:—

"*Savanna la Mar, March* 10*th,* 1837.

"GENTLEMEN,—It is with feelings of sincere pleasure that we welcome you to the shores of Jamaica, more especially on account of the generous and benevolent object of your mission. Several of us have labored in this island for many years, and have witnessed the horrors of slavery, and the oppressions and sufferings of the slaves. We lent our feeble efforts with the thousands of British Christians in England to accomplish the destruction of the cruel system, and sincerely rejoiced in the passing of that Act which professed to abolish slavery in every part of the British West Indies; 'though we deeply regretted the inter-

---

* See Appendix F, Sec. viii.

mediate state of apprenticeship decided upon by the Imperial Parliament, and have viewed with intense interest the working of that system during the two years and a-half that have elapsed. We feel ourselves called upon to declare to you our firm conviction that the apprentices have conducted themselves in the most tranquil and peaceable manner, and have shewn every disposition to be industrious where encouragement has been afforded them by fair and equitable remuneration, and where they have not been provoked by vexatious annoyances.

"We cannot refrain from expressing our deliberate opinion of the total unfitness of the apprenticeship system as an act of preparation for freedom; and that it is to the unparalleled patience of the apprentices, and not to its tolerant spirit, that the present peaceful and prosperous state of the island is attributable. To you we unhesitatingly declare our belief, that this mockery of freedom is worthless as a preparation for that state to which it can have no possible affinity; that while it represses the energy of the negro, it has rendered him distrustful of the British public, by whom he considers himself to have been cheated by a name; that it has entailed, and is still entailing, excessive suffering, especially on the mother and her helpless and unavoidably neglected offspring, and that to secure its termination, no effort can be considered too great. We do, therefore, most earnestly entreat you on your return to your native land, to exert your influence to effect the total abandonment of this system in 1838; but if every effort fail in procuring the abolition of the term of apprenticeship, to the predial apprentices, that those advantages may at least be secured to them, to which they are entitled by the provisions, imperfect as they are, of the Act for the Abolition of Slavery.

"We further urge you to watch with vigilance any law which may be introduced in the Imperial Parliament, or passed by any of the colonial legislatures, to curtail the liberty of the negro after the termination of the present system; and any enactments of a restrictive and oppressive nature calculated to keep them more degraded than any others of their fellow-subjects for one moment beyond that period.

"Your own observations in this colony must, we think, have convinced you that the costly apparatus by which it was intended to secure a measure of protection to the negro, is in many instances, made instrumental in carrying on a system of coercion and oppression as odious as that from which he was intended to be freed.

"We cannot but express our regret at the apathy manifested of late by some of those friends in England, who so long and so zealously exerted themselves in behalf of the injured sons and daughters of Africa, and must consider that the responsibility rests on them, who have the power to obtain justice for this still injured people, for any consequences that may take place. Meanwhile we shall continue to exert our influence to tranquillize their minds under every disappointment, and to induce them to bear with patience the wrongs they are called upon to suffer.

"We are, Gentlemen,
"With much esteem and respect,
JOSHUA TINSON,

JAMES M. PHILLIPPO,	THOMAS F. ABBOTT,
THOMAS BURCHELL,	WALTER DENDY,
WILLIAM KNIBB,	JOHN KINGDON,
HENRY C. TAYLOR,	BENJAMIN B. DEXTER,
JOHN CLARKE,	JOHN HUTCHINS,
FRANCIS GARDNER,	JOHN CLARK;
WILLIAM WHITEHORNE,	SAMUEL OUGHTON."

The preceding letter, signed by all the Baptist missionaries in the island, is addressed through us to the British anti-slavery public, to whose attention we earnestly recommend its important contents, which express the deliberate and well-considered sentiments of men, who, of all others, are the best qualified to form an unprejudiced judgment of the condition of the negros under the apprenticeship, and of their capacity for a true appreciation of the blessings of freedom. The testimony which it bears to the abuses of the existing system is the result of painful, personal observation; and is but a reiteration of a similar and even still stronger statement forwarded last year by six of the same missionaries to the Secretary of their Board in London; and which, it is much to be regretted, was not published, as was doubtless the intention of its writers. In the course of the day, we saw a negro from Glasgow estate, the property of R. WALLACE, M.P., for Greenock, whose affecting narration is inserted here as a further illustration of the present state of negro slavery in Jamaica. In the Appendix will be found a statement* of the same negro to a gentleman resident in the colony, which corresponds with the subjoined relation of the sufferings of himself and his fellow-apprentices. We are quite willing to believe that the proprietor of this estate has been kept in ignorance of the treatment of his negros; and it is not without great regret, that we bring these facts under his notice and that of the public in the present manner; but we are strongly impressed with the conviction, that there are no estates more oppressively and even cruelly managed, than those of many liberal, humane, and even religious proprietors resident in England.

* See Appendix F, Sec. iv.

Statement of Cyrus Wallace, an apprentice, from Glasgow estate:—" The old living before was better than now. If we come to the Bay, (Savanna la Mar,) to make a complaint, we are punished for it when the magistrate come upon the estate. We are obliged to work on our Fridays and Saturdays. The magistrate threaten we and make we consent; he say, 'if any person deny working on Saturday, bring them down to the Bay, and I shall cat them.' About four weeks ago, on a Friday, shellblow, the busha, (overseer,) ordered the gang to work the next day, (Saturday.) I say, I can't work, because I have a pain in my back, and want to take a dose of salts, as it is my own day. The constable said, if I would not make the fire, (throughout the day at the boiling-house,) he would lock me up. I asked him to take me to the busha, who said I should be locked up, and to-morrow be taken down to the Bay to be catted. I was locked up that night, (Friday,) in my wet clothes, and all the next day without food or water; and when I was let out, it was so late I could not go to my own house, but was obliged to lie down in the floor of the hospital: I was not brought before the magistrate. The constable, (driver,) lock you up when him like; the bookkeeper lock you up when him like; when the busha come, they tell him, and he fasten you in the dark hole better. When the magistrate come on the property, they bring you before him, and he know all about you before you come. If you offer to speak for yourself, he hold his finger and say, 'not a word.' Mr. Wallace property, worse than any property in the parish; every property better than we. If any person was to say—hem, in the field, the constable take and lock you up; and if the magistrate don't send you to dance the treadmill, he send you to be cat, (flogged.) There are four men put down to get cat. We don't know what we do. Busha, where I working, he come there, and why the reason make him sure he get me cat; I work three Saturdays, and no pay and no day. I went up to him, and tell him I want a day. He says, devil a day you get. I said, I must have a day, I lose too much day; you take away three day from me, and this is four. He says, you were at the boiling-house, stealing sugar. I says, me Sir; I would not do that, because I know the property that I live upon, and would not make fool of myself. When he tell me he won't give me the day, I go away and take one day. He would not pay me, and I was in need. He told me, you went and took day yesterday; I said, yes Sir. He said, now you may be sure, so help me God, that you'll get cat. The magistrate has not yet been on the property; but whenever he does come, the day he comes, I get it; he does whatever busha tell him. They give more flogging now than when we were slave. Before, when they had the power of we, they overlook little thing; not now. After crop we are continually obliged to watch (at night, by turn,) and get no pay. Only those that watch get their six herrings every Monday; and those that won't watch get nothing. We don't get any pay for our half Fridays. The busha makes us work on Saturday when he likes by taking us before the magistrate. Sometimes we get every other Saturday. When we have worked out four or five Saturdays according to the magistrate's order, he send for the magistrate again, and say, we don't turn out soon, though we turn out at daylight. Since the law came in we have had only about half our Saturdays. We turn out to work at daylight, and are allowed half an hour for breakfast;

they promise we an hour and a-half for dinner; when plenty of gentlemen come upon the property we get an hour and a-half; but when nobody come, the shell-blow again, before we can well catch a we house (i. e. the signal is heard for their return to the field almost before they have had time to reach their houses, much less to dispatch their dinners.) We looking to all our neighbours and they not so. We never draw off till dark; all will not satisfy. Massa think, perhaps, I tell him lie; but take me off the property and bring the magistrate, the overseer, the bookkeeper, and the constable, and I would beg massa the favor to put the Bible before me, (put me on my oath.) In crop we set to work on Monday, and put the mill about at four o'clock. I am employed one time making fire, and another time in the boiling-house. They expect we to boil twelve coppers and twelve skips of liquor. The mill-house people (feeders of the mill, and carriers of cane and greentrash,) work one whole day; and if they are not able to finish they work all night. If they get done once before night, when they have good canes, they are not able to do it again for two or three weeks when they have dry canes. Next day they go into the field, and another fresh spell work the same. The mill-house people will generally finish by the middle of the Saturday night; but, we in the boiling-house, are employed till daylight on Sunday morning. Not long ago, the mill was about till after midday on Sunday. The boiling-house people work all night long; *sometimes they are in the boiling-house from Monday morning till Sunday morning.* When the millhouse stop (for a few minutes,) from sending liquor, you get a little sleep, then when it send down more liquor you budge again. The mule boys, like the boiling-house people, get no sleep. This is a thing we never were used to do. They put too much upon we. We get nothing for our nights. We get a maccaroni, (one and eightpence,) for the extra time the first four days; tenpence for our half Friday, and half dollar for Saturday. If we don't able to make the twelve copper, we get three bitts for Saturday, (one shilling and tenpence halfpenny.) When we meet good cane we make it, (the twelve coppers;) but when we meet dry cane, we don't make it, and yet they require it from we. Every little they pay we, obliged to go for our belly. We have no grounds but a bit of garden about our house, and to this there is no fence; the cattle get into it night and day. No gentleman so much fine woodland as massa; but we no time to work it. We were obliged to throw up our old grounds, because the neighbours' cattle trespassed in it. It is now common pasture. Before the first of August we had a fence to our old grounds; but since, we have had no time to put it up again. We used to have a watchman for our grounds, but now we have none. We heard magistrate say, if we won't watch cattle-pen, the watchman should be taken from our ground; but, if we would consent to watch the cattle, we should have a watchman for our ground; but busha take away our watchman, and we continue to watch the cattle. Sunday we used to attend church; but now when we have nothing to eat, no Friday nor Saturday, what time else for to cook victual. We have no time to go to church. On Sunday we take we hoe, and pick about a little, for we to eat through the week. We have nobody to lean upon, and so we do every thing busha tell us on purpose to see if we can get living with him, but he get worse and worse every day. We get our salt, (herrings,) very seldom; now we get none. We are worse off than before the first of August. We are all broken heart;

getting old before our time. If we go into the hospital we wish never to come out again. From morning daylight they swear and curse upon we till shell blow. If the parson, (one of the Scottish missionaries,) were not there to tell us good word, we should lie down like cattle in the pasture. Last week four people have been put in the dark room every night without magistrate's order. Men and women are put together in one dark room. One young girl was put in for three nights because when the bookkeeper cursed her sister, she asked him " what for curse her sister?" The hothouse is an ugly dirty place. When the Hanover magistrate, Mr. ODELLE came, he quarrel much about it, and said it was a hog place. Massa this is not all; it is more than what I can tell, I am obliged to forget."

13th.—A few days ago we received from GEORGE GORDON, a gentleman who has the control of many estates, and who is esteemed one of the most judicious and humane planters in the island, an invitation to visit the properties under his care. We this morning availed ourselves of his general permission, and drove over to Meylersfield estate. We saw there a negro, who had been punished, though apparently not with severity, to the extent of twenty-five stripes, by order of the Special Magistrate. He had been guilty of stealing sugar from the boiling house. The overseer shewed us over the works. A catechist attends twice a week to teach the negros, but his instructions are attended by few of the free children. Four of the latter have been apprenticed by their mothers to the estate till twenty-one years of age, which are the first instances of the kind that have come to our knowledge.

During our stay at Savanna la Mar we saw and conversed with a great number of apprentices from the estates and made memoranda of their statements.* Although each of these might be separately considered as *ex parte,* yet the the uniformity of complaint is so marked as to leave no doubt of their substantial truth. The principal grievances are such as we have repeatedly enumerated; their being deprived of former allowances and privileges; being defrauded of their time in and out of crop; the enforcement of compulsory taskwork; the habitual use by Overseers of illegal punishments and general ill treatment by Overseers and Special Magistrates. The conviction is forced upon us, that in this part of the island, upon the majority of estates, the worst abuses of slavery including the aggravated oppression of excessive night work during crop, still exist in an unmitigated form. We left Savanna la Mar in the afternoon for Hopeton, the residence of HUTCHINSON M. SCOTT, accompanied by —— Mc. MURRAY, one of the agents of the Mico Institution, who was going by the same route to his principal station in the interior. Hopeton is in the mountains on the border of the parishes of Westmoreland and Elizabeth. We were very hospitably and kindly received. In the evening most of the free children and many of the apprentices attended the family worship at the great house Some came also from the Bog, a neighbouring sugar estate.

14th.—We had the pleasure this morning of being introduced to two of the Moravian Missionaries, who have a station about a mile distant from Hopeton. Their church, which holds nine hundred persons, is too small for their congregation. The prosperity of their mission in this neighbourhood is to be attributed in

---

* See Appendix F, Sec. iv.

part to the zealous co-operation of the Hopeton family, but chiefly perhaps to the persecutions many of their members have had to sustain, before the introduction of the apprenticeship, from their overseers or proprietors. Some striking instances were related to us of the stedfast and consistent lives of the christian negros. One of them, who is a native African, and still an apprentice, was described as very successful in bringing numbers of his ignorant and degraded brethren to a knowledge of the gospel. A large number of the apprentices as well as the free children attended the family worship this morning. Some of the Bog negros also took advantage of their breakfast time to run to Hopeton to attend it. We were introduced afterwards to WILLIAM HAMILTON, a man of color, who is now the overseer of Lenox, the sugar estate adjoining Hopeton, and belonging to the same proprietor. He was formerly a slave on the Bog, and purchased his freedom soon after the introduction of the apprenticeship. Though self-educated, he is evidently a person of an intelligent and reflecting mind, which has been improved by reading and disciplined by a life of adversity such as rarely falls even to the lot of a slave.

We afterwards visited the school on Hopeton. It is supported at the expence of the proprietor, superintended by a young man and his wife, two excellent and competent persons, sent out from England by the "Ladies' Society." There were about eighty children present, of whom forty were free children or apprentices from Hopeton and Lenox, thirty free children from the Bog, and several the offspring of free parents. They were examined by their teacher and shewed great proficiency in reading and arithmetic, and answered scripture questions with great readiness. All the scholars are clothed, and in a great measure fed by their kind patroness, the lady of H. M. Scott. It is a rule that all shall labor during certain hours, when some of the elder children turn out into the field with their little hoes, and others go into the carpenter's shop. The little ones are employed to pick stones off the ground or to carry cedar shingles. The girls of suitable age remain in school to learn needlework. They work with the same cheerfulness with which they learn. This is the first instance we have met with of free children working on an estate; for not only do the free children of the apprentices on Hopeton and Lenox thus apply themselves to labor, but the free children from a neighbouring estate and even the children of free parents. On these estates the evils of slavery have, we believe, been mitigated to a greater extent, than on any others in Jamaica, and that not only by increasing the comforts of the negros, but by an anxious attention to their moral and religious welfare. Every ameliorating provision in the Abolition Act was introduced many years before 1834, and the introduction of the apprenticeship involved no change of system. Night work during crop had long been abolished, and the allowances of food and clothing were on the most liberal scale. The conduct of the Hopeton family towards their slaves has been marked by its disinterestedness. The proprietor voluntarily relinquished those forced methods of cultivation, which have proved so destructive of human life on other sugar estates. With what success, his system, so opposite to that generally adopted, has been pursued, may be imperfectly learned from the tables of the increase and decrease of population on the Hopeton and Lenox estates. In 1817, there were two hundred and ninety-one slaves, including fifty-six under ten years of age; in 1832, three hundred and fifteen including eighty-three under ten years.* The proprietor is accustomed to employ his own people and all others, who apply, to work in their own time, for wages. None who are willing to work are sent away. Even young children and infirm people are employed and remunerated in proportion to their ability. He is at present engaged in making extensive alterations in his house solely by free labor. Before the apprenticeship, as was observed to us, it was never contemplated to perform any work but by the labor of their own slaves. Now the negros are found to be glad to work for wages, and there is much less trouble and more satisfaction in employing them as free laborers.

In the evening we had the opportunity of conversing with WILLIAM HAMILTON, whose history has recently

---

* Much valuable information respecting his mode of management is contained in the evidence given in December 1833, by H. M. SCOTT to a "Committee of the Assembly appointed to enquire into the moral and religious improvement of the slaves." He observes "that his property is exclusively conducted by slaves. Keys of stores containing large stocks of rum and sugar are at this moment committed to the custody of a servant liberated recently." And again, "A generally received opinion, that the culture of canes is necessarily hostile to human life seems destitute of any solid foundation; it is contingent not inherent when it becomes so. Where in the circle of the globe shall we find an object of culture which contributes so largely to the direct sustenance of the laborer, and at the same time almost entirely supports every animal employed in the cultivation of it; or one that returns more to the soil in manure, while it supplies a redundance of fuel for the manufacture of sugar when it is not destroyed by ill-constructed machinery. Nothing then is wanting to make the cane what a beneficent Creator designed it to be—one of his chosen gifts to man—but the regulations of an enlightened Government, with some salutary check on the cupidity of the cultivator."

excited public attention, in consequence of circumstances which are elsewhere alluded to.* Soon after the first of August, he purchased his freedom by valuation for *two hundred and nine pounds;* and has since been employed as the overseer of the Lenox estate. He has recently purchased seventy acres of land for himself, on which he observed, "I employ as many laborers as I can get, and I find the free negros work far better and more cheerfully than the apprentices, and give more satisfaction. The negros will do any thing for money. On Lenox estate, the task is one hundred and four caneholes a day. They will occasionally do two days work in one, or more frequently three days work in two, and work for money on the leisure day." His testimony as to the effect of slavery on the free classes is equally striking; "in consequence of labor having hitherto been considered a degradation, many of the free colored people will stand a poor chance, (after 1840) in competition with the best disposed and most industrious apprentices, which is the reason that they are so hostile to Emancipation, as they see plainly that some of the negros will rise above them. There are many who have only two or three apprentices, upon whose labor they chiefly subsist, and fall themselves in consequence into idle habits and drunkenness."

In the course of the day J. STURGE proceeded to Black River, which is the town and port of St. Elizabeth's, where he visited the jail and workhouse. There were about fifty inmates, of whom six were life convicts. The treadmill is one of English construction. The prisoners sentenced to this punishment are put upon it for half an hour three times a day, a pun-

* See Appendix F, Sec. ix.

ishment probably less severe than a single spell of ten minutes length, on some of the treadmills in the other workhouses. He also visited the rector of the parish, attached to whose living are a pen or glebe, and a number of apprentices. In 1820, the number of slaves was sixty-five; at the present time there are about one hundred and ten apprentices and their children. This is therefore another conspicuous instance of the effects of kind treatment. The people are allowed one day in the week in addition to the time legally due to them, in lieu of all allowances, an arrangement satisfactory and profitable to both parties.

15th.—We took leave this morning of the hospitable family at Hopeton. Their residence is situated about two thousand feet above the level of the sea, and possesses a very fine climate. The mountain scenery on every side is grand and beautiful. We left at an early hour, accompanied by —— Mc MURRAY, who was proceeding to his residence at Comfort, in the parish of Manchester. Our first stage was Holland estate in St. Elizabeth, the property of —— GLADSTONE where we staid breakfast. It is a very fine estate with a large number of apprentices. During slavery the numbers rapidly declined, but are now supposed to be stationary. The estate school and the allowances of the free children have been discontinued in consequence, as the book-keeper informed us, of the children refusing to give one or two days labor in the week in return. We left this property about eleven A. M. and called on our way at a Mico School by the road side, which has been recently established. There were seventy children present, who were eating their "second breakfast," of cold boiled yams and cocoas, of which their parents had supplied them with a very abundant meal. We afterwards heard a class of intelligent little girls read and answer questions. The master, a colored man, was formerly the teacher of the Holland estate school. He told us it had been discontinued because the attorney was "dissatisfied with the work of the parents, and thought they did not behave as they should, considering their privileges." It is not without reason that the negros suspect that their proprietors and overseers in proposals made apparently for their benefit, have some ulterior object in view. We subsequently called at Wilton, the residence of —— Hylton, an estimable clergyman of the establishment. We visited a little Mico School, held on the premises, where thirty or forty children were collected. It had only recently been formed. but the scholars were in good order, and appeared to have already made some progress. We arrived at Comfort late in the evening.

16th.—This morning we visited the schools, which are held in wattled structures of the simplest and cheapest kind. The girl's school, which was taught by a colored young woman, was in excellent discipline. We heard the principal class read, and the whole school answer scripture questions. Some of the scholars were particularly clever and intelligent. The boys' school was in a like satisfactory condition. Before Christmas the children were required to make a weekly payment of five-pence, which has since been discontinued, and the attendance has in consequence increased from forty to one hundred and sixty. We afterwards saw the boys at breakfast. The children at this school bring their yams and other roots to be cooked for them at the institution. When ready, their meal is laid on a cloth in the middle of the floor. One of the elder boys portions it out with a knife, the children bringing their tins or little baskets one by one, till all are served, when grace is said, and the meal commenced. Sometimes children come without food; in which case the others always manifest the utmost willingness to share with them. We afterwards rode over to Fairfield, the principal station of the United Brethren, passing on our way through Spurtree, a large pen, on which there are about three hundred apprentices. We observed in the negro grounds, a considerable number of tombs, all neatly constructed, and many of them recently whitewashed. Some were ornamented with carved figures of idols. On this, and several other adjacent properties, a night school is held once or twice a week, by the superintendent of the Mico institution at Comfort, or one of his assistants. The parish of Manchester is of great extent, and very mountainous. It is chiefly occupied by pens and coffee plantations. It has only one spring of fresh water, and the effects of the present long period of drought, are in consequence severely felt. From the ridge which we crossed to Fairfield, we had a fine view of the parish of St. Elizabeth, through which we passed yesterday. Part of it is a level savanna, many square miles in extent, bounded by lofty hills. The alluvial plain is occupied with sugar estates and pens, and the light verdure of the cane fields, forms a beautiful contrast with the depth of the intervening pastures of guinea grass. At Fairfield we were introduced to two of the brethren and their wives. We visited the Refuge, an institution established for the reception of colored orphan girls. We had not the pleasure of examining the children in any of their school exercises, but they appeared to be in exact order, and under the care of a competent mistress. They are twenty-five in number, of whom two were among a cargo of African slaves, taken out of a small vessel, which was wrecked on the coast of Jamaica during the administration of Lord MULGRAVE. They were named Kitty and Susan MULGRAVE, after the Countess of MULGRAVE, who took them under her own protection, and placed them at the Refuge for education and maintenance when she left the island. The eldest of them is so far advanced in learning, as to take a part in teaching one of the schools supported by the "Ladies' Society." The children at the Refuge are at present brought up with a view of their becoming teachers, but when that class is sufficiently numerous, they will be placed out as domestic servants. The expence of supporting each child, is about ten pounds sterling per annum, but the funds of the institution are so limited, that its directors have been recently compelled to use money raised to defray the cost of building a suitable school-room, for the support of the children.— It is worthy of more liberal assistance, as in the present state of society in Jamaica, it presents almost the only means of rescuing colored orphan girls from a life of profligacy. There are many schools in the parishes of Manchester, St. Elizabeth, and Westmoreland under the superintendence of the United Brethren, of which the only one we have seen is the excellent school on Hopeton before-mentioned. Of the state of the other schools we are unable to speak from observation, but a statistical account of them, as well as of their congregations, has been obligingly supplied by Brother ZORN, the superintendent of their mission, which will be found in the Appendix.* The Mico institution at Comfort, promises to be an invaluable institution, as the labors

---

* See Appendix F, Sec. x.

of its agents will be expended among a people who have been hitherto neglected. Their establishment is situated at a considerable elevation, with a Bay called Alligator Pond for its sea front twelve miles distant. The intervening country on the right hand is an extensive savanna, formed by the gradual slope of a range of hills. It is studded with numerous locations of free brown settlers, who are coffee planters, many of whom cultivate patches of land merely sufficient to serve as cover, for the purchase and sale of stolen produce from the larger plantations. They are generally owners of two or three apprentices, and are very great oppressors, being extremely degraded, ignorant, and debauched. Their jealousy frequently prevents them from allowing the free children of their apprentices to attend the school at Comfort, while they refuse to send their own, because no difference is made between the brown and black children. In the parishes of Manchester and St. Elizabeth, the resident proprietors are more numerous than in other parts of the island; they are also generally married, and some of them and their families are persons of religious character. The only mission stations are those of the United Brethren, who, though their churches comprise numerous bright and lively examples of personal piety, do not appear to have pursued a system sufficiently aggressive, to make much impression on the general mass. We are credibly informed, by various persons acquainted with their state, that the negros generally in this part of the island, are more ignorant and unenlightened than elsewhere. During our brief stay in these parishes, we had little opportunity of ascertaining the physical condition of the negros, except that one gentleman in St. Elizabeth's, on whom we called, informed us that a neighbouring planter, who was also a magistrate, never suffered his people to leave the field till after dark, and that it was evident by the morning and evening shellblows, that he and others defrauded them of much of their time.

17th.—We took leave of our hospitable friends at Comfort, and proceeded to Mandeville, a little town, delightfully situated amidst the Manchester mountains. We visited the workhouse, but were told by the Supervisor, that no visitor could be admitted without an order from a magistrate. The only magistrate residing in the vicinity was absent from home. He told us that a short time before, "some sectarian parsons had come and talked to the prisoners unknown to him, and that five of the life convicts broke prison afterwards." On our making further inquiries, he added, that he did not mean to say they broke out in consequence of any thing the missionaries said to them, and that it was a convict driver or turnkey, who had escaped and carried the other four prisoners along with him. On leaving Mandeville, we called on our way at the house of a young man who was sent out two years ago, as a schoolmaster and catechist, with the London Society's missionaries. He informed us, that the order which had excluded us from the prison, was made in consequence of himself and two of the missionaries having gone to see an apprentice, a member of one of their churches, who had been recently flogged and sent to the workhouse, on a fictitious charge, brought forward in consequence of his giving notice to be valued, because his master wished to remove him from one estate to another, many miles distant from his home and family. They had shaken him by the hand, and given him some words of comfort, and the deputy supervisor was standing by, while they spoke to him.

One of the London missionaries comes over every fortnight to Mandeville to preach. Their school at this station is large and flourishing. It has been formed about a year, and few of the children knew their letters at the commencement. We now heard a class of them read in the Testament. The little negros pay pretty regularly two-pence halfpenny per week, which is the smallest coin in Jamaica. There are also some colored children of free parents, who pay one shilling and eight-pence per week. As this part of the island is nearly destitute of other means, the efforts of the London missionaries to extend education and religious instruction, are likely to be peculiarly useful. We arrived in the evening at Porus in Clarendon, the station of W. SLATYER, one of the London missionaries. He accompanied us to Whitney, an estate in the neighbouring mountains, belonging to Lord WARD. It is in point of scenery, one of the most beautiful we have seen, being perfectly level, and surrounded by a complete circle of hills. It appeared as if it had once been the bed of a lake, or rather was the bottom of an immense crater, whose innermost sides were covered with native forest. The overseer received us politely, and at our request shewed us the hospital. We found it locked, and waited till the key was fetched. There were in it two patients. It was very clean, having been recently whitewashed. The dark room was locked, but the overseer sent for the key. When it was opened, the light from the door just sufficed to shew that there was some one within. On being called, a woman came out, who was asked by the overseer, who sent her? She replied, "the bookkeeper." "What for?" "I have done nothing, Sir; the bookkeeper said I was laughing." The overseer said something about the bookkeeper's "stretch of authority," and ordered the woman to follow us to the boiling-house. He asked the bookkeeper why she had been sent, and charged him with an undue exercise of power. The bookkeeper said, "you ordered me Sir, to lock up the people for disobedience of orders." He could not however explain of what the apprentice had been guilty, while she asserted that he had called her obscene names, which he did not deny. We afterwards ascertained that locking up is a frequent punishment on this estate,* and it was evident that the bookkeeper had not exceeded the common usages on this occasion. By this unexpected occurrence we became eye witnesses of a common species of punishment, which is illegally practised on estates to a great extent, without any reference to the Special Magistrate.

18th.—We left Porus this morning for Four Paths, in the interior of the parish of Clarendon, the residence of W. G. BARRETT, another of the Independent Missionaries. We attended the Special Magistrates' Court, which is held here once a fortnight. There were several Overseers present, some of whom were local magistrates. Notice was given by four or five apprentices to be valued at a future Court. Two were valued to day. The first was a woman named Elizabeth Francis, whose owner, a man of color, swore she was worth two shillings and sixpence per day. Two overseers appraised her at the same amount. The woman herself and her husband both pleaded that she was sickly and not able to work regularly. In the course of the proceedings it incidentally appeared, that the woman was accustomed till recently to work out for

* We have a list of eight apprentices who were punished in this way without any order from a magistrate by this overseer in the short space of one week.

hire as a domestic, a circumstance which made it evident she was a non-predial. This conclusion was however carefully avoided, and the poor people were too ignorant of their own rights to be aware of the importance of the distinction. Her husband wished to give evidence to the state of her health, but one of the local magistrates silenced him by saying "Ar'n't you going to advance the money? We don't want your evidence:" although they had taken the evidence on oath of her master, a person equally interested on the other side. She was valued as a predial for sixty-three pounds. The next valuation was of a predial apprentice named THOMAS BROWN, who though a much stronger and more able negro, was also rated at two shillings and sixpence per day, or sixty-five pounds for his remaining term of apprenticeship. His case however was only comparatively less unjust than the preceding, as a coffee planter in the neighbourhood told us he could procure as much labor as he wanted at one shilling and eight-pence per day. In a case of complaint, which was decided at this Court, where the prisoner was sent for five days to the treadmill, the magistrate, J. K. DAWSON, observed to the overseer, "You will understand when I send apprentices to the treadmill, they are to repay the time." This, though a frequent practice, is grossly illegal and contrary to the express instructions of the Governor, and exposes the apprentice to the dangers and temptations of starvation, as in Jamaica the negros are now solely dependent on labor in their own time for subsistence.

In the evening we accompanied the minister to a station in the Clarendon mountains, about six miles distant from Four Paths. It commands a beautiful view of the adjoining parish of Vere, which is a level plain extending to the sea, and about twelve miles square, with a hill of singular form called "The Camps," rising alone in the centre of it. It is almost exclusively cultivated with the cane, and contains a population of twelve thousand apprentices. There is no resident missionary in the parish, a circumstance in part accounted for by the difficulty of procuring land for buildings, as it is altogether occupied by large estates. Vere is one of the most wealthy parishes, and one therefore in which there are not more than one or two resident proprietors. These are most numerous in the impoverished districts, a circumstance worthy of remark, as proving that the immense productiveness of the colonies, tends to enrich only the proprietors of the soil residing in splendor at a distance, and is of little benefit to their own agricultural population. We lodged at the house of a respectable colored woman, who cultivates a small coffee plantation. In her house the minister had a small evening congregation of negros.

19th.—This morning service was held at an early hour in a rude shed, which has been erected on the premises of an intelligent negro, who has purchased his freedom, and is now cultivating coffee and provisions on his own freehold. The congregation consisted of one hundred and twenty persons, and the service of singing and prayer, and the practical and familiar exposition of a psalm. As soon as it was concluded we returned to Four Paths, most of the congregation following on foot. The remainder of the day was almost entirely occupied in teaching and the usual public worship. The missionary and his wife and sister have taught nearly one hundred children who were ignorant of the alphabet, to read during their brief residence. They have also distributed the "gift book" to about sixty of the apprentices whom they have themselves taught to read. This magnificent present of the Bible Society still continues to be exceedingly useful in inciting children and even adults to learn to read. In one of the adult classes was an old African woman, who read intelligibly in the Testament, having been taught from her letters. The congregation at this station was composed of about two hundred persons, assembled in a small temporary shed, for this purpose, used till a chapel which is erecting shall be finished. They were very attentive to the sermon and exposition of the scripture.

A squalid old man came this afternoon to the missionary's house, and begged that we would give him a letter to his master, that he might return to the estate, having been in the *bush* (a runaway) five weeks. During slavery it was a custom for repentant runaways to get an intercessory letter from some friend of their masters, or even from a stranger, to save them from punishment. It was a point of honor and of policy to attend to such requests, as the planters, in a country of mountain fastnesses like this, were glad to get their laborers back on any terms. The account this negro gave was as follows:—He belongs to a neighbouring coffee planter, whose apprentices had to work at a distance of seven or eight miles from their homes. They were expected to be at the place of work early on Monday morning, though they had to carry a week's provisions on their heads besides their hoes. They were threatened with punishment for being late, on which they went to the Special Magistrate, CHAMBERLAINE, who gave them a letter to their master and told them that he must allow them sufficient time to go and return every week. Their master tore the paper up before their eyes and took them away to Chapelton, a distance of twenty miles, where a magistrate was to be found who gave general satisfaction to the planters, and who accordingly sent several of them to the treadmill for ten days, and required them to repay the time by working on their Saturdays. When they came out this man found his provision ground, which was near the pasture, destroyed by the cattle, and being now bereft of his time, he was left destitute of food. He ran away to Spanish Town to appeal to the Governor, but did not succeed in obtaining admittance at the King's House, and being afraid of punishment for his absence fled to the bush. We could not learn how he came to hear of our being at Four Paths, or to think of applying to us. His evident distress placed us in a painful dilemma, as we have hitherto suffered nothing to divert us from our resolution to pass through the country as spectators only. We at length concluded to give him a letter to the Special Magistrate, requesting his favorable interference.*

This district of Clarendon was favored till recently with the presence of a faithful magistrate, an intelligent young man of color named CHAMBERLAINE. About two months since he was removed by Sir LIONEL SMITH, by exchange with the present magistrate; who on the other hand, had been charged with oppressive conduct in his former district in St. Thomas in the East. Special Justice LYON, an intelligent and up-

* This gentleman has since informed us, that the runaway was at his request pardoned. His letter contains explanations intended to give a favourable impression of the treatment of the apprentices on the estate in question; but all the material points of the preceding case are admitted or feebly palliated.

right man, has also recently been removed from St. Thomas in the East, to the opposite end of the island, without any assigned cause. The planters, encouraged by their recent success in these two instances, and in that of Dr. PALMER, are again plotting against several of the unpopular magistrates, who persist in endeavouring to do justice to the apprentices. A planter, who is also a barrister and leading member of Assembly, has recently sent a circular letter to the overseers in his neighbourhood, requesting them to meet and prepare a memorial and affidavits against CHAMBERLAINE, who has scarcely been two months in his new district. He promises that he will lay the respective affidavits before the Governor and *enforce them by all means in his power.* If the upright magistrates continue to be thus left unsupported by the Home Government, and exposed to these intrigues in the colony, not one of them will be able to retain his commission.

We had several opportunities during our stay in Clarendon of conversing with the negros. Their statements will be found with others of a similar kind.* Several of them who had been sent to the treadmill exhibited on their legs the scars of the severe injuries which they had received. Their complaints were principally of frauds of time, and of as large or larger an amount of task-work being extorted from them than during slavery in spite of the legal restriction of the hours of labor. There were also several instances of a common but flagrant abuse, where women with six children or upwards, were compelled to work in the field, who had been accustomed during slavery to "sit down" or required only to attend to light work. From

* See Appendix F, Sec. iv.

the information we were able to obtain, it appeared that the eight hour system* was generally enforced in this parish; and that the apprentices were defrauded to a great extent of their time. There is one proprietor, however, ALEXANDRE BRAVO, of whom his negros invariably speak in terms of gratitude for his just and kind treatment of them. The state of things on many of the estates is indicated by the following anecdote. A liberal overseer of a large estate complained to our informant, that "he was compelled to defraud the apprentices every day of their time. If his make of sugar were to be reduced, it would be deemed no excuse by his attorney, to say that he could not produce more with the amount of labor, which the apprentices are by law required to give. The rejoinder would be, "What do they do on the adjoining estates?"

We did not go into Vere, and have no information of the state of the apprentices in that important parish, except that the non-predials are likely to be detained in slavery till the year 1840. Two of the missionaries of the London Society informed us that a local magistrate of Vere observed in their presence, that in that

---

* Where the negros, as is the case in Jamaica, support themselves by working in their provision grounds, they are required by the law to work only forty and half hours instead of forty-five hours per week. Under the eight hour system the forty and half hours are divided into five days of about eight working hours each; an arrangement by which the negros are effectually deprived of the half-day of four and a half working hours, which was given them by law as an equivalent for rations or supplies of food. As their provision grounds are usually several miles from their houses, the distribution of the time over several days destroys it for any useful purpose to the negros. The enforcement of the eight hour system is therefore oppressive, besides which it is frequently made the pretext of extorting five days labor of nine or ten hours each, instead of the legal amount of forty and half hours.

parish, "they had abolished the distinction between predial and non-predial, by making all the apprentices *predials.*"

20th.—We returned early this morning to Spanish Town.

22nd.—We observed to day in the streets six or seven women, several of whom were hand-cuffed, in the custody of the police by whom they had been apprehended as runaway apprentices. They were subsequently taken before a Special Magistrate, when it appeared, that there was no proof that they were apprentices except that they could not produce their "free papers." They were in fact free, and had been taken, some from their own houses and others from their peaceable avocations. They were of course liberated, and the police reprimanded, but the injured parties received no compensation for their loss of time, or for the outrage committed on them.

We were to day in the company of one of the Baptist missionaries who is a creole by birth, and one of a family who though they have all been brought up in contact with slavery, have cleared themselves from its contaminating connexion. His brother, now resident in England, has manumitted his apprentices and directed a considerable amount received as compensato be expended for their benefit. The present estimable individual mentioned to us, that one old negro is now a member of his church, who was formerly one of their domestic slaves, and whom, he was accustomed, when a boy, to strike and beat at his pleasure; and that the recollection of this makes him deeply feel the debt of kindness which he owes him.

23rd.—We arrived to day in Kingston where we

had the pleasure of meeting our friend and fellow voyager, Dr. LLOYD.

26th.—We attended this morning the Baptist Chapel in East Queen-street, the largest of their congregations in Kingston. The auditory comprised about two thousand persons, of whom a large proportion were negros. They were very attentive.

28th.—We rode over this morning to Papine, the estate of J. B. WILDMAN, and saw the school in which were about thirty children, many being absent in consequence of its being Easter week. Their proficiency was not remarkable, but the greater number were at its commencement, about a year ago, ignorant of their letters.

29th.—We visited the school connected with the Baptist church in East Queen-street. There were about one hundred and sixty children present, of whom thirty formed an infant school. The attendance was considered small in consequence of the Easter holidays. Many of the scholars had made considerable progress in geography, grammar, and cyphering, and wrote also very neatly. A large proportion were colored, and one or two were white. We were introduced to day to E. B. LYON. He informed us that he had valued one hundred and sixty apprentices, since the commencement of the present system. Nearly all of them had subsequently been under his own observation, and conducted themselves in the most industrious and orderly manner.* He remarked that in the early part of the apprenticeship, the valuations of predials by himself and the associated local magistrates, averaged five and six doubloons; now for a fraction of the term they are

* See Appendix F, Sec. xi.

appraised at nine and ten. Domestics were then valued at from four to five doubloons, who are now for the short remaining period of their service estimated at the same rate. These remarks entirely coincide with our own observations, and with the facts stated to us by many other individuals.

30th.—We saw to day DUNCAN PATERSON, an apprentice from St. Thomas in the East, who, five months ago, gave notice to be valued; and from that time to the present, has duly every week attended the Court of the Special Magistrate, but has been hitherto successfully baffled by his master. The following is his statement, and we learn from other authority that its particulars are true. "When my master took a a new partner he made the people very unhappy, and used frequently to lock them up in the dungeon and ordered their salt fish to be taken from them. Three times last year I was locked up in the dungeon from night till morning without food or water. He complained that we did not turn out early on Monday morning, though we had to go ten or eleven miles to work, with our tools and a week's provision on our heads. The magistrate ordered every other Saturday to be taken from us. The last time I was locked up was for complaining to the magistrate about our allowance. I became so unhappy that about three months before Christmas I applied to Mr. HEWITT to be valued. I went to the court house every Saturday, but my master got it put off every week till Christmas, when he got a magistrate who valued me at ninety-six pounds Mr. HEWITT spoke against it and wrote to the Governor. I have been down every Saturday to the Court since and have not been able to get it settled. I have now been to Spanish Town, but was not allowed to speak to the Governor, but am sent back to the same magistrate."

30th.—We visited to day several of the principal public institutions in Kingston, accompanined by R. OSBORN, who is a member of the Corporation. We went first to the General Hospital which is supported by the island at a large annual expence. The patients are in small wards containing three or four beds in each. There were nearly two hundred, of whom a large proportion were sailors, chiefly Europeans and foreigners. No class however is excluded, except the apprentices, who are presumed to be provided medical and surgical attendance by their employers. The arrangements of this institution, including the medical attendance, the diet, and the admirable cleanliness of the apartments, appeared to be well adapted to secure the comfort and convalescence of its inmates, except that the number of patients was too large for the accommodation. Adjoining the hospital were two ranges of buildings for the reception of violent maniacs. The want of space here also was an obvious inconvenience. Three or four patients being frequently confined in a single small apartment. We were informed that several homicides had been committed by these unfortunate people in their paroxysms—the most violent cases were Europeans.

We next visited Wolmer's Free School; a foundation endowed with a large sum of money, left many years ago by the individual whose name it bears, for the education of white children. The trust is administered by the Corporation, who in 1815 threw it open to all classes without any distinction of color. The present master, EBENEZER REID, is not only well qualified for the situation he fills, but deeply interested in the cause of education generally. As it was the Easter week the attendance at Wolmer's was not more than one hundred and fifty; the number on the list being about five hundred of both sexes, and the average attendance proportionably large. Our time permitted us to make only a cursory survey, but we are inclined to pronounce Wolmer's the best school we have seen in the West Indies. The plan comprehends a general instruction in the physical sciences in addition to the usual routine. The French and Spanish languages are also taught, being necessary acquirements for those who aspire to employment in the stores and counting houses of the Kingston merchants. The proportion of white to colored children is about one in five. The testimony of the master to the intellectual equality of the races is very striking. He observes "For the last thirty-eight years I have been employed in this city in the tuition of all classes and colors, and have no hesitation in saying that the children of color are equal both in conduct and ability to the white. They have always carried off more than their proportion of prizes, and at one examination, out of seventy prizes awarded, sixty-four were obtained by children of color." Adjoining Wolmer's is an infant school in an excellent state of discipline, which was commenced and for some years taught gratuitously by a daughter of E. REID. It is now supported by the Corporation out of the fund of WOLMER'S bequest. There are two other public schools in this neighbourhood, one under the patronage of the Bishop, and the other supported by subscription and called the "Union School." We are are informed that the Governor lately inspected these schools and expressed his surprise and pleasure at finding white children learning with those of color; observing that it was a step in advance of Barbados.

From the schools we proceeded to the workhouse. To say that the premises are neat, would be too feeble; they are really beautiful, and suggest to a casual visitor ideas of pleasure rather than punishment. There is a large square court, surrounded with a border of grass, in which are planted rows of pine-apple plants. In the centre of the court are the solitary cells, and the building for the treadwheels; and it is inclosed by ranges of buildings comprising the sleeping apartments, store rooms, dispensary, &c. The premises on the south side are close to the sea, and are devoted chiefly to idiotic and maniacal patients. There are seventy prisoners, of whom one third are white soldiers, and the remainder male and female apprentices. There were about thirty sentenced to the treadmills, of which there are two of humane construction, and whose speed is regulated by machinery. The prisoners are divided into two spells, and work alternate quarters of an hour, from six A. M. to five P. M. with the intermission of one hour only for breakfast. They are not strapped on the wheel. The women were not supplied with a suitable dress, which is indispensable to decency on the treadmill. The male apprentices only are chained within the workhouse, but the females are also chained who work on the public roads in the penal gang. No shackles or fetters are used at night. There was only one prisoner, a white soldier, in the solitary cells, which are better constructed and ventilated than any we have yet seen. There are eleven life convicts, who are chiefly slaves convicted of burglary. The diet of the prisoners is three pounds avoirdupois of ground maize, and one large shad per diem. In a room and yard detached from the other premises, were four patients, affected with the disease called "cocobay," one of the most dreadful forms of leprosy, which is happily not very common in Jamaica. One of them had lost most of the joints of his hands and feet, and his ankles appeared to have spontaneously dislocated; the faces of others were shockingly disfigured.

We next visited the county jail, in which also there are about seventy prisoners. The premises are so limited as to render classification impossible. Among those in confinement, are several crown witnesses against prisoners to be tried at the next session, who are unable to find bail for their appearance. Their case appears peculiarly hard, as they are cognizant of crime only as accidental spectators. One fine young man has been thus incarcerated for several months, who is evidence against some horse stealers. Besides the irksomeness of their situation, the confinement and society of the prison must exercise a most deteriorating effect on the energies and habits of laboring persons. The greater number of the prisoners were collected for us to see them, and placed in two separate rows; of which one consisted of those awaiting their trial, and the other of convicts under sentence of transportation, many of whom had been waiting for several years for their sentences to be carried into effect. The prisoners of both classes, with a few exceptions, had shackles and bolts on their feet. They are kept in utter idleness; the only relief to which is, that a humane visiting magistrate has recently ordered that one of the prisoners shall teach the others to read, which he does for a short time every night and morning. A separate department of the jail is appropriated for debtors, who are allowed two shillings and sixpence a day for their support, and the criminals one shilling and three-pence, which sums are paid them in money. The only agreeable feature in the present state of the jail, is the fact that there are only seven or eight women in the whole number of prisoners

4th. Month, 2nd. (April.)—We went this morning to the Kirk, which is the largest and most costly place of worship in the city. The minister is liberally supported at the public expence. His congregation is small, and composed almost exclusively of the wealthy merchants and their families. The number of black and colored persons in the small unpewed portion of the gallery, did not exceed twenty. There is but one service in the week.

3rd.—We were introduced to day to Alderman NETHERSOLE, an intelligent and public spirited citizen; and we are informed, it is principally owing to his exertions, that the Kingston Workhouse is in its present creditable state. He is the proprietor of a large establishment, for tanning and manufacturing leather articles of every description. His numerous workmen and apprentices in the manufactory, are nearly all black and colored free persons, and he considers that for skill and good conduct, they will bear comparison with those of any English establishment. We were shewn over the premises, and the respectable appearance and industry of the workmen, and the quality of their manufacture, as far as we could judge of it, corresponded with the account we had received. In the tan-yard, which we had not time to visit, native products are used for tanning, of which the principal are the mangrove, and the seed pods of a tree called the divey—divey, which is found on the Spanish Main. The latter contains seventy per cent. of tanners. The skins are tanned in six or eight months, and the leather is nearly, if not quite equal in quality to that of English manufacture. Alderman NETHERSOLE may be said to have introduced this new and valuable branch of industry into the colony. Artizans, who have learned their trade in his establishment, are now setting up for themselves in various parts of the island. There is also in Kingston a large manufactory, where cabinet work is executed in the native hard woods, in a style that would not discredit any European establishment.

We had to-day the pleasure of making the acquaintance of RICHARD PANTON, an estimable clergyman of the Church of England, now connected with the Church Missionary Society, but who recently resided in St. Thomas in the East. Some of the Special Magistrates in that parish, are in the habit of punishing the apprentices by the forfeiture of their Saturdays to the estates. The consequences of this practice came under his notice in the following manner: It was his custom at church, to read over the names of the apprentice members every Sabbath, and require a reasonable excuse on behalf of such as were absent. This practice was adopted in order to maintain the strictest pastoral oversight over convicts so peculiarly exposed to the unfavorable influences of a degraded state of society. A reason constantly given by the negros for absence was, that having been deprived of their Saturdays by the Special Magistrate, they were compelled to go to their provision grounds on the Sabbath. As an instance of their acumen, and of their sense of the degradation of slavery, he mentioned that some years ago, a clergyman preached in his church, who addressed the negros affectionately and appropriately, but introduced that portion of his discourse intended for them, with the words, "my slave brethren." At the conclusion, the negros appeared to manifest much displeasure, and on being asked the reason said, "strange minister too bad;" and that when they stood before God in his own house, there was no longer any distinction of condition. In proof of which, they quoted the text, "In Christ there is neither male nor female, bond nor free;" and enquired whether the minister in addressing his congregation did not always say, "my brethren," and never "my sisters." Our informant acknowledged that the idea suggested in this inquiry, though consistent with his own practice, had not occurred to him before.

5th.—We crossed the harbour to Port Royal, and late in the evening JOSEPH STURGE embarked on board the Orbit packet, on his return, via New York, to England.

CHAPTER XII.

JAMAICA.

JOURNAL OF WILLIAM LLOYD[a] AND THOMAS HARVEY.

8th.—We set out to-day on a journey to the east end of the island. Our first stage was Yallahs' Bay, in the parish of St. David, nineteen miles from Kingston. Our kind friend J. Tinson, has a station at Yallahs, where he was spending a few days with his family. We accompanied him to see an old African, residing a short distance from the Bay, in the negro village of a neighbouring pen. He was a man of venerable mien, and though he has been so long in this country, he can scarcely speak English intelligibly, but can read and write Arabic. He wrote at our request, his own African name Arouna, and also some words which he said were a prayer before meat, a formula, we presume, he was about to use, as he was just sitting down to dinner when we entered. He told us that he was one of the royal family of the Houssa tribe of the Mandingo nation, and enumerated the names of various tribes in the vicinity of Houssa, which he said was three months from the coast. It has been noticed that the educated

---

[a] Dr. Lloyd, not having yet returned to this country, the ensuing chapter has not had the advantage of his revision, and his companion is therefore solely responsible for its contents.

Mohammedan negros speak the worst English. They are less frequently converted to christianity; and in cases where they have become nominal believers, they have been found to blend it, with the superstitions of their forefathers. The employment of this old man was to keep his master's garden in order. A stream ran through it, one part of which he had made wider and deeper, and had thrown a bower over it. In this shaded reservoir he kept some mullets which came at his call to feed out of his hand.

One of the most interesting objects in this neighbourhood is a silk cotton tree, of an extraordinary size, growing on the bank of a rivulet. It is about one hundred feet in circumference and each of its branches is equal to a large tree. The trunk of the silk cotton tree is frequently smooth and rises gradually tapering to a great height, at which it throws out its arms at right angles. When the tree attains, as in this instance a very vigorous growth, the trunk near the root gradually expands into angular buttresses, which support the weight of its immense limbs. Two opposite arms of this tree extend to a distance of one hundred and seventy-three feet; and its huge roots, stretching out above the surface in every direction, appear to cover a rood of ground.

9th.—The Sabbath. We were awakened this morning by the notes of the mock-bird, which is the only one that can be properly termed a bird of song. It is a species of thrush, though universally in the West Indies known as the nightingale. The early morning, at a distance from town, is delightful. The fierce heat of a tropical sun is abated by the cool and refreshing dews of night, and all is hushed, but voices and sounds expressive of the happiness of animated nature. We were disappointed in our hope of spending a few quiet hours at our inn. Three or four parties of overseers in gigs, with servants following them with led horses, came in, in succession, to breakfast, and soon converted the place into a scene of bustle. They were on their way to Kingston Assizes; but it is not an unusual custom to travel in this style on the Sabbath, visiting their friends on distant estates. The morning service at the Baptist mission station, commenced at ten o'clock. The chapel, which is capable of holding about three hundred, was completely filled, and some remained standing outside; the whole were very attentive; at the conclusion, a couple were married, who had been long waiting in consequence of the refusal of the Rector of the parish to marry them without a permit from the attorney, which they could not obtain.* Not long after the ceremony, the Lord's Supper was administered to about eighty communicants. There was another short service in the evening, attended by a few who lived in the neighbourhood.

10th.—In the course of the morning, we visited the parish workhouse, which is situated about four miles from the Bay, in a valley surrounded by high mountains, near the bed of a mountain stream. At present, this rivulet is only a few feet wide, but in the rainy season, it occupies a plain, across which a chain bridge has been attempted to be thrown, but became a ruin before it was completed. Its span was three hundred and fifty feet. The workhouse is a neat, little building, recently erected. It has no treadmill, and its inmates, four or five in number only, were employed for hire as a penal gang, on the neighbouring estates,

* See Appendix F, Sec. xii.

with the exception of one invalid. Offenders sentenced to the treadmill, are sent to workhouses in the adjoining parishes.

We called on our return at the school recently established by the bishop. The master and his wife, two colored young persons, appeared to take an interest in their occupation; and the children seemed to have profited by the pains bestowed upon them, though the school has been established too recently for any marked proficiency to be manifest. There were fifty-one scholars on the list. This school is the only one in the parish, which comprises a negro population of ten thousand souls. A building is being erected on the premises of the Baptist mission station, for a school, but is impeded by want of funds. This appears to be one of the parishes most destitute of the means of instruction, and the negros are represented to be among the most ignorant and benighted.

11th.—We proceeded early in the morning to Morant Bay, in the parish of St. Thomas in the East, a little town and port about twelve miles distant from Yallahs. We were introduced to M. Hodge, a missionary of the London Society at this station, who is on the point of quitting the island. He kindly accompanied us to the parish school, where there were about forty children, chiefly colored. We heard a class conjugate a difficult verb, spontaneously selected, in a very creditable manner. We next visited the school attached to the London mission, which is conducted by a catechist. The average attendance of the children, is about fifty. They were in good order, but they did not appear as yet, to have made any considerable proficiency.

We saw the jail, a small, confined building, in which happily there are no prisoners. The state of it is such as infrequency of use alone can excuse. The workhouse is some distance from the town, and is a convenient and well arranged set of premises. The present number of inmates is twenty-nine, of whom seventeen are life convicts. Nearly as many more of these last have escaped, some of whom, we were told, had not been heard of for years. The penal gang, both men and women, work in chains. The treadmill was in operation. The prisoners work, as at Kingston, alternate quarters of an hour, from six to five, with the intermission of only one hour for breakfast. The mill is difficult to regulate, and of bad construction, though much better than many others we have seen. There were four prisoners on it, one of whom was a woman, and another a white man, a sailor. They had not suitable dresses. The Supervisor said, that both men and women were " touched with the whip" when they would not tread the mill; but they are not strapped to the handrail unless refractory.

In the afternoon we accompanied M. HODGE to Belvidere, a large estate, a few miles distant from Morant Bay. The apprentices have erected a chapel upon it, entirely by their own labor. It is a neat wattled structure, capable of holding five hundred persons. We regarded it with no little interest, as a convincing proof of the desire of the negros for religious instruction. M. HODGE has two estate stations, this, and one at an equal distance from the Bay on the opposite side, at an estate called Retreat. These stations are supplied every Sabbath by himself and the catechist in turn; and in the afternoon he preaches at Morant Bay. Besides the establishment of the principal school, he has also distributed some of the Gift Books to apprentices, who have learned to read. Belvidere is a very fine estate, and belongs to a French Nobleman, Count F<small>REE</small>-<small>MAN</small>. His late resident attorney was President of the Council, and on one or two occasions, administered the Government of the colony. He was kind and indulgent to the slaves. The present attorney also, is said to be liberally disposed, while the proprietor has directed certain allowances to be curtailed. We walked through a part of the negro village; many of the houses are large and comfortable. The whole were almost concealed in the shade of plantains, cocoa nut, and bread fruit trees. We conversed with a respectable and intelligent negro, who complained that the watchman had been taken away from their provision grounds, and the cattle of the estates turned into them. He said they were compelled to buy provisions from the Bay, for their support, and that their principal dependence was now upon their fruit trees. The overseer told them they would soon be free, and must not expect their old privileges. He said that during crop, they received ten-pence when they worked in the night, but that their half Fridays were taken from them, for which they received no pay. On our mentioning these circumstances to our companion, he said, that the negros on Belvidere were as fine a set of well-disposed laborers as could be found any where; and that the overseer had often told him, they did more work within the hours than formerly; it is therefore most impolitic, as well as unjust, to pursue such a course towards them. We looked over the hospital, in which were several cases of fever and measles. The latter disease has been very prevalent in almost every part of the island. We have seen many cases of it, but it appears to assume a very mild form. We have not heard a single instance in which it has proved fatal. The great house on Belvidere, is one of she best mansions we have seen, and is delightfully situated on an eminence, immediately above the cane grounds. It commands a fine view of the Bay, the shore of which is marked by a long line of cocoa nut trees. This beautiful palm is the first tree that greets the eye of the voyager, on approaching the tropics, and from being introduced in all representations of tropical scenery, it appears when first seen, at once a novel and familiar object.

12th.—We came this morning to Bath, through Port Morant. Our route to the latter place was principally by the sea side. This country is highly cultivated to the base of the nearest range of hills from the coast, which are cleared of their forest, and covered with deep rich verdure. Port Morant is situated on a very fine harbor. After leaving it we turned off into the interior, through a very beautiful country. The road is rocky and mountainous. Bath is so enveloped in its grove of cocoa nut, palmetto and bread-fruit trees, as to be invisible at a distance, though a site so marked indicates as certainly the presence of human habitations as a view of spires or chimneys in Europe. Bath is a beautiful little town and harmonises in every respect with the magnificent scenery in which it is embosomed. It consists of a single street of houses, placed at convenient distances apart, the road shaded on each side with trees, principally the palmetto and Tahitian apple, the dust of whose beautiful crimson blossoms almost covered the road. In the course of the morning we visited the Botanic Garden, which like the one in St. Andrews, has been formed for the reception of Eastern tropical trees and plants. The Assembly has recently discontinued its annual grant, and in consequence it is at present neglected, but still contains many fine trees and shrubs. There are several apprentices attached to it, one of whom, the head gardener, shewed us over it.

There are two schools in Bath, one a private day school and the other a Mico school; the latter has been established only three months. It is attended by upwards of sixty children, who are all taught on the infant system, though some of them are ten or twelve years of age. Some of the scholars have already made considerable progress in reading. Their instructor considers them quite as capable as European children.

On our return we partook of an early dinner which consisted in part of mountain crabs, which Bryan Edwards pronounces "the most savory and delicious morsels in nature;" a sentiment in which all creoles unite. On some estates in this parish, an apprentice is kept as a crab-catcher, and is expected to produce a tale of fifty or sixty crabs per week. In the afternoon we rode up to the Bath, which is distant about one mile and half from the town. The road is a mountain path by the side of a rivulet, the banks of which are covered with trumpet trees and bamboos of a great size, which keep the pathway in almost perpetual shade. The surrounding mountains are of immense height, and their precipitous sides are covered with the densest vegetation, such as is never seen even in the tropics except where there are numerous springs. The scenery is thought to bear some resemblance to Matlock, but possesses far grander and more extraordinary features. Among the most striking vegetable productions of the locality, is the tree fern, which grows to the height of from twenty to thirty feet. It is the most graceful of plants and appears like a beautiful palm in miniature, with its slender trunk and crown of gigantic leaves. The Bath is a plain stone building consisting of several bathing rooms. A few hundred yards beyond it the hot spring rises into a stone cistern, near which is a building in a ruinous state, formerly used as the residence of the poor patients. The water possesses a slightly sulphurous smell and a temperature of 120° Fahrenheit. It is conveyed down to the principal bath in a stone channel, and is there mixed at pleasure with the water of the cold mountain stream.

13th.—We left Bath early this morning on our way to Manchineal. Our road was through a part of the plaintain garden river valley, a level savanna of great beauty and fertility. It is ten miles in length, and from one to three in breadth, and comprehends the finest estates in the island. Both yesterday and this morning, in driving through the estates, we have noticed the negros generally at work in the field at half past five or before sunrise, some of them running in great haste to join the gangs. We remained during part of the day at Belle Castle, the residence of JOHN KINGDON, Baptist Missionary. He accompanied us to a neighbouring plantation, to the proprietor of which, GEORGE CODRINGTON, we had a letter of introduction. The cultivation on this estate consists of arrowroot, and it is the first instance of that article, being grown and manufactured on a large scale, that has come under our notice in the West Indies. It is usually grown by the apprentices, the free settlers, or the maroons. The experiment of employing a considerable capital and superior skill upon its production and preparation, has in this instance been a profitable one. One of the apprentices on this estate was pointed out as addicted to dirt eating. He was apparently a boy of fourteen years of age, but was really, we were told, upwards of twenty. Few large estates are free from negros who have this unnatural appetite, which ought undoubtedly to be considered as a disease, though it has ever been the custom to treat it as a crime. This boy was on one occasion taken into his master's house and fed on generous diet, with temporary success, but his craving for dirt returned when he left the "great house." We were informed that the alkaline earth which is so greedily sought for by dirt eaters, is sometimes made into cakes and sold in Kingston market. In the evening we proceeded to Manchineal Bay, where we were introduced to the special magistrate, RICHARD CHAMBERLAINE, jun., an intelligent colored gentleman. He kindly invited us to accompany him to-morrow to several estates.

14th.—The first at which we called with the magistrate, was Williams-field, a fine sugar estate, under the attorneyship of JAMES COCKBURN, a gentleman who bears a high character for humanity and respect to the legal rights of the apprentices. Complaints are here rarely brought before the magistrate. The overseer observed that he thought the indulgent system was decidedly more advantageous. The number of apprentices is one hundred and twenty-five, and of free chilpren twenty-three. We were shown over the hospital, which is a miserable building almost in ruin. There were in it several cases of measles. There was a small jobbing gang of negros working on the estate, belonging to another estate nine miles distant, who came to complain that they were not allowed any time for going and returning from work. The magistrate directed that their master should allow them an hour for every three miles, with which they appeared satisfied.

We next visited Hector's River, a fine estate belonging to MAJOR HALL, an absentee. The head bookkeeper said there were no complaints to bring before the magistrate. The number of apprentices on this estate is two hundred and sixty, and of free children fifty. The latter receive no allowance but medical care at the expense of the estate, for which the parents, we were told, give no equivalent. We are, however, informed that the apprentices are deprived of all their half Fridays throughout the year, and all the extra hours required by day and night during crop, without any payment, though nominally in return for the slave allowances. The hospital on Hector's River is an airy good building, but too small for its purposes. There were in it several cases of measles, and also of obstinate sores and ulcers. We afterwards called at Grange Hill, a fine estate belonging to Sir HENRY FITZHERBERT, which has recently been turned into an indigo plantation. The Overseer told us that he had made last year two hundred and forty-six pounds of indigo of fine quality, but at an immense expense of labor. He was persuaded it would never succeed in this part of the island, though it might perhaps in the Southern parishes. Indigo was formerly extensively produced in the West Indies; this is the first instance we have met with of an attempt to restore its cultivation, and the circumstance of this interesting experiment being confided to an Overseer, and one who has made up his mind beforehand that it will not succeed, forebodes an unfavorable result. This Overseer appeared much irritated; he broke out into bitter complaints againsts his domestics, and talked of the pride and indolence of the mulattos, of which class the domestic servants are generally composed. He said he had no complaints to make against his field people. During our stay the fisherman, an apprentice whose sole duty it is to supply the Overseer's table with fish, came in with the produce of his day's labor, consisting of several small fishes. This afresh excited the anger of the Overseer, who proposed to put him on *task-work*, asserting, in opposition to the pleas of the negro, that chance, weather, &c. had nothing to do with fishing on this favored coast. A negro, who was the cook at the great house, came forward and complained that his busha had violently assaulted and beaten him this morning for not preparing dinner with sufficient promptitude. It was agreed between the parties that the complaint should be decided to-morrow at the weekly court, held at the police station, at Manchineal Bay. The assistant of the principal medical man of this district resides on this estate in the Overseer's house. He accompanied us to see the hospital. It was locked, and we waited till the attendant with the key made his appearance. We found it in a wretched and dilapidated condition. There was one old man lying on the floor, who the doctor remarked was a patient that he had not seen before. He did not make, however, a single inquiry into his case. The negro himself said he had been this morning to the Overseer to say he was sick, who told him "go away to the field, sir." He knew, however, that he was unable to work, and had therefore come to sit down at the hospital.

On our return we called upon the Wesleyan missionary, W. Gregory. There is no school in this neighbourhood except his Sunday school, which is attended by about one hundred and twenty children and adults. This part of the island is therefore very destitute of the means of education. The special magistrate informed us to-day that he had settled many manumissions by valuation, and did not know one negro so freed who did not support himself creditably by his own industry.

15th.—This morning at an early hour, several apprentices came to complain to the Special Magistrate, whose lodgings are at the only house of public entertainment in Manchineal, and consequently under the same roof as our own. Several of them were from the arrowroot plantation we visited two days ago. They brought with them a large basket, which would contain a bushel or upwards, and complained that it was used to measure their task, and that they were compelled, both strong and weak, to dig six baskets a-day for five days in the week, and if they fell short, to make up the number on Saturday. Sometimes they said if they chanced to work upon a good bearing piece, they could render their full task, but otherwise they found it quite impossible. This case was appointed to be heard in court to day. Another negro came in great distress to complain that he was about to be flogged. He said, that he was an apprentice on the Grange, a property in this (CHAMBERLAINE's) district, and that he and the rest of the gang were compelled to job out at an estate called Williams-fiield, twelve miles distant from their homes. Their grounds had no provisions in them, the cattle having trespassed and destroyed every thing growing there.

He was required to dig seventy cane holes a day in new, stiff soil. He had no food to eat and no water carrier in the field was allowed to their gang. One day the week before last, he said as he was eaving the field, "they ought to have something to eat, and that a horse would not be served so." The book-keeper reported what he said to the Overseer, who locked him up and sent for the Special Magistrate, WADDINGTON, to hear the complaint against him, who sentenced him to be locked up again and to receive thirty-nine lashes the next morning. The Overseer told him " he would give him a back to take to shew Mr. CHAMBERLAINE, and see whether he could take it off." He broke out of the dungeon and ran away this day week for fear of the flogging. "The reason," he said, " why they had a spite against him, was because he went to Spanish Town to see the Governor, when they wanted to remove the people from the Grange. We subsequently ascertained that the account of this apprentice as to the state of starvation to which his gang was reduced, was literally true. However hard his case, as he is under a legal sentence, there is no alternative for him but to be sent back in custody of a police officer to receive his flogging and answer for his additional offence of desertion.

About ten a. m. we proceeded to the police office where the Special Magistrate holds his court. There is a court yard behind this building formed by the remaining walls of an old fortification, in two of the angular corners of which have been constructed, four solitary cells, which are the very worst we have seen in the island. They are so situated as to be very damp even at the present time after a long period of drought, and it is difficult to imagine their condition during the rainy season. They are about eight feet long, six feet high, and four wide; they are furnished with a miserable shelf for the prisoners to lie on, and the floors are the bare earth covered with the rubbish of masons' and carpenters' work. No Special Magistrate of common humanity would venture to direct any negro to be confined in them. The Special Court was numerously attended, the following notes of cases will shew the character of the proceedings.

1st. Complaint against LYDIA KING, an apprentice on Rural Vale Estate, by the proprietor, for leaving work at sunset, two hours before she ought to have done, as it was crop time, and for insolence to the constable. The evidence of the constables sustained the charges. She said she had a young child at the breast and could not therefore remain after dark. She also brought counter complaints against the constable and overseer, and in the absence of her witnesses, the case was deferred till the magistrate should visit the estate. 2nd. Two women from the same estate were charged with not feeding the mill with canes, so as to produce a pan of liquor after sunset according to a special agreement. This also was proved by the constables. The proprietor on his cross examination acknowledged, that the negros had not had their half Fridays, which was expressly stipulated in his part of the contract. The case was therefore dismissed. 3rd.—A complaint against an apprentice of Muirtown estate, that having been sentenced for theft to dig five hundred cane-holes in his own time, and to be degraded from his office of watchman to the rank of a field laborer, he had not dug the cane-holes, and when ordered to the field had refused to go. The defendant stated, that he had commenced to dig the cane-holes and applied to his overseer for the requisite tools for field-work, a bill and hoe, which had been refused. This was admitted by the complainant, the book-keeper of Muirtown, and the complaint was therefore dismissed.

4th. Against another apprentice of Muirtown. The head constable stated, that he had ordered him to yoke cattle in the cart early in the morning, when he declared that this service was put upon him oftener than the rest, and was so insolent that the overseer directed him to be locked up in the dark hole which was done. On inquiry he said the magistrate was not informed of this locking up, which it must be observed is permitted by the local apprenticeship law as a measure of security against the escape of offenders only, and not of punishment. This case was therefore dismissed. The constable laid great stress upon the insolence which he received, but could not repeat it in words. These constructive charges of insolence are very frequent, and draw down an immense amount of punishment on the unfortunate apprentices. 5th. An apprentice on Grange Hill, the plantation we visited yesterday, complained that his Overseer had boxed his face, repeatedly, and kicked him for not preparing some soup so early as was required, which was occasioned by his having to fetch the wood and water himself from a distance. The defendant admitted the assault, but pleaded aggravation. He was ill yesterday, and could not get the soup, and does not think he should have got it by this time if he "had not kicked up a row." He was fined two pounds, on which he pulled out an island check for five pounds, which he held up in complainant's face, and said, "here, would you not like to get some of this," as if exulting in the fact that the award would give no reparation to complainant. 6th. The defendant in the above case, preferred a counter-charge against the same apprentice, for disobedience of orders and idleness, which for want of evidence was deferred till the magistrate's next visit to the property. 7th.—

An apprentice of Dr. BELL, complained that his master had flogged him. He said also that the doctor had prevented a fellow apprentice from coming down to the court, as a witness of the assault. This the doctor indignantly denied. The magistrate offered to ride up to his house and decide the case, which was agreed to. 8th. An apprentice from Elmwood, the estate of EDWARD PANTON, the judge advocate general, complained, that though he was a cripple, he had been ordered to go to the field. He produced a large heavy hoe, which had been given to him, and which he had been forbidden to sharpen in his master's time. His former employment was tending hogs and minding the gate, which it was his duty to open to all visitors, but he had been strictly forbidden to admit the Special Magistrate when he came to the estate, and his offence consisted in having disregarded these orders. He was told that he could not be compelled to work in the field as a punishment, and being also a cripple, was directed to return to his former employment. 9th. Another negro from the same estate said, that one of his fellow apprentices had received serious injury from a fire in the stillhouse, where he was working under the superintendence of the Overseer's son. He said this man was a very active, valuable negro, and had often saved his master's property, when it had been on fire before; but that now he was in the hospital, neglected, and with no one to attend him. The two medical men attending the estate were present, and contradicted this statement warmly. The result of the conflicting testimony was, that the man was very seriously burnt. He could not feed himself, but was lying in the hospital, which was locked up, and his mother was not allowed to be with him, nor any one but the negro attendant called the hospital doctor. The accident occurred through the wilfulness of the bookkeeper, in refusing to take the advice of the man who was accustomed to work the still. This complainant also repeated coarse abuse, lavished upon the Special Magistrate, by the Overseer and others. 10th. Two pregnant women from Hartford estate, complained of being compelled to perform field work. One of them was far advanced in pregnancy, and had a diseased leg, which alone would incapacitate her from severe labor; the other said she had been very sickly during her pregnancy, and yet was required to turn out as early as the rest. The medical men present were asked to give an opinion, but declined, as they did not attend the estate. The magistrate received a note from the Overseer, stating, that the doctor declared one of the women was only in her third month, and might continue to perform her ordinary work; and that the other, (the one affected with elephantiasis,) was between six and seven months gone in pregnancy, and might work another month in the second gang. It must be observed, that the second gang works the same number of hours as the first, and its labor is frequently as severe. The case was deferred till the magistrate's next visit to the estate.—11th. An apprentice, on Happy Grove plantation, the property of GEORGE CODRINGTON, complained that he and his fellow apprentices were required to dig six baskets of arrowroot per diem, for five days in the week, as before stated; also that they were compelled to watch at night by turns, and if a man missed a night, he was made to watch for six nights in succession, although they received no pay for watching: also, that when they were able to complete their task of arrowroot, they were compelled to go and pick grass: also, that having worked by agreement, for three days in their own time, for one shilling and eight-pence a day, their master had refused to pay them for more than two days. He said the apprentices had made no agreement to work by the task; their master had forced it on them, and the former magistrate, (DAWSON) would not hear a word they had to say. When they complained recently to their master, he told them, they might go to Mr. CHAMBERLAINE; that it was their turn now, but would be his by and bye; that he would have justice done him, and would send for Major BAINES, (a magistrate very popular with the planters in an adjoining district.) Complainant also repeated offensive expressions used by his master in reference to the magistrate's complexion. The defendant in reply, admitted the expressions attributed to him, except the last, which he denied. He said that his people had worked by the task of six baskets a day, *for the last fifteen years*, and on the introduction of the Apprenticeship had continued to do it, under the sanction of CHAMBERLAINE's predecessor, (DAWSON,) " who was a very fair magistrate," and he should insist on their still giving him the same quantity. On the magistrate remarking that it was illegal to impose taskwork without the consent of the apprentices, he said he *would do it*, adding, " Sir LIONEL SMITH is of a different opinion to you Sir, and we shall seee presently whether you will be able to prevent it." On being asked respecting his imposing six nights continuous watching, as a punishment on his apprentices; he said, " he considered himself as their *protector*, and desired that they should look up to him as such, and that the magistrate should not come on the property; but now they had called him in, they should have enough of him." He enquired in his turn whether the magistrate would enforce him a proper amount of labor, and whether he would punish for insolence. He did not affect to defend the imposition of grass picking, and acknowledged they had a right to refuse to do it. With respect to the disagreement about the three days, he admitted the fact alleged, but said they had left the work which they had agreed to do unfinished, and if they had been free laborers, he could have had them punished. He brought forward his bookkeeper, and another witness, to prove that the task of arrowroot digging, was what they frequently performed by two o'clock in the day; but as the case affected the entire gang, it was concluded, apparently by consent of all parties, that the magistrate should visit the property, and hold a Special Court to decide the case. 12th. Another apprentice on the same property came forward to be valued. His master said that he was one of his most valuable men, that he was a mason and carpenter, and occasionally worked in the field. His bookkeeper deposed, that during a two years residence on the estate, he had never known him employed except in the field, but that he was a very active, valuable man. Another bookkeeper deposed, that he had once seen him some years ago plastering a cottage. The next witness was a colored man, who had been a slave, and had been manumitted by the father of its present proprietor, for his valuable services, and is still employed on the estate. He swore that the negro in question could handle both a trowel and a saw, but was not a good workman with either. The apprentice himself said, he had only been sent to learn to be a mason for a short period, several years ago, and that he had bad health. His brother confirmed this statement. An Overseer who was standing by, rated his services at forty pounds per annum nett. A dispute next arose, about the class to which he belonged, as he had been employed as a domestic servant some time previous to August, 1833. The local magistrate, appointed as valuer by the proprietor, pulled out of his pocket, the island Act recently passed for regulating classifications, and read the clause which gives the master the right of nominating a local magistrate, to associate with the Stipendiary, and in case they cannot agree, to appoint a second Special Magistrate as umpire. This he very truly observed, "gave great power to the master" in all disputes about classification. He said he should insist in case of dispute, that the case should be decided in that manner. It appeared at length pretty clear, that the man was a predial, and after some further difficulties, the valuation was at length fixed at sixty pounds. Two important features of the system, were disclosed to our observation during these proceedings. The Special Magistrate reminded the proprietor of the fact which had been elicited in the previous case, that he paid his negros only one shilling and eight-pence for their Saturdays, and he remonstrated with him on his placing an exhorbitant price on their services, when they came to be valued. The latter replied, that whatever the time of his apprentices was worth, it was nothing to any body, if they chose to sell it to him for one shilling and eight-pence a day. The local magistrate, before referred to, remarked that every planter must get a profit by the labor of his people; so it appears, that in valuations, the local magistrates take the market price of labor; adding thereto the real or imaginary profit, which the master would realise upon it during the remainder of the apprenticeship. The other was on a doctrine propounded by the same local magistrate, to the following effect:—that the Stipendiary ought if required to administer the law *literally*, and to require the forty hours and half labor per week, from the apprentices in cases of sickness, or pregnancy, and that all needful relaxations should emanate from the bounty and humanity of the proprietor. Against these sentiments the Stipendiary protested, and declared that he would never violate the law of nature in any such manner. 13th.—The last case was the valuation of ALLICK, an apprentice to JOHN ROSS, of Mullatto River estate. This apprentice was a fine, intelligent, negro, who has been employed for ten months past as an overseer on the estate, at a salary of twenty pounds per annum, giving up all his extra time. He was, however, so good a house servant, that his mistress had persuaded her husband to reduce him again to that capacity, which was the cause of his wishing to be valued. His master, who was present, employed another gentleman, the same local magistrate, to act for him on account of his age and deafness. An agreement was produced to fix the class of the apprentice as a predial. The purport of which was, that fourteen apprentices therein named, of whom ALLICK was one, should receive the same time and the same quantity of provision ground as the predial apprentices, on condition of their remaining apprentices till 1840. This had been verbally settled between them and their master on the first of August, 1834, and a year afterwards confirmed by the memorandum now produced, which was signed by their marks, and by the Special Magistrate, DAWSON. The agent for the proprietor observing, that the Stipendiary disregarded this agreement, again produced the new classification law, and proposed as a local magistrate the proprietor of Happy Grove estate, to associate with Special Justice CHAMBERLAINE, and a neighbouring Special Justice of notorious character, to be the umpire. To this the Stipendiary objected, observing, that the dispute was not as to the usual employment of ALLICK for the year preceding the 1st of August, 1833, which cases alone were the object of the Classification Law, but as to the character of the document produced, which he contended was neither legal nor valid. He deferred the question with the intention of submitting it to the Governor. The old gentleman who was a principal party in the cause, paid at this time five pounds; an amount, which he had been fined on a previous occasion for an assault on one of his apprentices.

At this Court, we could not but observe the very great difficulties the magistrate had to contend with, nor sufficiently admire the manner in which he discharged his duties. The room was filled with planters and overseers, some of whom were spectators only; and when any low, vulgar abuse of the magistrate was stated in evidence by the negros, it created a general laugh. The animus of the whole proceedings on the part of the planters was odious, and this single day's experience convinced us, that for general and systematic violations of the Apprenticeship Act, this is not behind any district in the island.

16th.—The man who was valued yesterday from Happy Grove, came to day in distress to complain, that his master had found out the person who was going to lend him the money, and had been to him to induce him not to do so.

We attended the services at the Baptist mission house at Belle Castle. The congregation consisted of about three hundred persons; many of them apprentices from distant estates.

17th.—We paid a visit this morning to Windsor Forest, the property and residence of Captain Quelch. It is on the borders of the parish of Portland, nine miles distant from Manchineal. The coast by which our route lay is very bold and rocky. The vegetation of the hills immediately above the sea is of the most luxuriant character. A parasitic species of orchis is found in great abundance on the trees, and the fragrance of its flowers at this season, perfumes the air for a considerable distance. Windsor Forest is an abandoned sugar estate of six hundred acres. There are only ten apprentices attached to it, who grow provisions and tend cattle. So small a part, however, is cultivated, that trees and brushwood are fast regaining possession of the land. The proprietor is naturally anxious for the labor of the community to be thrown into a market open to fair competition, in order that he may turn his property to better account. He bought this estate a few years ago after the negros had been removed to another by the former proprietor; and the first thing he saw on coming to take possession, was a negro suspended from the bough of a tree, which he pointed out to us, near the gate. This man was the most intelligent and valuable slave in the gang, and had been heard to say he never would remove alive. Instances scarcely less striking of the strong local attachment of the negros are by no means infrequent. From this estate we accompanied the Special Magistrate to the Grange in the parish of Portland, the estate to which the negro belongs, mentioned in our journal two days ago, as having broke out of confinement to escape flogging. There are about forty people on it, who are a jobbing gang and are at present working at Williams-field twelve miles from their homes. They had complained that they were destitute of food and clothing, and had scarcely a shelter over their heads, and two Special Magistrates, CHAMBERLAINE and WADDINGTON, who were directed to inquire into their case, had ordered that they should have time allowed them to build themselves new houses and make new provision grounds, and in the mean-time be supported by their owner. We saw several of the people at their huts. It would be difficult to conceive any thing worse than their condition, and impossible to describe its wretchedness. Both their appearance and that of their dwellings were truly miserable. They have only two or three habitable houses among them, in each of which several families are obliged to shelter themselves. They are nearly destitute of clothing, and having no provision ground, have consequently no food. Their grounds had been entirely destroyed by cattle while they were absent by the week together at their work, and the only watchman, who had been allowed them, was a crippled young man, whom we saw, and who was not only unfit for that service, but incapable even of attending to his own wants. The proprietor on being asked to day by the Magistrate whether they had been supported agreeably to his directions, replied that they did not require it as "they had plenty of friends and neighbours who would assist them," meaning the negros on neighboring properties. We may add, that this individual is a local magistrate.

During our stay in this part of the island we conversed with a number of the negros from different estates in the Manchineal and Plaintain Garden River districts, whose statements will be found with others of similar character,* and not inferior to any in their painful interest. We wish we could convey the impression of the appearance and demeanor of the individuals with whom we conversed, and the natural pathos with which many of them related their distresses. In no part of the island are the abuses greater than in this. The cases in the Appendix will be found to include almost every variety of oppression, legal or illegal. The negros throughout all the estates in this part of the island, we believe, without a single exception, have been deprived of their half Fridays, and on the greater number of properties, they have been extensively defrauded, by being compelled to work more than the legal number of hours per diem. Instead of forty hours and half, they are made to work about fifty hours of severe uncompensated labor per week out of crop, and in crop a large amount of night-work has been exacted from them for which they frequently receive no remuneration, except what are called the extra allowances or indulgences of slavery—viz. salt fish and medical attendance for their free children. It might be argued, that both in law and justice those allowances are due to the apprentices, but were it otherwise, this compulsory exaction of a most disproportionate amount of labor in lieu of them, would characterize the system as one of gross fraud and oppression. On many estates these arrangements are enforced under the authority of pretended agreements, which have been made not with the people, but between the Stipendiary and the overseer or proprietor. And even if these agreements had been made in a *bona fide*

---

* See Appendix F, Sec. iv.

manner, their conditions have been rigidly exacted from the apprentices, and very imperfectly fulfilled by the overseers, the distribution of salt fish having been on many estates very irregular. We have obtained a copy of a scale drawn up by a planting attorney residing in this parish, upon which *agreements* had been enforced by the late Stipendiary Magistrate on several estates, and which is a specimen of the manner in which the apprentices have been treated throughout the whole district. Its avowed object is to obtain their half Fridays and extra labor during crop, in exchange for what are called the indulgences of slavery, without any pecuniary remuneration. This table with remarks upon it will be found in the Appendix.* The present Special Magistrate, R. CHAMBERLAINE, has been about two months in the district. His predecessor was J. K. DAWSON, the character of whose administration may be inferred from the present state of the district. The refusal of the former gentleman, to sanction the pretended agreements of the latter, and to carry on the same system of coercion, has excited a combined hostility against him on the part of the planters; and the strongest efforts are being made to effect his removal. There is in fact, a conspiracy in the district, to re-enact the proceedings, which terminated in the removal of Dr. PALMER, and the issue of that enquiry, has inspired the planters with strong expectations of success. In the midst of profound quiet, the minds of the irritated predial population being tranquillized by the just policy of their new Stipendiary, the district is beginning to be represented as in a state of insubordination, and these rumors may be expected to increase till the

* See Appendix F, Sec. xiv.

credulous at a distance believe the eastern extremity of
the island to be in rebellion; while in fact all the violence, turbulence, and defiance of the law, are committed by the white overseers, proprietors, magistrates,
colonels of militia, and assistant judges.

A practice exists in Jamaica, and it is hoped exists
there only in the civilized world, of making representations against Special Magistrates, and other obnoxious
persons, founded on expressions used in the freedom of
social intercourse or *quasi* friendly correspondence.
These representations are sometimes employed to prejudice the public mind, through the newspapers, and
sometimes, embodied in the solemn form of affidavit,
are forwarded to the King's house, to effect their purpose with the Government. Several instances have
come under our notice in different parts of the island.
A gentleman called not long ago on the Special Magistrate of this district, and in the course of a *friendly*
conversation, complained that his negros were taking
in too much land to cultivate; the magistrate replied,
that they would pay him more rent for it after 1840.
Soon afterwards, the same individual wrote a letter to
the Governor, stating, on the authority of this conversation, that the Special Justice was disseminating ideas
among the negros, that they were to forsake estate labor, and to rent independent parcels of land after 1840.

18th.—We left Manchineal this morning for Bath,
on our return to Kingston. Nothing that we have
seen in the West Indies is equal to the vale of the
Plaintain Garden River, seen in its whole extent from
the neighboring heights; its level bed being covered
with cane fields, studded at intervals with extensive
estates' buildings and works, partially hidden by cocoa
nut trees. This beautiful savanna is about ten miles

in length, and terminates at the sea coast, in a fine harbour called Holland Bay. It is bounded on the south by a low range of hills, and on the north by an ascending series of heights, terminating in the lofty range of the Blue Mountains. The Plaintain Garden River, at this season an inconsiderable stream, intersects the savanna. Owing to the nearly uniform succession of fine seasons, this district is one of the most affluent in the island, but is reputed to be very unhealthy, and has been sometimes termed the grave of Europeans. We were accompanied by J. KINGDON, with whom we called at Amity Hall, a fine estate near the centre of the savanna, and were introduced to —— KIRKLAND, the resident overseer, and joint attorney of the estate. This estate is managed with more lenity than most others in the district, a circumstance which is owing to the proprietor and his family residing upon it for a short time, and to his selection of the present overseer. The apprentices obtained their half Fridays, when their owner was in the island, but have again been deprived of them since his departure, without, as we learned from the overseer himself, any agreement having been entered into, to compensate them for the loss.* We were shewn over the works, which are very complete. The boiling-house has been newly arranged, and is the best we have seen for economy of

---

* This fact had been mentioned to us previously by two individuals acquainted with the circumstances. The change was made through the influence of the other attorney, one of the members for the parish. The motive could have been no other than a determination to preserve a uniformity of system throughout the district, as the example of one estate legally administered, would tend to excite discontent and resistance on the neighbouring properties. This is one reason why the directions of humane absentee proprietors are rarely carried into effect.

labor. There is a patent *teach*, as the last boiling copper is called, from which the granulating liquor is drawn off, instead of being laded out, by which means, a saving is effected of time and fuel. The hospital is a very poor building, and was full of cases of measles. The population of Amity Hall decreased fast under the old system. We were told that the number of apprentices is two hundred and fifty, and of free children only sixteen, a proportion that appears incredibly small. The "great house" is situated on the brow of one of the neighbouring hills, and is occupied by a catechist of the Church Missionary Society, who teaches about one hundred and twenty children in a school room, which has been built for the purpose. He appeared to be an excellent young man, and devoted to his duties. He made the unusual complaint of the inattention of parents and their children to education. There are, he observes, two hundred and seventy children of suitable age, within two miles of the school on different estates, while he has not half that number on his list. The attendance was thin to-day, on account of the extraordinary prevalence of the measles. We next visited Golden Grove, an estate on the other side of the Plaintain Garden River, over which is thrown an elegant suspension bridge. Canals are conducted from the river, through the different estates, which set their works in motion, by means of large undershot wheels. The present time of drought, impedes the progress of the crop, and renders it impossible to plant, so that its effects will be still more sensibly felt next year than they are at present. The attorney of Golden Grove, THOMAS MC. CORNOCK, who is also the Custos of the parish, received us very kindly, and requested the overseer to shew us over the works. Golden Grove is one of the most productive estates in the island, and has upwards of five hundred apprentices. The buildings are very complete, and on an extensive scale, and the mill is on an improved plan. Instead of being placed in a raised building, for the purpose of allowing the cane juice to run down into the receiver in the boiling-house, so as to require all the canes to be carried up in bundles, the mill is placed on the level, and the cane juice is raised by a wheel hung round with buckets, moved by the water wheel that sets the mill itself in motion. It must be remarked of this and similar improvements, which are at length beginning to be introduced, that they not only save the labor of many hands, but abolish altogether those kinds of labor, which were the most painful and destructive of life. It is remarkable, however, that such improvements are scattered singly over the island, and we believe, no estate can be pointed out, which combines them all. The hospital at Golden Grove is roomy, clean, and well ventilated. It is full of cases of measles, and the patients are locked in till convalescent. The practice is general throughout the island, of permitting the apprentice attendants, called hospital doctors, to bleed and compound medicines. The most interesting building on this estate, is a handsome, little, brick church, built by the proprietor, with materials supplied from his estate, and with the labor of his own slaves. It is now thrown open to the public, and the minister is paid by this and several adjoining estates. There is a clock in the tower of the church, and we enquired of the attorney whether the people drew off when it struck six; he replied no, they draw off at sun-set, and as that is earlier than six on the short days, one season compensates for the other. He also acknowledged they did not have their half

Fridays, and received in lieu, their allowance of salt fish. The overseer mentioned to us, that the apprentices did not cultivate their provision grounds, nearly so well as during slavery, and now rarely have any to send to market. On Amity Hall, we were informed on the contrary, that the negro houses and grounds were more industriously attended to than before. In the evening we proceeded to Bath.

19th.—Very early this morning we rode over to Altamont, the new immigrant settlement situated in the heart of the Portland mountains, about eleven miles from Bath, and fifteen from Port Antonio. We proceeded by a bridle path over a ridge three thousand feet high, called the Coonah-Coonahs. After the first four or five miles all traces of human interference with the wild domain of nature had disappeared excepting only the track we followed. Below us was a valley of immense depth formed by a long ridge on the opposite side, and by the one impending over our heads. All was one vast forest, whose solitude was broken only by the deep-toned voices of birds. That delightful and cheerful songster, the mocking bird is a lover of human haunts, and its wild and merry notes cease to be heard in these deep recesses of the mountain forests. Here the multitude of mountain springs and rivers give ten-fold luxuriance to the productions of a fertile soil vivified by a tropical sun. On the side of the precipice, above which we were travelling, were huge trees, rooted at a great depth below us, but far over shadowing our heads with their arms and foliage. Above us on the other side was a canopy sometimes so dense as to exclude the sky. Among other beautiful trees, we observed the down tree, with full crops of its curious pods of vegetable beaver, and the tree fern frequently covered the sides of the hills for a considerable extent. Our path was as thickly strewn with decayed leaves as in a northern autumn, while all else bore the aspect of summer; for in this climate few of the trees become wholly or even partially denuded. After a long and difficult ascent of several miles, and a still steeper descent, we came to a place where the valley opened into a wider basin, in which traces of cultivation began to appear. We crossed a mountain torrent, the commencement of the Rio Grande, and entering a beautiful glade covered with turf on which cattle were grazing, we came to a farm house belonging to a person of color, near which is the settlement of Altamont. A single family have been sole tenants of this wilderness, for a long period, during which their only neighbours were the Maroons, living at Moore Town, about four miles distant. They were formerly accustomed to exercise free hospitality, but are now compelled to become hotel keepers in self-defence. The new settlement is formed on six hundred acres of land which was a part of their estate, and has been purchased from them at thirty shillings an acre. We were fortunate enough to arrive soon after the Superintendent of the immigrants, A. G. JOHNSTON, to whom the Custos had given us a letter of introduction. He is a gentleman of great intelligence, and very sanguine temperament, and appears completely devoted to his new undertaking. Under his auspices the immigrants certainly appear to have a good prospect of successfully contending with the difficulties of their new situation. The location is delightfully chosen in an irregular valley about one mile and half in length, through which flows the Rio Grande. The climate is very fine, and the only obvious disadvantage is the difficulty of transporting produce to a port or market. The sides of the mountains being crown land, afford ample scope for the extension of the settlement. The soil is virgin land of the most fertile description, well suited to the cultivation of coffee and ginger. The attention of the Superintendent is turned to the introduction of indigo, tobacco, the mulberry, and various other descriptions of profitable cultivation. The colony consists at present, of only six families, who have been about two months in the island. The commissioners anticipated their arrival, by building some neat little white cottages, which the people themselves have since further improved, and enclosed in little plots of ground, by neat fences of young rose trees. They are all married persons with young families, from the neighborhood of Aberdeen, selected by a minister, who is the brother of a member of Assembly in this island, one of the chief promoters of the colonization of Europeans. They have hitherto enjoyed good health, with the exception of one family, who were detained on a sugar estate, near the coast, where the husband found employment as a cooper. There his wife and children were attacked by intermittent fever, from which they have not yet recovered. Each family, besides being permitted for the present to occupy a house rent free, cultivates any quantity of land they think proper. They have also a cow and certain allowances of food till they are able to support themselves. An account is kept against them for the two latter items which they will be expected to repay. They are offered twenty acres of land in fee, as soon as they can erect a house upon it, so as to leave their present dwellings for new occupants. About twenty houses are either built, or in progress, and an additional number of families are shortly expected. The Superintendent appeared delighted with the industry of the immigrants, and indeed shewed us sufficient proofs of it, in the quantity of land they have already brought into cultivation. The men are fine, athletic peasants. They seemed cheerful, and expressed themselves satisfied with their new country; they were employed in making a piece of road, towards the expence of which the island has granted a sum of money. Their children looked happy, and their blue eyes, laughing faces and bare feet, reminded us of their native mountains. Their wives, however, generally appeared home-sick. The circumstance which gave us the least satisfaction was the destitution of the means of religious instruction. There was formerly a resident minister, connected with the Church Missionary Society, stationed at the Maroon Town, four miles distant, but he has recently been withdrawn by the bishop. It is the intention of the legislature to form a colony of white immigrants in each of the three grand divisions of the island; the eastern part of it called the county of Surrey, the central Middlesex, and the western Cornwall. The one in Cornwall has already been formed, and is called Seaford Town. We did not visit it, but heard a very unfavorable account of its progress. The Middlesex colony is not yet in existence. This, of Altamont in Surrey, has probably the best promise of success, as considerable attention has been paid to the selection of the families. While, however, we have thus expressed the agreeable impressions we received from our visit to Altamont, we cannot but consider the artificial system, upon which the settlement has been formed, as most unlikely to produce good results of a permanent nature. In addition to the formation of the settlements, European colonization has been encouraged, by the grant of an indiscriminate bounty of fifteen pounds a head, to the importers of immigrants; a plan which could promote no other end than the introduction of the European vices of drunkenness, and housebreaking; so that in some of the parishes a further expence has been incurred in order to deport them. Europeans have also been settled by individual proprietors on many of the estates almost uniformly, with an unfavorable result. Notwithstanding, however, the experience of the past, the mania for immigration still continues as if there were a charm in a European birth, and white complexion. These attempts may be traced to the boasted knowledge, but real ignorance, of the colonists, of the negro character. The present condition of the low, white population of Barbados has been forgotten or disregarded; as well as the fact that the introduction of Europeans, as laborers, must in the first instance be attended with an enormous waste of life, and when this difficulty is overcome, they can never compete with the superior adaptation of the negros to a tropical climate. The true motive of the immigration policy, appears to have been to create such a considerable body of whites as to neutralise the anticipated political importance of the enfranchised negros. Such schemes, involving the most lavish expenditure of money, deserve the scrutinizing attention of the *bona fide* proprietors of the soil, whether resident or absentee, as it is generally believed that the "power of the purse" is in the hands of men in the colony, whose fortunes are no longer susceptible of injury, either by private or public extravagance. About mid day, we proceeded to Moore Town, which settlement is as beautiful in situation as Altamont. It consists of about one hundred cottages, larger and more finished than negro houses on estates, scattered over a considerable extent of ground on the side of a hill. The residence of the superintendent, Captain WRIGHT, is on an opposite height, which overlooks the town. On a still higher eminence is a large house, belonging to one of the Maroons, which was lately occupied by the clergyman. The Maroons are a fine race of people, tall, and elegant in person, with features more European than the negros generally possess, and with the independent bearing of men who have been for generations free. Some of the women are decidedly handsome, and except their complexion, more like gipsies than negros. The inhabitants of this settlement, the largest Maroon town in the island, have lately acquired a reputation for industry. We saw a number of women employed at Altamont, in carrying lime on their heads a considerable distance, to the top of a hill, on which a building was in progress. A troop of the men sometimes turn out, with their negro captain at their head, to clear the pastures of such of the neighbouring planters who are willing to employ them; they work with their cutlasses, having a sort of disdain for the implements degraded by slavery. They also cultivate their own grounds industriously, and surround themselves with many domestic comforts; and bid fair in short, to become industrious citizens. Their improved condition and habits, do great credit to their present superintendent. It is to be desired, when their bloodhound occupation of hunting out runaway negros shall have ceased by the abolition of slavery, that their exclusive character and privileges may be abolished, their land divided among them in fee, and themselves left to merge into the general community of free persons. We called at the residence of Captain WRIGHT, who was from home, but his lady politely gave us what information we desired. The present number of maroons is about six hundred. Moore Town, and Altamont are most accessible from Port Antonio, from whence there is a carriage road, to within five miles from the former.

21st.—We returned this morning to Bath; and in the afternoon to Port Morant.

22nd.—We returned to Kingston early this morning, where we had the pleasure of meeting J. A. THOME, and J. H. KIMBALL, of the United States, who have been engaged in an inquiry into the results of complete emancipation and the apprenticeship, in Antigua and Barbados.

23rd.—The following instance of the inhumanity with which the free children and their mothers are treated, even at the seat of Government, was related to us, by an individual, intimately acquainted with the circumstances. A few days ago, an apprentice at the country property of a medical man, residing in Spanish Town, came to her master's town residence, a distance of nine miles, with her infant in a dying condition; he refused to look at the child, and ordered her to return immediately to her work. An individual to whom she applied in great distress, saying her child would die on the way, if she attempted to return home, suffered her to remain in his house, at the risk of a prosecution, for harboring an apprentice, under a clause of the Act in Aid. The child died two days afterwards, and she returned to her labor.

4th Month, 2nd, (April.)—We went this morning to pay a visit to CAPT. KENT, R. N. a Special Magistrate, in the Port Royal Mountains. His residence is the great house of Robertsfield Coffee Estate, and is a spacious and convenient mansion, though very difficult of access, being situated on the breast of a hill, several hundred feet high, the sides of which are excessively steep. There are many such dwellings in Jamaica, which excite our wonder, at the industry displayed in the conveyance of building materials, for many miles of road, which might be deemed almost impracticable for such purposes. Robertsfield commands a view of an immense valley, formed by the highest mountains in the island, through which runs the river Yallahs, contracted in this dry season within very narrow limits, though its spacious and rocky bed bears witness to its usual size and impetuosity. The mountain scenery of Port Royal and St. Andrews, has a different character from that of Portland and St. Thomas in the East. The sides of the hills are cleared of their native timber, and their huge masses and towering peaks are fully exposed to view. So clear is the atmosphere, that they are seen with a distinctness that lessens considerably their apparent height and distance.

3rd.—After breakfast, we accompanied Captain KENT to Clifton Mount, a large coffee estate near the summit of St. Catherine's Peak. The great house of Clifton Mount, is situated four thousand two hundred feet above the sea, at an elevation greater than that of almost any other residence in the island. The Peak rises immediately before it, and as seen from this point of view, is perfectly conical in form, and covered with forest. It is a conspicuous landmark at sea. The distance to the summit does not exceed a mile, but it is nearly seven hundred feet higher than Clifton Mount. Next to the Peak is the outline of the still loftier mountain, called John Crow Hill; and the eye traces in the same line, the three Peaks of the Blue Mountains, the highest summits in Jamaica. The attorney of Clifton Mount, COLIN CHISHOLM, accompanied us to the pass called Content Gap, from whence is seen a magnificent prospect of the plain and mountains of Liguanea, the city and harbor of Kingston, and the adjacent coasts. We rode through the "Gap," and ascended by a spiral path to Cold Spring, the ruins of the property and seat of the WALLENS, celebrated by BRYAN EDWARDS. The thermometer at this elevation, ranges throughout the year from 44° to 70°. The coffee and tea trees, the Magnolia, English and American oaks, firs, cedars, broom, and furze grow here together. The oaks commence their hybernation regularly at the same season as in our own climate. There are two of the old English variety, of which the largest, though still vegetating, was laid prostrate by the tempest of 1815, a period so memorable in this mountainous district, that it is employed by the negros, as an epoch, from whence to date all subsequent events. Its effects are still visible, the swoln torrents having torn away masses of rock, and carried off the soil from the sides of the mountains, leaving in many places, the bare rock or the original earthy strata fully exposed. We ascended from Cold Spring nearly to the summit of the Peak. The small wild strawberry and blackberry of our own country are common at this height, but the coffee tree ceases to flourish at a greater elevation than four thousand or four thousand five hundred feet.

4th.—We left Robertsfield early this morning, and called on our way to Kingston, at the house of S. BOURNE, where we met R. CHISHOLM, a planter in his district, who has the credit of governing his apprentices with kindness, and without the need of Stipendiary interference. His estate is in excellent order, and very productive, and he assured us he would not take for it one shilling less than before the introduction of the apprenticeship.

6th.—Two Special Magistrates related to us instances of the wanton destruction of the goats belonging to the apprentices, by the overseers. In one case, a goat belonging to one of the negros, which was tied up in a gulley, was destroyed by an overseer with his dog. In the other, a goat similarly secured, which was big with young, was beaten to death by a brutal overseer with his stick. Numerous cases have been mentioned to us of the hogs and poultry of the negros, being shot by the overseers. This species of persecution frequently follows as an act of retaliation, when the apprentices seek the protection of the law.

9th.—Yesterday we came to Jericho, in the parish of St. Thomas in the Vale, to pay a short visit to JOHN CLARKE, the Baptist missionary, and called with him this morning on NICHOLAS GYLES, the proprietor of Recess plantation, an individual prominent in the recent contest, which terminated in the dismission of Dr. PALMER from the magistracy. He received us courteously, and conversed with us for some time on the state of the island. Among other signs of the decline of its prosperity, he mentioned the decrease of litigation, which he considered a proof that there was little left worth contending for. He read to us a long letter, he had just written to a friend in London, describing the ruin of the colony, which concluded with the expression, "that without coercion, no good could be done after the termination of the apprenticeship." He did not believe that his negros were a worse set of people than on any other property, and when a proprietor praised his apprentices, he considered it a proof that he did not manage them himself, for in his own opinion, they could never be changed nor improved "so long as they were black." He said that his negros, whom Dr. PALMER had instigated to rebellion, were now building new houses for themselves, which was a proof they did not mean to leave the estate after 1840, though he intimated they might then intend to take forcible possession. Such was their inconsistency, that when he advertised Recess a short time since for sale, his apprentices came to him in a body, and said, they did not want to belong to any one else. He advertised it as "in a high state of cultivation, notwithstanding circumstances," an expression which had been laid hold of, to disprove the charges he brought against the administration of Dr. PALMER; but this high state of cultivation was secured, he observed, by the sacrifice of a part of last year's crop. We requested to see the negro houses and hospital, to which he assented. Several of the former which we entered, consisted of three small apartments, which were rude, ill-constructed, and dirty; the floors of bare earth, the walls were unplastered, and the whole had an air of extreme discomfort. He said they were proofs of the idleness of the people. In another cottage, we noticed and praised the healthy appearance of the free children. The proprietor said it was nothing like what it would have been in slavery; in 1834 he returned twenty-four children under six years of age, out of one hundred and twenty slaves, and that *there were fewer free children on the property now*. In another cottage was a man lying on a mat on the floor, evidently very ill from fever, with his arm bound up. His master asked him why he did not go to the hospital, he replied, "because you treat me so ill there, and struck me and gave me a kick on the back." We looked at his arm, it was affected with erysipelas, and seemed almost ready to suppurate; his illness will probably be fatal. The proprietor afterwards gave us his version of the affair; the man had come up to the great house to say he was sick, and refused to go into the hospital, because it was a place of confinement. He was put in by force, but only staid about half an hour, when he got out and went down to his own hut. The statement of the sick man, that disgraceful violence was used towards him was very faintly denied, and indeed rendered still more probable by the explanation which was offered. The great house on Recess stands on the barbecue on which the coffee is dried, and the basement story consists of store rooms and the hospital. This last is a small room without a window, about six and a half feet high, furnished only with an inclined plane of boards, on which the patients sleep. The door is kept locked, but is worn full of holes, which admit light and a little air. There was no patient in it, but the effluvia of the apartment was still perceptible. One side of it is a place of confinement, which has been most appropriately named by the negros "the coffin." It is constructed by a strong, wooden partition, thrown across the room at a distance of fourteen or sixteen inches from the wall, and with a floor elevated sixteen or eighteen inches from the ground, so that it is not more than five feet high. From these dimensions it is evident, that a person could not stand upright in it, nor sit without being wedged, nor lie in any other position than on the side. When one or more prisoners were confined, the heat must have been excessive, and the absence of light total. The door had been removed, and we were assured by the proprietor that it had not been used since 1834. He told us that it had saved the life of many a poor dirt eater, and also many a negro from more severe punishment. He said that it was made many years ago, to punish a woman after whose name he had called it, but the negros, always ready with a nickname, had called it " the coffin." He also gave us an account of the attempt of PALMER* and HARRIS, acting under the direction of Lord SLIGO, to see this celebrated place of punishment; which attempt had created much excitement, having been made the foundation of actions in the Island Courts, and a prominent part of those proceedings which terminated in the dismission of Dr. PALMER, and the removal of HARRIS to another part of the island. The proprietor of Recess was very bitter against LEWIS GRANT, one of his apprentices, who was a Baptist, and as he described him, a great leader among the other negros. He regretted that he had not shewn us a chapel, which the negros had built in the negro village, and in which, he informed us, they meet every other night, and make a great disturbance. On a recent occasion, he said he went there while they were holding their meeting, with a cutlass in his hand, and ordered his man to follow with a fowling piece, which latter, however, was for the purpose of killing a hog; and that LEWIS GRANT had since made an affidauit, that his master had come to the chapel with loaded pistols, and that he was afraid of his life.

10th.—We took leave this morning at our very kind friends at the Mission House at Jericho, and proceeded to Sligoville, a station in St. Catherine's Moun-

---

* See Appendix F, Sec. xiii.

tains, attached to the Baptist mission in Spanish town. We were kindly welcomed by J. M. PHILLIPO. This mountainous district, though possessing great advantages of situation, soil and climate, has been hitherto neglected, and is still wild and uncultivated. The population however, is sufficiently large to supply a numerous attendance at the mission chapel and school. The premises are situated on an eminence, about two thousand five hundred feet above the sea, and command an extensive prospect on all sides. The whole breadth of the island is visible from Old Harbour, on the south to Port Antonio, on the north side. Sligoville derives its name from a finely situated mountain residence of the late Governor, in this neighbourhood.

11th.—We returned to Spanish Town early this morning by a mountain ride, which is not surpassed by any in the island. From their contiguity to the capital, these mountains offer delightful situations for villa residences, and accordingly, within the last few years, an active spirit of improvement has been manifested in the district.

A numerous meeting of the custodes and other leading persons from the different parishes, was yesterday held to establish a scale of labor, which is a favorite project with Sir LIONEL SMITH, who carried it into effect in Barbados contrary to law. Soon after his assumption of this Government, he directed the planters to form committees in their respective parishes, to agree upon labor scales, and the present meeting was summoned to reduce these to a general standard. No project can well be conceived more absurd and impracticable, as the greatest variety of soils is found in Jamaica, no two parishes, nor scarcely any two estates being precisely alike. Notwithstanding such difficulties, a uniform scale would probably have been adopted, which would have been an engine of cruel oppression, but the design was happily defeated, by the influence of a planter of superior intelligence and liberality, who pointed out its absurdity, and declared that he found no difficulty, by kind treatment, in obtaining a fair and equitable amount of labor from the apprentices. As an instance of the use, to which a scale would have been applied, it may be mentioned, that almost immediately after the Governor issued his first circular to the parishes, one of the Special Magistrates reported that, certain overseers in his district were filling up the ranks of their first or strong gangs with weaker laborers; and compelling people to turn out, who had previously ceased to labor on account of age or infirmity; under the expectation of being able to extort the work of able-bodied laborers from the gangs under the projected scale, estimated by their number without any reference to their efficiency.*

13th.—We saw to day in Kingston, two intelligent negros who had run away from their estate for fear of being flogged, pursuant to a sentence of the Special Magistrate. They applied to W. W. Anderson, who found their case to be one of peculiar hardship, and consented to endeavour to bring it by *certiorari* under the cognizance of the Court of Assize. We obtained a copy of their affidavit which relates the follow-

---

* Although the project of a scale of labor for the whole island was thus abandoned, it by no means followed that the parish scales would not be adopted in their respective parishes. The Governor has since sanctioned the scale drawn up by the planters of St. Andrews, and directs that it shall be used by the magistrates as a standard, by which to judge of complaints of insufficiency of work. For the results which may be expected from this measure see Appendix E, Sec. iii.

ing particulars. Their names are JOSEPH and CATO SMITH, and they belong to ROBERT JOKIN, of Torrington Pen, in St. Thomas in the East. They are part of a jobbing gang of negros, who work at a distance from their homes, to which they return only once a week. Their provision grounds were repeatedly trespassed in, and their provisions destroyed by the cattle of the estate, which were not penned up, nor sufficiently attended to; and although they did what they could by making fences, it was impossible for them, on account of their long absence from home, to prevent or repair the damage sustained, and they consequently had not sufficient provision for their maintenance. Their master refused to afford them any remedy or compensation. They applied to Special Justice WILLIS, who told them their master was not liable for the damage, and they must attend to their grounds themselves. On his refusal to redress their grievances, these apprentices and about sixteen others, men and women, went to Spanish Town to see the Governor, but he was absent on a tour of the island, and they returned with a letter from Special Justice HILL to the Governor, whom they saw at Golden Grove, where he was staying, near their master's property. They stated the treatment that they had received, and further, that the police had been upon the property for some time, destroying and living upon the hogs and poultry of the apprentices. The Governor directed ALEXANDER BARCLAY, a local magistrate, and member of Assembly for the parish, to go upon the property with Special Justice WILLIS, and see the provision grounds of the apprentices, and report their state to him. They accordingly visited Torrington some days afterwards, when the gang were called up before them. BARCLAY told them he thought they had a good right to what they asked, but that it was impossible to give it them, as it would be a bad precedent for all the jobbing gangs in the parish. Special Justice WILLIS asked their master, which were "the two Governor's men," and these two negros were pointed out to him. He then said that no King or Governor should prevent his punishing them, and proceeded to sentence seven of the women to the treadmill, and these men, and four others, to receive fifty lashes each, which sentences were carried into effect, except in the case of these negros, JOSEPH and CATO SMITH, who again ran off to Spanish Town. They had obtained a letter from the Governor's Secretary, to the Special Justice. They had never been flogged during slavery, and seemed to be in such terror, that it appeared as if they could not be induced to return home, as in consequence of the expressions used by the Special Justice, they were certain they should be flogged, notwithstanding any instructions to the contrary, in the letter of which they were the bearers.

14th.—We embarked for New York, in the J. W. Cater packet.

Before concluding our journal, it may not be improper to mention an official investigation, that took place during our stay in the colony, and which affords some important illustrations of the condition of the negros. On the 18th of February, an apprentice named JOE DAWKINS, from Spencer's Pen, in St. Catherine's parish, came to Spanish Town, to complain to Special Justice RAMSAY; that he was threatened with punishment, by JAMES DUNDASS, the overseer of Molynes, an estate in St. Andrews, belonging to ANTHONY DAVIS, residing in England, who is also the proprietor of Spencer's Pen. On the 13th instant, he, (DAWKINS) was employed in taking lime to Molynes, with a mule and cart, when the axletree broke and he was obliged to put up the cart on an estate by the way. He went on and reported the accident to DUNDASS, who behaved with such violence towards him, that he ran off to Spanish Town for protection. In order to explain his fears, he stated that, the said DUNDASS was in the habit of maltreating the apprentices on Molynes; that some of them wore rivetted iron collars; that DUNDASS put others in the stocks and chained them by the neck to a post in the hot house; that he beat them with his supplejack, and that a fortnight ago he had caused one of the apprentices to be laid down by two of the negros, while a third gave him a severe flogging. On the same day an apprentice from Molynes, named JAMES WINE, came to Spanish Town to complain to the Governor, and was referred to the same Special Justice. He complained that he had been turned out of the hospital, and compelled to work during severe sickness. He confirmed the statement of the preceding witness, with the addition, that the use of rivetted iron collars on the estate, was sanctioned by LLOYD, the former Special Justice of the district, who was afterwards removed to another part of the island, and by his successor, Captain BROWNSON, who was at this date, in charge of the district as Special Magistrate. These depositions were reported to the Governor, who ordered Special Justices, KENT and MORESBY, to proceed to Molynes estate, and inquire into the facts and into the penal discipline in use on the estate. The following is an abstract of some of the affidavits of the apprentices.

JOHN CUMSO, " a miserable object with diseased

feet," states, that he had an iron collar put on his neck by order of Special Justice LLOYD some time after August, 1834, and does not remember when it was taken off. In the time of that magistrate, he was frequently put in the stocks by DUNDASS, during his half Friday.

ELSEY LEWIS deposes, that she was compelled to wear an iron collar nearly a year and a half, and that LLOYD saw DUNDASS screw it on.

WILLIAM LAKE deposes, that four weeks ago, he received thirty-nine lashes by order of Captain BROWNSON, who also ordered that the blacksmith should rivet an iron collar on his neck, which he has worn ever since, and worked in the field. Before he was brought before the Special Justice, he was kept five days and nights in the hot house, handcuffed and in the stocks, and was chained to a post one of those nights. He did not hear DUNDASS tell the magistrate that he confined him, and he, (LAKE) made no complaint to the magistrate himself. In reference also to WILLIAM LAKE's case, there is the following entry in the complaint-book of MOLYNES' estate:—"January 9th, 1837. WILLIAM LAKE charged with being a runaway, *to receive thirty-nine stripes*, and to *pay back eighty days*, that he has been absent, and to *wear a rivetted iron collar for six weeks*. Signed W. H. BROWNSON."

SUSAN PORTER deposes, that since christmas she was confined in the dark room from one o'clock on Wednesday, until ten o'clock on the following Friday, (two days and nights,) during which time, she had *no food of any sort*. She told Captain BROWNSON, but he took no notice of her complaint. She was locked up once before, but did not complain to the magistrate. About ten months after the 1st of August, 1834, she was severely flogged by Mr. DUNDASS, but did not complain to the magistrate. She did complain twice to Captain BROWNSON about two months ago, that she had *no allowance of food and no days*. He said he would see to it, but he did not, and *she has nothing to live upon but what her children give her.*

ALEXANDER NOTICE, states, that about four weeks ago DUNDASS caused two of the other apprentices to lay hold of him, while a third *flogged him* severely on the bare back with a cat. He was not tried by the Special Magistrate, and did not go to complain. The same day DUNDASS had *previously, severely beaten* him over the head and neck with a horse-whip.

RICHARD DAWKINS deposes, that he was flogged by DUNDASS, and did not go to complain, but ran away; for which, when taken, he was locked up in the dark room two days before christmas. *He was chained to a post and handcuffed, the chain ran through the handcuff.*

EDWARD DAWKINS deposes, that he has seen WILLIAM LAKE and RICHARD DAWKINS, in the stocks, with iron collars round their necks, and a chain passed through the collars and fastened to a post, and knows that SUSAN PORTER was locked up for several days. They have never gone to the magistrate, *as they knew they would get no right.* Never saw DUNDASS strike any *but the little children*. The apprentices are often locked up at night, and let out in the morning, without ever being brought before a Special Magistrate.

WILLIAM NAAR states, that he has been so locked up himself. He remembers DUNDASS flogging RICHARD DAWKINS, he, (NAAR) brought the cat out of the house to flog him. DAWKINS ran away, and when he was taken, he was confined in the stocks and chained to a post.

The same facts are reiterated by numerous other witnesses. The room in which the apprentices were punished by being handcuffed, put in the stocks, and chained by the neck to a post, is described by the following witnesses.

THOMAS MUMFORD, the second constable, says "the lock-up place is the *hospital* in which *is the stocks*."

JAMES DANIEL, the head constable,—"knows of several instances of the apprentices being placed in the stocks by order of Mr. DUNDASS, and chained to a post in the place of confinement. It is a close place but not so dark."

FREDERICK KRAMMA, a German, employed as a mechanic, and occasionally as a book-keeper, on Molynes, states " that the windows in the hospital were built up and loop-holes made, and that the fire-place has been lately closed, in consequence of a female apprentice making her escape up the chimney.

JAMES DENNISON, the book-keeper, deposes; " the hospital was closed up before I came to Molynes; what were formerly the windows, have been converted into loop-holes; it is in fact a dark room. *Heard* Mr. DUNDASS *flog the stable boys last Sunday*, because they left the grass piece open. Has never *seen him flog any but the house people*.

DUNDASS himself handed in a written statement to the magistrates, in which he asserts, the iron collars were rivetted on the necks of the apprentices, by order of the Special Magistrates; that WILLIAM LAKE was confined in the stocks and chained to a post *for security*, till Captain BROWNSON should visit the property, and try him as a runaway; that JOHN CUMSO was locked up on Friday night, by order of Special Justice LLOYD. He admits having struck SUSAN PORTER with a supplejack; he admits having locked up some of the apprentices without calling in the Special Magistrate; he admits having flogged ALEXANDER NOTICE.

The sole remark, we think it necessary to make on the above disclosures, is, that it is apparent, that whatever cruelty the negros on Molynes endured, whether flogged, kept without food, put in the stocks, or chained by the neck, they never thought of applying to the Special Magistrates of the district, who, they well knew, would afford them no protection. The above inquiry was the result of the accident of DUNDASS having threatened and assaulted an apprentice on another property, Spencer's Pen, who lived in the district of WILLIAM RAMSAY, a magistrate of a very different character from LLOYD and BROWNSON. We now come to the immediate bearing of this painful subject upon the present condition of the apprentices generally. The two Stipendiaries, LLOYD and BROWNSON, were dismissed from office by Sir LIONEL SMITH, for having employed the illegal punishment of rivetted iron collars, and for *having suppressed those sentences in their official reports.* The character of their general administration of the law may be appreciated from the fact, that while they were each accustomed to report monthly, about one hundred and fifty cases of punishment, of which a large proportion were by flogging, their successors reported at the end of the first month, the one nineteen and the other fourteen cases, in none of which corporal punishment had been inflicted. On the occasion of his former removal from his district by Lord SLIGO, LLOYD received an address of thanks and approbation, from the magistrates of St. ANDREWS; and BROWNSON who succeeded him in that parish followed in the same steps, and became equally popular. On their final dismissal as above mentioned, they received the strongest expressions of sympathy from the planters, by whom their past conduct was eulogised in the most emphatic terms, as will appear from the following extracts:—"A farewell dinner was given to Captain BROWNSON at Halfway Tree, on Thursday, for the purpose of presenting him with a testimonial of the parishioners' respect. A subscription has been also raised for the purchase of some memorial, as a *tribute of gratitude* for his impartial conduct in administering the law as Special Justice."

Jamaica Despatch, May 1*st.,* 1837.

His colleague received a still more signal mark of approbation. The whole parish of Clarendon was moved to do him honor, and he was presented with the following address:—

"To SAMUEL LLOYD, ESQ. late Special Justice for the parish of Clarendon, &c. &c.

SIR,

We, the magistrates, freeholders, and other inhabitants of the parish of Clarendon, beg leave to offer *the expression of our unfeigned regret at your dismissal* from the Special Magistracy of this island. *We deplore this event as a public calamity;* and when we reflect on the disorganised and unsettled state, in which you found many of the properties in this district, (arising from circumstances which led to the removal of your predecessor,) we feel that to your exertions, and to the faithful discharge of your official duties, we are indebted for our present comparative tranquillity. *Your vigilance, active habits and address, were peculiarly calculated to restore order;* and we venture to affirm, that the result of the strictest investigation, would prove creditable to yourself, and shew that your great object was the maintenance of proper discipline, with the least possible severity. We shall always be happy, individually and collectively, to bear testimony to your impartiality as a judge. With you, the rich and poor, the master and apprentice, had upon all occasions an equal hearing; and if at any time you have erred, in not rigidly fulfilling all the provisions of the Abolition Act, we are satisfied that such error was of the head, not of the heart. In the execution of your arduous duties, you have succeeded in conciliating the good opinion of all classes of this community; and we trust you may have also gained the approbation of God and your own conscience. Wherever fortune may lead you, be assured our best wishes will always accompany you.

WILLIAM COLLEMAN, CHAIRMAN.

At the meeting at which the above was agreed to, the report of the Despatch states:

"A subscription was immediately entered into, for the purpose of affording Mr LLOYD a substantial proof of the estimation and regard he was held in, by the community in general; when the following sums, (amounting to two hundred and forty pounds,) were instantly subscribed by the gentlemen present; and there is not the slightest doubt, that treble this amount will be raised in the other districts of the parish, and *this laudable example followed throughout the island.*" The above shew that the pro-slavery feeling in Jamaica, is as general and as malignant as ever.

Besides dismissing the magistrates, the Governor directed the Attorney General to prosecute DUNDASS, and accordingly seven indictments were sent up to the Grand Jury against him at the ensuing Assizes. True bills were found in two of the least important cases only, cases in which DUNDASS had committed himself by admitting the facts. The Grand Jury *ignored* the other five, and made the following presentment.

" With feelings of the deepest regret, we have to observe, that in the examinations of the several witnesses from Molynes estate, we have found great discrepancy and contradiction, particularly as relates to five of the seven indictments, preferred against JAMES DUNDASS, overseer of the said estate, *the evidence not at all bearing out the charges set forth.**

"We also humbly conceive, *that charges of so light and frivolous a nature,* as appeared from the evidence adduced, should have been referred to the Special Magistrates, who are the judges appointed by law to take cognizance of them, or to the Petty Courts of the country.

"·We feel the greatest pride on all occasions, fearlessly to perform our duty to our country, *but we view with alarm these appearances of persecution, and we*

---

* An intelligent individual, intimately acquainted with the circumstances, writes as follows. "Mr. DUNDASS, immediately on the investigation closing, was so satisfied, that he must stand condemned before a jury of his country, that he got his brother to write a letter to Mr. DALY, the county Inspector, requesting him to use his influence with the Attorney General, to instruct that the prosecutions should be tried in the Court of Quarter Sessions; alleging that some personal dislike which the Chief Justice had towards him, gave him no expectation but that of a severe sentence at his hands. At this time, there was no imputation of perjury against the apprentices, on whose evidence he and the magistrates were judged guilty, nothing on which he could raise the cry of persecution, no features in the proceedings to be deprecated, as calculated to destroy all confidence between the extreme classes of society; yet how strikingly does the scheme of persuading the Attorney General to turn over the cases to the Quarter Sessions, tally with the presentment of the Grand Jury, that they were of a nature for reference to the Petty Courts of the country. This looks like artifice and contrivance, not on the part of the apprentices, but on that of the overseer and the Grand Inquest of the country.

deprecate the introduction of a system, so effectually calculated to destroy all confidence between the employer and the employed, so ruinous in point of expense to the subject, and so prejudicial to the interests of the island at large.

THOMAS Mc. CORNACK,
FOREMAN."

We would call attention to two points in this presentment; the atrocities with which DUNDASS is charged, are characterised as "light and frivolous;" and secondly, it is glaringly evident from the concluding paragraph of their presentment, that this Grand Jury of planters, looked not solely to the evidence laid before them, but to the bearing of the proceedings against DUNDASS, on the planting interests of the island at large; interests which are thus identified with a system of cruel and hateful coercion.

CHAPTER XIII.

THE RESULTS OF THE APPRENTICESHIP IN JAMAICA.*

The preceding chapters contain our own observations on the condition of the negros; and in the Appendix F will be found authentic information on various important subjects included in our inquiry. In the 14th Section of that Appendix, there is especially a large amount of the testimony of the negros themselves, respecting their sufferings and treatment. Such is the nature of the evidence we have to lay before the public, as the result of a personal investigation of the mode in which the present system is administered, in almost every part of the island, and on plantations comprising every kind of cultivation.

The reader will form his own opinion, respecting what we deem to be, the internal evidence of the authenticity and truth of the statements of the apprentices themselves; but it is important to add that the great majority of the negros whose testimony we have cited, are intelligent, and of good character; many of them are connected with religious societies, and are known

---

* Although the following observations relate only to Jamaica, there is reason to believe, that the condition of the negros in some of the other colonies, particularly in Demerara and Trinidad, is still worse than in Jamaica itself.

to the missionaries, or other persons of respectability, with whom we had the advantage of communicating. Their statements are consistent with each other; they are in accordance with the facts which came under our own notice, and with the concurrent evidence of other resident witnesses of unimpeachable veracity. It only remains, therefore, that we should present the results of our mission in a condensed form, so as to enable the public to judge how far those benefits have been realised to the negros, which were purchased for them by the nation, for the sum of twenty millions sterling.

It is well known, that the measure so undeservedly termed, an Act for the Abolition of Slavery,* was opposed to the views of those who objected on principle to slavery; whose exertions had excited general public sympathy for the oppressed, and at length urged the question of Abolition, on the attention of an unwilling Government. They could not have done otherwise than protest as they did, against a law, which declared slavery to be for ever abolished, and the slaves set free, subject to such exceptions, as created a new kind of slavery, under the name of Apprenticeship; an anomalous condition, in which the negros were continued, under a system of coerced and unrequited labor. Nor, although they might have concurred in the grant of a liberal relief to the proprietors, whom slavery had ruined, in order to enable them to commence a better system,

---

* " We entreat His Majesty's Ministers not to contemplate any imperfect measure of Emancipation. We are deeply convinced, that the negro must be fully restored to his rights, and that no scheme of Emancipation, which would leave him half a slave and half a freeman, would tend materially either to his own benefit, or to the tranquillity of the Colonies."—Memorial to Earl GREY, signed and presented by the three hundred and thirty-nine Anti-slavery delegates, April 19th, 1833.

under more favorable auspices, could they have avoided protesting,* against the acknowledgment of their claim to "compensation," by which, for the first time, the British statute book was disgraced, by the formal recognition of the right and lawfulness of slavery. These were fatal objections to the new scheme; and the event has proved, that they were not merely of a theoretical character.† The simple declaration by the Imperial Legislature, of the inherent personal and civil rights of the negros, as fellow subjects under the British crown, as equal members of the human family, and endowed with the same physical and moral capacities, would have ensured those rights some degree of respect from the local authorities and the planters, by whom they are now trodden upon.

However, for the sake of our argument, we will suppose that the Act for the Abolition, was such a measure as the public voice demanded, a measure consistent with humanity and justice. In this point of view, it appears in the light of a great national *compact*, in which the British Nation covenanted to pay twenty

---

* "The Metropolitan Committees feel it expedient to call your attention pointedly to the distinction they have drawn between compensation and relief. They wholly and absolutely disclaim the principle of compensation: they deny that it is due: they protest against its payment: they consider compensation to be directly opposed to the very principles upon which the title to Emancipation is founded."—Circular of the London Anti-slavery Committees, April 4th, 1833.

† "If the debt of immutable justice be paid in full to the injured slave, a humane and considerate people will readily concur in all such reasonable measures for the relief of the planter, or of individual cases of distress, as may meet with the approbation of the British Parliament."—Memorial to Earl GREY, signed by the three hundred and thirty-nine delegates, April 19th, 1833.

millions sterling, for the purchase of the liberty of the slaves in the West India Colonies, the Mauritius, and the Cape of Good Hope, in the years 1838, and 1840; and for the establishment, in the interim, of a modified and mitigated servitude, which should be an advantageous state of transition to unrestricted freedom. It remains therefore to enquire, how far the provisions of this costly measure have been carried out, and to compare the condition created in theory, by its stipulations, with the actual state of the slave population in Jamaica.

The first clause of the Act, premising the justice and expediency of the abolition of slavery, and of compensation to slave masters, declares, that it is expedient to make provision for securing the industry and good conduct of the manumitted slaves for a limited period; and that it is necessary to afford time for the adaption of the local colonial laws to a state of freedom. It therefore enacts, that all persons who, on the first of August 1834, shall have been duly registered as slaves, and shall appear on the registry, to be six years old or upwards, shall from that day become apprenticed laborers. We have already shewn, that the *non-registered* slaves are also detained in apprenticeship in direct violation of this enactment.

The second clause enacts, that all persons, who would for the time being, have been entitled to the services of the slaves, if this Act had not been made, shall be entitled to their services as apprenticed laborers. No other services are thus transferred to the slave-masters, than what the colonial laws secured to them, under the previous system. By those laws, the mothers of six or more living children, were exempted from field labor, and provided with "an easy and comfortable maintenance;" but under the Apprenticeship, this class of slaves, including, in numerous instances, individuals who have been for years in the enjoyment of their exemptions, have been turned into the field, and coerced to the performance of the severest kind of labor.

The fourth clause of the Act divides the apprenticed laborers into three district classes :—*predials attached*, or those, " who, in their state of slavery, were usually employed in agriculture, or in the manufacture of colonial produce, or otherwise upon lands belonging to their owners :"—*predials unattached*, who were employed in like manner, " upon lands not belonging to their owners ;" and *non-predials*, " comprising all apprenticed laborers, not included within either of the two preceding classes." It is also provided ; " that no person of the age of twelve years and upwards, shall be included in either of the said two classes of predial apprenticed laborers, unless such person shall for twelve calendar months at the least, next before the passing of this present Act, (viz. from August 28th, 1832, to August 28th, 1833,) have been habitually employed in agriculture or the manufacture of colonial produce." The fifth clause declares, that the predial apprentices shall become free on the 1st of August, 1840 ; and the sixth, that the non-predials shall be emancipated on the 1st of August, 1838. The slaves between the ages of six and thirteen years, are left by these clauses, to be classed as predials or non-predials, at the pleasure of their owners. The classification of the apprentices has been hitherto left undetermined, on a vast majority of the estates in Jamaica, and in the mean time great numbers of the non-predials have been defrauded of their rights. The very numerous body of apprentices called estates' tradesmen, including the coopers, carpenters, masons, smiths, &c. are by common consent, deemed and taken to be *predials;* notwithstanding the express words of the Law, that none shall be so classed, who were not, during the twelvemonth specified, " habitually employed in agriculture, or the manufacture of colonial produce." Such of them as have purchased their freedom by valuation, have been rated at an excessive daily or yearly value, multiplied by the full term of days or years, of the predial apprenticeship. In many instances even the domestic slaves, have been made predials;* and numerous cases are given in Appendix F., and in other parts of this volume, of domestics being turned into the field by their owners or overseers. A local Act was passed during our stay in the colony, to enable the planters to carry a fraudulent classification still more extensively into effect. The rights of the *non-predials* have been hitherto violated with impunity; and the great majority of them will be forcibly detained in bondage beyond the 1st of August, 1838.

The 7th clause of the Abolition Act empowers masters to manumit their apprentices. A few noble-minded individuals have availed themselves of this power of manumission, the only privilege which a slave-master, as such, can exercise with a safe conscience. Many members of the Baptist churches in Jamaica, some of whom were dependent on the labor of a few negros for subsistence, have recently, from conscientious motives, set their apprentices free, and the missionaries

---

* We have already quoted the expression of a local magistrate of Vere, that in that important and populous parish, the class of *non-predials*, has been abolished by the planters.

of that denomination anticipate, that their several churches will soon be clear of the sin of slave-holding. If it be unlawful to take the fruit of the laborer's toil without payment, whether he is called a free man, a slave, or an apprentice, we would commend the conduct of these few, poor, despised, colored christians, to the imitation of the wealthy, liberal and professedly christian apprentice-owners, residing in England. The 7th clause provides, that in case of the voluntary discharge of aged or infirm laborers, the masters are to continue liable for their support; a provision which might have been spared in Jamaica, as the aged or infirm apprentices on the plantations are supported by their own relations and friends. They receive nothing from their owners, but a few shillings'-worth of clothing once a year, medical attendance during illness, and, where the proprietor is unusually indulgent, a small weekly allowance of salt-fish.

The 8th clause relates to the compulsory manumission of apprentices by valuation; which it enacts, shall be effected in the manner and form to be prescribed by the local laws of the colonies. The mode adopted in Jamaica is the following.—A negro informs the Special Justice of his district, of his wish to purchase his discharge from apprenticeship. The Special Justice gives fourteen days' notice of the intended valuation to the owner, who appoints a local magistrate to unite with the Special Justice; these two magistrates choose a third local magistrate, and thus constitute a tribunal for determining the valuation. It is needless to offer any comment on the character of a tribunal composed of two local magistrates, who are almost invariably planters and friends of the master, and one Special Magistrate, who possibly may be an impartial and humane functionary, but who is too often completely subservient to the wishes of the stronger party. The master and other witnesses give evidence on oath of the daily or yearly value of the negro's services, which is multiplied by his term of apprenticeship. The result, from which one-third is generally, though not always, deducted for contingencies of life and health, is the amount of the valuation. When the three magistrates differ in their estimates, it is customary to add their several amounts together, and take an average of the total sum as the value of the apprentice. Having witnessed numerous valuations in different parts of the island, we are enabled to speak with confidence, respecting the considerations, which in the estimation both of witnesses and magistrates, usually determine the value of the services of apprentices. The contingent loss is taken into account, which the master may sustain from the difficulty of replacing a laborer. If the apprentice is stated to be honest, intelligent, and industrious, he is rated proportionably higher. If he has ever been employed for a short time, as a mechanic, or if by his own ingenuity, he has taught himself any handicraft business, he is valued accordingly, although his habitual employment may have been that of a common field laborer. Lastly, the the profit, real or imaginary, which the master would have made by the labor of the apprentices, during the remaining term of years, is taken into account; and a temporary advance in the price of colonial produce, in the European markets, though it would not affect the price of labor in the colony, would instantly occasion an increase in the valuations. The negros, in short, who wish to become free, are rated at higher prices, than they were worth as slaves; and these prices do not diminish as the term of apprenticeship lessens. In many instances, a negro could have purchased his freedom for a much smaller sum on the 1st of August, 1834, than that which, after one or more years of uncompensated service, he has been compelled to pay for the remaining term. In these proceedings, the colonists stand self-convicted of fraud; for the wages, which they pay for the apprentices' extra labor, is in no kind of proportion to the price, which they put upon their services at valuation. During crop time, extra labor, equivalent to from two to three working days per week, is often remunerated by a sum, scarcely equal to the sworn value of half a day's labor. Notwithstanding, therefore, the immense sacrifices, which the negros are willing to make for freedom, numbers who are anxious to be valued, are still detained in bondage, and those who succeed in effecting their release, are crippled in their resources, or involved in debt, from which years of assiduous toil may fail to relieve them.

Instead of continuing to examine the clauses of the Act *seriatim*, we will devote our remaining space to a few principal considerations.

The Imperial Act regulates the labor of the apprentices in the following manner. (c. v.) No predial apprentice shall be bound or liable, to perform any labor in the service of his master, for more than forty-five hours in the whole, in any one week; from which, in case the apprentice supports himself by cultivating a provision ground, (c. xi.) such portions of time shall be deducted, " as shall be adequate for the *proper* cultivation of such ground, and for securing the crops thereon grown." The time deemed sufficient for these purposes, is four hours and a half per week, so that the amount of labor, required from the apprentices in Jamaica, is forty and a half hours in the week. The Colonial Legislature is required (c. xvi.) to frame the necessary regulations, for ensuring to the apprentice the enjoyment of his own time for his own benefit; for securing exactness in the computation of the time, during which he is required to labor for his owner; to make the necessary provision for preventing the imposition of task-work, without the free consent of the apprentice to undertake the same; and for enforcing the due performance of voluntary contracts on the part of the apprentice for labor in his own time. The reader will find numerous proofs in this volume that, instead of forty hours and half per week, from forty-five to fifty hours are statedly exacted from the apprentice in ordinary course. The enjoyment of his own time for his own benefit is not ensured to him. No regulations exist to secure exactness in the computation of time; and his days, instead of eight and nine working hours, frequently extend from nine to eleven hours. Compulsory task-work, so expressly declared to be illegal, is frequently enforced; and to an extent, as it has been our painful duty to record, in numerous instances, avowedly equal to what was exacted under the former system, when there was no legal limitation of the hours of labor. We have also seen, that it has been a favorite policy with Sir LIONEL SMITH, to cause the adoption, throughout the island, of "a scale of work," by which labor would be regulated by quantity and not by time, in such a mode, as would render the oppressive exaction universal. In crop time, which extends on sugar estates over a period of from three to six months, the negros have to perform an immense amount of extra labor, sometimes by spells of twelve, sixteen, and even twenty-four hours length, and estates are instanced in the Appendix, on which the mule boys and sugar boilers work continuously for six days and nights, snatching a few minutes rest during the short intervals of their toil. All this extra labor and night work is sometimes obtained by the coercive powers of the Special Magistrate, without any remuneration; sometimes it is extorted for a trifling and most inadequate payment, under the sanction of pretended agreements. Very efficient regulations have been framed to enforce voluntary contracts, and the same are used also to enforce fictitious and pretended contracts, for the labor of the apprentices. The Act declares, (c. xxi.) that apprentices shall not be compelled to work on Sundays except in certain specified cases of necessity, but in consequence of their being fraudulently deprived of their time, as above stated, and of the mulcts imposed on them by the Special Magistrates, they are frequently compelled by want, to work their provision grounds on the Sabbath. With regard, therefore, to the labor of the apprentices, we are brought to the conclusion, that not only is every provision of the Imperial Act violated, but the requirements of a much higher law are openly contemned. The planters may be emphatically addressed, in the language of the apostle JAMES: "The hire of your laborers, who have reaped down your fields, which is of you kept back by fraud crieth; and the cries of them which have reaped, are entered into the ears of the Lord of Sabaoth."

We come next to consider the maintenance of the apprentices. By the Imperial Act (c. xi.) a proprietor is required to provide his apprentices, with " such food, clothing, lodging, medicine, medical attendance, and such other maintenance and allowances," as by any local law he was required to provide his slaves. The burden is thrown (c. xvi.) upon the Colonial Legislature, of making the necessary regulations to *secure* punctuality and method, in the supply to the negros, of such food, clothing, &c: and for determining " the amount and quality of all such articles, *in cases where the laws at present existing in any such colony, may not, in the case of slaves, have made any regulation, or any adequate regulation, for that purpose.*" Where the apprentices are supported by the cultivation of provisions for themselves, the master is required to provide them " with ground adequate both in quantity and quality," for their support, and within reasonable distance of their usual places of abode; and to allow them, out of the forty-five hours per week, a portion of time, adequate for the proper cultivation of such ground, and for securing the crops thereon grown. The Colonial Legislature is required (c. xvi.) to make the regulations necessary to secure these several objects. The Jamaica Abolition Act, sanctioned by the Home Government, enacts, (c. xvi.) that the apprentices shall be supplied with the same food, clothing, lodging, &c., as by the Slave Act, the master was required to supply to his slaves; and (c. xlvi.) that all grounds hitherto allotted to the slaves, shall be deemed suitable in quantity, quality, and distance from their homes, for their maintenance as apprentices; that (c. xlviii.) four hours and half, out of the forty-five hours labor per week, shall be allotted for the cultivation of such grounds; and (c. xlviii.) where the grounds from drought or other casualty, become unproductive, that the owner shall, by other ways or means, make " good and ample provision" for the support of his apprentices, in the trifling penalty, in this last case, of twenty-four shillings sterling for each infraction of the law.

The agricultural slaves in Jamaica, were always maintained by cultivating provision grounds, and by the weekly distribution of an allowance of herrings or other salt fish; and in the case of invalids, pregnant women, and mothers, of a small quantity of flour or oatmeal, rice, sugar, &c. Certain other arrangements, necessary to the welfare and even the subsistence of the negros, were sanctioned by general custom in the colony. Thus a watchman was provided for the provision grounds, in order to prevent the crops from being destroyed by the trespass of cattle, or plundered by idle and improvident slaves; and one of the women was employed as a field-cook and water carrier, to prepare the breakfasts and dinners of the gangs in the field, in order that their mealtimes might be also intervals of rest, and to carry water for them, to quench the thirst created by exhausting labor under a burning sun. "The first act of the proprietors after the first of August," observes Dr. MADDEN, (who attentively watched the progress of events, during a period immediately preceding and following the introduction of the Apprenticeship,) "was to take away all those allowances and customary gratuities from the negros, which were not *literally* specified in the new law." It must be observed, that it was the local Abolition Act, that was deficient in these particulars, as all those allowances were continued to the negros, by the spirit and even the letter of the Imperial Act, as above quoted. The Attorney General, DOWELL O'REILLY, who has discharged the difficult duties of his office, in trying times, honestly and firmly, at the expense of his private interests, and with little support from the government with which he is associated, gave his opinion, that the apprentices were entitled to the slave allowances, and for the following reasons:—that the Abolition law was a remedial act, and could not be so construed, as to place the apprentices in a worse situation than they were in before; that slavery itself, is and was contrary to common law; and as it derived its validity from custom, so might the apprentices invoke custom in support of their claim to these allowances. The planters immediately submitted a case to the Ex-Attorney General, himself a planter, who gave his opinion in the following terms:—"I am of opinion, that under the Abolition Act, the apprentices are *not entitled* to the indulgences and allowances above alluded to. The 16th. Section of the Act gives them the same 'food, clothing, medicine, medical attendance, and such other maintenance and allowances,' as the owner was required to supply a slave by the 'Act for the government of slaves.' Now, on referring to this Act, it will be found, that the only clauses on the subject are the 11th, 12th, 13th, and 17th, neither of which specify or require the allowances above mentioned, (salt fish, &c.) to be given to the negros. The 11th provides, that owners, &c., shall inspect the provision grounds, and where the negro grounds are unproductive, or there is no land proper for provisions, shall by some other ways or means, make 'good and ample provision for all such slaves as they shall be possessed of, in order that they may be properly maintained and supported,' leaving the mode and nature of the support to the discretion of the owner. The 12th clause requires every owner to provide proper and sufficient clothing, to be approved by the vestry. The 13th requires an affidavit, that the grounds have been inspected, and that every negro is sufficiently provided with grounds, or, 'where there are no grounds, with ample provisions,' as required by the 11th section. The 17th section compels every owner to provide infirm and disabled negros, with sufficient clothing and wholesome necessaries of life." Such are the vague and valueless provisions, which have been accepted by the British Government, in satisfaction of the stipulations of the Imperial Act. The Ex-Attorney General continues,—" The 8th section of the Act in Aid of the Abolition Act, passed the 2nd of July last, has no clause respecting allowances to the apprentices, except the 8th, relative to sick apprentices, who under it, are to have the same medical care and attention, as has heretofore been customary. It is clear therefore, that by the Slave Act, an owner is *not obliged to give any of the above allowances, but merely to provide sufficient grounds, fit for the cultivation of provisions.*" It will now be asked, which of these opposite opinions prevailed on a question, affecting so nearly the interests and welfare of the apprentices? We regret to say, that the Government did not enforce that of its own responsible legal adviser; and that the extracts, we have given from the opinion of his rival, have decided the condition of the apprentices with regard to maintenance, in fact as well as in law. The negros have either been generally deprived of these allowances, now called with bitter truth, " the indulgences of slavery;" or their partial continuance has been made the pretext of extorting a far more than equivalent value in extra labor, over and above that, which the apprentices are required by law to perform. These indulgences, it must be remarked, were not *indulgences* under the former system; they were granted by the master for his own interest's sake, as necessary to the health of his slaves, who subsisted as they do still, chiefly on farinaceous roots, cultivated by their own hands. With regard also to the four hours and a half, allowed for the cultivation of the provision grounds, it cannot be for a moment believed, that that amount of time is sufficient for the negros to provide the means of a week's subsistence. In this point also, the planters stand self-convicted of fraud, for on most sugar estates, the half Friday ostensibly granted, as adequate to provide food for an entire week, is taken back for a trifling weekly allowance of five or six herrings, the least considerable part of his necessary support. In those parts of the island, where the eight hour system of labor is adopted, a system which is usually a mere pretext for defrauding the apprentices of time; the four hours and a half are so distributed over several days, as to render it impossible, that he should employ the time for the purposes assigned. The provision grounds of the apprentices, are from one to fifteen miles distant from their houses; but in no case, is any allowance of time made, on account of their distance, for going and returning. The watchmen have in numerous instances been taken away, and the provision grounds consequently ruined by plunder, or the trespass of cattle, for which injuries, though reduced to starvation, the apprentices have no redress. In some cases, they have suffered to such an extent from these causes, as to be compelled to throw up their grounds, and to depend for subsistence on the most casual and insufficient resources. On many estates, the negros have been deprived of their field cooks, and thus compelled to labor throughout the day without food. The domestic apprentices, who were, and still are supported in the same manner as the agricultural slaves, by cultivating provision grounds, were entitled under the former system to the same amount of time for their own benefit; viz., one day in a fortnight, in addition to the two Sabbaths, or two days in lieu of them; now they are allowed only one day in a fortnight, to provide themselves the means of subsistence, and are liable to render service at all other times, by day or by night, as well as on the Sabbath. To these several considerations it must be added, that during illness, the apprentices are supported by themselves or their relatives, and that their young families and aged relatives are also dependent on them for support. Their poultry and other live stock, are frequently wantonly destroyed by the overseers; and the small portion of time which is left to them for procuring the necessaries of life, is diminished not only by the frauds practised on them by their owners, but by the mulcts of the Special Magistrates. The great bulk of the apprentices therefore, are not, and under such a system cannot be, sufficiently maintained. A large proportion of them are wholly, or in part, dependent for support on their fellow apprentices, and many of them are suffering from the pressure of actual want.*

In the article of clothing, the authority, already quoted, requires "every owner to provide proper and sufficient clothing, to be approved by the vestry." The distribution is in effect regulated, in quantity and quality, by the disposition of the owner or his repre-

* While these sheets are passing through the press, the Jamaica papers recently arrived, contain the most serious complaints of the scarcity and excessive prices of provisions. The markets are chiefly supplied by the apprentices, with the surplus produce of their grounds, but from the causes we have cited, these supplies have gradually diminished, until the effects of the new system are at length severely felt even by the free population of the island.

sentative. A considerable proportion of the expense of their clothing, falls upon the apprentices themselves. The head negros, in particular, do not wear the coarse articles which are distributed to them. It is well understood, we believe, by the merchants, that the demand for these coarse fabrics, will not long survive the apprenticeship, but will be replaced by others of better manufacture.

The medical attention to which the negros are legally entitled, is accorded to them in the same imperfect and grudging measure, as the means of subsistence. The neglect and oppression of the sick, is a frequent subject of complaint with the negros; and of comparisons of the former and present system, very unfavorable to the latter. The medical men, imbued with colonial habits and prejudices, and dependent on the planters for professional income, are in most instances subservient agents of oppression. On many of the smaller properties, there is no hospital nor medicine chest, and the apprentices are frequently left destitute of medical treatment, or have to sustain the expense of it themselves. The Act in Aid of the Abolition Act, (c. viii.) declares, "that the apprentices shall be subject to all such necessary sanatory restraint and control, as the medical attendant shall direct." This clause is made the pretext of converting many of the hospitals into places of confinement. They are kept locked by day as well as by night, the inmates being deprived of even the occasional attentions of their nearest relatives. "Sanatory restraint" has been sometimes held to include confinement in the stocks and bilboes.* An upright Special Magistrate is in these

---

* One of the missionaries informed us, that on one occasion, having been requested to visit an apprentice member of his church, who

cases, brought into angry collision both with overseers and medical men. Invalid apprentices are not supplied with any allowance of food from the estates.

The condition of the free children, is another important feature of the present system. All, who, on the first of August, were under six years of age, were declared unconditionally free, but were left liable, (c. xiii.) in case of destitution, to be apprenticed by the Special Magistrate, to the owner of their parents, till twenty-one years of age. This was undoubtedly one of the most dangerous parts of the Abolition Bill; as such an apprenticeship of the rising generation, involved the indefinite continuance of slavery. Through the constancy of the parents, all the attempts to procure the apprenticeship of the children, have been defeated, though at an expense of infant life, and of an amount of suffering to mothers, which cannot be computed. Let it not be forgotten, that the free children are solely dependent on their mothers for support, and that the latter have only one day and a half in the week to cultivate ground for this purpose; an insufficient amount of time, which is still further reduced by the frauds of overseers, and the mulcts of Special Magistrates. The evils and the suffering, which spring from this state of things, are becoming daily more aggravated as time advances. Every birth increases the difficulty to the negro mother, of providing maintenance for her offspring, and of escaping punishment herself. The injurious consequences to the interests of proprietors, and of the public, from the present position of the

was very ill in the estate's hospital, he found him with his feet in shackles. We have already mentioned a medical order, entered in a plantation book, as quoted in one of the Special Magistrates' reports, " that the patients with sore feet should be kept in the stocks."

free children, have been adverted to in various parts of the present work.

The treatment of pregnant women and nursing mothers, is another feature of the apprenticeship, by which it is unfavorably distinguished, even from the worst aspect of slavery. The indulgences which their situation required, were, under the former system, imperfectly guaranteed to them, by the sordid interests of their owners. Women advanced in pregnancy, were confined to light employment, and for weeks immediately preceding and succeeding their delivery, they were suffered to cease work; and when at length required to return to the field, were permitted at proper intervals, to quit their labor and attend to the wants of their infants. All these indulgences have been curtailed, and in many instances abolished, to the very extent of the capacity of the human frame, for the endurance of suffering. On many plantations, they are kept in the field, sometimes working in jobbing gangs many miles from their homes, to the day of their delivery, and are hurried back again to field labor, as soon as exhausted nature can be tasked to the exertion. In many instances, nurses and midwives must be provided at the expense of the apprentices themselves, and they receive none of the minor "indulgences" of flour, rice, or sugar, and mothers are not suffered to leave the field to give nourishment to their infants. If the Abolition Act possessed a single feature, which tended more than another, to reconcile the nation to the costly sacrifice of twenty millions, it was the advantages it appeared to confer on the weaker sex, whom it professed, by exempting them from degrading punishment, to elevate at least one step towards that position which reason and humanity require that they should occupy. Widely different, however, is the law enacted by the Imperial legislature, from the same law as carried into effect by the executive government, and by which the oppression and degradation of females are sanctioned and aggravated. The Imperial Act (c. vi.) expressly interdicts the flogging of females, yet the present volume contains proof, in addition to much that has already come before the public from other sources, that females have been and still are flogged upon the treadmill, and that the treadmill itself is an instrument of torture. They are publicly worked in the penal gang, chained to each other, and with iron collars on their necks; besides being liable to the punishment of solitary confinement with an insufficient diet, and to mulcts of time, by which they are deprived of the means of providing food for themselves and their children. All these punishments, women in a state of pregnancy, and others with infants at the breast, endure in their full proportion. We leave it to those who may be qualified for the decision, to balance the severity and degradation of the treadmill and the chain gang, with the punishments by which the unrequited labor of females was formerly extorted.

As the principle of fair and honest remuneration for work performed, has no place in the apprenticeship scheme, our next object will be to take a general view of the penal discipline, by which the labor of the negros is enforced. The Imperial Act abolishes the powers of punishment, heretofore irresponsibly exercised by the master and removes the apprentice from the jurisdiction of all authorities in the island, except the superior civil, and criminal courts. It lodges the necessary powers both for his coercion and protection, in the hands of a class of magistrates specially appointed by the King, and salaried by the British nation. The task of arranging the details of their administration is imposed upon the Colonial Legislature. Of the local Abolition Act, in reference to this subject, it may be observed, that while it does not contain a single explicit enactment securing to the apprentice the necessaries of life, and the enjoyment of his own time for his own benefit; and while, so far as his interests and protection are concerned, it is destitute of an "executory principle;" yet such is the number and severity of its penal enactments, for the offences of apprentices, both circumstantially defined, and of a vague and general character, that it is probably the most highly penal law that ever disfigured the statute book of the colony. Our present concern, however, is rather with the practical administration of the law, than the law itself. We would first observe, that the local magistrates in violation of the law, still exercise a jurisdiction over the apprentices, both in their individual capacity, and when sitting in petty and quarter sessions; and that in particular, when an apprentice is sent to the workhouse, he is taken for the time being, out of the jurisdiction of the Special Magistrates. The masters and overseers still exercise direct coercion, by putting the apprentices in confinement. The local Act grants them this power for the security of the person of an offender, till the arrival of the Special Magistrate, but provides, that the imprisonment shall not exceed twenty-four hours, and that the Special Magistrate shall in all cases be informed of the matter of complaint. The practice on the part of the owners and overseers, of punishing negros by confinement at their own caprice, without any previous or subsequent reference to the Special Magistrate, is general in every part of the island. The planters have also perpetuated their irresponsible authority, by the exercise of indirect powers of coercion, in withholding the slave allowances; destroying the goats, poultry and hogs of the apprentices; pulling down their houses; taking away the watchmen from the provision grounds, and suffering them to be destroyed by the trespass of cattle; taking away the field cooks; locking up the sick in the hospitals, and other acts of cruelty and oppression, against which the apprentices have no protection. The amount of suffering and punishment inflicted in these modes, is placed on no record, reported to no authority, but it is not therefore less oppressively and keenly felt. It affords us little satisfaction to turn from illegal to legal oppression. A limited and imperfect idea of the amount of punishment inflicted by the Special Magistrates, may be learned from the fact, that during the first two years of their administration in the colony, sixty thousand apprentices were punished to an extent, in the aggregate, of a quarter of a million of lashes, and fifty thousand other punishments, by the treadmill, chain gang, solitary confinement, and mulcts of time. We would repeat here the remark, that we have neither the power nor the wish to institute a comparison between the present and former system. To do this would require an unenviable faculty of imagination, or a personal acquaintance with slavery, during which, the mind should have become familiar, without becoming reconciled, with its scenes of violence and wretchedness. We are not therefore in a condition to state how much the negro has gained by the substitution of the Special Magistrate for the negro driver, and of the discipline of the parish workhouse, for the stocks and bilboes of the plantation; but we can and do assert, that the new system is efficient for the purposes of perpetuating the enslaving influence of terror, and rendering owners and overseers independent of the law of kindness and justice. Many of the treadmills, as we have shewn, are instruments not of punishment but of torture. From their construction, they are not capable of their legitimate object, the enforcement of a species of severe labor. The prisoners are put upon them for one or two short spells in the day, for the sole purposes of torture, and to diversify the horrors of the dark cell, and the chain gang. Another feature of the workhouse discipline, is its demoralising tendency, which is as complete as if it had been devised for the purpose. The prisoners of both sexes, of all ages, and for all offences, are thrown together indiscriminately. At night the males are crowded into one sleeping room, and the females into another, their security being sometimes ensured by shackles. Of the temporary inmates of the workhouses, thus associated together, besides young persons of both sexes, a fair proportion are members of churches, individuals of irreproachable conversation, who are sent for offences occasioned by accident, inability, or sickness; or for those of a fictitious and constructive nature, which, if true, fix no stain on their moral character, though they are thus visited by punishments, implying the deepest moral degradation.

The forfeiture of time to the estates, is the last mode of punishment, which our brief summary enables us to allude to. It is one which involves as much irritation and suffering as all others combined, from the circumstance, of its reducing the negros to absolute destitution. The law has given the master a direct interest in convicting his negros of crime, by affixing a penalty, which gives him their labor without payment, for a variety of offences, some of which do not, in the least degree, trench upon his interests. This evil is increased by the practice of some of the Special Magistrates, of ordering the apprentices to pay back the time, which they lose when sent to the workhouse; a practice repugnant to justice and utterly illegal.

Next to the consequences of the excessive activity and severity of the *coercive* powers of the apprenticeship, must be considered the far greater amount of suffering occasioned by the imperfection of its *protective* powers. We have shewn in our remarks on labor, maintenance, condition of the females, &c. that the negros are unprotected in the rights most expressly secured to them by the British statute. The local Abolition Act imposes no greater penalty than three pounds sterling, for the utmost injury which an apprentice can sustain at the hands of his master; and even the petty pecuniary mulcts, which the Special Magistrates are permitted to inflict on owners and overseers, are paid into the *Island Treasury*. The law does not recognise the right of the negro, to compensation for any personal injury. Defective, however, as the law is, its administration is still worse. Personal observation, and the testimony of multitudes of the negros themselves, force the conviction on our minds, that many Stipendiary Magistrates act as if their sole duty was to coerce labor, and to maintain at any cost the authority of the planters. When apprentices are brought before them as offenders, they refuse to hear a word in defence or explanation, and when the negros are complainants, they award them punishment, instead of redress. Where this system has been carried to perfection, it has produced a state of things, known and described by the colonists, as "a state of order and tranquillity;" and its authors have been rewarded with substantial marks of public and private gratitude. Desolation may be as justly termed peace, as this condition of things described by names, to which it has no resemblance, but in its *silence.* The negros are silent, because they have learned by experience, that it is better to make any sacrifice, and to submit to aggravated oppression, than to appeal to magistrates, who will crush every complaint by adding to their yoke and increasing their chastisement. Such quiet " is not the complacent quiet of contented enjoyment, but the portentous quiet of despair."

We would not throw all the blame, nor even the chief blame, of this disastrous working of the apprenticeship, upon the Special Magistrates. Their administration of the law may be considered a fair transcript of the policy of the Government itself; for in their relation to the Governor, and their immediate responsibility to his authority, they more nearly resemble subordinate military, than civil officers. They have also peculiar difficulties to encounter, to which we have had frequent occasion to advert. The duties imposed on them, by the local Act, it is impossible for human strength to fulfil. They are inadequately remunerated, and are thrown by unavoidable circumstances upon the hospitality of the planters. It must cease, therefore, to surprise us, that the greater number of them are as completely subservient to the colonists, as if they had been selected and paid as their agents, instead of being the independent and responsible officers of the British Government. But of all their difficulties, the greatest is the absence of countenance and protection on the part of the executive. A magistrate was some time since removed by the Governor, ostensibly and avowedly, "for administering the law in the spirit of the Imperial Act." This decision has been confirmed by the Secretary of State,* and by a necessary consequence, it is now understood, by every Special Magistrate, that if he so administers the law, he does it at the peril of his office. There are yet some holding the Special Commission, who at least endeavour to do their duty; men of tried worth and strength of character, who have displayed rare qualities of the heart and intellect, under circumstances of unexampled difficulty. These will long be held in grateful remembrance by the negros. They are few in number, and we would gladly record their names, but from the fear of omitting a single individual, who may deserve praise for the conscientious discharge of his difficult and responsible duties.

We have now completed our review of the condition of the negros under the apprenticeship, and with a few additional remarks on the Imperial Abolition Act, we shall leave the reader to decide how far the terms of the compact have been respectively fulfilled by the nation and the planters. The clauses relating to compensation are by far the most ample, the most minute, and the most accurately worded, of any part of the Bill. They have been carried into full effect. Not a single slave-owner can complain of being defrauded, either in whole, or in part, of his share of compensa-

---

* The late Governor, the Marquis of SLIGO, after he became acquainted with the oppressions to which the negros were subjected, endeavoured with great firmness and magnanimity, to protect them in the enjoyment of their rights. He experienced far less difficulty from the turbulent violence of the colonists, than from the apathy or concealed hostility of the Colonial Office, which subsequently led to his resignation of the Government.

tion. Some, indeed, have been defrauded by their fellow colonists,* but, by the British nation, the sum of twenty millions sterling, has been paid with accumulated interest, and free of all charges. In addition to which, the apprenticeship has been upheld by the presence of British regiments, and administered by a legion of magistrates, paid out of the British Treasury. The nation, therefore, has fulfilled its part of the compact, and even exceeded its stipulations. The negros, though no parties to the agreement, have yet fulfilled all its onerous and unjust conditions. But on the other hand, in every essential particular, it has been violated by the planters, with the connivance and even the active participation of the Executive Government. A remarkable proviso is appended to that clause (c. xvi.) of the Imperial Act, which enumerates the various objects which it will be necessary for the local Legislatures to provide for in detail, to the following effect :— that it shall not be lawful for any subordinate Legislative authority, by any Act, Ordinance, or Order in Council, to make or establish any enactment, regulation, provision, rule or order, which shall be in any wise repugnant or contradictory to the Imperial Act, or any part of it; and such enactments are declared to be absolutely null, void, and of no effect. This proviso appears to have been intended as an emphatic assurance to the nation, that the conditions of the Act should be fully complied with by the colonists. No law, however, has been more utterly disregarded than

---

* Soon after the passing of the Bill, reports were actively circulated in Jamaica, that the compensation would never be paid. Some of the great alarmists were meantime speculating in estates and compensation claims. Many of the poorer and more ignorant colored slave-holders sold their claims for less than half their value.

this specious proviso. It has been, in itself, absolutely null, void, and of no effect. The very minister who introduced and carried the Imperial Act, who inserted in it this proviso, subsequently advised the sanction of the Jamaica Abolition Bill, as " adequate and satisfactory," to entitle the colonists to compensation, and to carry out the provisions of the Imperial Act ; a Bill confessedly so inadequate, and so little satisfactory, that he himself in the very act of announcing his acceptance of it, called upon the Assembly to remedy both its excesses and deficiencies. Each succeeding colonial minister has trodden in the same steps, and the concealment and defence of successive errors, have led to the establishment, by authority, of the new system such as we have described it. At the present moment, the shelves of the colonial office groan under accumulated evidence, of the wrongs and sufferings of the negros.

One provision of the Abolition Bill, the freedom of the apprentices in 1840, is yet to be fulfilled. With the experience of the past before us, what security has the nation, that this last and principal instalment in satisfaction of the twenty millions will be paid? There can be little doubt, that the name of apprenticeship will cease at the appointed time, as did that of slavery; but that its substance will not remain; that coercive, penal and restrictive laws, exclusively affecting the negros, will not be passed; and if passed, sanctioned, and carried into full effect, there is no security, unless the British public demand the effectual redress of past grievances, and existing wrongs; and thus discourage the attempts, which will undoubtedly be made, to perpetuate under a new form and specious designation, some system of violence and unrighteous oppression.

CHAPTER XIV.

CONCLUSION.

There are some exceptions to the description we have given in the preceding chapter of the condition and treatment of the apprentices. There are some resident proprietors, some attorneys and overseers, whose conduct to the negros under their charge is in striking contrast with the general management. Our pages bear witness of our anxiety to do justice to those with whom we became acquainted, who merit this honorable distinction. Such individuals have uniformly experienced the industry and good-will, with which, the negro renders, what becomes under such a yoke, almost a voluntary service, and his readiness to work for reasonable wages in his own time. The willingness and even anxiety of the apprentices to labor for pecuniary remuneration, have been fully demonstrated wherever they have been fairly put to the test; and the circumstance is important when viewed in connection with the prospective results of emancipation, should the change in the social system, which has been so inauspiciously begun, be carried out to its desirable completion. It would be almost idle to speculate on the agricultural prospects of the colonies under present circumstances. Those prospects are clouded by the Apprenticeship, which threatens, if not the ruin of the island, or the disorganization of the community, partial or complete loss of property, to those, who now wantonly outrage the rights of their dependent bondsmen.

Few will be prepared to dispute the advantages, which the division and combination of labor, under the direction of capital and skill, offer in comparison with that simple condition of society, in which each individual supplies all his various wants with his own hands. It is, therefore, desirable that the cultivation of the great staples of the colonies should go on with uninterrupted success. Such has been the result in Antigua, such might have been the result in Jamaica; and if the Apprenticeship should be brought to an early and peaceable termination, such perhaps might be the result still. Nothing can exceed the disposition manifested by the negro population, to acquire the comforts and even the luxuries of civilized life. The world has seen no example of so general and intense a desire for education and religious instruction, as has been shewn by the apprentices on behalf of themselves and their children within the last few years. Their conduct and their character are full of promise for the future; full of tokens of their capacity to become, when free, a well ordered, industrious, and prosperous community. Their oppressors continue to malign them, but the shafts of calumny have spent their force. None of those dreams of danger and difficulty, which were put forth as pretexts for delaying the Abolition of Slavery, ever had any other basis, than fraudulent design or guilty fear. From the time, when it was maintained, that the negro was of the lower creation, to the present day, when he is recognised as of the common brotherhood of man, every pro-slavery dogma respecting his character and capabilities, has been disproved by experience; every pro-slavery prophecy has been falsified by the event. We are entitled, therefore, to doubt the intimate acquaintance of the planters with the negro character; to turn a deaf ear to their speculations on the future, and to listen to those reasonable considerations, which are deduced from the supposition, that the apprentices are governed by the motives and interests common to human nature, and which are in accordance with our experience of the past.

It is undeniably established, that the Abolition of Slavery does not effect the safety of the state, nor the well-being of the community, except by ensuring the one and establishing the other. The question is liable to no difficulties, but those which are raised by the sordid interests of individuals. It is a false view of such interests alone, which demands the perpetuation of violence and fraud. It is already proved that the community, the state, the whole body of the people, would be more prosperous under a state of freedom. It is not necessary to shew, that the present order of things will be so little disturbed, as to leave every plantation cultivated as it is at present, yielding an equal amount of produce, an equal revenue, to be as unequally distributed. The production of excessive wealth, in a slave community, does not alleviate misery, nor lighten toil; it serves but to heighten the contrast between the splendor of the slave-master and the wretchedness of the slave. In the British Colonies, wealth has been the cause of non-residence, the origin of a system of mercenary agency, which has aggravated even slavery itself. The continuance of such vicious parts of a bad system is neither probable nor desirable in a state of freedom. A view of the evils resulting from the non-residence of land-holders in Ireland, would afford a very imperfect exemplification of the effects of a similar cause in the West Indies. If, however, in the heart of the empire, and under the immediate inspection of Government and the nation, a vast amount of suffering and civil disorganization, is found to result from absenteeism, it will not be doubted, that the same consequences, aggravated in a ten-fold degree, exist in the colonies, where absenteeism is far more general and uninterrupted; where the Imperial Government possesses limited means of information, and consequently a very limited control; and where the legislative, and for the most part the executive powers of the local administration, are confided to the same mercenary agency, which has been created to superintend the private interests of the absent proprietors. The immense export of corn and cattle from Ireland cannot be adduced as a proof, that her peasantry are living in comfort and abundance; nor do the amount and value of the exports from the West Indies denote, under present circumstances, the happy condition of their agricultural population.

We would not, however, be understood to favor the supposition, now so generally exploded, that slavery is consistent with the permanent agricultural and commercial prosperity, either of the aggregate community, or of the few individual proprietors. From the date of the Abolition of the slave trade, the population of Jamaica gradually declined, and its yearly amount of agricultural produce has lessened in a still more rapid ratio. In 1807, it exported more than one hundred and twenty thousand hogsheads of sugar; in 1834, less than seventy-eight thousand; and the returns for intervening years, shew that the falling off is not accidental, but the result of permanent causes, gradual, yet certain in their operation. Such a state of things tended not to prosperity, but to ruin. Were the results, therefore, of change, more doubtful than they are, and were economical interests solely involved in the question, it would be sound policy to substitute freedom for slavery. Experience has shewn, that the negros will follow those employments by which they can realise money for the purchase of articles, which cannot be grown or manufactured by their own hands. Under present circumstances they can earn most money by cultivating ground provisions for sale in the markets; yet the immediate pecuniary reward, obtained by working for wages, is frequently preferred to the larger yet deferred profits, which would result from the cultivation of their grounds. In a state of freedom, it may be anticipated, that the condition and resources of an agricultural laborer, working for regular wages, will be, as they are in England, superior to those of the petty agriculturist, cultivating his little plot of land with the labor of his own hands; and it is evident, therefore, that the negros will generally prefer working on the estates. Their strong attachment to the place of their birth, to their houses, gardens, to the graves of their parents and kindred, exceeding what has been recorded of any other people, is another circumstance, which favors their continuance as laborers, on the estates to which they are now respectively attached.

From such general considerations, we are led to infer, that the cultivation of the present staples of the island will be continued. No planter who has treated his apprentices kindly, and has habitually employed them for wages in their own time, entertains a doubt, that he will be able to carry on the cultivation of his estate by free labor. Such, it may be confidently anticipated, will be benefited, rather than injured by Emancipation. Those, however, who have pursued a contrary course, will suffer a deserved retribution. It cannot be anticipated, that every individual laborer should continue in his present employment; and it needs no extraordinary foresight to point out the parties who will sustain the loss, resulting from the diminution of laborers. That diminution may be expected to be occasioned chiefly by the gradual, voluntary withdrawal of women from regular field labor, to domestic duties; a change, not more essential to the happiness and improvement of the negros, than to the future, permanent, advancing prosperity of the whole community.

To such views as these, is opposed the fear that the negros will be tempted, by the abundance and fertility of the waste lands, to become small settlers, and independent cultivators. We do not think such an alarm reasonable, and we deprecate any attempt to evade the difficulty, by lessening the free agency of the laboring population. It would be possible to deprive freedom of its substance and value, by restrictive laws, devised with subtlety, and executed with violence. It would be possible to reduce the negros to a hybrid condition in the social scale, which should possess neither the efficiency of slavery, nor the energy of freedom: to erect a new state of society in the room of the present, possessing, like the image of mingled iron and clay, neither tenacity nor strength, but wanting every element of durability and safety. But the die is cast upon freedom: nothing less than unfettered freedom can save the colonies; freedom, protected, not circumscribed, by new laws. In a country of mountain fastnesses, the negros can only be prevented from *squatting* on the crown lands, by being suffered to acquire them honestly by purchase. They will not occupy them to a greater extent, than the demand for agricultural produce for the island markets, will enable them to do with pecuniary profit. Mutual competition will speedily abate the desire for independent cultivation. Throwing open the ports to Haytian produce, would also tend, by a legitimate mode, to attach the people to estate labor. The trade between these fine islands is still prohibited, though they are almost in sight of each other, and capable of carrying on commerce with immense mutual advantage. The Haytians would supply yams, plaintains, fruits, poultry, hogs, goats, cattle, mules, horses, hides and mahogany, in exchange for British manufactures. Such a measure would essentially promote both the commercial and agricultural prosperity of Jamaica; the price of labor would be lowered by the abundant supply of provisions, and the desire of the negros, for independent cultivation, were it even stronger than it is, would give place to the disposition to render cheerful and continuous labor, on the estates, for adequate wages.

We have heard the sentiment frequently expressed, that the negro population of Jamaica, is more unintelligent and degraded, than that of Antigua and Barbados. Comparative observation has left a contrary impression on our minds. There are undoubtedly, in Jamaica, a greater number of benighted negros, both Africans and Creoles; but there are also a larger proportion, who evince intelligence, energy and independence of spirit, similar to what are manifested by the peasantry of a free country. The cause of this difference need not be traced further, than the several modes in which the slaves have been subsisted in the colonies named. In Antigua they were formerly fed by rations; in Barbados they are still chiefly supported in the same way; but in Jamaica, they are dependent solely on their own exertions, in their own time, for the necessaries of life. Their children, their aged and infirm relations, look up to them for support; and though under present circumstances, the pressure of such claims, frequently occasions intense suffering, yet these wholesome cares and responsibilities, develope an intelligence of mind, a firmness and self-reliance, which are marked characteristics of many of the apprentices of Jamaica.

We are unable, within our allotted limits, even to attempt to render justice to missionary efforts in Jamaica. Representation cannot picture the happy results of those efforts; description can convey no idea of their excellence and magnitude. A few years ago, the negros were heathen and benighted, now they are to a great extent enlightened and christian. The Sabbath, once desecrated, is now devoted to public prayer and thanksgiving, and to the enjoyment of christian communion. A few years ago, education was unknown; now it is making progress under many disadvantages, and waits but for freedom, to become soon more generally diffused than in our own country. The success of missionary labors among the servile population, has been general and striking; much has been done, yet more remains to be done. The work requires to be deepened, strengthened, and extended; and we earnestly commend those benefactors of the human race, the missionaries, to the more earnest prayers, to the deeper sympathies, and to the yet more liberal support of British christians.

APPENDIX.

[A]

ANTIGUA.

SECTION I.—POPULATION.

		1787	1805	1817	1821	1832
Whites.	Male / Female	2590	3000		1140 / 840 } 1980	
Free Colored and blacks	Male / Female.	1230	1300		1549 / 2346 } 3895	
Slaves.	Male. / Female.	37808	36000	15053 / 17216 } 32269	14531 / 16533 } 31064	13992 / 15545 } 29537

The above table, compiled from the Antigua Almanac and official and parliamentary returns, exhibits a gradual decline in the Slave Population. About three-fifths of the decrease were occasioned by manumissions; leaving still a fearful waste of life to be carried to the account of sugar cultivation by *slave labor*.

The excess of females over males is a marked feature in the predial population of this and other colonies. The causes of the discrepancy are yet unexplained; as during the slave trade the importations were composed of a large excess of males. The fact seems to denote the existence of another element of social disorganization peculiar to slavery in sugar colonies.

As no general census has been taken in 1834 or subsequently, we are in want of the data necessary to exhibit the effect of the *Abolition* of Slavery, upon population; but it may undoubtedly be calculated, that the result of a statistical comparison would be favorable, as the Negros are confessedly more careful of their health, and far less frequently require medical aid, than during slavery.

A very intelligent and experienced resident, connected with many estates, writes to us on this subject as follows.—" The health and longevity of the laborers are likely to be improved and increased; because they need not submit to be overworked, nor, when recovering from illness, need they return too soon to their accustomed daily labor; both which evils existed under the old system, especially on those estates which were weak-handed. From these evils, with an insufficiently strengthening diet, sprang that early decrepitude, which often struck with surprise persons who knew the age of some who appeared old. I expect the population to increase from the foregoing causes, combined with the greater care that pregnant women will take of themselves; for it is notorious that, under the old system, such women, when exempt from working for their owners, would, for themselves and their connections, stagger to town under such loads of wood, grass, fruits, vegetables, &c. as scarcely even the rough means then used to enforce labor, could have induced them to carry for their owners, when in a state of perfect health."

SECTION II.

COMMERCE AND AGRICULTURE.—The gentleman above quoted, informs us "that the amount of imports of dry goods (articles for clothing and domestic economy) has increased; so also has the import of rice, flour, mackarel and dried codfish. Other fish, as pickled herrings and alewives, are not in the former demand; nor is indian corn, nor in my opinion, from which others differ, is corn meal."

From the preceding, and from much other testimony to the same effect, we learn that there has been a general increase of import trade; and that the character of it is considerably changed; the coarser articles of food and clothing, formerly distributed to the slaves, being displaced by superior qualities of grain and fish, and cloths of a finer and costlier fabrication

The only articles produced for export in Antigua are sugar, rum, molasses and arrowroot, of the last, of which the quantity is inconsiderable, and is chiefly grown and prepared by the negros on their own separate account. The yearly average export of sugar, for ten years preceding emancipation, was thirteen thousand four hundred hogsheads, of about fifteen hundred pounds net each. The exports, for the seasons of 1834—5 and 1835—6, have been about fourteen thousand and ten thousand hogsheads respectively. A still greater reduction, it is to be feared, has taken place in the produce of the season of 1836-7. From this circumstance, occasioned by a drought, of great severity and of eighteen months duration,* the planters have not derived all those benefits which might have been expected to result from emancipation in a period of agricultural prosperity. This severe visitation has, however, pressed far less heavily upon them than if it had occurred before 1834. During

---

* In Antigua the yellow or Bourbon Cane is exclusively cultivated. In the parish of Vere, and other parts of Jamaica, which are subject to uncertainty of climate, this variety has been displaced by the Violet Cane, which sustains drought better, rattoons for a greater number of years, produces much more leaves for fodder and manure, and stalk or magass for fuel, and is generally a more vigorous and hardy plant. The sugar made from it is little inferior, in quantity or quality, to that of the Bourbon Cane.

slavery, a general failure both of the crops of sugar and provisions, in successive seasons, occurring, as this has done, simultaneously with the scarcity and excessive prices of those imported supplies from British America on which the island depends, would have given the final blow to the embarrassed fortunes of a majority of the planters. This will appear more evident from the fact that supplies of meal and fish, when purchased at a credit of a few months only were charged by the merchants at an advance of one-third upon the cash price.

From the statements we have already given of the opinions of practical planters it appears, that the cultivation of the greater number of estates is carried on at a less expense than during slavery. We are not disposed to insist too strongly upon the saving which has thus been effected; because several of those estates have yielded the largest revenue since 1834, on which there has been a judicious *increase* of expenditure, and also because a statement of comparative outlay, even if it could be obtained for the whole island, would afford too narrow a basis, on which to form a judgment of the respective merits, in an economical point of view, of *free* and *slave* labor. The following statements therefore, selected from a number kindly put into our hands by several planters and managers, are subjoined rather as illustrations than as proofs in addition to what has already been advanced on this subject. The amounts are given in currency.

COMPARATIVE VIEW OF THE EXPENSES ON ——— ESTATE.

Expenses from 1st. *January, to* 31st *December,* 1833.

	£	s.	d.
Nourishment, &c. for sick	18	14	10
57 Barrels of Herrings	155	9	6
40 Puncheons and 92 barrels of Meal and Flour	771	7	0
*139439 lbs. of Yams, at 7s. per 100 lbs.	488	0	8
*14880 lbs. of Sweet Potatoes, at 7s per do	52	1	7
4 Hogsheads of Codfish	44	7	6
Wine, &c. for the sick	2	10	0
9 Barrels of Pork for christmas	81	0	0
10 Ditto of Flour ditto	45	0	0
Cotton for Nurses	1	19	0
Osnaburghs and Blankets	95	14	10½
Caps	30	0	0
Paid to women for bringing out children	2	12	0
To Parish Taxes on 321 Slaves	44	2	9
To deficiency Tax on ditto	80	0	0
To Medical care of ditto	136	4	0
	£2049	3	8½

* These are grown on the plantation, and are charged at the market price.

APPENDIX.

Expenses from 1st. January, to 31st. December, 1836.

	£	s.	d.
To Clothing for old people	8	9	10½
Blankets for ditto	7	16	0
Disbursements for Sick	0	17	6
8 Puncheons of Meal, allowance for old people and Stock Keepers	87	19	6
14 Barrels of Shads for ditto	30	5	9
Hire of Agricultural Laborers	1250	9	3½
Medical care of ditto	70	0	0
Balance in favour of free labor	593	6	8½
	£2049	3	8½

It may be doubted whether the parish and deficiency taxes should be introduced as above; since the revenue derived from them is made up from other sources, while the maintenance of worn out slaves, charged on the other side of the account, does not properly form a part of the cost of the free system.

COMPARATIVE VIEW OF THE EXPENSES ON ——— ESTATE.

ONE YEAR OF SLAVERY.

	£	s.	d.
70 Puncheons of Meal	819	0	0
52 Barrels of Herrings	163	16	0
4½ Ditto of Pork at christmas	40	10	0
5 Ditto Flour ditto	22	10	0
910 Yards Osnaburgh	56	17	6
529 Ditto Blue napped clothing	92	11	6
8 Dozen Kilmarnock Caps	9	12	0
50 Yards White Flannel	5	0	0
75 lbs of Fresh Beef	5	12	6
Medical care of 108 Slaves, at 9s. per head	47	12	0
Extra labor of Coopers	98	0	10½
	£1361	2	4½

ONE YEAR OF FREEDOM.

	£	s.	d.
Paid Laborers from 1st. Jan. to 10th Dec. 1836	777	15	7½
Computed for the two remaining weeks	29	18	3
Medical attendance on laborers	28	16	0
Support of three annuitants	17	11	0
Clothing for ditto	3	11	3
Balance in favour of free labor	503	10	3
	£1361	2	4½

In addition to which the manager observes, that out of the one hundred and eight slaves supported on the estate, twenty two were the property of another party, who received hire for them; which is not charged in the above account. The one hundred and eight were distributed as follows:—

  1 Ranger.
  2 Foremen.
 10 Tradesmen. (coopers, carpenters, masons, &c.)
  6 Picking grass for horses.
  6 Caring cattle, mules, &c.
 41 Field laborers.
 13 Infirm people able to work a little; and some of whom since emancipation are employed.
  6 House servants
  8 Superannuated.
 15 Infants.

108

Our informant adds,—" Of the forty one field laborers, if the estate mustered one half in the field it was well—pregnant women, nursing mothers, runaway, lazy, sick, and attendants on lying in women, fully taking the other half or more.

"The estate makes equally as good crops with free labor, and with less trouble to myself. The work is also much more forward, although we have had a great deal of building. The cultivation of provisions is decreased, that of canes increased. I have been prevented, by the building, from putting another piece of land in canes.

What laborers we now have are all effective, and we do all that we can with the plough, having very little land that the plough cannot work.

"During slavery we had *three coopers*, who never did supply the estate with hogsheads. We used to hire others on the saturdays to make them at *four shillings* each. We purchased all our puncheons for molasses and rum ready made. We have now *two coopers* who make all the hogsheads and puncheons we want, at *two shillings* each."

SECTION III.

RELIGION, MORALS AND EDUCATION.—The Establishment has six parish churches, and five chapels of ease; which are attended *habitually* by about three thousand five hundred persons, of whom eight hundred are communicants.

The Wesleyan society has " seven principal stations; besides a great number of preaching places on the estates." It has upwards of three thousand members.

The United Brethren have a chapel at each of their five stations; which collectively are capable of accommodating two thousand seven hundred persons. The number of their members is, of adults about ten thousand three hundred, and of children about three thousand five hundred; the number of communicants about five thousand one hundred. They have nine missionaries; so that, besides supplying their regular congregations on the Sabbath, several ministers are at liberty to preach the gospel at the more distant estates. The insufficient accommodation afforded at their stations for so large a body of members tends to create among them habits of irregular attendance. This evil is partially counteracted by the pastoral oversight of the ministers, exercised in the manner already described.

We cannot express our own sentiments respecting the effect of emancipation upon the religious state of the people better than in the words of our excellent friend J. Morrish, one of the Moravian missionaries.

He says in a letter to us—" My opinion regarding the morals of the Negros since emancipation, compared with the two previous years, is, that there is as great an improvement as could reasonably be expected, in so short a time from a people emerged from a state so degrading; there is a greater desire to be married than formerly; and the husband and wife more generally reside together, which in many instances they could not do in slavery.

" There is a more general attendance on the means of grace than during slavery; and there is a manifest improvement in the morals of children."

There are several societies in the Island, to promote benevolent and religious objects. Of those more immediately connected with the negros, the Friendly Societies are the most important. There is one in connection with most of the Wesleyan and Moravian congregations; and with several of those in the Establishment. Their beneficial results have already been adverted to.

Temperance societies have also been formed in the town of St. John's, and on several estates by the Wesleyan missionaries; and have been very useful. Intemperance is not however the same overwhelming evil in this Island, as in the United Kingdom. There are few shops for the retail sale of spirits; the spirit dealer's licence being in the town of St. John's as high as £160 currency per annum, and £100 currency in any other part of the Island.

Pawnbrokers' shops are unknown in Antigua.

The ministers of the Established Church have under their care,

    1 day school in St. John's, attended by 200 boys.
    1 ditto   in   ditto   150 girls.
    1 ditto   in English Harbor   150 children.

And fifteen Infant Schools, situated on estates, or at the different parsonages, attended by about eleven hundred children.

Sunday Schools are kept in all the churches and chapels; and the adults have the privilege of attending school at noon and in the evening, on the estates where infant schools are held.

The above schools are chiefly supported by funds derived from the "Negro Conversion Society," and the "Ladies' Negro Education Society;" and from the Government through the Bishop of the diocese.

The United Brethren have schools at each of their five settlements, attended by about six hundred day scholars, and seven hundred sunday scholars.

They are in great need of pecuniary means to enable them to enlarge their present school-houses, and to erect new ones; as well as to pay the salaries of teachers. Five colored persons are at present employed by them in that capacity; but much of the labor of instruction falls upon the missionaries themselves. With one or two exceptions, their schools are not in the same efficient state as those of the Established Church, and Wesleyan society.

The state of the Wesleyan schools will appear from the following remarks kindly drawn up by Charles Thwaites for our use. Most of his observations are applicable to the schools of the Island generally.

"The schools in connection with the Wesleyan stations are as follows:—

Sunday Schools, 7 in number, attended by 1800 children.
Day ditto 18 ,, ,, 1365 ,,
Night ditto 24 ,, ,, 500 ,,

The total number under instruction is about two thousand five hundred; of whom about two thousand two hundred are children of slaves, liberated on the 1st of August, 1834.

No regular system of instruction is pursued in the sunday and night schools. The infant school system is *imperfectly* taught in the day schools

The children's capacities to learn are equal to those of any other class of people. They excel in reading, and the girls in needlework. They are deficient in writing and arithmetic.

"Adult schools have repeatedly been established; but, for want of regularity in the attendance of the scholars, have been given up. There are notwithstanding many adults learning to read in their spare time; some of whom are taught by their own children.

"The funds have never been sufficient to hire teachers of competent ability. Of those we have (twenty three in number) three are very capable; the rest are liberated slaves. Some of them receive four dollars per month, others three and a half, and some three dollars. This pay is much too small; and some of them suffer from pecuniary difficulties. They are pious and indefatigable in their duty, and love their work, which makes them engage in it at so reduced a sum. Many of them have also greatly improved themselves since they have been employed.

In most of the schools each child is required to pay three farthings sterling per week; and those taught writing and needlework three half pence per week.

"The schools have been supported chiefly by the 'Negro Education Society;' who have given an annual grant of £50 and sometimes £60, besides paying the rent of the Church Mission Society's premises in Willoughby Bay, for the use of the superintendent and Willoughby Bay school. The Ladies' Antislavery Societies at Chelmsford, Birmingham, Westbromwich, Clapham and Liverpool have also given considerable assistance in money and articles of reward. The regular funds are notwithstanding very inadequate; and a continual reliance on God is necessary, not only for the regular supply that it may be kept up, but also for the deficiencies; and it is a matter of gratitude that we can say hitherto He has helped us."

Besides the schools under the superintendence of the three religious bodies, there are several on particular estates supported by the proprietors or managers.

The want of a normal or model school is felt by all in the Island who take an interest in the subject of education. The rector of St. John's, previously to his recent visit to England, raised an amount by subscription sufficient to bring out a master and mistress to establish such a school for the training of teachers. On his arrival in London, he learned that the trustees of the Mico institution were about to appoint an agent to carry that object into effect. Their agent subsequently sailed; but his destination was suddenly changed from Antigua to Barbados, to the great disappointment of the friends of education in the former island.

SECTION IV.

LOCAL GOVERNMENT.—The constitution of the chartered colonies is so generally known, that it would be needless to refer to it but for its important bearing at the present crisis upon the welfare of the enfranchised negroes. The following remarks on Antigua will also illustrate the state of things in the other colonies.

The legislative and administrative departments of the local government, comprising about one hundred and sixty important officers of trust, are filled by the governor and forty eight colonists; of whom thirty six are landed proprietors, five engaged in mercantile pursuits, and the remaining seven members of the medical and legal professions.

The Council is composed of ten members appointed by the governor. All but one are proprietors. It possesses the same place in the legislature as the House of Lords.

The House of Assembly consists of twenty five members, of whom all but three are proprietors; they are chosen by twelve divisions of the island, of which ten send two members each; one, one member; and the town of St John's, four.

The Assembly is elected for seven years, and meets for the despatch of business once a month, or oftener, by adjournments. It is thus always in session; a circumstance which invests it with a power of imprisonment for an almost indefinite period; a power which has, on more than one occasion within memory, been exercised in the most arbitrary manner.

The elective franchise, in the absence of any specific law, was formerly regulated by an Act, which defines the extent of freehold necessary to qualify an individual for the exercise of *other* political privileges, to be the possession of ten acres of land, or a house of the yearly value of £20 currency. Under this Act, the number of electors in the country divisions' does not, in many instances, exceed two or three. By the nominal concession to the colored classes of their political rights, the electors of St. John's were increased to upwards of two hundred. The house, some time afterwards, by a *simple resolution* defined the qualification for the exercise of the franchise to be the possession of a freehold of ten acres of land, or a tenement of the yearly value of £50 currency, or of the dimensions of thirty by fifteen feet; the latter singular standard having apparently been adopted for the purpose of excluding a large class of substantial dwellings, and of including coach houses, and other similar buildings, which might be used by the wealthy to confer fictitious qualifications on their dependents.

After the election, following the adoption of this resolution, two of the four liberal members, chosen by the Metropolis, were unseated by a committee of the whole House, on the petition of their opponents; the committee not only acting on the resolution, but carrying it out still further by the most strained and partial interpretations. The aggrieved electors, adopted at a public meeting a series of resolutions strongly condemning these arbitrary proceedings. They likewise addressed a petition to the three branches of the local government, setting forth in forcible and perspicuous terms, the injurious consequences of the unconstitutional conduct of the Assembly. Finally they made their appeal to the Home Government.

The reply of Lord GLENELG to their memorial arrived during our stay in the Colony, and was to the following effect.—

'The redress of the grievances of which the petitioners complain, is beyond the power of His Majesty's executive government, and the petitioners are also advised to seek protection from encroachment "in the peaceful and temperate exercise of the right of petition, and of free public discussion."

The Colonial Secretary by *this counsel* displays a remarkable ignorance of the state of society in the smaller Colonies; by his decision he *charters* the unconstitutional assumption on the part of the Assembly of a power which belongs jointly to the three estates; he sanctions an invasion of the Royal Prerogative; and contributes to continue the Assembly what it has long virtually been—*a self-elected body*.

Such is the legislature of the Colony. The administration of the laws possesses counterpart features.

The Chief and Puisne justices of the Court of Common Pleas

are Planters, without any legal education. They are liable to be concerned in civil suits in their own persons, or in those of their creditors and debtors: On one or two occasions an embarrassed *chief justice* has been the *defendant* in actions for debt in this court.

The Court of Chancery consists of the Governor and the members of Council; many of whom being Planters are suspected, justly or otherwise, of being under the influence of a certain wealthy merchant and mortgagee resident in the Island.

These two Courts do *not* possess the confidence of all classes in the Colony.

The Court of King's Bench is composed of the Justices of the Peace, who are thirty three in number, and are appointed by the Governor with the approbation of the Council. Twenty of them however, are magistrates *ex officio*, viz. all the members of Council, Judges in the Court of Exchequer and Common Pleas, the Speaker and Crown Law Officers. Three are persons of color, all of whom owe their appointment to Sir EVAN MAC GREGOR, the late governor.

The justices also dispose of all petty offences at the Police Courts, and occasionally at their own houses. At St. John's, the offences of disorderly persons in the town population, form the bulk of these minor cases. At the country stations of Parham and English Harbour, nine-tenths of the cases decided come under certain Acts, which have been passed since the Abolition of Slavery, to enforce the observance, on the part of masters and servants, of their respective duties; as the Contract Act, Malicious Injuries to Property Act, General Hiring Act, &c. &c.

The administration of these important Acts, has strong features of resemblance to that of the English Game Laws, a few years since, by certain owners of game preserves.

The complaints against employers are very few, and they are generally dismissed by the Magistrates. Complaints against the laborers are numerous; they are rarely dismissed and are punished with a severity disproportionate to the offences. The penalties usually imposed are, however, far more lenient, when the Magistrates are highminded and wealthy proprietors, than when the presiding Justice is an individual not immediately connected with planting, but dependent on the Planters for professional income. We are happy to add, that there has been a considerable decrease of cases of this kind since the commencement of the new system; but it is doubtful whether these Police Courts will ever be equitable and efficient until an *independent* Magistracy is appointed. There are individuals in the Colony, who for moderate stipends would discharge the duties of Police Magistrates with vigour and impartiality.

From the preceding statement it is evident, that the Local Government of Antigua is an oligarchy composed of an exclusive class; whose private and personal interests are inseparably intertwined with their public duty. Their legislation is essentially of a vicious character; and their administration of the Laws still more partial and objectionable. Much of this evil tendency of the constitution might undoubtedly be counteracted by the powerful control of the Home Government; but unhappily that control has rarely been exercised honestly and firmly. The change, in recent years, in our Colonial system has been forced by a generous people upon an unwilling Government; which, while adopting in profession a humane and liberal policy, continues to retain in its service a host of functionaries who aid in obstructing all measures of reform. This grand defect runs through the whole series of Colonial appointments; but is most conspicuous in the selection of Governors; to whose want of capacity, indifference or virtual coalition with the Planters, the difficulties which the Colonial Office experiences in carrying out its policy, are chiefly to be attributed.

An old resident in Antigua thus expresses himself on this subject,—

"It has been the unhappy lot of this island to be ruled, for the last thirty six years, by such representatives of the King as were imbued with high tory notions of Government, and at the same this time, addicted to company and pleasure. The only exceptions to remark throughout that period, have been Mr. HUGH ELLIOT and Sir EVAN MAC GREGOR. The consequences of these appointments have been at all times oppressively felt by the inhabitants of the island; and, ever since measures began to be in progress for the "Abolition of Slavery, they have occasioned *not a little embarrassment to the Government itself.*"

The same general remark, with similar exceptions, applies to all the Colonies.

SECTION V.

LAWS OF ANTIGUA.—The Act for the Abolition of Slavery swept into oblivion an entire series of those disgraceful laws which disfigure the Statute Book of every slave community. The framing of new enactments, adapted to the changed circumstances of the colony, was commenced with great industry by the Colonial Parliament. New laws were fast multiplied; of which some appear to have been intended to obviate evils and inconveniences, the remedy for which is in the province of *time*, and not of legislation. But let it be observed that this legislative activity was exercised in a particular direction; and, consequently, several necessary reforms remain yet in abeyance. Among these are, the legal recognition of marriages, performed by Dissenting Ministers; an entire change of the judicial system; and a revision of the laws affecting property. These several and most necessary changes have been pressed upon the attention of the Colonial Legislature by Lord GLENELG; and it is probable, that Acts will ere long be passed in conformity with his views. We would only now emphatically observe, that all interested in the welfare of the Negro population

APPENDIX.

should immediately use their influence to obtain a Marriage Act, having a retrospective as well as prospective effect.

The Acts which have been passed, to meet the immediate exigencies, created by the entire change in the social and political condition of the Colony, demand a very serious examination; as they are so many precedents which will affect hereafter, the rights and interests of the enfranchised population of the other islands. We would make on these important laws the general remark—that they contain many clauses which press with undue severity on the working classes, and that the penalties they impose are usually excessive; evils which are not mitigated by the manner in which they are interpreted and administered. We will select, for more particular attention, and as an illustration of the one-sided character of Colonial Legislation, an Act which was passed immediately before our arrival in the Colony; and which received the Royal sanction by an Order in Council, dated April 26th, 1837. It is entitled "an Act for preventing a clandestine deportation of laborers, artificers, handicraftsmen and domestic servants from this island, and for establishing regulations concerning their departure from the same."

The preamble sets forth the evil practice of designing persons coming to Antigua, and, by delusive promises of great gain, inducing the laborers to enter into Indentures or Contracts to serve in other Colonies; and that it is much to be apprehended that the Laborers become victims to such mercenary speculations; and that they are frequently thus induced to emigrate when in debt or under contract in the island, or when they have infirm relatives, wives and children depending on them; and finally, that such practices are detrimental to *the interests and well-being of this island, as well as of the laborers themselves.*

The first clause enacts that every laborer, wishing to emigrate, shall before leaving his parish, state his intention to *one of the nearest Justices of the Peace,* who, joining himself with another Justice, shall inquire whether the person has any grandfather, or grandmother, father or mother, wife, or child under fourteen years of age, legitimate or illegitimate, dependent upon him for support, and who may become destitute on his departure. If the Justices find that the said laborer has no such kindred or claims upon him, and that he is not bound by any existing contract for service, they shall give him a certificate to that effect, which shall authorize the Island Secretary to set up his name in the Secretary's Office, as a person about to leave the Island. If, however, they find that the laborer has any such kindred, or claims upon him, and that he refuses to make *satisfactory* provision for their support during his absence, they shall refuse their certificate, and shall apprize the Island Secretary of the name of the person, an of the obstacles existing to his departure.

The third clause gives the laborer an appeal to the Governor and Council; who shall have power to overrule any intentional, improper, or unnecessary obstruction on the part of the Justices.

The fourth imposes a penalty of one hundred pounds, and six months imprisonment, on any master of a ship, or other individual, endeavouring to induce any laborer to emigrate without complying with the provisions of the Law.

The sixth requires the Island Secretary, after receiving the certificate of the Justices, to publish weekly, for thirty days, in one of the newspapers, the name of any laborer intending to emigrate, together with the name of his last employer and last place of residence.

This Act is intended to obviate a real and pressing evil; but the remedy here proposed is far worse than the disease. A different measure, of a simple and unobjectionable nature, is completely within the power of the Colonial Department; because Demerara and Trinidad, where alone labor is sufficiently dear to afford a premium on the speculations of the above mentioned " designing persons,"· are both Crown Colonies.

The Editor of the Antigua Herald and Gazette, in announcing that this Law has received the royal sanction, observes, " that it is reported to be considered *very efficacious,* and to be viewed by the country gentlemen as an Act likely to prove highly beneficial *to the Colony."* It appears to us, on the contrary, that the tendency of it is to convert the free agricultural peasantry of Antigua into *adscripti glebæ.* The landed proprietors have already combined as individuals, to enforce a low tariff of wages. By this Act they combine, as legislators, to exclude foreign competition, by placing insuperable obstacles in the way of their laborers carrying their industry to the best market. That a peasant desirous of emigrating, should be able to make, for the numerous relations specified in the Act, a provision *satisfactory* to one of the nearest Justices of the Peace, viz. his own employer, or one of his own employer's friends, is very unlikely. The duty of a laborer to support his parents and grand-parents, has never, we believe, before been enforced by legal penalties. He may be so circumstanced as scarcely to be able to earn necessary food and clothing for his wife and children; in which case, emigration, under a reasonable prospect of improving his condition, may become his interest and duty; even though he should leave behind him other near relations in a state of destitution. This Law however declares, that in such a case he shall remain, and witness their misery without being able to alleviate it.

The preamble speaks of the well-being of the island, as distinguished from that of the laborers, and this spirit is carried out through all its provisions, which press exclusively on the laboring classes; creating a permanent legal distinction and barrier between them and the other classes of society. It is impossible to be too jealous of laws like these—we cannot forget the condition, a few years since, of the Hottentots at the Cape; who, nominally free, were reduced by a single injurious ordinance to a state of villanage, which left them at the mercy of a ruthless taskmaster, without giving them any protection even in his self-interest,—a state which exposed them to the exactions of slavery without its slender indulgences, to its worst horrors, without any of its mitigations.

Upon our Colonial Government has devolved the superintendence of the most interesting political experiment, recorded in the history of our country, and what responsibility can be more sacred, than that of preventing the young liberties of a suddenly emancipated people from degenerating into license, and of protecting them on the other hand from the encroachments of superior power and intelligence? We would ask whether Government has discharged its high duties worthily, and in such a way as to secure that complete Emancipation for which the English people have so earnestly contended, and for which they have made so costly a sacrifice? Do not the laws, passed in this and other Colonies since the Imperial Act for the Abolition of Slavery, and *sanctioned* by Royal orders in Council, bear witness, that the Colonial Department is *not* at the present moment, filled with men to whom the sacred interests of negro liberty can be safely intrusted, without the exercise of increased vigilance on the part of the public? There is nothing in the situation of the Colonies, or in the character of their population, to warrant even temporary deviations from a sound, legitimate and equal legislation. The great principles of political economy are as applicable to them, at the present crisis, as they are to the mother country; and any wide departure from those principles, will not only inflict much present evil, but create serious difficulties for the future.

SECTION VI.

THE ABOLITION ACT.—The debates of the Assembly and Council, as reported in the Island newspapers during the sessions of 1833—4, and 5, cannot be said to exhibit the entire body of Antigua Legislators in the character of highminded and disinterested philanthropists. The passing of the Emancipation Act, was barely secured by the unwearied efforts of a small, but benevolent and enlightened, majority; to whom also is owing the defeat of subsequent measures, which would have virtually undone all that the Bill professed to effect. The first Act was rejected by the Home Government, in consequence of its containing a clause repealing the four and a half per cent duties. A second was introduced in a remodelled form; and ultimately carried by a *casting* vote. The Governor, Sir EVAN MAC GREGOR, took the warmest interest in the measure, and employed all his legitimate influence to effect its passing. He was undoubtedly the means, under Providence, of determining the nicely balanced scales of liberty and apprenticeship in favor of the former.

SECTION VII.

THE FOUR AND A HALF PER CENT DUTIES.—It is to be regretted

that the Home Government did not acknowledge the full surrender on the part of the Antigua Colonists, to the wishes of the parent country, by the desired cession of the 4½ per cent duties; a tax which cannot in any point of view be defended, and which is objectionable in its origin, mode of collection, and application. It is an impost from which Jamaica, Demerara and others of the more fertile Colonies, are exempt; and which presses unequally upon the older and comparatively exhausted islands. It originated in Barbados. That island, having been first granted to the Earl of CARLISLE, was, during the abeyance of his patent, in the parliamentary war, colonised by numerous bodies of refugees. At the Restoration, the respective claims of the actual possessors of the soil, and of the Earl of CARLISLE, were submitted to the arbitration of KING CHARLES II, who confirmed the titles of the occupants, on condition of their paying a duty in kind, of four and a half per cent on all exports, first to the creditors of Lord CARLISLE for a series of years, and afterwards to the Crown. Every means was industriously employed to extend this precedent to the other colonies. Antigua fell under the yoke in the following manner. In 1666 the island was surprised by a petty French force from Guadaloupe, which retained possession of it till the following year, when it was recaptured by the British. The 4½ per cent duty was made the condition of the Colonists receiving new grants of their estates, which they had forfeited by taking the oath of allegiance to the French Monarch. This duty became a fund, out of which successive sovereigns granted pensions to their favorites, until it was recently placed with the other Crown revenues, under the control of Parliament. The episcopal establishment for the West Indies is charged upon it, and the new judicial system is proposed to be provided for out of the same fund. This tax operates as a protecting duty in favor of the newest and most fertile soils; and it is, with manifest injustice, levied upon a few of the colonies to defray charges incident to the whole. It ought to be at least exchanged for a civil list, raised at the discretion of the local legislature; and appropriated to defray the charges of Government. Among other reasons for giving the claim of Antigua for the abolition of these duties a favorable consideration, it ought not to be forgotten, that the rejection of the Apprenticeship has saved the mother country about twelve thousand pounds sterling in the salaries of stipendiary Magistrates.

SECTION VIII.

WASTE LANDS.—There are several thousand acres, of which the title to possession appears to be indisputably vested in the Crown by the reconquest of this island. The statute book contains many Acts of appropriation of land, by the three estates jointly; a fact which can scarcely be held to impair the original, sole right of the Crown; as Colonial Bills are enacted in the form of petition. The sale of these lands from time to time, in small parcels, would probably have a more powerful tendency than any other measure in the power of the Home Government, to elevate the emancipated population in character and condition. The monopoly of land, which at present exists in the hands of large proprietors is injurious to every interest in the island.

[B]

DOMINICA.

SECTION I.

A TABLE, SHEWING THE INCREASE AND DECREASE OF SLAVES ON THREE ESTATES OF RESIDENT PROPRIETORS, AND ON THREE OTHERS OF NON-RESIDENT PROPRIETORS, FROM 1817 TO 1834.

N. B.—*The increase, from other causes than Births, means by purchase, inheritance, &c.; and the decrease from other causes than Deaths, means by sale, bequests, &c.*

PROPRIETORS—RESIDENT.

Morne Rouge Estate, St. Mark's, producing Sugar and Coffee.

1817	No. of Slaves		69
1817	Increase by births	42	
	Decrease by deaths	21	
to	Difference	—	21
	Increase from other causes	27	
1834	Decrease ditto	20	
	Difference	—	7
1834	No. of Slaves		97

Bête Rouge and Coulibri, St. Mark's, producing Coffee.

1817	No. of Slaves		64
1817	Increase by births	36	
	Decrease by deaths	21	
to	Difference	—	15
	Increase from other causes	16	
1834	Decrease ditto	9	
	Difference	—	7
1834	No. of Slaves		86

APPENDIX.

Pointe Mulâtre Estate, St. Patrick's, producing Sugar.

1817 No. of Slaves		175
Increase by births	89	
1817 Decrease by deaths	53	
Difference	—	36
to		211
Increase from other causes	1	
1834 Decrease ditto	6	
Difference	—	5
1834 No. of Slaves		206

PROPRIETORS—NON-RESIDENT.

Good-will Estate, St. George's, producing Sugar.

1817 No. of Slaves		200
Increase from other causes	78	
1817 Decrease ditto	19	
Add difference	—	59
to		259
Decrease by deaths	142!	
1834 Increase by births	63*	
Deduct difference	——	79
1834 No. of Slaves		180

Canefield Estate, St. Paul's, producing Sugar.

1817 No. of Slaves		163
Increase from other causes	61	
1817 Decrease ditto	9	
Add difference	—	52
to		215
Decrease by deaths	145!	
1834 Increase by births	41*	
Deduct difference		104
1834 No. of Slaves		111

Castle Bruce Estate, St. David's, producing Sugar.

1817 No. of Slaves		281
Increase from other causes	57	
1817 Decrease ditto	3	
Add difference	—	54
to		335
Decrease by deaths	224!	
1834 Increase by births	51*	
Deduct difference	——	173
1834 No. of Slaves		162

* The reader will not fail to observe the fewness of the births as well as the fearful number of deaths on these estates.

SECTION II.

Local Government.—The administration of the laws is of the same character as in Antigua, and in the same urgent need of reform.

The strong hold of abuses in the Local Government, is in those departments, both legislative and executive, which are filled by the appointment of the Colonial Office. The representative branch is not liberal, but in future elections it may be expected to become so, as the colored class are numerous and influential, and the members whom they return have been hitherto the consistent supporters of measures of improvement. Nothing can be said in praise of the Legislative Council, which is nominated by the Crown; and it would be difficult to reprobate too strongly the appointment or retention, in the most responsible offices, of men who perpetuate the worst Colonial abuses. The present Attorney General is a conspicuous example of the persons, who are distinguished by the confidence of the Home Government. It will be remembered by some of our readers, that a statement was made public in England, in the early part of 1835, that two female apprenticed labourers had been punished by flogging, in the market place of Roseau; and that a free colored man, convicted of an assault, had been worked in the chain gang amongst felons, and left to depend, during a long imprisonment, upon the charity of his fellow prisoners for food. This report excited public indignation in England, which caused the House of Assembly to investigate the matter in a Committee of the whole House, in the hope, doubtless, of falsifying or explaining away the statements which had been made. From their printed report we extract the following:—" The result of this investigation, in respect to those points to which the inquiry was directed, establishes in the opinion of the Committee, the following facts:—First, that two female apprenticed labourers, named Dongouse, and Mary Clarke, were severally indicted, &c.—and were sentenced by the Court, to receive, the former, thirty nine, and the latter, thirty stripes in the public market place;—that the punishment was inflicted on them, *without any improper exposure of their persons*, and without any further exposure, than was necessary to carry the sentences into execution.

" The Committee have not thought it incumbent on them to enter into any examination of the legality of the sentences pronounced; they have thought it sufficient, that those sentences proceeded from the highest Criminal Court, and were sanctioned by the legal opinion of the *first law officer of the Crown*, in this Colony." The examination of the witnesses is appended to this report. The following are two of the questions proposed to the Attorney General and his replies.

"Were you called upon by the Court to give your opinion as to the legality of awarding punishment by whipping, in the cases of DONGOUSE and MARY CLARKE?"

"I do not recollect that I was called upon to give my opinion, but I did give my opinion, that the punishment of females by whipping, was, *legal.—I pointed out to the Court, that that mode of punishment was still in their power, and that the cases of the two parties warranted its exercise.*"

"Upon what Law do you ground your opinion that women may be flogged in this Colony for certain offences?"

"*Upon the Law of England.*"

The Provost Marshal was asked,

"When were the sentences put in execution? and on what day?"

"In the market place, on the 7th of February, between twelve and one o'clock."

"Was it on the market day, and was the market full of people, men and women?"

"It was on a market day, and there were a great many people, men and women, as is usual on those days.

The Attorney General, who thus deliberately avows, that these female apprentices were publicly flogged, on his unsolicited recommendation to the Court, is still, through his own talents, and the favor of the Government, the most influential person in the Colony.

From the investigation into the other case of the free man of color, it appears that it is not the custom in Dominica for *free* criminals to receive any food; and that this prisoner was actually dependent on casual charity, and on the pity of the apprentices in the chain gang. One of the town wardens, on being asked, in reference to this case, "Why do you consider the punishment by the chain gang not a severe punishment?" replies, "In the first instance, I consider the chain is put about them as *a badge of shame*, to which, in my opinion, the generality of them are perfect strangers, &c." he adds, "I have latterly observed, that the chain is so *folded up, or covered,* that you cannot discern whether it is a chain or not!" This is a striking illustration of the unconscious simplicity with which a thorough-paced advocate of colonial oppressions, will sometimes supply facts in refutation of his opinions. It would, indeed, not be surprising if the sense of shame were obliterated by slavery; but it is a fact, that many of the females manifest as deep a feeling of the degradations to which they are subjected, as could be shown under the same circumstances, by the wives and daughters of more happy England.

SECTION III.

THE LATE GOVERNOR.—We have had occasion in the preceding pages, to speak in terms of praise of Sir EVAN MAC GREGOR, and it is our grateful task to record here, that those in Dominica interested in the welfare of the apprentices, attribute the accomplishment of some good, and the prevention of much mischief, to his brief residence among them as Governor. In his farewell address to the Legislature, on his departure to assume the Government of the Windward Islands, he recommended the Abolition of the Apprenticeship in 1838. We would gladly write nothing but eulogy of the author of so benevolent a proposition, but a sense of what is due to impartiality, compels us to notice two acts which disfigure his administration. First, an attempt to introduce *compulsory* taskwork, in imitation of Sir LIONEL SMITH, and in opposition to an express enactment of the Apprenticeship Law. Secondly, his decisions, on a number of charges preferred by JOSEPH FADELLE against certain individuals, high in office, in Dominica. We have before us a pamphlet, which may be considered to contain an *ex parte* view of this subject in favor of Sir EVAN MAC GREGOR. Since it consists entirely of his own statement of the several charges, his references to the evidence, his citations and interpretations of the Laws, his decisions on the separate charges, and his concluding "general remarks." A careful perusal of it has brought us to the conclusion, that his interpretations of the Abolition Law are destructive of the spirit and intention of the English Act, and that his decisions and "Remarks" display a strong bias in favor of the accused parties. Sir EVAN thus speaks in his "General Remarks" of the success likely to attend efforts to protect the apprentices by the exposure of the oppressions to which they are subjected. "Unless through the kindness and favor of their masters, whom they ought rather to be encouraged to propitiate by submission, than goaded to exasperate, by impotent resistance, the apprenticed laborers may look in vain, for an amelioration of their lot." This striking passage explains what is the actual condition, in law and fact, of the apprenticed laborers. They have no rights, which they can effectually maintain in opposition to the despotic will of their owners. The Abolition Law so far from being largely interpreted in their favor, as an Act intended for their benefit, and on the theory, that subject to certain well defined restrictions, they are *free* men, is interpreted largely in favor of their masters, and on the theory that with certain ill-defined immunities, they are still *slaves*.

SECTION IV.

COMPARATIVE CONDITION OF THE APPRENTICES.—It appears evident that the negros in this Colony have gained nothing by the exchange of Slavery for Apprenticeship. It is the general belief of many residents and eyewitnesses, that their yoke during the earlier part of the new era was even heavier than before. Some good subsequently was effected by the favorable influence of Sir EVAN MAC GREGOR; and more recently some of the Planters, including one gentleman who is Attorney for the majority of the estates of the absentee proprietors, have themselves pursued a more indulgent course. With all these alleviations, we believe the negros to have gained nothing by the twenty millions but the hope of freedom in 1840.

In many instances they are deprived of the old slave allowances of salt fish and meal, &c. Their children are neglected, and mothers are compelled to repay the time lost in attendance on them when sick. Pregnant women are sometimes kept at labor in the field nearly to the day of their delivery. The people are often kept at work in the field in heavy rain, at the risk of their health. The power of imprisonment in the estates' *cachots*, conferred by the Local Act, as a security against the escape of offenders is frequently employed by the Managers as a *punishment;* and lastly, they have no protection against ill-treatment from persons who are not their employers. The Special Magistrate has not power to summons before him, on the complaint of an Apprentice, any person of free condition, other than the person entitled to the services of the Apprentice. He has power, however, to punish an Apprentice on the complaint of any person whatever. An Apprentice, therefore, in case he is ill treated by any free person, other than his master, must resort to the General Justices of the Peace, or to the Supreme Courts of the Island. We have before us thirteen examples of the practical value of this privilege, in a list of as many cases of Apprentices, assaulted by free persons, not their owners, within the short space of one month, who, after making many applications, could get no Justice of the Peace to entertain their complaints.

APPENDIX.

[C]

MARTINIQUE.

Copies of the Petitions of the Colored Proprietors of Martinique, for the immediate Abolition of Slavery.

No. 1.

Abolition de l'Esclavage. Les Hommes de Couleur de la Martinique aux deux Chambres.—Les cris de liberté qui se sont fait entendre dans les îles voisines sous la domination Brittanique en faveur d'une classe si nombreuse de notre population, ont retenti dans nos Cœurs.

Nous savons par expérience que les garanties promises par les lois et les ordonnances de la Métropole, sont inefficaces dans la pratique, et qu'il n'ya pour ceux auxquels le législateur a dénié l'immense bienfait de la liberté, aucune compensation, aucune moyen de faire respecter en eux les droits de l'humanité. Malgré l'etat de dégradation où la servitude les a placés, le sentiment de la liberté vit impérissable au fond de leurs cœurs et met aujourdhui plus que jamais en péril la sécurité des biens et des personnes libres.

Nous croyons qu'il est impossible de retarder plus long temps sans de graves dangers l'entierè abolition de l'esclavage.

Nous sommes prêts comme propriétaires à faire tous les sacrifices que la Métropole voudra nous imposer à cet égard, et à concourir avec les gislateurs à l'émancipation morale autant que physique de la population au milieu de laquelle nous sommes placés.

Que des lois généreuses et sages fixent les principes de cette régénération. Quelles se confient à notre fidélité, à notre amour pour la Métropole et la réussite en est assurée.

Quand les esclaves sáuront que nous n'avons pas mis obstacle a ce que leurs cháines soient brisées, ils croiront à nos paroles, et ne refuséront pas les travaux dont nous leur donnerons l'exemple.

No. 2.

Saint Pierre, 25th Novembre, 1836.
Pétition dernierè, aux deux chambres.

M.

Nous venons rendre hommages aux nobles sentimens qui animent les chambres et le Gouvernement envers la classe la plus malheureuse, la plus nombreuse de nos Colonies.

Les promesses solemnelles de S. E. le Ministre de la Marine et des Colonies à la Chambre des Deputés dans sa séance du 25 Mai dernier, nous ont pénétré de la plus vive reconnaissance ; nous voyons avec le plus profond intérêt que le Gouvernement est déterminé a faire cesser l'esclavage, en ce qu'elle est contraire au principe fondamental de toutes les Sociétés, et n'etant utile ni au maitre ni a l'esclave. Nous applaudissons à sa généreuse résolution ; nous y concourirons autant qu'il sera en nous, nous soumettant a tous les sacrifices qui pourront nous être imposés.

Quand il n'y aura plus d'esclaves aux Colonies, il ne sera plus nécéssaire d'y envoyer ces fortes garnisons transportées à grands frais pour maintenir la soumission des ateliers, l'autorité et la sécurité précaires des màitres. Devenus soldats et Citoyens, les affranchis seront intéressés au maintien de l'ordre public et à dèfendre le pays qui les a vus nàitre.

Enfans du sol, ils n'auront pas à redouter les effets d'un climat destructeux qui enlève chaque année de nombreux defenseurs à la merè patrie !

Ainsi l'emancipation des esclaves sera un acte d'humanité, de justice et de bonne politique ; nous l'appelons de tous nos vœux, réprouvant à l'avance toutes résolutions opposées. Avec elle, renaitront la sécurité, l'ordre et la tranquillité ; avec elle, le travail libre et salarié remplacera le travail forcé et humiliant qui démoralize, et le màitre et l'esclave ; par elle se formeront des liens de famille incompatibles avec l'etat d'esclavage quel quil soit !

Mais en promettant notre concours au Gouvernement, nous émettons aussi le vœu qu'il adopte des mesures tendantes à accroitre l'industrie coloniale et qu'il lui accorde la liberté commerciale, au moins pour les objets les plus nécéssaires à la vie des habitans de toutes les classes.

Nous avons l'honneur d'etre, &c. &c. &c.

APPENDIX.

[D]

BARBUDA.

Of the three seamen in our little Schooner who were Barbadians, two were exiles from their homes, and the third was a colored boy, the son of the late Superintendent of the Island, who is menitoned by Sir BETHEL CODRINGTON in his public correspondence on Slavery with T. F. BUXTON. Many of our readers will remember, that Barbuda is the private property of Sir BETHEL, and that the happy condition of its inhabitants was brought prominently forward by him, in the correspondence referred to. The boy, above mentioned, is left without any education, to earn his bread as a cabin boy in a small coasting schooner, a life of all others, distinguished by hardship and privation. Before Emancipation, there were five hundred slaves in Barbuda; none would have quitted it voluntarily as they are attached to their native soil, to their fertile gardens, and varied employments of agriculture, hunting, fishing, piloting and diving. At the present moment, however. upwards of a hundred of them are in banishment in Antigua. The will of the Superintendent is law, and for every real or supposed offence they are liable to be ordered off the Island. Our Captain, who is employed by the Superintendent, and has evidently no sympathies for the negros, told us, that on one occasion since they became free, when their labor was not wanted, in consequence of a dry season, the people were all dismissed but thirty, and that they were pardoned and permitted to return as soon as seasonable weather set in! They receive wages from the Superintendent, but as he is the sole shopkeeper, much of the money circulates back again into his till.

During our stay in Antigua, we had several opportunities of conversing with persons acquainted with the state of Barbuda. It was originally granted to the ancestor of its present proprietor for ninety nine years, and at the expiration of this period was regranted by GEORGE IV, for a term of fifty years, on the condition that the grantee should present the Governor of Antigua annually with a fat wether sheep. The Island is nearly as large as Antigua, and very fertile. The cultivation of the cane is not permitted by the terms of the tenure, but a large revenue is derived from its timber, corn, cattle, sheep and deer. The salvage of wrecks is another productive source of income, as the island is low and nearly surrounded by a coral reef, running out for miles into the sea. A daily look out is kept, and the negros are very active in rendering assistance to wrecked vessels, being familiar with the intricate navigation, and very expert in the use of boats, and in swimming and diving. During slavery, Barbuda was also a nursery for slaves, to supply the waste on the Codrington estates in Antigua, from whence a few families, the ancestors of its present numerous population, were originally brought. They are the most robust islanders in these seas, and distinguished by the primitive simplicity of their character. Heinous crimes are unknown among them. They have no Laws, and the sole authority is the Superintendent, who holds the commission of a Justice of the Peace from the Governor of Antigua. They have no resident religious instructor. Several years ago, the Wesleyan missionaries of Antigua, paid occasional visits to the Island, until they were prohibited, and their congregation violently dispersed by the late Superintendent. The Bishop of Barbados, soon after his arrival, appointed a resident catechist who staid a short time and was followed by several others in succession. We met the last of these in Dominica, an energetic young man, who, like his predecessors, had been compelled to relinquish his charge by disagreements with the Superintendent. Most of the people, both old and young, are able to read, and a few to write. Many are married, but concubinage, one of the many evils resulting from the absence of a resident minister, prevails to a great extent. The island has no resident medical man, until recently one of the emancipated slaves, an intelligent colored man, acted in this capacity, but he has lately left it to seek a more extended sphere for the exercise of his skill.

Barbuda is within the legislative power of the Government of Antigua—but the parliament of that island has always refused to undertake the responsibility of legislating for it. Their neglect, at the time they abolished slavery in their own island, to enact the apprenticeship in this, is said to have induced the proprietor to adopt the graceful alternative of emancipating the slaves by a deed under his own hand. It is reported that an individual of known liberal sentiments has recently been appointed, and is expected shortly from England, to take the office of Superintendent. Should this happily be the case, we trust that this little despotism will be administered with more regard, than it has hitherto been, to the temporal and spiritual interests of its inhabitants.

APPENDIX.

[E]

BARBADOS.

SECTION I.

PAUPER POPULATION.—There is a class of several thousand poor *whites* in Barbados, known by the name of "red shanks;" many of whom are dependent on parochial and casual relief, and even on the charity of the apprentices. The competition of the colored people has driven them out of almost every field where free laborers were wont to exercise their skill and industry. From their idle and dissolute habits they are more degraded than the negros, but are proud of their caste as whites. There are only a few individuals of the colored class receiving parochial relief.

SECTION II.

STIPENDIARY ADMINISTRATION OF THE ABOLITION LAW.—The following is an analysis of the record of complaints and decisions made in one month in a single district. The document from which it is extracted was taken up at random, and was subsequently ascertained to be in no respect distinguished from the journals of several of the other Magistrates, either in number of cases or nature and severity of punishments.

BARBADOS—District D. December, 1836.

I.—Complaint of apprentice against employer, in which the latter was fined £5 currency for flogging complainant. Two hundred and twenty-six complaints of employers against apprentices. The sum total of the penalties inflicted on the apprentices is;—

Imprisonment and hard labor	,,	,,	697 days.
Ditto ditto on the Treadmill,			180 ,,
Solitary confinement	,,	,,	127 ,,
Saturdays forfeited to the estates	,,	,,	517 ,,

In addition to which the apprentices must repay to the estates, pursuant to a clause in the Local Act, upwards of seven hundred of their Saturdays, being the amount of working days lost by them, when at hard labor, in solitary confinement, or on the tread mill. The total is more than two thousand two hundred days in which two hundred and twenty-six negros were mulcted in one district in a single month. The character of the Law under which these punishments take place will appear in its true colors when it is considered that there are seven districts in the island and that the apprenticeship extends over a period of six years.

APPENDIX. xxvii.

The following cases, from various Journals of the Stipendiary Magistrates of the date of December, 1836, are a fair specimen of the offences, which are considered to require magisterial interference. They need no comment.*

COMPLAINANT.	DEFENDANT.	COMPLAINT.	DECISION.
G. R. Doyle, vs.	Eight males, fifteen females.	Indolent performance of labor.	To perform three days extra labor.
Jane vs.	Rachel Clark.	Not supplying complainant with provisions for seven days.	To pay double value amounting to 6s. 3d. currency.
Thomas Francis, vs.	Tom Cullen.	Harboring an apprentice. Defendant states that the apprentice was his wife.	Sentenced to pay £6 5s. or to receive twenty-four stripes on the 1st. January.
Rebecca Story, vs.	Mary Eliza.	Defendant has been a runaway for the last six weeks. Defendant acknowledges the complaint, and says it was in consequence of not being able to get any thing to eat.	Thirty days hard labor.
Miss N. Seals, vs.	Sarah Francis.	Inattention to work, and disobedience of orders. Defendant acknowledges complaint, but says complainant ordered her to throw her child on the wharf.	Ten days hard labor.

* It will readily be conceived that under such an administration of the law the apprentices must often have cause to appeal to the Governor. It is therefore with great regret we learn, that Sir EVAN MAC GREGOR has made an arrangement by which they are precluded from appealing to him unless they are furnished with a ticket from their stipendiary magistrate, the very individual against whose decision the appeal is made. Their right of appeal is thus virtually taken away.

xxviii.   APPENDIX.

COMPLAINANT.	DEFENDANT.	COMPLAINT.	DECISION.
Mary Frances, vs.	Mrs. R. Tapshan.	"I am apprentice to the defendant who hires me out to Mrs. GALLOP and takes all my wages; she has not given me any clothes for the present year, and also refuses to give me lodging." Defendant says complainant is hired out with an agreement to pay her* five bits a week (2s.) and receive two for herself (9½d.) for food and clothes, and that the complainant owes her at this moment 1¾ dollars for wages.	Defendant to remit the 1¾ dollars and pay 11s. (9s. 6d. sterling) besides, in lieu of clothes.
Blossom, vs.	William Adamson.	For not providing wholesome lodging.	*Complainant* ordered to solitary confinement for three days.
John Myers, vs.	Seven pregnant females.	Indolent performance of duty.	Three days solitary confinement. Medical certificate said they could do some work.
Wm. A. Moore, vs.	Nine predial apprentices (five women and four men.)	Idleness.	The men to work one Saturday each, the women two.
E. L. Hinds, vs.	Five apprentices.	Idleness in resorting to the Hospital under pretence of sickness. Certificate of medical man produced to that effect.	To work four Saturdays each.

* In this case it will be observed that a poor woman earning less than three shillings a week, pays two shillings to her mistress, who requires her to find herself *in food and clothes* besides.

APPENDIX. xxix.

COMPLAINT.	DEFENDANT.	COMPLAINT.	DECISION.
J. T. Hutchinson, vs.	Matty.	Disobedience of the superintendent's (driver's) orders and telling her he lied.	Seven days confinement and hard labor.
R. N. Smith, vs.	Eight women.	Idleness and bad work.	Two sentenced as above, six to forfeit three Saturdays.
A. Toderingham, vs.	Charles King.	Absence from his duty six hours.	To work two Saturdays
R. W. Harding, vs.	Eighteen apprentices, four males and fourteen females.	The Manager being sworn, convicts the prisoners by deposing that their general conduct is exceedingly idle and that chiding them for their improper conduct avails nothing.	All to work three Saturdays.
On the following day the same manager apparently well satisfied with having obtained fifty-four days from the negros summons twenty-eight men, viz.	Twenty-four women and four men.	Witnesses complainant, WILLIAM DANIEL, Superintendent (driver) and Jemmy, first row man "convict prisoners by deposing that their general conduct is exceedingly idle, but was especially so on the 12th inst. and this morning, although threatened yesterday to be complained of to-day; and that there appears to be a combination amongst the laborers of this estate, to resist the authorities placed over them and the law itself, and that ALICK and DUCHESS are ringleaders of this conduct amongst the laborers of said estate."	Alick and Duchess, one month's confinement with hard labor each. The rest to work six Saturdays.

APPENDIX.

COMPLAINANT.	DEFENDANT.	COMPLAINT.	DECISION.
Edward H. Taylor, vs.	Eve.	Prisoner refused on the 7th instant to carry manure as directed by himself and the superintendent in common with the other laborers; and neglected to work on the 10th instant, as was her duty to make good the time she was at the House of Correction:	Fourteen days confinement with hard labor.
H. G. Bayley, vs.	Dick William.	Prisoner on the 3rd inst. declared several times in the presence of the whole gang that *he care nothing for manager.*	To work three Saturdays.
W. A. Moore, vs.	Kitty Ann, and Mercy Kate.	On the 2nd inst. they disobeyed the orders of the manager by singing aloud in the field contrary to his positive directions, and that they would not desist when directed so to do by him.	To work two Saturdays.
J. H. Alleyne, vs.	Eight apprentices.	Disobeyed the sub-manager's orders and performed their work very negligently, especially POLYDORE who set all his orders at defiance, although a first row man from whom a better example is expected.	Polydore to work four, the other three Saturdays.
Ditto, vs,	Three apprentices.	Deporting themselves very disorderly in the yard, on the 16th instant, to the great annoyance of their master's family.	To work three Saturdays.

APPENDIX.

COMPLAINANT.		DEFENDANT.	COMPLAINT.	DECISION.
W. T. Barton,	vs.	Ben Hagar.	Sammy, Superintendent deposes that on the 16th inst. he detected her with a cane which had been recently cut from the field.	To work three Saturdays.

The comparative leniency of the law in the case where a master maltreats an apprentice is remarkable; yet this disproportion is increased in the administration of the Magistrates. We have before us the particulars of a case where an entire gang, composed of thirty-two negros complained against their master, a wealthy proprietor and member of assembly, that they were kept in the field at work on one occasion, from 6 A. M. till 1 P. M. without food or water, (under a burning sun) and again from 3 P. M. to 6 P. M. being ten hours, or one hour more than the legal time. The defendant admitted that he ordered the driver not to allow any of the gang to leave the field, and that they worked 9¾ hours. He was fined in the moderate penalty of one pound currency in each case, which the Governor Sir LIONEL SMITH was pleased to remit, at the same time approving of the conduct of the Magistrate. Had the laborers been a few minutes after time they would have been punished, without appeal, by the forfeiture of several of their Saturdays to the benefit of the estate. Many other instances might be quoted to shew the contrasted leniency and severity of the law in the opposite cases of planters and apprentices.

SECTION III.

SCALE OF LABOR.—The system of taskwork, however desirable in itself, requires to be regulated by so many special circumstances, that it can never be introduced without injustice except by mutual and voluntary agreement between masters and laborers. This was so universally admitted that the Apprenticeship Law expressly declared that taskwork should not be imposed without the consent of the apprentices. It was, however, a favorite measure of Sir LIONEL SMITH to regulate the labor of the apprentices by a fixed standard; notwithstanding the insuperable obstacles created by differences of soil, and fluctuations of weather, and inequality of strength of individual laborers. He appointed a Committee of three Planters to draw up a " Scale of Labor," which he forwarded to each of the Special Magistrates with the following instructions.

" You will be furnished with printed copies of the scale; and I have to desire that it may be constantly hung up in your respective offices for public information. You will also have the goodness to distribute copies to the several estates in your district, with a request to the proprietors or managers, that they may be placed in some situation in the buildings of the estate where they may be easily referred to by the apprenticed laborers. As there are few or no estates where there are not some among the negro population who can read, I am in hopes that this measure may prevent many complaints arising from misunderstanding and ignorance being brought before you."

The scale is entitled " A Scale of work to be performed by effective apprenticed laborers in the Island of Barbados, drawn up by the undersigned, appointed a committee for that purpose by his Excellency the Governor General, and subsequently approved by His Majesty's Council."

The principal column in the scale is headed, "quantity of work to be performed by *one or more* laborers in one day of nine hours," which means that a gang is required to perform as many times the quantity of work set down as there are negros composing it. The intention of the scale was to facilitate the introduction of taskwork, which was accordingly generally resorted to when it was first issued, but soon we believe as generally abandoned. The scale, in the event of the failure of its first object, was intended to prevent complaints and as a standard of punishments. Hence the facility, with which the numerous vague and general complaints of idleness and insufficiency of work, are disposed of by the Special Magistrates. We took much pains to ascertain the real character of the scale, and the result of our inquiries in the Colony, was that "it is such a scale as the *strongest* negros could not work upon for a twelvemonth together." In order still further to satisfy ourselves, we forwarded a copy of it to Antigua, and requested a friend to obtain for us the opinion of planters residing in a part of the island where the soil is very similar to that of Barbados. In reply, one manager, speaking of the number of cane holes required by the scale says, "We usually bank our land with the plough and crosshole afterwards (with the hoe.) Our laborers would open in nine hours the quantity prescribed." What a comment is this on the severity of the Barbados scale, when the fact is stated, that the plough is not used in that colony, but that the laborers must both bank and crosshole with the hoe! Some remarks are made by our informant on other items of the scale, and the following general observations. "The quantum of labor to be reasonably expected must depend upon the land, not only being stiff or light, but wet or dry, foul or otherwise, and other circumstances;" and in the boiling house, "the quantity made must depend on the wind, if a windmill is used, quality of the canes, distance of cartage, &c." "This plan must give a great deal of trouble and be a source of irritation." Another observes, that he agrees with the observation of the previous manager, "about the facilities for squabbles afforded by the scale submitted," and observes, that in the scale "there is more required than can always be yielded, and therefore it is oppressive if insisted on."

When to these considerations is added the fact that the planters distribute the negros into the various gangs at their own pleasure, it is evident, that the scale affords them opportunities of exacting a most oppressive amount of labor. We have before us a case, the other particulars of which are of a gross character, where a girl ten years of age, was sent by her master into the first gang with a heavy hoe as a punishment. The first or able-bodied gang may thus be augmented in number by the addition of young or weakly persons, and yet the full aggregate amount of labor required from it; and by reference to the preceding section in this appendix it will be seen, that the practice of bringing entire gangs before the Magistrate for punishment is not infrequent. This scale "hung up" in their respective offices still regulates the decisions of the magistrates.

SECTION IV.

THE LATE GOVERNOR.—Sir LIONEL SMITH, administered the affairs of this colony in such a manner as to acquire the confidence of the colonial minister, and to obtain promotion to the Government of Jamaica, and several other marks of distinction and favor. He arrived in the colony before the agitation of the Abolition measure. The strong opposition which it encountered, threw the Governor into a position from whence he derived a reputation that his subsequent proceedings have by no means supported. His early policy, however, was decidedly in favor of the negros, and to him it is mainly owing, that the efforts made to bring about a general compulsory apprenticeship of the children soon after August, 1834 were defeated. A marked change was subsequently visible in his Government. He adopted what he was pleased to consider a policy of *conciliation,* by which the interests of the negros were sacrificed to the views of the planters. The stipendiary magistrates did not receive from him that support to which they were entitled, and when about to leave the Island, in a farewell speech which he made to them, he intimated in terms which could not be mistaken, that Government was weary of the irritating controversies that the system created, and that, as the magistrates valued their places, they must conciliate the planters and keep things quiet, as they well knew the agriculture of the island must be kept up.

The disgraceful state of the jail at Bridgtown, under Sir LIONEL's government has already been described.

The same change was visible in his conduct towards the colored people. Though their political disabilities had been nominally removed some years before by a legislative enactment, they had as yet obtained a very insignificant share of power and influence in consequence of the value of freehold conferring the franchise having been raised simultaneously with the cession of their political rights; while the qualification of the existing voters was undisturbed; so that the colored freeholders in the towns are required to possess a house of the yearly value of thirty pounds, while a great body of white electors are qualified by the possession of tenements of the value of only ten pounds per annum. Sir LIONEL SMITH's professions of impartiality and freedom from prejudice excited great hopes in the minds of the colored people. They expected at least that some of their number, men of wealth, education and superior qualifications, would receive commissions in the magistracy. In this they were disappointed; the only attempt made by the Governor in their favor was, by inviting a colored gentleman to his table. One of his white guests manifested his offence by leaving the room, which created so much alarm that the Governor immediately relinquished his aggressive policy and fell back upon *conciliation.* The real difficulties which he encountered, may be estimated from the fact, that his successor who made no promises, placed two colored men on the bench of magistrates, a few weeks after his arrival in the colony with the consent of the council.

Sir LIONEL SMITH embarked for Jamaica amidst the execrations of the crowds of free blacks and apprentices assembled on the beach.

SECTION V.

NOTE ON THE APPRENTICESHIP OF THE FREE CHILDREN.—We have intimated in the Journal that the plan of procuring a general apprenticeship of the free children, was revived in Barbados soon after the arrival of the present Governor. As this important subject has subsequently taken a favorable turn in the legislature of the Island, we have omitted some important memoranda relating to it that we made during our stay in the colony. We are, however, prepared to prove, if called upon, that we have ample reason for asserting the existence of the designs referred to.

APPENDIX.

[F]

JAMAICA.

SECTION I.

NOTE ON PRISCILLA TAYLOR'S CASE.—The statement in our Journal having been taken down in the public room of the Ferry tavern, a garbled report of the investigation was published in the island newspapers. The facts of the case are much stronger than what originally appeared in England. We took much pains on subsequent occasions to verify them, and have in our possession more detailed statements which explain the motives in which these disgraceful proceedings originated, and contain particulars of a still more revolting character than what are now laid before the public. We were also favored, during our stay in the island, with a letter from the Special Magistrate implicated in the transaction, who admits the fact of PRISCILLA TAYLOR having been chained to a man, but denies his participation in it. She subsequently purchased her freedom by valuation, under the fear of further persecution in consequence of our having seen her, for *sixty nine pounds*. The money was lent to her by a friend, on the security of a verbal promise of repayment from herself and her husband, who belongs to a different master. The gentleman alluded to informs us that part of the amount has already been repaid out of the produce of their labor in cultivating provisions.

SECTION II.

HALFWAY TREE WORKHOUSE.—We have before us the report of an action, (WILKINS vs. LIDDELL) instituted by a person on behalf of herself, her son and her daughter, against the Supervisor of this Workhouse for trespass. The complainants were apprehended as *runaway apprentices,* and confined for nearly a week in chains *before they were taken before any special magistrate,* during which time the son was worked publicly in the penal gang. The facts were incontrovertible, and the Jury gave a verdict of thirty five shillings; *an amount too small to carry costs.* In the same Court the complainants succeeded in proving that they were not apprentices.

We have also the copy of a "brief in support of motion for criminal information vs. WHITEMAN," which comprises the affidavit of a female apprentice to the effect, that she was worked in the penal gang chained to another girl; that frequently while on the treadmill, she was flogged by the drivers, (who are all convict slaves,) and once severely flogged and kicked by the defendant, (who was the Overseer or deputy Superintendent of the Workhouse.) WHITEMAN in his affidavit denies that he ever struck complainant, but does not deny that she was flogged by the drivers. He accuses her of having once thrown herself off the mill, at the same time "taking the whip out of the driver's hand" in his presence. The affidavits of the four *drivers* give defendant a high character; declare they never saw him strike complainant; and that "on one occasion she took the cat out of the driver's hand," when defendant took it away and restored it to the driver. Throughout these affidavits the flogging of females on the treadmill is not denied, and it appears from the affidavits of the accused, himself and his witnesses, that the convict drivers carried a cat when superintending women on the treadmill. At the Court (June, 1836) at which this motion was made, the Custos of St. Andrews, whose residence is near the Halfway Tree Workhouse; and who, as Chief Magistrate of the Parish, was in some measure implicated in its abuses, sat on the bench as one of the assistant judges. He publicly reprobated the conduct of the parties who brought the case forward, saying, "It was an infamous proceeding." The Attorney General besides insisting that the affidavits of WHITEMAN and the convicts were not conclusive, observed; " I have serious doubts as to the legality of chaining women in workhouses, and I want the court to say whether it be legal or illegal to do so." The Chief Justice replied, " We will give you a decision on that point, if we must do so, *but not otherwise.*" The application was subsequently refused, the Chief Justice observing; "The affidavit comprehends chaining and corporal punishment; but the *only real ground of complaint is the latter.* We are not called upon to pronounce as to the chaining. There are four affidavits denying the principal charge, the preponderance of evidence is therefore in favor of WHITEMAN, and we must deny the application." This is one of several instances where the attempt to procure the redress of gross abuses in the houses of correction, by instituting suits of criminal information in the Island Courts, has proved abortive.

SECTION III.

THE NON-REGISTERED SLAVES.—It has been stated in our journal that in one parish, several hundred non-registered slaves have obtained their freedom, while in other parts of the island they are still held in slavery. A proprietor in St. Andrew's parish has fifteen of these negros, some of whom, as the Magistrates of the district refused to coerce them, were brought down to the Special Court at Halfway Tree, where they were sentenced to be flogged. The recent Jamaica papers report another case in the parish of Hanover, where a negro, about two years ago, being ill, and not likely to live, was turned adrift by his master, who informed him that he was free, as he was not registered. The man recovered, and was then reclaimed, brought before a Special Magistrate and flogged for refusing to work. He ran away to Spanish Town, and appealed to the Governor, who instructed the Stipendiary that he could not coerce a non-registered slave as an apprentice. The negro thus obtained his freedom, hired himself to work on an estate for half a dollar a day, but when he applied for his wages was told by the overseer that they should be paid over to his owner. He appealed to the petty sessions for the recovery of the amount, but was told by the local Magistrates he was an apprentice. He was then employed by the rector of the parish, who has recently been fined ten pounds by the same local Magistrates for harbouring an apprentice, under what is called the inveigling clause of the Act in Aid.

In the June Grand Court of Assize, a case (BAYLEY vs. EWART) was brought forward for the purpose of obtaining a formal decision, whether a non-registered slave was an apprentice, or legally free. The majority of the Bench decided that he was an apprentice. The Chief Justice rested his argument to this effect, chiefly on the decision of the Privy Council in the Mauritius case. The Hon. THOMAS J. BERNARD one of the assistant judges, and a planter, dissented from this decision, and maintained, in a candid and able argument, that non-registration did confer freedom. Should the attempts become general, to carry out this decision, and to re-enslave the few non-registered negros who have recovered their liberty, the worst consequences may be expected to ensue; and meanwhile, the precarious freedom which they enjoy, is nothing better than an unprivileged outlawry.

The Law fraudulently entitled an "Act for the Abolition of Slavery," enacts in express terms that "all persons who *in conformity with the laws of the said colonies respectively, shall have been duly registered as slaves,* &c. shall become and be apprenticed laborers." The Chief Justice of Jamaica has decided that those also who were *not* duly registered according to law are apprentices. It is scarcely necessary to remark, that in the respective colonies, proprietors who neglected to register their slaves, incurred heavy penalties; so that the effect of the Abolition Law, as interpreted by the Chief Justice of Jamaica, is not to emancipate the non-registered slaves from the bondage, in which they were illegally held, but to relieve their masters from the penalties which they had incurred by so holding them.

APPENDIX.

SECTION IV.

STATEMENTS OF APPRENTICES.

PARISH OF ST. THOMAS IN THE VALE.

1.—WALLEN AND ROSE HALL ESTATES.—The negros on these properties work on the eight hour system out of crop. In crop time they work eleven hours a day, for five days, viz: from four to eleven A.M. and from one to five P.M.; being fifteen hours extra per week for which they receive two shillings and one penny. The head boiler-man receives five shillings, and the three next four and two-pence, but the latter frequently work till ten at night. Under the old system, the salt fish and syrup which they received were worth more than their present wages. They said, with regard to the mode in which this arrangement was introduced, "when the master want any thing done out of the people, he send for the Magistrate, and the Magistrate open it to the people, and they are obliged to agree to it, else they are bad servant, and might get punished if they did not agree." On Rose Hall the people refused the bargain; but the men were promised a new shirt, and the women a new petticoat, if they would do their work well, and not steal. They then agreed, but do not expect to receive them, as salt fish was always promised to be given them after crop was over, which they never received. One of the apprentices has a watch. He says sometimes the shellblows, (in the morning, at mealtimes and in the evening,) are very correct, and sometimes they are an hour, at others half an hour behind time, but the people are always summoned back to the field in good time. He said, "if a gun was placed at Rodney Hall, and a soldier was sent from town to fire it every day at the shellblows, every things would go on right." Before the apprenticeship, the negros on these estates used each to receive six shads a week, and the head men twelve shads and a quart of rum. These allowances are now discontinued. The yearly distribution of clothes during slavery was six yards osnaburgh, six yards coarse cloth, four of baize, one hat and one handkerchief; now, it is only seven yards of osnaburgh, and three of baize, besides the hat and handkerchief. The cooks, who used to prepare their meals in the field, and to carry water for them to drink while at work, have been taken away. The sick are often turned out of the hospital before they are well. The doctor attends once a week, but treats the people very roughly. They used, when sick during slavery, to have oatmeal and sugar allowed them, and occasionally a little wine; now, not a morsel of food is given to them; they must support themselves, or be supported by their relations. No longer ago than to-night, a girl who was very sick was told by the overseer that she might go to the hospital, but there was no medicine for her, and a fellow apprentice was obliged to give her some "out of his own expense." If a free child is taken ill, parents have to pay back the time they spend in attending to it; if the doctor sees it they have to pay him, and some of them have been charged ten shillings. Before the first of August, pregnant women used to draw off (from work) six weeks before they laid down. Now they are allowed no time before delivery, and only four weeks afterwards.

GEORGE DAVIDSON, the head carpenter on Wallen's, has been twice valued, first time about a year ago, for three hundred and fifty-two pounds; he appealed to the Governor, who directed a fresh valuation, when he was rated at two hundred and thirty pounds; but this second valuation was set aside. He says his master brought a great number of persons "to swear against his character; who put trades upon him that he knew nothing about, and made out there was nothing he would not do." He has now given up all idea of purchasing himself. He is getting on for sixty years of age, and "thinks the freedom will not come soon enough to do him much good." His master wanted to make him a constable, but he declined it on account of his being weak in strength, "and because he did not like to take the Bible in his hand too often."

BENDLEY'S.—Five apprentices from this property state that their extra work during crop and remuneration for it, are the same as on Wallen's and Rose Hall. They would not agree at first, but the Special Magistrate threatened and abused them till they consented. Out of crop they work from seven o'clock in the morning till five, and sometimes six in the afternoon, *without any intermission for meals.* They get no time to prepare their food, except by rising early to cook their breakfasts before they go to the field at seven o'clock. We cross-examined them about the time, and their accounts were clear and consistent. They said they knew the time by the shellblows on the neighbouring estates, and by the "gunfire" at six o'clock in the evening. They said the apprentices were better treated in the hospital than on Wallen's, as they sometimes received oatmeal, &c; but the pregnant women are allowed no time before delivery, and only nine days afterwards. They complained also of the injury they sustained by the trespass of the estates' cattle in their grounds.

DAWKINS'S TREADWAY.—Two apprentices state that in crop time, they work from four in the morning till eight at night every alternate day, with the intermission of only half an hour for breakfast, giving up also their half Friday. For this amount of extra labor, they received last year two shillings and sixpence a week, this season their only pay is six herrings a week. They were told they should not have their Christmas allowance if they did not agree, and last year they did not receive any allowance at Christmas (1835—6.) Out of crop they work from six to six, with the intermission of only one hour for breakfast. They have every alternate Friday but have been deprived of the salt fish, which was distributed to them weekly during slavery. It may be easily imagined that this system of depriving the people of their time during crop without remuneration, (a system of gross fraud and oppression which is carried into effect by the coercive powers of the Special Magistrates,) does occasionally excite some expression of a sense of the injustice with which they are treated from the negros. Some weeks after the above statement was made to us by the apprentices from Dawkins's Treadway, a neighbouring missionary was compelled to appeal on their behalf to the Governor. The following is a copy of his letter, addressed to the Secretary for the Stipendiary Magistrates' department.

" Jericho, St. Thomas in the Vale,
March 31st. 1837.

" SIR,
I beg you will please make His Excellency the Governor acquainted with the case of the apprentices belonging to Treadway estate in this parish. I was last evening informed that the whole of those engaged in taking of the crop meant to repair to Spanish Town to night, in order to complain to His Excellency of the usage they are receiving. On hearing this, I sent to request them to remain at home in perfect quietness and submission, and promised to make known to His Excellency their situation; and also their account of the conduct of Captain REYNOLDS, the Special Justice of their district, towards them. The account they give is, that one spell works (at the boiling house) from four o'clock, A.M. to eleven o'clock, A.M. and is then relieved by the second spell, which continues till eight o'clock, P. M. That the first spell is sent into the field to cut canes soon after it is relieved (at 11, A. M.) and works until six, P.M. or thereabouts; that the second spell previous to relieving the first, (at the sugar works) works in the field from six o'clock, A.M. to near eleven o'clock; that those in the field are required to cut down canes and tie them up in bundles for the wains, and so to supply the mill that one of the spells may occasionally go to clean young canes; that for this amount of extra time and labor, (about six working hours per diem,) they receive six herrings, most of them broken ones in the week; that when they objected to this remuneration as being too small, the value of six herrings being only five pence, Captain REYNOLDS told them roughly that he did not care if they would not take it, but they should do the work, or he would send for the police to make them work, or carry them to Rodney Hall Workhouse to be punished, or words to this effect: that on Monday last, they were called up before Captain REYNOLDS, who heard the charge of the overseer against the people for insufficiency of work, but would not here a word from the apprentices in their defence, and sentenced them all *to lose five alternate Saturdays.* That an apprentice named SALLY HUTCHINSON attempted to speak. They state that Captain REYNOLDS said, ' I don't want to hear a word.' She then said, ' You

can't make we speak and hear one word from we, to see whether we for right or wrong.' Capt. R. replied, 'Woman, hold your tongue; if you don't, I will send you straight off to Rodney Hall! The woman without noticing the threat, proceeded; 'Massa, we have to cut cane, then tie, we can do no more; we not have enough of prentice to carry on the work.' She was ordered into the charge of the constable, and sent to be locked up in the hot house. As she was going, Capt. R. called her back and required her to beg pardon, She replied,'' Massa, me no do nothing to beg your pardon, Sir.' She was then sent off to Rodney Hall to be confined for a week, as it is said, in the dark room. "The people went to their attorney, Mr. BERNARD, when he visited the property after sentence had been passed, to complain to him of their usage, but they say he would not hear them, nor give them the least satisfaction; and as this was the case, they agreed to wait until this evening, when they expected Saturday would be their day, and then proceed to lay their grievances before his Excellency the Governor; but one of them thought it best first to consult with me, when I gave the advice above stated, and promised to represent to you in order to be laid before his Excellency, an account of this matter.

I have the honor to be, Sir,
Your obedient Servant,
JOHN CLARKE.

P. S.—Having obtained a copy of the commitment, I take the liberty to transcribe it to accompany the above case.

"Jamaica, ss.
To the Keeper of the House of Correction,
Rodney Hall.

Receive into your custody the body of SALLY HUTCHINSON, an apprentice of Treadways, this day brought before me for using violent language, and endeavouring to persuade the gang that they were sentenced to pay back too much labor to the estate by the Magistrate. I therefore sentence SALLY HUTCHINSON to six days confinement in the House of Correction, &c.

Signed,
T. REYNOLDS. S. J."

Given under my hand,
this 27th day of March, 1837.

To the above letter, the writer, at the time we saw him about six weeks after its date, had received no answer from the Governor.

BERWICK ESTATE.—Sir A. C. GRANT, Proprietor.—Three apprentices state, that Dr. PALMER came four times on the estate, but only punished the people twice by taking away sixteen hours of their time. The owner said that would not do for him, and complained to the Governor, who ordered Mr. COOPER to take charge of BERWICK. When he paid his first visit, the owner complained to him that the people had been idle during Dr. PALMER's time, for which COOPER sentenced them to pay four days. The people refused, and went to PALMER, who told them to do every thing that COOPER said. The latter came with the police and flogged one man, and sent a woman to the treadmill for fourteen days. Dr. PALMER always told them to work well, and said if they did not he would punish them. He did not flog them like the other Magistrates, nor take away their Saturdays to give to the property. They do work well, but their overseer is never satisfied, and is continually complaining to get their time taken away, though there is not a cane piece on the estate that is not in good order. Since August, 1834, they have never had a field cook till two months ago. They get no salt fish, except in crop. In crop, the people give up their half Fridays, and receive for their extra work, the mill people two shillings and sixpence, the boiler-men three shillings and four pence, and the cattle boys one shilling and eleven pence a week. They work about sixteen hours a day. The watchman for the negro grounds was taken away about a year before August, 1834, and they have thrown up their grounds on account of the trespass of cattle. They have now only little gardens about their houses. The hospital is surrounded by a fence like a jail, which is kept locked all day. The pregnant women are not allowed to sit down, but go home from the field and are delivered the same night. They are allowed about four weeks afterwards.

RIO MAGNO.—Belonging to the same proprietor.—An apprentice complains, "that they are living very hard. They have had no salt fish since christmas; they are employed jobbing on Berwick. Their grounds are mashed up by the cattle, and they are obliged to go far into the woods and cut out a little place for grounds."

PALM.—GUTTERES, proprietor.—Two apprentices from this estate, state that their provision grounds are on the line of the Recess plantation, belonging to Mr. GYLES. GYLES's cattle got in and eat it down smooth. They caught them, and drove them down to their overseer, who would not send them to the pound, but ordered them to take them back to Mr. GYLES. Neither GYLES nor their own overseer would give them any kind of satisfaction. The latter said he would not put a stop to Mr. GYLES's cattle eating their provisions, because when they had plenty to live on, they would sit down and not do any thing for him. They were compelled to give up their grounds, and content themselves with a little garden about their houses, but the estate's cattle trespass in that, and they can get no redress. They cannot take them to the pound without a written paper, and they can get no satisfaction from the overseer. "We were better off in Dr. PALMER's time. We made many complaints to him about the cattle, and he scold the busha. The busha used then to give us a paper to take cattle to the pound."

The parish of St. ANN.—Apprentices from New Ground, Chester, Banks, Drax Hall, Blenheim and Windsor estates, and Carlton Pen, state as follows:—

On New Ground the people work from six to nine, from ten to half-past twelve, and from two, to ten minutes before six every day. The overseer breaks them off a little before six, in order that he may call it eight hours, and thus deprive them of their half Fridays. He frequently strikes the apprentices, and if they complain they get no redress. He also puts them in the dungeon at his pleasure. The Magistrate hears nothing they have to say. He is always drunk. In crop time the apprentices work by spells, and not in extra time, except the boilermen, who receive six shillings and eight pence, the mill feeders five shillings, and some others three shillings and fourpence per week. These work night and day. The night work has been added since they made the agreement, and they are still compelled to abide by it. The allowances of salt fish have been taken away, as well as their field cooks. They are not allowed to draw off during heavy rain, even if it lasts the whole day, because, "their masters do not mind much now if they get sick and die." The old negros are not supported by the estate. The free children have not the privilege of the hospital. The apprentices receive no food from the estate during sickness, and the hospital is kept locked. Sometimes invalids are ordered out too early, and then if they remain, they are required to repay the time. The pregnant women are worked in the field to within a few days of their confinement, and are allowed three or four weeks afterwards. The overseer lately sent to order a woman into the field, who had staid at her home because of her advanced pregnancy; and when the driver arrived, he found her actually delivered. The apprentices not long ago had to pay two Saturdays because they took the Tuesday at Christmas.

BANKS AND RICHMOND.—Both these estates are under one attorney, the latter is the property of RALPH BERNAL, M. P. Out of crop, the apprentices work from six to six, with intermissions of two hours and a half for breakfast and dinner. They have no half Fridays, no payment for extra labor, no salt fish, no field cooks. Invalids get no food, nor old people any support from the estate. Pregnant women are allowed no more time than on New Ground. They say it is useless to complain to the Magistrate; "his hand shake so" that the overseer always has to write his sentences for him.

DRAX HALL.—Similar complaints, except that the apprentices receive their salt fish, though irregularly. They are compelled as on New Ground to work in the rain.

CHESTER.—Similar statements, and in addition there is no "hot house" (hospital) on this estate, no doctor, no medicine; when the people are sick, they have to provide these themselves. They are defrauded of their extra time during crop.

BLENHEIM.—The hospital is locked during the day. Apprentices are compelled to watch at night without any remuneration. *All* the negros on Cranbrook and Blenheim were mulcted five Saturdays recently, because some canes were stolen, and it could not be discovered by whom. They have been obliged in consequence to work their grounds on the Sabbath for a subsistence.

WINDSOR.—The apprentices have been sentenced to pay three Saturdays to the estate for not turning out early in the morning, which they declare is a false accusation.

CARLTON PEN.—The apprentices make no complaints. They receive their salt fish, &c. as during slavery.

PENSHURST, the property of G. W. SENIOR.—THOMAS BROWN states, that "ever since Lord MULGRAVE came into the country, Massa has turned out very savage. In Lord MULGRAVE's time I went up to hear the law; when I returned, he took a cowskin and beat me severely upon my back. Since he found that he can't raise his stick and mash us to pieces, he is worse than ever. I once went to Captain CONNOR to complain; after he left, my Master brought me before Dr. THOMPSON for it, who ordered me thirty lashes. He would not hear a word we had to say. The gang turn out at six, and draw off at six; they have one hour for breakfast, and one for dinner. They are not allowed a cook to cook their victuals, or bring water to them in the field. They never used to get their half Fridays till this Governor came, and their minister wrote to him about it. Since then, they have been compelled to work on Fridays from six till one, being allowed one hour for breakfast. They know the time by the shellblow on neighbouring properties. The present Magistrate (RAWLINSON) will not listen to their complaints. If Massa tell him the work is not going on well, and we working as hard as ever we can to oblige Massa, and still not able to please him, the Magistrates side with Massa, and take away our time. He took away three Saturdays from the whole gang about five months ago, because he said they did not work enough on a rainy day, though they staid in the field till shellblow. They once had to go to Chester, a distance of twenty miles to pick pimento. They were ordered to be there by nine o'clock in the morning, but could not reach it till twelve. The master complained also of the quantity they picked, although they had picked all there was on the trees. They were sentenced to lose one Saturday. On one occasion, the whole gang were sentenced to clear five acres of land of heavy bush in their own time. It took four half Fridays. I had to build a wall, and built eight yards a day, having to pull the old one down myself. He gave me a woman to pull the old wall down and then I built eleven yards a day. He complained I did not build enough, and the Magistrate sentenced me to build thirty yards in my own time, which takes away all my half Fridays. He ordered me to be tasked, and my master set me to build twelve yards a day. I have to work from sun rise to sun down and can't finish it. I have scarcely time to eat my breakfast. I tell him, Massa, I try to oblige you and you won't be satisfied, he answer me, "You lie, you devil." If he tell we do any thing we never refuse it, we only want for Massa to be satisfied. The people have never had salt fish since the apprenticeship, nor any christmas allowance, except of clothing. The pregnant women are allowed only one week before delivery and three weeks afterwards. The hospital is a little bit of a hut. Dr. E. TUCKER attends well to the people; but the free children do not go to the hospital; several of them have died. The Master thinks very hard of allowing their mothers time to suckle them. The negro houses are very wretched, all of them let in water. The Master says they can be punished for not keeping their houses and grounds in order, but he refuses to allow them time to do it, or to give them shingle or any other materials.

LAVINIA TROWERS, Penshurst, has three children and has been sick these four years, and can neither do any thing for herself or for her master. He has several times put her in the dungeon for three or four days at a time without speaking to the Magistrate. Sometimes when locked up she has never seen her child to give him suck for a whole day and night. She is fed by her fellow apprentices and by her husband who lives on Knapdale estate. Once Mr. SENIOR ordered her off the property and told her she might go where she liked. She went to Knapdale, and lived with her husband. When she had been away eight weeks the constable fetched her, and her master brought her before the Magistrate as a run away, but she was "in such poor condition" that he told the constable to take her back to the hospital. The Magistrate said, if she went to Knapdale again, he would have her husband punished severely. Her master gives her no medicine. He can't bear a sick person on the property. "Two times I ask him for medicine, and he tell me to go to the baptists." This woman was a poor, miserable looking object. Her statement was confirmed by eight or nine apprentices from the estate who were present.

AMELIA LAWRENCE, Penshurst. "When Massa find fault, she said she did not know how to work to please him. For this she was sent to the treadmill for seven days, and danced it night and morning, and worked on the road in chains. One day afterwards, on a Friday, the master ordered them to draw off for breakfast. She said the people would rather work on; (to finish their halfday.) He said that she seemed a mistress at the top of the first row, and cursed and abused her. After breakfast, he put her in the dungeon till next day, and when Mr. RAWLINSON came, she was sent to the workhouse for ten days. She has a lump on one of her wrists from being strapped to the rail, and was bruised on her legs by the mill. She came out the week before Christmas, and is still ill from its effects. She has been obliged to pay the doctor her own self, and has had to pay back the ten days to the estate. The driver at the workhouse beat the people well that could not dance the mill as well as in the penal gang.

MARIA DALLING, Penshurst. "Before the first of August, I was in the small gang, and was afterwards ordered to go into the great gang. I went to Captain CONNOR, who said I must stay in the small gang, as I had six children living. When he left, I was ordered to the great gang, where I remain till now. I did not complain to Mr. RAWLINSON; he is such a thick friend with massa. He eat, drink, and sleep at massa's house."

WILLIAM DALLING, Penshurst. "I and massa used to be very good friends before August, (1834.) After August, we fall out, because I join the baptists, and he can't bear the baptists near him. I am a house servant. All the allowance I received last year was six herrings twice. I have only eight yards of osnaburghs at Christmas, which is not sufficient to clothe me. I am almost starved, as my ground is eaten up by the hogs." There were several other of the Penshurst apprentices who all said that "their master is constantly in the habit of putting people in the dungeon without any authority." He takes them on Friday just before shellblow, and takes them out on Saturday morning. The late magistrate, Captain CONNOR, did them justice, and heard what they had to say. "He never dined with massa; but massa and the present magistrate agree well together."

There were, also, two free men, who had bought their time from Penshurst, in consequence of being treated harshly. One of them says his "master pulled his house down, broke up about half his furniture, and took away the rest." He got back the rest of his furniture, after a long time, by going to the magistrate. One of the men bought his time for fourteen doubloons. The other was asked eleven doubloons the first year of the apprenticeship. *He worked fourteen months and was then valued at twelve doubloons.* He was obliged to sell all he had to raise the money. The apprentices from Penshurst gave the following account of the treatment of a man named HENRY JAMES:—" He was a watchman to a corn piece, which had no standing fence. The hogs and cattle got in. Massa complained to Dr. THOMPSON, who ordered him twenty stripes. The police were fetched to flog him. He was tied to a cart, and his hands and feet were stretched so wide that he was strained. He coughed blood four days afterwards. He was ill about a month off and on in the hospital. They would not give him any medicine. He went to Brown's Town to complain to Mr. DILLON. When he came back, the doctor ordered him some medicine, but he did not get it. He went again to the magistrate, who said he did not know what to do as the doctor was not there. The man told him he did not think, from the way he felt, that he should see him again. He threw up blood, and dropped down dead a little while after he had left the Court House."

Rose Hill Estate.—"The apprentices work from sun to sun. Their grounds are not protected, and the cattle trespass and destroy all their provisions. They used to be allowed a watchman. They get no salt fish. An apprentice says, his wife is sickly and unable to work. He beg massa to sell her time, but he said if she worth only fivepence he would not."

Knapdale Estate.—An apprentice states, "I have had eleven children; seven are living, three of them are free. I was allowed to leave the great gang and sit down for two years, and was sent into the field again a month before the law. The month before Christmas I got a little child, and had a swelled breast for three months. The doctor ordered me physic, but the overseer did not give it me. I was in the hospital two months, when I was ordered out to dig cane holes, which brought on fever. I tell the overseer, I don't able to work in that gang because I had so much piccaninny. He said, the law before and now quite a different thing; and would not take me out of the great gang. I am obliged to work in the rear, and am not able to keep up with the rest. Magistrate sent me for seven days to dance the treadmill because the constable abused me and then said I was insolent to him. When I came home my two foot was just big, and I was in the hospital three weeks. I am scarcely able to walk now, and if I sit down I can scarcely get on my feet again. When I was put on the treadmill, the first day the driver gave me three licks on my back. I worked on the road in chains. When I was laid up with piccaninny, I was delivered the very same day that I came from the field. I was ordered into the field three weeks afterwards. We do not get six half Fridays since the law came in."

The husband of this apprentice made the following statement, at a different time:—"Since my wife had the child, she had a troubled breast; I was like to lose her three times. The doctor order a poultice and other little things; busha would not give her nothing at all. I tell the doctor, my wife have seven children and ought to sit down. He say, this time the law don't allow that. My wife was laid up for a month after being at the treadmill. We get no half Fridays. They say they give we the hours every day in room of Friday, but they never blow the shell till sun down; we can't get no hours."

Ballantyne.—An apprentice says, "they have a good busha. They receive, however, no salt fish, nor flour, nor sugar, for their children, as before the apprenticeship. They get their half Fridays, and the pregnant women have a month before and a month after confinement."

Tripoli.—Two apprentices state, "the apprentices on this property are a jobbing gang, and work about nine miles from home. They work from six till five, one hour being allowed for breakfast. Never get a half Friday. On Friday when they go home, they don't draw off any earlier than other days. No field cook allowed.

Pregnant women work in the field, and go home and lie in at night. Aftewards they are only allowed two weeks. Mothers take their children on their backs to the field; no nurse, no flour or sugar allowed. Last year we complained to Mr. SOWLY about our half Fridays. He fined us eight Saturdays for complaining."

SOUTHAMPTON.—An apprentice states, "we turn out at half past five and have half an hour for breakfast, and draw off at five. The cattle broke in and destroyed our ground and left we nothing to eat. I showed massa my ground. He said, 'we must find soft stone and eat it; we ought to make a high fence to keep out the cattle; it's no use complaining to him.' If any women's children very sick and mothers attend them, they have to pay back the time. When the people are sick he wants them to pay back the time, and gives them no medicine. If it rain ever so hard the people must work in it or pay up the time. All this is since they got a new master."

PARISH OF TRELAWNEY.—OXFORD ESTATE, the property of E. BARRETT.—A number of intelligent apprentices say, "that there is more work done on this estate than formerly. There used to be forty or fifty jobbers constantly at work, who dug all the cane holes; now, the cultivation is carried on by the estate's people only, and the crops are increasing. In crop, they work from 4 o'clock, A. M., to 10, P.M., snatching their meals as they can; and for this amount of extra labour for five days, receive six shillings and three-pence per week. They agree to this arrangement for the sake of peace, but could earn more by working in their own grounds or on adjoining estates. Out of crop, they work from six to six, or even half-past six, with two hours intermission for meals. The overseers blow the shell when they please. They get their half Fridays. Their mountain grounds are from seven to nine miles distant. They are allowed a watchman for them, and field cooks, but have had no salt fish these six months. The pregnant women are allowed to sit down two months before delivery and a fortnight afterwards. The free children receive nothing from the estate."

Several apprentices on Cambridge, an estate of the same proprietor, say they are similarly circumstanced, except that they have a bad overseer. They are never allowed more than an hour and ten minutes for dinner. They would not agree to the arrangement for their extra labour during crop, except to keep them quiet, for which purpose they are willing to do all in their power, but the "overseer is a man of war." They observed, "we know we got a good massa in England, and we wish to do every thing to oblige him; but if the overseer continues to worry us none of the apprentices will remain when the time is up."

RICHARD BARRETT, one of the negros present, has been a carpenter on Cambridge for twenty-eight years, and has been recently turned into the field for preferring a respectful complaint to his attorney against the overseer. He has given notice, in consequence, to be valued. These people said, although the free children are less attended to, they do not die more than before; "God Almighty takes care of that himself, and there are more births than ever there were." They assured us, also, that their children were not brought up in idleness, and that they had plenty of little things for them to do at home or in their grounds. They said they heard that some of the people on other estates were worse off than before the apprenticeship. For themselves, in answer to an inquiry, they said, "how can we like the old system? We are well satisfied with the present, *when we think when the whole come.*" In conclusion, they spontaneously expressed their thanks to their friends in England, for the exertions they had made for them to secure the abolition, and for sending out missionaries, and teachers and books.

A gentleman acquainted with RICHARD BARRETT, the negro above mentioned, subsequently gave us an account of his release from apprenticeship by valuation. He had always borne a good character, and had been head carpenter for seven years, and second carpenter for two years—having been superseded, as head carpenter, by a free person. About the middle of last month, (February,) he was ordered into the field by the present overseer, — HAWES, to perform field labor, and had *taskwork* set him, the same as the rest of the gang, in digging cane holes. Although not desirous of leaving the estate, yet, being unaccustomed to field labor, and unable to perform it, he determined to obtain his discharge. When he came to be valued, he stated to the Magistrates that his only reason for seeking to obtain his release was his having been made a field laborer, and, therefore, that he ought to be valued as such. To this one of the *Local* Magistrates agreed, but the *Special* Justice, PRYCE, and the other Local Magistrate, said that he must be valued as a carpenter. He was accordingly valued at £67. 10s.

This case illustrates several important points :—First, that the practice of sending mechanics and domestics into the field, ever considered by the negros the severest and most degrading punishment, is still practised; secondly, that the overseers sacrifice the property and interests of their absent employers, without scruple, to gratify their own tyrannical dispositions; and, lastly, that valuations are conducted without any regard to justice, or even to a decent respect for the rights of the negros, as guaranteed to them by the Abolition Law.

THE PARISHES OF ST. JAMES AND HANOVER.

SALT SPRING ESTATE.—An apprentice complains that "after being allowed by the doctor to sit down two months last year during her pregnancy, she was ordered afterwards to pay back one month. She worked out all the Saturdays but two, on which her

APPENDIX.

husband and another relative worked for her. The overseer refused these two days, and brought her before the Magistrate, who sent her to the workhouse for three days, and ordered her to repay the time. When she came out, she worked two Saturdays, but on the third was obliged to go to her provision ground for victual. *The negro grounds are fifteen miles distant from the estate.* For going to her ground for food, she was brought before the Magistrate, and sent to the workhouse five times in succession, one after another. The Magistrate will not listen to her. She is now pregnant again; and he says, after her confinement she must pay back all the days she spent in the workhouse. She says, nursing mothers are not permitted to leave the field to suckle their children. When she and others have complained to the busha, he says he does not care a pin, because they are free."

The brother of the preceding apprentice gives the following account of the first complaint above noticed:—" His sister was ordered by Mr. FINLAYSON to work every other Saturday from the first of May to the first of August. The overseer refused to allow her husband to work for her, and when she had repaid all the days up to the first of August, he said she had not finished, and brought her before the Magistrate. He complains, that if two or three of the apprentices lose five minutes in the morning, Mr. FINLAYSON stops the whole gang for two Saturdays."

NEW MILL ESTATE.—Two apprentices state, "that in the two last crops the people have not received any thing for their half Fridays; and this year they are again squabbling with busha about them. The negro grounds are about ten miles from the estate. Pregnant women are allowed four weeks before and after delivery, and then are allowed to turn out an hour later in the morning. Nursing mothers are allowed an hour a day to go to suckle their children, one at a time. Field cooks and salt fish are continued; but if the overseer finds the least fault he stops their allowance for a month or two. If mothers take their free children to the hospital they are not allowed to have any medicine, and must pay back any time they take to nurse them. These negros mentioned to us the cases referred to, in the Journal, of Lucy Anne Stephen and Judy Evans, two old women, each mothers of eight children, being compelled to work in the field. They also mentioned two other old women who have been put in the dungeon now these ten days past. They both of them came to this country three years before ninety-five, and one of them was then 'a good prime woman,' (who must now, therefore, be upwards of seventy,) the other a girl. The former being weak and unable to cut grass, was ordered to be locked up by the Magistrate, (PRINGLE,) for absence from work; the other is unable to work from illness, and is also ordered to be locked up."

COVENTRY ESTATE, the property of — HIBBERT.— SUSAN MACKENZIE, an apprentice, says that "during the rebellion she was sent for because she was a 'great baptist woman.' They tried to make some men swear against her to hang her, but did not succeed; and because she would not say any thing against Mr. BURCHELL, three men, with three new cats, were ordered to flog her. They gave her about three hundred lashes, and she remained in the workhouse for three months. On the first of August, 1824, the attorney, Mr. GRANT, said she must go into the field. She said she was not able, and showed him her back; but he said that was nothing, and for her refusal she was sent three times to the workhouse: they then allowed her to cook for the children, which is her present employment."

This woman is an individual of superior intelligence for her station, and bears a very high character as a person of amiable and mild disposition, and consistent in her deportment as a professor of religion. She is almost blind from the effects of flogging; the upper part of the back is covered with white patches, where the *rete mucosum* has been entirely obliterated by the horrid punishment described above.

Speaking of the condition of the apprentices on Coventry, she said, that "the people are compelled to do taskwork in the field, and so much is given them, that they cannot finish it, though they work from sun rise till dusk without intermission. Their breakfasts are cooked for them, and they eat them in the field without sitting down. If there is a patch left, they are compelled to finish it on the Saturday. The Magistrate won't hear what they have to say. They receive no salt fish."

PORTO BELLO.—An apprentice states, "the people turn out at half-past six, they get forty minutes for breakfast and an hour for dinner, and leave the field at a quarter to six. He has a watch, and knows the time exactly. The people have no field cooks; never received any allowance of salt fish. Their provision grounds are very bad land, and eight miles distant. He never went into the field till December, 1835, when he was made a predial. The Special Magistrate, Mr. FINLAYSON, will scarcely allow the people to speak. He went to him this morning, but was told he (Mr. F.) could do nothing for him; he had better get a friend, and go to the Governor."

WORCESTER ESTATE.—One woman, with ten children, six apprentices and four free; another with seven children; and a third with six, had withdrawn from field work before the first of August, 1834. After the first of August, they were ordered to the field again, and because they did not turn out with the rest of the people at six o'clock, they were brought before the Magistrate, and sent to the workhouse. One of them had twins, and, being ordered to the field, was obliged to leave them in the care of their little brother; he went to play, and when she returned she found them lying in their own filth, and eating it. At present, the picaninny women are allowed to take turn in minding their children, and to have half an hour in the morning. The people on the estate generally turn out at six, and draw off at half-past five, and sometimes six. They have had no salt fish these two months. In crop, they work five hours extra per day, for four days in the week, for which they receive one and eight pence. When the people complained, Mr. CARNABY would not allow them to speak, but said if they did not grind eight coppers of liquor a day they would be punished."

PROSPER PEN.—RICHARD SHEPPIE, an apprentice, states, "that there were two steers that could work, two young steers, two cows, and one bull calf, belonging to himself and his sister. Mr. GRANT, the attorney, said he must sell them, as he would not allow them to stay any longer on the estate. He compelled RICHARD to brand the cattle himself with the estate's mark. When he went for his money, he was offered £16. for the two steers, and £16. for all the rest, which he refused, as the steers were worth £18. a piece, and the cows £16. a piece. The steers have been working for the estate ever since. He does not know what Magistrate to apply to."—The head negros on many estates are allowed to raise cattle, mules, and horses, for themselves; and instances of the possession of this kind of property to a small extent by apprentices, are frequently to be met with. The above case is an example of the insecurity of such prosperity, which depends at all times on the caprice of overseers or owners.

GREAT VALLEY.—Apprentices complain that if they are sick no notice is taken of them. The doctor does whatever pleases the overseer; and if they continue in the hospital, they are required to repay the time, and when they refuse, are taken before Mr. PRINGLE, who sends them to Lucea workhouse, to dance the treadmill and be flogged. A man present says his wife has been treated thus. The head driver says, when they are not cutting canes, they work regularly on taskwork, and sometimes so much is set them they are not able to finish it. They get no breakfast or dinner time, but go into the field at day clear, and return sometimes at four o'clock, sometimes at night. The people never agreed to work by the task, but are afraid of being taken before Mr. PRINGLE and punished. In crop time, they work from six till eight or nine at night, giving up their half Fridays, for which they receive two and sixpence per week. They have never made this agreement, but do the work for fear of punishment. Three cases of jackets were brought up, which had been injured by the salt water; they were opened to be sunned. The people said they were glad they had a massa in England to send them this present, but the overseer said it was not for them, but to be sent to Lucea and sold.

FAIRFIELD.—A ranger on St. Catherine's Hall says, he married a woman on Fairfield, by whom he has had seven children, four of whom are living, one an infant in arms. She is compelled to come to Catherine Hall every night to lodge. He went to her overseer to ask him for a little place to make a house for her, but he would not allow him to do it. Last year she was pregnant and they took her before the Magistrate and said she would not work. She was in the sixth month, and not able to do anything but light work. The was sent to the workhouse, and had a chain on, and was made to dance the treadmill for a week.

BAMBOO ESTATE.—Apprentices say they have not had a half Friday these two years.

FLOWER HILL.—Apprentices state, they receive no salt-fish, and have no mountain ground; are obliged to take land in the pastures, which is very bad, and trespassed in by the cattle. No notice is taken of those who are sick, and they are compelled to repay the time. The doctor does what the overseer says.—A boiler man complains that they do not get paid for their time. He went to the Magistrate, who said he must be paid, but the busha refused, and abused him and called him a bad negro for complaining about his time. The overseer, and a ranger also, struck him and pushed him down. He came to the Bay to complain, but the Magistrate refused to hear him; and when he comes on the estate he will not hear a word after the busha's story.—An old woman was put in the field, for the first time, in May last. She has had grand-children, and refused going to the field. She was sent to the workhouse by Mr. FINLAYSON, where she worked in chains in the streets. The Magistrate said, whatever the master said, she must do.—Another apprentice, a girl, was sent into the field at the same time, who had been taken out of the field three months before the rebellion, and has been in the house ever since.—Another woman complains, that the overseer has put her children into the field since the first of August, who never were in the field before. The Magistrate says, what the busha tell, they must go by it.

CHILDERMAS.—The apprentices are compelled to work extra hours for ten pence a day during crop, though they have made no agreement.

DEARNE HILL.—An apprentice says, "Mr. COCKING (S. M.,) does not allow you to speak at all, but takes and cats you." The people have no attention paid them when sick.

BEVERLEY.—An apprentice says, about a year ago she was confined, and her child was sick. She took him to the overseer, who refused to do any thing for him. The child died. She was two months sitting down before she was confined, for which she was brought before the Magistrate about two weeks after the child died. She commenced on the 13th August, and worked every Saturday till a few weeks ago, since which time she has worked on her half Fridays. She has not had her salt fish or allowance like the rest these two years.

PITFORE PEN.—Apprentices complain, that taskwork has been set them without their being consulted. They work from six to six, and can get no breakfast or dinner time on account of the amount of work that is set them.—A woman, with a child four months old, is required to do the same work as the rest.

ROUND HILL.—An apprentice says, he is obliged to be with the cart every Sunday. When Mr. PRINGLE comes he will not listen to the people, after hearing what busha says.

HARTFIELD.—The apprentices are a jobbing gang, and work twelve miles from their houses and grounds. A pregnant woman from this estate complains, that she has to work up to the time that the pains seize her, and has to find the midwife herself, and to repay all the time she is in the house. No time is allowed them to suckle their children. Mr. FINLAYSON tells them they must do whatever busha tells them, and when she replied, Mr. NORCOTT told them they should not do so; he said, she had no business to mention Mr. NORCOTT, and sent her to solitary confinement for six days, where she was kept on short allowance and nothing allowed for the child. If the child is sick, she has to pay four dollars to the doctor.

CATHERINE MOUNT.—In the short days, the overseer used to say the apprentices did not work the nine hours, and stopped a little of their time; now, in the long days, they are scarcely ever allowed to leave work till dusk. The Magistrate ordered them to have their proper dinner and breakfast time, but the overseer said they should not get it. The Magistrate won't hear what they have to say; the busha speaks to him first.

LEOGAN.—Apprentices complain of being compelled to remove their grounds. There is no mountain land belonging to the estate, but they had good grounds before on Amity Hall, seven miles distant; when the present attorney (HISLOP) came, he gave them grounds on Dearne Hill, his own property, nine miles from their houses, and only gave them a month's notice to remove their grounds. Their provisions were unripe, and of no use. They got no compensation for removing, and their new ground is very bad. They did not complain to the Magistrate, Mr. COCKING, because he is as good as living upon the property, and will never hear what they have to say. The head constable, who has a watch, says if the people lose three or four hours in turning out in the course of the week, the Magistrate takes away as many of their Saturdays. The overseer, besides taking back the time himself, by keeping them in the field later at night, frequently complains to the Magistrates and gets their Saturdays. The pregnant women are allowed one month after delivery, but are sometimes worked till within a day or two of being confined.—The nursing mothers turn out with the rest. The hothouse is locked up day and night. There is a dungeon on the property, with a stone arch, dark, and so confined that damp drops upon the prisoners like dew. It was not used during slavery. Apprentices are put in without any orders from the Magistrate.—EMMY MACKINTOSH was locked up for a night, by the attorney. She was a nurse to the child of his concubine, and he complained that she did not prevent the child from crying.—MARGARET SAMUEL is the washer for the house. She washes for the attorney, his concubine, and for his daughter by another woman, and for Mr. COCKING, the Special Magistrate. When she had to wash for Mr. C. she complained that the clothes were too much. She was locked up in the dungeon by the attorney, and when she came out was threatened, and now is obliged to wash the clothes.—A cow died from weakness and age, which was being used to carry sugar to the wharf. The head cartman, THOMAS FOWLER, was ordered by the Special Magistrate to pay £16. for it, or to be sent to Lucea Workhouse for three months, to dance the treadmill three times a day, and receive fifty lashes going in and coming out. The people offered to assist him; and all of them (about fifty) worked three half Fridays and three Saturdays to pay for the cow—being rated, carpenters at three and fourpence, and first-gang negros at one shilling and eight pence. THOMAS FOWLER is still working in his days, and they won't give him any account, or tell him whether the amount is paid or not. In crop time, they work from 4, A. M., till 8, P.M., for five days, for which the trashmen and cane carriers receive five shillings per week. They were brought into this arrangement by being threatened to be worked on the "nine hours' spell."

THE PARISH OF HANOVER.

Statement of SARAH NELSON and BESSY GRANT, from PHŒNIX ESTATE.—They were sent here (Savanna-la-Mar Workhouse) because they were not able to grind sixteen coppers of liquor a day. The apprentices on that estate are divided into two spells, each of whom were ordered to grind eight coppers of liquor. They often worked from 1 o'clock, P. M., to four the next morning. There was only one spell of mules, who sometimes laid down from fatigue, and so stopped the mill. Last year the people received tenpence per day for their extra work, but this year they receive nothing. The Magistrate (HULME) at first said, they could not be compelled to do night work; but afterwards he d—d them, and said if they did not grind the eight coppers, they should work all Friday, Saturday, and Sunday. He lives on the estate, and has all he wants from it. He will never listen to the apprentices, and does whatever busha pleases.—We obtained a copy of their commitment, in which their offence is stated to be "combining, and resisting work," and "insolent and disorderly conduct." They are sentenced, together with a man named WILLIAMS, to hard labor in the penal gang, and to the treadmill twice a day for twenty minutes, for the space of two calendar months.—A gentleman has communicated to us notes of complaints made to him at various times, by oppressed apprentices, of which several relate to Phœnix Estate. On the 14th of last month, six apprentices, including the three above named, made to him the statement of their being divided into two spells, each of which was tasked to grind eight coppers of cane juice a day, which compelled them to work continually through the greater part of the day and night.

During this week, they state, the first spell made short work, and, in consequence, the mill feeders and cane carriers for *both* spells were ordered by the Magistrate to work on two Saturdays, which they did on the 4th and 11th instants—on which days they worked without breakfast or dinner time, and had none to cook for them or to bring a drink of water. They complain that the task of eight coppers a day for each spell is too much, especially as the cattle and mules are not sufficient for the work. They sometimes lie down in the mill and keep the people waiting a long time. One of the complainant's states, that *he works day and night, and never goes to his house through the week.* On a subsequent occasion, five boys stated to the same individual that "they are the cattle drivers, (at the mill,) and that they drive constantly through the week, day and night, and get no rest until the mill stops on Friday. They get no pay. The apprentices charge one shilling and three pence for their half Friday. The attorney came and abused them all for a set of rascals, and complained that they worked two years, and never charged for their half Fridays. Some of them told him that the beasts would be worked to pieces by the work busha put upon them. He said, 'I will give you plenty of beasts.' None have come to this time, which is four weeks, and four cattle have since died.* Before he went away, the constable asked the people whether they agreed to go upon the same plan as last year. They said, for the goodness of Master QUARREL (the proprietor residing in England) they would give up the Friday, although they were not getting any salt fish." This almost incredible amount of nightwork is also exacted on Glasgow estate. See the statement of an apprentice from that property, in the Journal, and the following account, previously given by the same negro, to the above-mentioned individual.—CYRUS WALLACE says, " he is a boiler; *boiled sugar till past one o'clock on the afternoon of Sunday,* the 29th January last. The bookkeeper told them (the boilers) that unless they finished boiling off the sugar left on Saturday, they and the busha will have it out —meaning, as WALLACE thinks, that busha would get them punished. He has boiled sugar all the week, and *never has time to go to his own house, by day or night, until the end of the week.* They work every Saturday, *and sometimes finish boiling off at daybreak on Sunday morning."* Next follows an account of the circumstance mentioned in the Journal, of his being locked up on Saturday for refusing to work when he was ill. He says, also, that he " had the measles last year, and was ordered to pay the time back that he lost by sickness, and that this is a common practice on the estate. Overseer puts them in the dark room any time. Among others, ANNA BUCHANAN STEVENS had sore throat and

---

* Our informant, in a letter recently received, observes, "I have heard that sixty head of cattle have died during this crop season at Glasgow. It is on this estate, as on Phœnix, if the apprentices were not more able to endure fatigue and privation than their cattle, they would die off in like manner."

pains before Christmas, and Mr. MURDOCK, the overseer, had her confined in the dark room for six weeks. At the end of that time, she and another woman named SARAH DALRYMPLE, broke out through the flooring, and went to the Magistrate, Mr. OLIVER, who said they must go back to the estate, and he would get Mr. PHELP, the Magistrate of their district, to settle it. When Mr. PHELP came to the property they were taken up by the constables, and asked by Mr. PHELP what they had to say? A. B. STEVENS told him how long she had been locked up. He said he wished not to hear it, and sent them to the treadmill at Savanna-la-Mar for about two weeks and a half. During the time they were locked up on the estate, the Magistrate visited the property, but they were not brought before him.

HANOVER AND WESTMORELAND.

FROME ESTATE.—Two apprentices state, that "in crop, the mill is put about at four o'clock in the morning till seven o'clock the next morning—no breakfast time or shell-blow being allowed. The coppers are kept boiling through the night. A spell of people come out of the field at seven o'clock, to relieve the boiling-house people. They thus get every other night to sleep, but must be in the field the next morning by daylight. They work on Friday, and sometimes on Saturday. The apprentices receive nothing for all this extra work, and if they go to ask for anything, are brought before Mr. PHELP to get punishment. The only men who have been paid are two of the boilermen and the head cartmen. About two or three weeks back Mr. PHELP came, and Mr. MACFARLANE, the overseer, went and called two or three overseers, who valued the people's work, and said it was not enough. Mr. PHELP commits the whole gang to pay four Saturdays. Through the year, they are constantly taking away our Saturdays. When busha wants to hire the people, and they say they won't, because they know he won't pay them, he sends for the Magistrate directly and values the work, and says, you won't hire, and now I shall take your Saturdays for nothing. We don't get a day to work our mountain grounds, which are six miles from the estate; we are obliged to go to them on Sunday. We receive no salt fish. We have had no clothes these two or three years, except two or three yards of canvas this Christmas. The busha has shot several of the people's hogs. If a man raise a little fowl, when they want one for dinner they send for it and kill it. Before last August, the busha came to the negro houses, and took away one fowl belonging to one of us, two of the other, and three of a third apprentice, who is not present. —— says he went up to ask for his fowl, and the busha said he would not give it back, but should eat it for his dinner. I went to the field and was talking about the fowl, when he said I was making a noise, and sent the constable to lock me up in the dungeon.

"A week after, he brought me before the Magistrate, and said I was making a row in the field. He sent me for fourteen days to the workhouse, to work in chains and dance the treadmill. When I came back, I had to pay four days. I had been before to the Magistrate about the fowl, and could get no satisfaction. ——— also says, he and his wife have been sent to the dungeon a good many times. His wife was sent when quite big with child two days and nights. The prisoners are fed on four heads of dry corn and a pint of water a day. His master and busha hate him because he is a baptist."

GROVE PLAIN.—An apprentice says, the negros turn out the same as in slavery, and work from sun to sun, getting half an hour for breakfast and an hour for dinner. In crop, their Fridays are taken away, without payment. The boilermen only are paid for nightwork. Their mountain grounds are eight miles from the estate. No watchman is allowed; any beast may go and destroy them. Their master sends out salt fish, but the people get none of it from month to month. "The fish is there, and we perishing for want of it." No notice is taken of the sick, who are sometimes locked up in the dungeon, which is a shocking place. "The busha locks up plenty of people, without telling the Magistrate."

FRIENDSHIP, the Estate of LORD HOLLAND.—Apprentices make the following statements:—"In the first offset, (August 1st, 1834,) the agreement was that we were to receive our salt-fish. Some have got none from that day to this. We get none unless we do extra work beyond what the law obliges us, as watching at night by turns. Those old women that have been serving a long time, and are not able to keep spell in crop, get not a grain of salt-fish from one year's end to the other. The people turn out to work the very same as during slavery. They get their half hours for breakfast and one hour and half for dinner, and never draw off at night till a quarter past six. On Friday we draw off at eleven, and get no breakfast that morning. In crop time, one spell goes in at four o'clock on Monday morning, and keeps there till six o'clock at night, when another spell comes in, and stays till six the next night—working a day and a night without dinner or breakfast time. For this, they receive two bitts a day, (fifteen pence.) No agreement was made. We have to give up all our half Fridays in crop, and get no pay and no time for them. Some women refused to work in this way, viz.: BETTRISS HOLLAND, KITTY JONES, DOLLY FERGUSON, CHRISTIAN WILLIAMS, and RUTH ALLEN. They were brought before the Magistrate for disobedience of orders; he would not allow them to speak, but sent them to the treadmill for fifteen days. One of them complains of pains in her joints to this day. This is two years ago, and since then we can't refuse. —Another apprentice, GEORGE BLAKE, when he was ordered to go to watch, in the first year of the apprenticeship, said he would go if they would pay him. They said he should do it without, as there was a law for it. He said, 'we heard we should never have to do anything in our extra time without being paid for it.' He was put in the dungeon four days and nights, when the Magistrate came and committed him to the workhouse for fourteen days, to work in chains and collars. He had to pay the time back in his half Fridays and Saturdays. His wife, CATHERINE BLAKE, was at that time employed in the house as a washer, but on account of her husband's offence she was sent into the field, where she remains from that day to this. She also gets no salt-fish. About five months ago, she was kept in the bilboes, day and night, for four weeks, without any Magistrate's order. Even when she went to work she had to carry the shackle. The punishment was for objecting to go to the field when she was a domestic. She is still lame from the effects of the bilboes. In the time of our last overseer, we could hardly eat our own bread, we were getting so uneasy. If the new overseer goes on well, we shall be comfortable; for as for the Magistrate of the parish we shall get no sort of satisfaction from him. As soon as the overseer makes his complaint, he makes out the writing of punishment. Missis (Lady HOLLAND) has been kind to we. We know that, whether we get the gifts that she sends or not; and we should wish to remain on the estate as long as we live. There was at one time a talk of a school on the estate, but lately we hear nothing about it. We should be thankful to get a lesson ourselves as well as our children."

GREEN ISLAND PEN.—The busha, BENJAMIN CAPON, "is constantly in the habit of striking, collaring, and kicking the apprentices—men, women, and children. They never complain to the Magistrate, because they get no right. The Magistrate takes away their days whenever the busha wants them. The apprentices have had no salt-fish for three or four months. Their grounds are destroyed by cattle, as no watchman is allowed for them. There is no hospital on the estate. If the people are sick, their days are taken away to pay back the time. They turn out to work at daylight, and never draw off till seven o'clock. Their half Fridays have been taken away since Christmas, without payment. Yesterday the busha ordered a girl to be switched by the constable, and locked up at night. Her mother, ORIANA WEBSTER, just said, 'hi! this picaninny work so hard from morning to night—no breakfast, no dinner time; and you go lock her up:' then he collared her, and ordered her to be fastened in the dungeon."

PETERSFIELD ESTATE.—"The people turn out from six, A. M., till seven, P. M., and get half an hour for breakfast and an hour for dinner. In crop time, they have to keep spell through the night, for which they are paid as on Friendship Estate. Sometimes their Fridays are taken away, without payment, and they are always made to work more than half the day. Their provision grounds are seven miles off, and trespassed on by the cattle, as there is no fence. No attention is paid to the sick. The flogging is the only thing that makes it different from before. The busha tries everything to get we punished. The Magistrate won't allow you to speak for your right."

ROARING RIVER.—The apprentices, out of crop, work about the same hours as on Petersfield, and in crop, they work from four, A. M., to seven, P. M. In crop, they get no half Fridays, and receive only two bitts for all their extra time during the week. They are compelled to work by the task, though they have made no agreement to do so. When the canes are dry, and will not produce the tasked number of coppers of juice, they have to work in the night to make it up. Out of crop, they are not allowed to leave the field on Friday till three or four o'clock in the afternoon. The busha sometimes says they turn out late in the morning, and gets four Saturdays taken away from them. Mr. OLIVER won't hear what the people have to say. "The busha tell we many way to choke dog without hang him : he would work we law fashion, and he would work we field fashion." The people had no salt-fish last year, and have only had it three times since Christmas. Sometimes the field cooks are taken away, and the people remain without food till night. When apprentices go to the treadmill they are obliged to work out the time. Mothers have to repay the time when their free children are sick, or if they take a day to bury them.—CATHERINE LEWIS and three other women were handcuffed and sent to dance the treadmill for sixteen days, because they asked for a little sugar and rum, as payment for their breakfast and dinner time during crop.

SHREWSBURY.—"Busha frequently locks the people up in the dungeon, even women with child. They are sometimes kept two or three days; sometimes he gives them a little corn, sometimes nothing. Sometimes he applies to Magistrate; at others, punishes without applying to Magistrate. Magistrate never comes on the property, except when busha writes him a letter; and then, right or wrong, he gives the busha satisfaction, and won't allow the people leave to speak. Out of crop, the apprentices are not allowed to draw off till two o'clock in the afternoon. In crop, their half Fridays are taken away, without payment. They are tasked to grind so many coppers of liquor, and if the canes don't yield, they have to work till daylight. They have only tenpence for their nightwork. For weeks before Christmas, the busha ordered the people to pay a Saturday, because he said they did not turn out early in the morning. They refused, because Saturday was their own day. He sent for Mr. PHELP and Mr. OLIVER, who came the noonday after with the police. WILLIAM SQUARRY and two other young men, and five of the principal women, were picked out, and the men catted, and the women sent to the treadmill for ten days. The police gave WILLIAM SQUARRY thirty-nine lashes on his bare back in the field. He was a constable, and was flogged as an example to the rest."

CORNWALL.—" When Mr. MULGRAVE was here he told we no more slavery, but apprenticeship; and that we were to get an hour for breakfast and two for dinner. We go on pretty well that year, but after, we only get half an hour for breakfast, and one hour and half for dinner. In crop time, we get no half Friday, nor any day or pay for it. One spell goes in on Monday, at four o'clock in the morning, and works till nine at night. The next morning the second spell does the same, and the first goes to the field. One spell thus works three long days and two short ones every week, and the other, two long and three short. The first gets two and sixpence a week, the last one and eight pence. No agreement was ever made. Mr. OLIVER says, we ought to do what master bids. After crop, last year, he wanted to take our half Fridays and give us the time on Wednesday. We refused because our mountain grounds are seven miles off, and we could not go and come back on the Wednesday. For this, two men were flogged by Mr. OLIVER, and another sent to the workhouse as an example to the rest. Apprentices sent to the workhouse have to pay back the time. 'The master sends out two puncheons of oatmeal for the children; they take it to feed hog, and say, the free children no use to massa. If you have any eggs, the overseer will give you a little oatmeal in exchange.'"

DEAN'S VALLEY DRY WORKS.—" We have not had a single half Friday since the new year came in. One of the apprentices, JAMES GRINDFIELD, went to Mr. Mc'NEEL, the attorney, and asked if he had stopped the half Friday. He came down to the property the next day, and began to quarrel and make such a racket, and told the overseer we were not to have it. Lord MULGRAVE told us we should get one hour for breakfast and two for dinner, but now we get only half an hour and an hour. We have had no salt-fish from the middle of last year till a fortnight ago; though we have been obliged to watch the cattle pen at night, without payment. If we leave work in the rain, they take away a Saturday to pay for it. In crop time, the people work in two spells, (see Cornwall,) the first gets twenty pence, and the other fifteen pence, for all extra time through the week. No agreement was ever made to work in this way. 'We give up all our time to make things easy, because we have no one to complain to. The only good thing is, that they can't lay we down and flog we on the estate.' The estate's cattle trespass in our provision ground. Young picaninny mothers get no oatmeal or sugar, and are obliged to come out to work at daylight with the rest. The people are sometimes kept in the field till blind dark. JAMES GRINDFIELD was sent to the treadmill for ten days, two years ago, for having prayers in his house. Mr. OLIVER said he had no right to do it."

FONTABELLE.—" On the first of August, the former attorney, Mr. GEORGE COLLO, agreed with the people to work one Friday and take another. When Mr. SHALLITO came, before Christmas he took away one Friday entirely. When we say it is a hard case, he takes us to the Magistrate to dance the treadmill for fourteen days. Mr. PHELP won't hear a word; he says, 'they brought him to Jamaica to put it quiet, and he shall put it quiet.' When he comes, if the overseer tells him we have not worked enough in the field, he takes away three or four Saturdays. Our mountain grounds are seven miles off, and are sometimes trespassed in. We go to work at sunrise, and have half an hour for breakfast and an hour for dinner, and never draw off till candlelight in the great house. In crop, the people work in two spells, and are tasked to grind seven coppers of liquor a day. If the canes are dry it can't be done. Nothing is ever paid, except to the boilermen. The busha puts the apprentices in the dungeon as he likes, without meat or drink, except sometimes he gives them two heads of corn and a pint of water. If the picaninny women don't turn out with the rest, they are locked up. 'We are worse off than before, only just the flogging.'"

SMITHFIELD.—ANN CAMPBELL is a house servant. "She has no allowance of food, no provision ground, no salt-fish. She has only one Saturday in two weeks. She has no support but what she receives from her Christian family (fellow apprentices, who are members of the same church.) She has no relations. She lost one of her legs by disease some years ago, and was obliged to get the carpenter to make her a wooden one, but has nothing to pay him. Her master said last week that a law came in to bring back flogging, and he should put a hoe in her hand and turn her into the field. All the domestics are treated in the same way."

CONTENT PEN: JAMES RANKIN, master.—"Before the law came in, nine or ten of us were expected to split one thousand shingles a day. About three months ago, master sent six of us to work, and said we must split one thousand a day. We could not do it, though we worked all day without taking fifteen minutes for our meals. He took us before Mr. KELLY, who said we must do it. Master took five of us down to the Magistrate, and got us catted—forty stripes each, and ordered us to make up the thousand a day. We made it up in our own time for five days; he then said it was six days, though he knew in his conscience it was only five. He then sent for the Magistrate, who ordered us to make up seven thousand. The women who are employed to scrape ginger, have to scrape thirty pounds a day out of forty pounds. Their friends are obliged to assist them through part of the night. Two weeks ago, the task was so great that eight women were obliged to take Sunday to finish it. The apprentices never agreed to work taskwork. When Mr. JAMES RANKIN came to the property, after his father's death, he told the people they were too rich and had too much time. He said they were too religious, and he should see if he could not make them work their grounds on Sunday. He used to make them come down to the Court House on Saturday, whether he had any complaint against them or not. When he saw one of them coming down from the ground on Sunday, where she had been to look for a little food, he laughed, and said, 'what you can work now on Sunday?'"

PROSPECT ESTATE.—This is under the same attorney as Fontabelle. The people perform a similar amount of extra labour in crop, for scarcely any remuneration; nightwork and taskwork, by compulsion, without any agreement: a heart-sickening story, corresponding in all its details with the preceding. Invalid women get no salt-fish, even those that can make themselves useful. An apprentice states, The former attorney, — COLLO, used to treat the people kindly; but now, if it were known that we were here, some of the people would come on crutches to tell their story to us.

THE PARISH OF CLARENDON.

GREEN PARK.—"We get no salt-fish, and are compelled to watch at night, without any payment. This is since Mr. CHAMBERLAINE left. They say, it is not Mr. C.'s time now. Since this Magistrate came, we live very unhappy; massa knows if we complain we shan't get our right, that makes him take away our time and do every thing."

YORK PEN.—Statement of ELIZABETH FRANCIS. (See our account of her valuation, page 270.) "Before the first of August, I was never in the field, but belonged to Mr. SCOTT's mother, who gave me ten shillings a week wages. Afterwards, Mr. SCOTT used to send me to Kingston to buy cloth, which I used to sell, and carry him the money. I was very sickly with a complaint in my stomach and my side. Mr. SCOTT sent me into the field the year before last. I was very often ill, sometimes for two or three months at a time. The doctor was a black man, from Parnassus Estate; we never had a white doctor. Because I was so sickly, and not able to do field work, I wanted to buy myself; and my husband, who is a free man, asked my master what he would part with me for. He ordered the constable to turn him off the property. He sent for Dr. RITCHIE to examine me, who said I was not so bad. When I spoke to the Magistrate on the property, he would not hear a word I had to say, but said, 'shut your mouth; if you are impudent to your master, I shall send you to the workhouse and have you catted!' When I came to be valued to day, they said I was a field negro, and valued me so high."

SHECKLES PASTURE.—This property has been recently sold, and its late proprietor, the Hon. WM. ROWE, President of the Council, has ordered all the people to remove to his other property, in Manchester, about thirty miles distant. One of them, THOMAS GALE, says, "he is living with a free woman, by whom he has five children. He would rather die than remove. He will not, cannot go and leave them. Many of the people have proposed to be valued. Their master says they must come into Manchester to be valued. The Magistrate there is his cousin."

BELLE PLAIN.—An apprentice states, "that he is employed chipping logwood. In the old time, four cwt. a day was considered straining work; now their master demands four cwt. and a half. They were unable to do it, though they gave up their breakfast time. Their wives, who belong to another property, offered to assist them to make it up in their own time, but they said we would rather go to the Magistrate, for if we do it once, we shall have to do it again. He told the constable, it is not worth while to impose upon us; we are not able to do it. For this, he was charged with impudence, and sent by the Magistrate to the treadmill for five days, and ordered to pay back the time. He came home last Sunday, and was so sick that he was unable to work all the week. Yesterday the master charged the constable to bring him to the Magistrates' Court to day. He was not, however, called up, for the constable told him he might go home, as the Magistrate would visit the property on Tuesday."*—Another apprentice from Belle Plain is a boy, about sixteen or seventeen. Four years ago he met with a serious accident. The doctor told his master if the boy lived he would never be of any use to him. His father, also an apprentice, took him home, and was at the expense of his medical treatment, and has supported him entirely till now. After having so long neglected him, his master, about two months ago, compelled him to turn out to work. He is evidently unfit for labor. His knee is much enlarged; he has not the proper use of his arm; and walks as if his spine was seriously injured.—Another apprentice from Belle Plain says, that he is a domestic, and hires himself out, paying five macs. (five shillings sterling) a week. He wanted to buy himself, and then his master told him he had been rated as a field negro.—Another, from the same property, complains of being compelled to chip four cwt. of logwood a day, which is the task of the old time. They never made any agreement to do it; and though they turn out at sunrise, and work till four o'clock, without breakfast or dinner time, they cannot do it.—Another is the mother of nine children—one free, and eight on the estate, most of whom are grown up. She has sat down for several years, but since Christmas has been ordered into the field, and is compelled to turn out with the rest."

WOODSIDE PLAIN.—Apprentices complain that they turn out at six, A. M., have an hour for breakfast, and do not draw off till five, or, on Friday, till one or two in the afternoon. One of them has nine children, of whom four are free, whom she has to support. Since she had the sixth child she was not expected to do much, but now she must turn out with the rest. She was taken before Mr. DAWSON, and though she showed him one of her children, which had the measles, he said it did not signify, she must turn out with the rest. The apprentices are allowed no field cook, no salt-fish. Their provision ground has no fence nor watchman, and is destroyed by the cattle.

BELMONT.—THOMAS THOMAS is a penkeeper. "His master

---

* We have reason to believe, that this and other cases on similar occasions, were deferred in consequence of our being present at the Courts.

brought him before Mr. GORDON, at Chapeltown, and charged him with insolence, disobedience, and refusing to work on Sunday. When he wanted to speak, the Magistrate told him to shut his mouth, and sent him to the treadmill for ten days. Before that, he never got his Saturdays or Sundays, or any payment or time in lieu of them; since then, he has refused to work on Sunday, and gets about half Saturday. When he came out of the workhouse, his legs were much injured. He was kept on for an hour at a time. The mill used sometimes to take the skin off the belly of the people. When they could not tread it, (and when hanging by their wrists,) the driver used to pull them from the mill by their legs, and throw them against it." The women had their clothes tied, and were served in the same way."—Other negros from Belmont informed us, they had been sent to the treadmill, "where the driver beat them on the soles of the feet with a bamboo."

THE PARISH OF ST. THOMAS IN THE EAST.

HECTOR'S RIVER.—An apprentice states, that "she has seven children—four apprentices and three free, and that she is compelled to work in the first gang, though she is old and infirm. Her youngest child, about two years old, has got the yaws. The overseer made her take it to the yawshouse, and there leave it. She is allowed to turn out an hour later than the rest to attend it, but does not see it through the day, except at dinner time. The people on Hector's River are worse off than any. Just after the first of August, they got their proper meal-times, but it was soon altered. They have never had their half Fridays."—Another apprentice on Hector's River has chronic rheumatism to such an extent that her joints are indurated and enlarged. She complains of being compelled to do work that she is not fit for.—Four apprentices from the same estate say, 'we turn out at sunrise, and draw off for dinner from eleven to one, and then work till dusk. Our houses are so far off that at dinner time we often have to return when the shellblows, with a hungry belly. Sometimes when sick, we are locked up in the dark room, and fed with three ears of dry corn and one pint of water. The hospital is kept locked on Saturday and Sunday. When the Magistrate comes upon the property, the constables are afraid to speak the truth. "Since the busha came all the best of the slave died." There was a young man, a domestic, who had the charge of a sick horse which died,—the busha took a spite against him, and when he fell sick, would take no care of him, nor allow him to go into the hospital. He died in the cane paths. "When any body dies belonging to you, if you beg the busha to give you the four o'clock, he won't listen to you, but work you till dark, and you are obliged to bury the dead when you cannot see your hand." The busha's table is sometimes supplied with provisions from the negro grounds. One woman complained to the Magistrate, who said the young man who fetched the provisions from the grounds, must pay for them; but he said he did it by the busha's order, and she got no satisfaction.—Another apprentice says, that her daughter is in the great house. Sometime ago she broke a glass goblet. Her mother procured two from Kingston to pay for it, but the busha deprived the child of her allowance and days for a month; and because the Magistrate of the district would not punish her further, he sent for Mr. WILLIS, who sent her to the treadmill. Not long ago, he threatened to horsewhip her, on which she ran away. The Magistrate sentenced her to be locked up for five days and nights.—JAMES PURTON, another apprentice on Hector's River, states "In the first year after August, the busha sent and took away eight fowls from me, and said, I had nothing to do but raising fowls. He put them in his own fowl house. About the same time, I caught two fish one Sunday night at the rock, having nothing to eat. The busha came to the rock, and took away one of the fish, and cut it in two, and took it to the great house to cook. I asked him if he was going to pay me for it; he said, he ought to punish me well, instead of paying me for it. After he came upon the property, about seven years ago, I was a shepherd, and he used to send me to punish at dinner time, at night, and on the Sunday, if any of the sheep died. If he want one to kill, and I tell him none properly fat, he punished me for not making them well fat. I had more than I could do—watching goats, sheep, and cattle, and cutting sticks to mend fences. My arm began to swell, and he would not take me into the hospital; and through his neglect I come to this ailment. About five weeks ago, my leg began to swell. I went to him, but he would not take me into the hospital. I then went to the white doctor, who said I must have a few days' rest. I was in the hospital for a week. He said I must make rope to pay for the time. Through the head man's goodness I escaped. He only made me work regular time, and passed the word for me as if I had done it."—The appearance of this negro was deplorable. His arm was about three times the ordinary size, and very much ulcerated. His leg was also very large, and apparently dropsical.—Another infirm woman complains, "that she is locked up in the black hole a week at a time, and only let out at shellblow. She is afraid to complain to the Magistrate. The manager won't attend to the doctor's orders, and the weak are forced into the field. Their provision grounds are distant, and their provisions are often stolen."—Another negro says, "that the busha sends a man to the grounds to dig provisions for himself.—LOUISA BURTON, a very infirm, dropsical woman, who is quite unfit for labor, has to pick cotton, or she would get no salt-fish. Four apprentices on the estate died last week."

ELMWOOD.—Apprentices from this estate complain, "that they never get their half Fridays. They turn out at six o'clock, and turn in from eleven to two, and then draw off at sunset. They get their salt-fish, but never made any agreement, nor were ever asked about giving up their time. Mr. DAWSON put down whatever busha wished. He would not allow them to speak, and gave orders to kill all their hogs. Mr. CHAMBERLAINE gave the people right. Mr. HENDY, the overseer, ordered the gate to be chained, and the Magistrate not to be allowed to go in. He went to Portland the day that he knew the Magistrate would come; but the book-keeper, his son, saw CHAMBERLAINE coming, and ordered a crooked man by the gate to put the chain on. Some of the apprentices cried out, why don't you open the gate to the Magistrate? Then he opened it, and for this the book-keeper ordered him to take a hoe and work in the field. *When the Magistrate comes, they cannot leave the field to go to complain to him.* When apprentices are in the hospital the door is kept locked, and their own brothers are not allowed to go to see them."

HAYNING.—Two apprentices from this estate say, that their master, — CARGILL, is anxious for them to have what is right. They work from sunrise till ten, and from one to six o'clock. Their master scolds the overseer when he does not give them their time. They do not, however, get their half Fridays.

MULATTO RIVER.—BECKFORD Ross "belongs to Belle Castle, but works on Mulatto River, nine miles distant. They turn out before sunrise and work till ten; go to work again at one, and work till quite dark. They have no half Fridays, and have to return to their homes after dark on that day—no time being allowed them for their distance. Mr. CHAMBERLAINE said they were to have their Fridays, but Mr. Ross said he would not let them. They have had no salt-fish this five months."

WILLIAMSFIELD.—" After the first of August, the apprentices were allowed three hours for breakfast and dinner; now they work from six till six, and are allowed only from ten to twelve for both meals. Their provision grounds have no watchman, and their provisions are stolen. Their attorney, who lives at Kingston, is good to them, but the overseer compels them to watch the curing house and cattle pen, without any allowance. Their turns come round every five nights.—One woman complains, that she is not allowed to see the child to give him suck, except at shellblow and at night. Mr. COCKBURN, the attorney, said she was to have time, but when he was gone the busha would not suffer it."

HAPPY GROVE.—" The apprentices have to dig six baskets of arrow root a day, although they made no agreement to work taskwork. Their Saturdays are often lost in making up the deficiency, as they sometimes can't dig two baskets a day; though on a good bearing piece, they can sometimes finish six baskets by four o'clock."

The apprentices from various estates in the district say, " they are more comfortable in their minds since Mr. CHAMBERLAINE came. He hears what they have to say, and does them justice."

WHEELERSFIELD ESTATE.—"The apprentices turn out at day dawn, (five o'clock at this season;) half an hour is allowed for breakfast, and an hour and a half for dinner, and they leave off work at dark, except that this week they have been drawn off just at sundown, about half an hour before dark. Soon after the first of August, the people who had been to hear Lord MULGRAVE explain the law, began to complain about the time; but they got no satisfaction, and now they never dispute about it, as they find it the best to let busha have his own way, and they try to be satisfied. The busha locks the people up for trifling faults. The Magistrate takes no notice of it, but goes by whatever the overseer says. They never get their half Friday."

AMITY HALL.—The apprentices say they are treated well by their overseer. They work the same number of hours as on Wheelersfield. When the master and mistress were here, they used to get their half Fridays, and for some time afterwards, but they have since been taken from them.

DUCKINGFIELD.—The hours of work are the same as at Wheelersfield. The people have never had their half Fridays. No agreement was made to give their time in exchange for the saltfish. Some of their Saturdays have been taken away from them for not turning out earlier than six o'clock. The women with six children are made to work in the field. Their provision grounds were so destroyed by the cattle that they have thrown them up, and depend now upon a little place which they have fenced off about their houses. The overseer puts people in the dark hole frequently, without sending for the Magistrate. No attention is paid to the free children.

HOLLAND ESTATE.—They work the same hours per day as at Wheelersfield. They got their half Fridays for about two months at first, but have never had them since. They never made any agreement to give up their extra time. The Magistrate frequently takes away their Saturdays, and, therefore, though they have good grounds, they are badly off. They are often obliged to go to their grounds on Sunday. Mr. DAUGHTREY and Mr. BLAKE used to hear what the people had to say, but Mr. WILLIS goes by what the overseer says, and will not allow any to speak. GEORGE WALTERS, a tradesmen, has been sent into the field to dig cane holes.

SECTION V.

JAMES WILLIAMS's CASE.—His statement to us on the occasion alluded to in our Journal, is as follows. "My master has an old grudge against me. I have been flogged seven times since the new law came in. He complained to Dr. PALMER against me for insolency, but Dr. P. gave me the right. He complained frequently to Captain CONNOR who also gave me the right, and never punished me. Massa said, 'Thank God, Dr. THOMPSON is come, and we have got a Magistrate who will see justice done.' He bear false witness against me and said, that I advise JOHN LAWRENCE not to be a constable, because he was so young. I never said any thing of the kind to J. L. Dr. THOMPSON order me thirty nine lashes. Finding him, and afterwards Mr. RAWLINSON so severe upon me, I went away to the King's House. I was away seven weeks, but I did not see Lord SLIGO because he was up at Highgate. When I returned, I was put in the cage at the Police station for a day and a night. I was then, by order of Mr. RAWLINSON confined for ten days in the dungeon on the property— Afterwards sent to St. Ann's Workhouse, where I received fifteen lashes, and danced the treadmill every morning and evening for nine days. I worked in chains on the road. I bruised my shin (on the treadmill) the first day, but on the second day I caught the step. Many people were sadly cut. You could not see any thing on the mill but blood. The prisoners on the mill, men and women were catted most miserably. When I came out of the workhouse, I was put in the cell for four days and nights, and ordered to pay fifty days to the property. This was a year ago last September. I was afterwards ordered fifteen lashes again for not turning the horses into their right pasture. I had so many different kinds of work to do that I neglected it. My master met me and held his stick over my head, and threatened to strike me three times. I said, it was not an earthly man that made the world, but that the man that made the world would come again. For this I was charged with insolence, and sent to the house of correction to dance the treadmill for seven days, and receive twenty lashes. When I came out, my massa send me to climb bread-nut tree, and cut bread-nut. I told him I am not able, my stomach ill, you flog me so severely since the new law came in. He said, if I did not make an end of him, he would make an end of me. I set off to Sir LIONEL SMITH, but was taken up by an overseer on my way and sent to Rodney Hall on Saturday, and kept there till Thursday; a constable fetched me, and I reached home on Friday late. I came before the Magistrate, who ordered me to receive twenty five lashes, and to be sent to St. Ann's Workhouse for a fortnight to dance the treadmill. My master says, he will bet £1000 he will make an end of me. He threatens me every day for my life, and I don't know how soon he may kill me. What make me so much afraid is, that he did kill a man; he got him ordered a severe flogging, and, because the constable did not flog him enough he ordered the policeman to take the whip. The man coughed blood. He went afterwards to Brown's Town to complain to Captain DILLON, and died in the town."

JAMES WILLIAMS also represented himself as being destitute of food in consequence of the cattle having trespassed in his ground while at the treadmill; and from his having to pay so many days to the estate. We saw several of the most intelligent and respectable negros from the same estate, who confirmed his statements assured us that his veracity might be relied on, and that he was as he represented, in a state of starvation. The money was subsequently advanced to him to purchase his term of apprenticeship, when he was valued for upwards of £46, though he had only seventeen months to serve till he became free. The "Narrative of Events," contains a much more detailed account, though the reader, who will compare the above statement made to us in Jamaica, with the "Narrative," dictated to a third party in England, will find them perfectly consistent. The "Narrative" has been published at length in the Jamaica papers, and has excited abusive and angry comments, but not one of its facts has yet been disproved. His master, G. W. SENIOR has published a letter on the subject which contains the strongest confirmation of the truth of the "Narrative." He admits many of the details, and does not deny the truth of a single one of JAMES WILLIAMS's statements; contenting himself merely with vilifying his character. The sum at which he was valued is a sufficient answer to these calumnies. It was the price not only of a capable and industrious, but of an honest and orderly apprentice. On the other hand, the baptist minister of Brown's Town in a letter, dated August 8th, 1837, has furnished us with the most convincing proofs of the truth of the Narrative. He observes; "I have carefully read the narrative as given in the Patriot; and though not an eye witness of what he (JAMES WILLIAMS) narrates, *I had heard from others most of the particulars, none of which had he at all exaggerated or misrepresented.*" He also states, that he read the Narrative to three fellow apprentices of JAMES, of whom he says; "In these three men I can place the strongest confidence. They declare that JAMES WILLIAMS's Narrative is true. In reading it to them, *the only error they could discover was, that Thomas Brown Lawrence* (called in the Narrative, THOMAS BROWN) *was not one of the three flogged by the Police. He was flogged by the constable of the property.*"

Documents relating to JAMES WILLIAMS have already been laid before the public, viz; the certificate of his pastor as to his veracity and general good conduct; a certificate to the same effect, signed by thirty three free men and apprentices who are acquainted with him, some of them residing at Penshurst; and lastly, the declaration of three intelligent and respectable apprentices on Penshurst, that they have heard the Narrative read, and that it is an unexaggerated statement of facts. In addition to which, we refer to the statements of negros from Penshurst in the preceeding section of the Appendix, some of which are the relations of circumstances mentioned by WILLIAMS.

We have thus adduced what appears to us incontrovertible evidence of the truth of the Narrative; and it only remains to ask, whether the flagrant perversion of the law by Special Magistrates, who are the table companions of the planters, and the present horrible workhouse discipline of Jamaica are to be permitted to continue. Can any one read JAMES WILLIAMS's Narrative, and persuade himself that the negros could have been liable to greater oppression, or endured a greater amount of misery, when they were slaves in name as well as in fact?

SECTION VI.

ARCADIA ESTATE.—In 1833, the proprietor of Arcadia published a pamphlet vindicating himself as a Christian slave owner, from the charges brought against him in the Anti-slavery Reporter. (No. 104.) When we contrast his sentiments with the past history and present state of Arcadia, we cannot but regard his experience as one of the most unhappy examples, of the consequences resulting from the dereliction of the plain principles of Christian duty, for a course of expediency and compromise. Of all the partners in colonial iniquity, none are more guilty than the professedly liberal, and especially the Christian proprietors, resident in England; and it is in discharge of a most painful duty, that we presume to place them, in the person of an eminent individual of their number, at the bar of public opinion.

Of the subjects discussed in the pamphlet alluded to, our present concern, is solely with those, which refer to the author's opinions on slavery; or to his defence of his course of conduct as a West India proprietor.

He intimates that he is opposed in principle to slavery, and anxious to see it abolished; due regard being paid to the interests of the planters, and to the fitness of the negros for freedom. Were we to judge, by the comparative earnestness with which, on the one hand, he describes his hatred of slavery, and, on the other, his repugnance to immediate abolition, and his views of the difficulties of a general emancipation, we should certainly come to the conclusion, that his sense of the former is feeble indeed, compared with his impressions of the latter. His remarks on the unfitness of the negros for freedom, shew an inexcusable ignorance of the facts of the case. When he speaks of the innate indolence of the negro, of the far more elevated natives of our eastern territories, in the scale of civilization; of the negros as the least fit of all human beings for entire freedom of person and action, and declares, that they are still only to be regarded as in their pagan state, he shows, evidently, from what "practical source" his information has been derived. Surely his tremendous responsibility, as the owner of three hundred human beings, ought to have impelled him by a sincere investigation, (we would say, by a personal inquiry if no other way were left open,) to ascertain, whether the premises were true, from which consequences are deduced, so important to the destinies of his slaves. We will, however, test him on his own principles. There are a number of men on every large estate who are entrusted with employments requiring great skill and intelligence. These men display prudence and industry, not to say acquisitiveness, in the management and increase of their own little property. Who will dare to deny that they are fit for freedom? and, if so, on what principle has the proprietor of Arcadia continued to retain them as slaves, profiting by their uncompensated labor?

An examination of the practical conduct of the proprietor of Arcadia, has brought us to conclusions equally painful. We will consider his statements *seriatim*. He denies, however, the right of any one "to intrude into his private affairs."* We disclaim any such intention; and in our turn deny, that the interests of the Slave Population of our Colonies, are the private concerns of any individual proprietor.

Charges contained in the *A. S. Reporter,* quoted from the "*Letter to Thomas Wilson, Esq.:*" with observations thereon:—

I.—"'Above all,' it is alleged, "he might have provided religious instruction; though to this hour nothing effective, we fear, has been done for that paramount object.' I ask the reader of my evidence, whether there be any plea, however futile, for such an insinuation? Does it not hold out, as plainly as possible, that Mr. KNIBB had been engaged as a religious instructor, and that I *then* was ready to renew the engagement if he had found it expedient to return to Jamaica?"

At the time the attorney of Arcadia gave Mr. KNIBB leave to go upon that estate and instruct the negros, he expressly forbade him to teach a single slave to read or write; and when J. VINE first went to reside on Arcadia, he found only one slave who could read.

II.—"'Mr. H. might have had, at least, an elementary school on his estate; he might have found a man and his wife competent to the task, &c., upon it. Had I told the Committee, 'even when urged,' all I had done, they would have known that, as such persons could not be obtained of the Baptist Society, I had applied to the Moravian Committee in London, for a resident instructor and his wife, and that if such persons are *not* on the estate it is only because I could *not* obtain them."

It is extraordinary that such persons could not be found, seeing the numbers who have subsequently been engaged under similar circumstances; but experience has shown that had such individuals been sent out, their efforts would have been successfully obstructed by the attorney of Arcadia.

III.—"'Did he wish to rescue his slaves from all necessity of Sunday labor?' Yes; he did: and it was among the first and chief things pressed upon the attention of the attorney on the estate; and further urged in the personal intercourse I had with him in London, just before the late insurrection, which has put every thing, for the present, out of course."

See the remarks on No. 4.

* " I require them to show what right the constitution of their own, or of any public institution, gave them to intrude into my private affairs, and found charges against me of having violated my own principles in the management of my *property!* ' *Letter to Thomas Wilson, Esq.*

IV.—"'He might have introduced regulations as to marriage.' I can only say, that if the greatest encouragement is not held out to the slaves on that subject, it is in direct contravention of my instructions: and I have no reason to imagine that on this point at least, the disposition of the attorney differs from my own. Married persons have, with other encouragements, all that very comfortable dwellings can give. Mr. KNIBB will bear testimony: he states; 'the estate is the most comfortable one, in every respect, that I have ever seen. The houses in which the laborers live are excellent, and every thing connected with the estate, has the appearance of comfort.'"

In a number of the Christian Record now before us, mention is made of a proprietor, who "concluded that giving instructions by letter in Scotland, and carrying them into full effect in Jamaica meant the same thing." The editor observes; "This is a misconception, to which the West India proprietors, resident in Great Britain, are notwithstanding so prone, that we know not how to avoid considering it a *determined self-deception*." We are credibly informed, that there is a row of good houses in front of the negro village of Arcadia, but that these are not allotted to the married people as an encouragement. The head people dwell in miserable hovels, a fact, that W. KNIBB could not have been aware of, when he wrote in praise of the negro houses of Arcadia. We can scarcely reconcile our author's remark on the favorable disposition of the attorney on this point, with the information he possessed of his character and conduct.

V.—"'He might have established compulsory manumission!' It is not needed. The power granted to the attorney gives him power to manumit any that are inclined to purchase it. A slave has recently been manumitted, who had no other ground of claim than the alleged verbal promise of the former proprietor, made several years ago."

The general reply to the charge of the A. S. Reporter, on this and the two preceding points, is weak and evasive. The example which is given, is most incorrectly stated. The facts of the case are as follows; "During the time of the former proprietor of Arcadia, one of the slaves was anxious to procure the freedom of his daughter. He bought two valuable male slaves, and placed them on the estate, in purchase of his daughter and her children. At that time a proprietor could not manumit a slave, without giving bond to the extent of £100 for the good conduct of the freed man, and for his maintenance, in case he should prove unable or unwilling to support himself. To evade this difficulty, a formal *written* document was executed, declaring the slave in question and her children exempt from labor for ever, and at liberty to reside on the estate, and receive their maintenance from it as formerly. This is what is called "*the alleged verbal promise of a former proprietor.*" When the present proprietor came into possession, this woman and her children were *re-enslaved.* They were worked, flogged and treated in every respect like the other slaves on Arcadia. Will it be believed, that at the very time the "Letter to THOMAS WILSON, Esq." was published; and until a recent period, she remained in bondage; and regained her freedom at last, not by the act of the proprietor of Arcadia or his attorney, but through an investigation ordered by Lord SLIGO into her case. The Governor also directed that, her claim, and that of her children, to wages, should be determined, *from the date of the apprenticeship;* and £200 currency was subsequently paid to her, for their wages from the first of August, 1834. She and her children have received no compensation for their labor, from the time when they were re-enslaved, till the commencement of the apprenticeship; and the value of the estate itself, would be no adequate recompense, for the cruelties and indignities, to which they were subjected during that long interval. This is an instance of slave holding and something more.

VI.—"'He might have entirely interdicted the flogging of females.' He has done so; and has the written assurance of the attorney, that his directions have been complied with."

VII.—" 'He might have given his slaves fifty-two week days in the year; he might have put down the driving whip in the field; he might have abolished (with Mr. WILDMAN) the night labor of crop.' I have yet to learn that Mr. W. has discontinued the night sugar boilings. (see his answer, Parl. Rep. No. 7993.) As to the rest, I have avowed, that such measures were only incipient:' indeed, time had not allowed for any thing beyond, and I cannot myself yet say what has been effected. Indeed my answer, No. 4635, shews how little confidence I have at present, in my own judgment, as to the practical consequence of extensive changes."

The proprietor of Arcadia, pleads ignorance, inexperience and want of confidence in his own judgment, " as to the practical consequence of extensive changes." In matters of such importance, none of these pleas have the smallest weight. He might have ascertained, without leaving his own counting house, that the number of slaves on Arcadia, was decreasing, though there was no disproportion of the sexes, and that this was owing in great part to the night labor during crop. Also that night work had long been generally discontinued in the Danish colonies, and in several of our own; and that this alteration, with the abolition of the driving whip, and many other improvements had been adopted on several estates, even in Jamaica, without any disadvantage.

Our author subsequently speaks of the honorable conduct of his negros during the late insurrection. Had he known all that transpired on Arcadia at that eventful period, he would have desired to blot out the remembrance of it for ever. Much might be written on this subject but we forbear. The proprietor of Arcadia has not been uninformed of the character of the individuals by whom his property has been administered. He must have been aware, that, from his attorney to the lowest book-keeper, all the white men on his estate, were living, some in concubinage, and others in promiscuous debauchery. Has he testified any displeasure at these things? Has he withdrawn his confidence from the actors in them, or manifested any gratitude to those who have brought them to his knowledge?

When the London Missionary Society concluded, soon after the introduction of the apprenticeship, to send out six missionaries to Jamaica, one of them was selected to reside on Arcadia. This individual was a man of well known reputation, the pastor of a numerous and increasing church, and one therefore, who made great sacrifices to embark in the missionary work. Few indeed, in the estimation of those who know him, of his own as well as other denominations, are more richly endowed with missionary qualifications. On his arrival on Arcadia, he was compelled to reside for a time in the same house with the overseer, who was living in the unhallowed way of the country. He endured indignities, and encountered obstacles; but meantime his spiritual labors were blessed. He and his wife taught upwards of sixty of the negros to read, and their church was prosperous and increasing. It was attended by numbers of the white inhabitants, a class that few missionaries have been favored to benefit, or to number among their spiritual children. One overseer was converted, and is now usefully employed in the Mico Institution, in promoting religious education. Among the negros, his services were equally useful, and, a circumstance, we believe unexampled hitherto, were not rendered unacceptable by the attendance of the whites. He has been compelled to break up his station, in the midst of a scene of distinguished usefulness, and to seek one where he may commence anew.

We have placed these things on record, not without painful feelings, nor from any other motive than a sense of duty; and we cannot conclude without stating our deliberate conviction, that a christian slave owner can only exercise a conscience void of offence towards God and towards man, by emancipating his slaves; and that that duty is not the less imperative at the present moment, because the era of complete freedom will soon be ushered in by Act of Parliament. The attempt to discover and pursue a middle course, demands not only a sacrifice of principle, but, if they are non-residents, involves them in the participation of evil, which it is fearful to contemplate.

lxxvi. APPENDIX.

SECTION VII.

STATISTICAL TABLES.

EXTRACTS FROM TABLES COMPILED BY HENRY HUNTER, ATTORNEY OF LATIUM ESTATE, JAMAICA.

Increase and Decrease, &c. on a Sugar Estate.

+ Increase. — Decrease within given period.	No. of Negros.	Date.			Births within given period.	Of those born, No. living on the 28th Dec. 1836.	Time.
— 23	523 500	June "	28th, "	1817 1820	36	6	16
— 18	500 482	" "	" "	1820 1823	38	21	13
— 9	482 473	" "	" "	1823 1826	36	20	10
— 26	473 447	" "	" "	1826 1829	23	12	7
— 8	447 439	" "	" "	1829 1832	30	18	4
+ 2	439 441	" "	" "	1832 1835	32	20	1
+ 3	441 444	" Dec.	" 28th,	1835 1836	24	23	—

INCREASE AND DECREASE ON A COFFEE AND CATTLE ESTATE BELONGING TO THE SAME PROPRIETOR.

Increase, within given period.	No. of Negros.	Date.
	177	1800
+ 29	206	1810
+ 47	253	1820
+ 61	314	1830
+ 23	337	1836

APPENDIX. lxxvii.

TABLE OF MEDICAL ATTENDANCE ON THE SUGAR ESTATE.

Through the years	1829	1830	1834	1835	1836
Visits of Medical Attendant	217	237	131	115	111
Patients prescribed for	4516	4067	834	554	867
Sides of foolscap written upon	398	276	77	50	66

DISTRIBUTION OF LABOR.

On 1st Jan.	1832	1833	1834	1835	1836
In Agricultural labor, viz.					
First gang	135	131	135	134	122
Second do.	60	60	60	59	64
Third do.	34	33	34	38	30
Fourth do.	27	27	27	11	16
Caring Stock	16	17	16	13	14
Various Jobs	19	17	19	16	13
Grass Cutters	15	17	15	19	18
Watchmen	24	25	24	25	26
	330	—327	—330	—315	—303
Mechanics, &c. viz.					
Domestics	15	15	13	16	15
Carpenters	9	9	9	11	11
Coopers	10	8	10	9	8
Masons	7	7	7	6	7
Smiths	1	1	1	1	1
	—42	—40	—40	—43	—42
Total that work	372	367	370	358	345
Diseased	4	3	4	4	1
Invalids	12	16	12	18	24
With six children or upwards	7	6	7	6	3
Servants at Great House	14	13	14	12	9
Young children	45	46	45	50	64
Total that don't work	—82	—84	—82	—90	—101
No. of Negros	454	451	452	448	446

COMPARATIVE VIEW OF TIME DUE FROM THE NEGROS TO THE ESTATE.

	Slavery.	Apprenticeship.
No. of working days in the year	280	231
Negro days	33	82
Sundays	52	52
Total	365	365

APPENDIX.

AMOUNT OF CROP IN VARIOUS YEARS.

N. B. The inferior items of Molasses and Rum are omitted, being in proportion to the Sugar crop.

1832			1833			1834			1835			1836		
hds.	trs.	brls.	hds.	trs.	brls.	hds.	trs.	brls.	hds.	trs.	brls.	hds.	trs.	brls.
369	35	8	238	36	7	363	2	0	290	4	5	*256	3	10½

EXTENT OF LAND IN CANES.

A.	R.	P.	A.	R.	P.	A.	R.	P.	A.	R.	P.	A.	R.	P.
374	0	26	352	3	31	361	2	31	324	0	20	317	1	10

* The Hhds. of 1836 were made of 44 inch staves, and those of preceding years of 42 inch, making a difference of 3 cwt. per hhd. in favour of the hhds. of 1836, the crop of which was in reality somewhat larger than that of 1833.

TABLE OF LOSS OF CATTLE AND MULES IN EACH YEAR.

	1832	1833	1834	1835	1836
Loss...	6	6	6	7	*13

* Five of this number being old Mules shot on account of disease. The loss of stock during crop on many estates is very great. See note at foot of page lvi. in this appendix.

From one of the preceding tables, it appears that the time legally due from the negros to their owners, has been diminished one-fifth by the apprenticeship law, and from the table of crops, that there has yet been no consequent diminution of produce or revenue, and this, notwithstanding the employment during slavery of a jobbing gang of slaves, to dig the greater part of the cane holes, which are now entirely dug by the estates' people. The difference is more than supplied by the apprentices on the estate working in their own time for wages, and in their master's, on a judicious system of task-work and remuneration, arranged by mutual consent. See the following table:—

COMPARATIVE TABLE OF CANEHOLES DUG BY JOBBERS AND ESTATES' NEGROS, FOR THE CROP OF 1831, 1832, 1833, 1834, 1835, 1836, 1837, 1838.

N.B. The acres of caneholes are placed, not under the years in which they were dug, but under those in which the plant canes from them were or will be cropped.

	1831.			1832.			1833.			1834.		
	A.	R.	P.	A.	R.	P.	A.	R.	P.	A.	R.	P.
Acres dug for plant canes by jobbers.	70	1	15	47	3	10	32	1	10	49	3	5
By estates' negros.	14	2	0	34	2	26	42	1	30	42	0	35
Total	84	3	5	82	1	36	76	3	0	72	0	0

(Continued on next page.)

	1835.			1836.			1837.			1838.		
	A.	R.	P.	A.	R.	P.	A.	R.	P.	A.	R.	P.
Acres dug for plant canes by jobbers,	28	1	30	0	0	0	0	0	0	0	0	0
By estates' negros,	29	3	10	35	0	10	58	3	5	76	3	36
Total	58	1	10	35	0	10	58	3	5	76	3	3⅙

To secure continuous labor in the digging of cane-holes through the fall season 1836, an agreement was entered into with 40 cane-hole diggers as under:

Every labourer to dig 405 cane-holes in the 4½ days due to his master, and to receive 10lbs. of salt fish and a daily allowance through the week of sugar and rum for beverage; the salt fish to be diminished in the ratio of 1 lb. for every 40 holes short of 405; and to work in the 1½ day of his own time, at the rate of 3s. 4d. for every 90 cane-holes.

The greatest labor performed by one laborer, was in three weeks or 13½ days,

Dug in estates' time — — — — — — 1130 caneholes
In his own — — — — — — — — 1017
—————
Total — — — — — — 2147 about 0 3 7 (A. R. P.)

For which he received 28lbs. of fish, and cash £1. 15s. 0d.

The whole quantity of 58 acres for the season was finished in 44 days, being 1A. 1R. 10P. to each laborer, at the following cost:

	£.	s.	d.
Rum, ¾d. per day for 6 days, for 40 Negros	0	15	0
Sugar, 1d. ,, ,, ,, ,,	1	0	0
Fish, 3s. per week, for 405 holes	6	0	0
Money wages Friday and Saturday	10	0	0
Expense of digging eight acres	£17	15	0
The cost of digging the 58 acres was therefore	£147	10	0
Had jobbers been employed, the cost would have been, viz. 58 acres at £8 per acre,	£464	0	0
Or had jobbers dug half, as would probably have been the case, under the old system	£232	0	0

Being in either case a considerable saving of expense, besides the increase of the prosperity of the estates' negros, by distributing the wages among them, that formerly went to the owner of the jobbing gang.

APPENDIX.

COMPARATIVE EXPENSE OF CLEANING PASTURES, &c. BY SLAVE AND FREE LABOR.

In cleaning of pasture land, what a jobber would demand £3. to £4. per acre for, the plantation laborer has done at £1. per acre, and made 2s. 6d. per day wages.

In falling a piece of woodland, the first gang of one hundred and forty-three laborers cleared in one day 10A. 2R. 0P. at three and four-pence each per day, or £23. 13s. 4d., or £2. 5s. 0d. per acre, which a jobbing gang would not have undertaken for less than £8. to £10. per acre.

Task-work in cleaning of canes has yet to be tried.

COMPARATIVE EFFICIENCY OF SLAVE AND FREE LABOR. FALLING WOODLAND.

The piece of woodland above-mentioned was cleared by laborers to the acre — — — — — — — 14
During slavery it would have required laborers to the acres — — — — — — — — 25 to 30

DIGGING CANEHOLES.

During slavery were required to dig in light soil in a day, laborers to the acre — — — — — — 31 to 35
During slavery were required to dig in clay soil in a day, laborers to the acre — — — — — — 40 to 47
The first being at the rate of holes per laborer, 87, or one hole in — — — — — — 8 to 9 minutes
The second being at the rate of holes per laborer, 68, or one hole in — — — — — 10 to 12 minutes

Since the introduction of the Apprenticeship, under the system of remuneration described above.

1 man, a strong laborer, has dug caneholes, averaging, per hole, 1½ minutes
1 woman, ditto ditto ditto 2¼ do.
1 man, an ordinary laborer, ditto ditto 3½ do.
1 woman, ditto ditto ditto 5 do.

During Slavery the daily labor by male and female averaged 70 minimum to 90 maximum.

For wages the Negros have dug in one day { Males 270, Females 200 } In Nov. 1834. { Males 280, Females 190 } In 1835 and 1836.

APPENDIX.

PARTICULARS OF WAGES PAID AND EARNED.

The rates paid for Cane-hole digging, &c. have already been stated.

WAGES FOR TRANSIENT LABOR.

A prime head man	3d per hour
An inferior do.	2d do.
First gang, able	1½d do.
Ditto, weakly	1¼d do.
Second gang, able	1¼d do.
Ditto, weakly	1d do.
Third gang, active	¾d do.
Ditto, lazy	½d do.

WAGES EARNED FROM 5TH JUNE, TO 1ST AUGUST, 1836, BY TEN LARGE FAMILIES.

				£.	s.	d.
1 ... 11 individuals	10 workers		43	14	2
1 ... 4	do.	2 do.		18	4	1
1 ... 17	do.	10 do.		31	4	2½
1 ... 9	do.	8 do.		35	8	0¼
1 ... 2	do.	2 do.		11	5	4
1 ... 12	do.	10 do.		24	8	0½
1 ... 26	do.	19 do.		42	5	2½
1 ... 3	do.	1 do.		19	18	1½
1 .. 10	do.	7 do.		18	13	0
1 ... 6	do.	4 do.		7	1	4

The following are instances of the highest wages and means among the whole population of the Estate; they are constantly held up as cases of imitation for others to follow by:—

	A prime Head Man.			Inferior Head Man.			First Gang Laborer.		
	£.	s.	d.	£.	s.	d.	£.	s.	d.
Estates' Allowances	38	5	4	21	6	8	8	3	9
Salary	10	0	0						
Wages for digging Caneholes				10	0	0	6	0	0
Ditto Spellkeeping				9	0	0	7	0	0
Value of house, estimated	5	0	0	5	0	0	5	0	0
Provision grounds, value of crop	32	0	0	21	6	8	16	0	0
Yearly Resources	85	5	4	66	13	4	42	3	9

RELIGION AND EDUCATION.

There are 83 married couples, who, with their children, amount to 293 of the population. "The whole are Baptists, who attend Salters' Hill Chapel, upon the line of the property. About 50 of the children are at school, which is encouraged as much as possible."

lxxxii.   APPENDIX.

GENERAL VIEW OF THE CHARACTER OF THE NEGROS AS LABORERS FOR TWO YEARS FROM 1st. AUGUST 1834, to 1st AUGUST, 1836.

Good workers of their provision grounds ~ ~ ~	60	Good workers for wages ~ 60
Indifferent ditto ~ ~ ~	106	Indifferent ditto ~ ~ ~ 145
Bad ditto ~ ~ ~	203	Bad ditto ~ ~ ~ 164
Free Children ~ ~ ~ ~	76	Free Children ~ ~ ~ ~ 76
Total	445	Total 445

SECTION VIII.

THE BAPTIST MISSION.

Statistics of the Baptist Churches and Schools in Jamaica, for the year ending March, 1837.

Number baptized during the year 2950
Number of members 16821
Number of inquirers 16146
Clear increase of members during the year ... 2800
Total number in connection with the Mission   32966

SCHOOLS.

Number of Day scholars 1622
,,   Evening do. chiefly adults .. .   451
,,   Sunday do. 5594

A history of the Baptist Mission in Jamaica would be a valuable addition to the more permanent records of missionary enterprise, which we already possess. Its commencement was obscure, but it has grown to a height and magnitude, within a comparatively short period, which has struck beholders with surprise; and none probably have been more impressed with silent wonder, than the individuals who have been the means, as feeble instruments in the hand of Divine Providence, of effecting so great a work. There are at present sixteen missionaries of this persuasion in the island, the majority of whom have a principal and several subordinate stations, under their care; or, in other words, they are the pastors of three or four distinct congregations.

It is impossible to suppose that labors so multiplied and extensive can be advantageously sustained by so small a number of missionaries, and we would affectionately suggest the importance of supplying additional aid to carry on the work, to the Directors and Christian supporters of the mission in this country. In addition to their more immediate duties, the Baptist and other missionaries have bestowed much effort upon the education of the apprentices and free children. We have already observed, that the extensive diffusion of education, by the missionaries, at a small expense, and by a very limited agency, is truly remarkable. An increased liberality, on the part of the Christian public in England, would enable them to multiply their schools and extend their efforts in promoting this grand object, with greater effect, and still more extraordinary results.

SECTION IX.

WILLIAM HAMILTON.

The sufferings of this individual during the last years of slavery, were alluded to by J. M. TREW, the agent of the Mico Institution, in a letter to T. F. BUXTON, which was subsequently given in evidence before the Apprenticeship Committee of the House of Commons. This letter was published with the other evidence appended to the report of that Committee, and was recently made the subject of a debate in the Jamaica House of Assembly, which afforded certain of the members an opportunity to vilify the man, who had thus dared to lift the veil that concealed the true lineaments of slavery. The following are characteristic examples :—

"Mr. Trew is "worse than a Baptist—the blackest sheep among them."—Speech of Mr. Hamilton Brown, in the Jamaica House of Assembly, 23rd February, 1837,

"An old offender."—Mr. Dallas.

"The publisher of a vile fabrication and of a wanton and malicious falsehood."—Mr. Leslie.

"The whole tale was got up for stage effect, and nothing else; it was not true—it could be nothing else than a deliberate falsehood."—Mr. Guy.

"Altogether a fabrication."—Mr. Watt.

"The work of imagination."—Mr. Hodgson."

The dispraise of such men is an honorable distinction, and accordingly J. M. TREW has placed the above at the head of a letter to one of the island newspapers, in which he has given a history of these proceedings of the House. A committee was appointed to enquire into the facts, by whom J. M. TREW and WILLIAM HAMILTON were examined; but as this long-threatened inquiry was conveniently deferred till near the close of the Sessions, no result of its labors is ever likely to be made public. It is more than possible, that the evidence of HAMILTON, as tending to prove more than was desired, has been expunged from the Minutes. Any but the most cursory mention of the atrocities perpetrated during slavery, would be incompatible with our present object, nor should we have alluded to HAMILTON's history, but for the above mentioned circumstances which connect it with the present system. HAMILTON was the only slave on the Bog Estate who dared to attend a place of worship; the only one of upwards of 400 negros who dared to live with his partner in marriage. For these offences he was degraded from being a first-rate mechanic and coppersmith, to the rank of a common field laborer, and sent to a swampy estate, thirty miles distant from his wife and family, where he narrowly escaped with his life. He had learned to read and write when a boy, by stealth, and during his banishment he kept a journal, which, though it is chiefly the record of his spiritual conflicts and his religious labors among the neglected heathen negros with whom his lot was cast, yet contains many incidental allusions to the sufferings of himself and his fellow slaves. A copy of this painfully interesting manuscript is in our possession. It is an interior picture of slavery, which exceeds perhaps, any that the world has yet seen, and has forcibly impressed us with the conviction, that the worst features of that horrible state of society, neither have been, nor can be laid open to public view.

On the introduction of the Apprenticeship he purchased his freedom; in reference to which transaction he stated to us, that during the time of his persecution, he was looking forward very anxiously to the new system; but when he heard that the power was to be taken out of the managers' hands, he gave up the idea of purchasing his time. His Overseer renewed his ill-treatment, and the Special Magistrate threatened to flog him. He then gave notice to be valued, and was appraised at £209, being at the time in ill health. Mr. TATE, his Overseer, then gave him one of the best characters in the country. He said too, that to be deprived of HAMILTON's services, would be a loss of £500 a-year to his proprietor, though he had been employing him as a common canehole digger. As TATE placed so high a value on him, he offered to be employed by him as a freeman, but was refused. HAMILTON stated—"Since this system, negros of my acquaintance have often applied to me to be a witness at their valuation. On one occasion a negro was to be valued who proved that he was a nonpredial. His master endeavoured to make him a predial so as to increase his amount. I said, the man has proved himself a domestic, at which the Special Magistrate took offence. Soon after I carried my son to be valued, when I was not allowed to say anything in his behalf. The boy was about fourteen. My witness valued him at £8. a-year. Mr. TATE browbeat the witness, and said he was not going to stand by to see a man's property taken away without its full value. He called upon Mr. STONE, a neighbouring proprietor, to be witness for him, who valued the boy at £26. a-year. I said—Sir, you are valuing the hair on people's heads. The Special Magistrate, Mr. KELLY, got into a passion, and threatened to put me in irons, and fined me £3. 10s. for disrespect to his Court, which I paid. The valuation was at length fixed at £22. 10s. I have not heard of a single case since of an apprentice purchasing his time in this district. The Magistrates and Proprietors appear to have leagued together to put a stop to it. Previous to that Mr. C. and Mr. S. both had apprentices who were purchasing themselves. Mr. C. sat as a magistrate to value for Mr. S., and Mr. S. for Mr. C. I heard that Mr. S. said we must value these people high, to prevent this habit of purchasing themselves. When the apprentices saw how they were treated in the valuations, they wanted to commission me to go to England to represent their case. I did not encourage it because I was not sure it would be right, and did not know how it would succeed. They would soon have raised money to take me and bring me back."

SECTION X.

RELIGIOUS INSTRUCTION AND EDUCATION.

The United Brethren have eight Stations.

The number of persons in their religious care is as follows:—

Communicants	1738
Members not yet admitted to communion	1451
Children	2209
Catecumems	3731
Total	9129

They have also under their superintendence—

25 day schools, chiefly on estates, some of them very small, but attended in the aggregate by	1043	children
10 Sunday Schools, chiefly attended by older children and adults	1220	
A number of Evening Schools, in which are receiving instruction	483	
Total	2746	

The statistics of the Baptist Mission have been elsewhere given. In addition to these two societies, there are the Rectors of parishes and island Curates, a few of whom are exemplary in the discharge of their duties. There are also Missionaries and Catechists of the Church Missionary Society, Wesleyan Missionaries, Scottish Missionaries of two societies, and Missionaries of the London Missionary Society; many of whom are successfully employed in promoting education among the negros, as well as in diffusing a knowledge of the saving truths of Christianity. Each society can number faithful and zealous laborers in the missionary work; each can recount the names of brethren whose praise is in all the churches. We do not possess the necessary documents from which to furnish statistics similar to those of the Moravian and Baptist Missions; but we cannot dismiss the subject without recording our deep sense of the value of their labors among the negro population.

In addition to the above, there are the agents of the Mico Institution, whose attention is more immediately limited to education. Their schools are numerous and efficient.

SECTION XI.

VALUATIONS.

" From the 1st August, 1834, to 31st May, 1836, 998 Apprentices purchased their freedom by valuation, and paid £33,998. From the 31st May, 1836, to the 1st November, in the same year, 582 Apprentices purchased themselves, and paid £18,217, making in all £52,216; a prodigious sum to be furnished by the negros in two years. This makes a large community of persons of provident habits, spread through the country, who are establishing themselves as small proprietors." (Communicated.)

From the above statement it appears that the desire to be free is daily becoming more general and more intense, and that the price of liberty remains the same, although the term of Apprenticeship is decreasing. The amount paid by the Apprentices, is a proof of the extent of the exertions and sacrifices they are willing to make for freedom, which can scarcely be appreciated, by those who are unacquainted with the disadvantages of their previous condition. The negros frequently raise the money by loans to purchase their freedom, and they are scrupulous in repaying money lent them for that purpose.

One of the most intelligent of the Special Magistrates, E. B. LYON, has furnished us with some information concerning the numerous valuations effected by him, during the first two and half years of the Apprenticeship. He adds, " I have particularly and anxiously watched the conduct of those, who have released themselves by purchase from their apprenticeship, not alone from the influence their example would naturally have upon the remaining bondsmen; but also as an indication of the disposition of the laboring population after 1840; and the result has been, that I firmly believe the island would have been in a far more prosperous condition, had there been no intermediate state; that the apprenticeship has rather tended to retard than develope the energies of the peasantry. I have had the opportunity of knowing that, of those who had freed themselves by purchase in my district, the tradesmen were engaged at first-rate wages, and the field laborers as managers of small plantations, or were settlers of plantations of their own. The women had husbands or families, who required their services for the promotion and increase of their domestic comforts; very few were under the necessity of hiring themselves out to service, but such as were, have conducted themselves creditably. I know of some receiving ten shillings per week as laundry maids and nurses.'

There are, however, other and less pleasing circumstances to be noticed in connection with valuations. The same magistrate in one of his official reports makes some important observations, from which we extract the following in a condensed form :—

"The narrow minded factionist refuses to adapt the laws to the new relations of a state of general and unconditional freedom; and discountenances and checks by persecution every approach to this condition. One species of opposition, is the exclusion of the husband or wife, freed by purchase, from the society of the wife or husband, who remains in bonds. It is not a mere threat of exclusion, but a proceeding systematized under the formalities of notices served, in which the parties are declared tenants, charged with an exorbitant rent; or in which they are warned to depart under the pains and penalties of the law. The Special Magistrate, in his struggle to protect the apprentice in his domestic rights, is then brought into collision with the Local Magistrates exercising jurisdiction over the persons released from apprenticeship. To mention a case or two : two female apprentices, to Mount Vernon, the property of Mr. McPherson, a local magistrate, both of whom were old African women, were purchased by their husbands, who were desirous that their lives should be devoted to the domestic comfort of their families; and that they should enjoy that necessary ease, which their years and infirmities required. The moment their certificate of freedom was granted, they were directed to leave the estate, and forbidden to enter the houses of their husbands, unless they paid a weekly sum for the privilege. My endeavour to protect them in their civil rights has created a considerable degree of irritation against me, among the magistrates and attorneys of the district generally. Mr. McPherson has threatened to issue his warrant under the Trespass Act for their apprehension. At Island Head plantation, Robert Graham purchased the remainder of his term, and was immediately ordered off the property, and forbidden to enter the house of his wife. A few weeks ago he crept into the house in the night. He is a Baptist, and they joined in prayer and sung a hymn. His arrival was reported to the overseer, who instantly ordered the constables to watch the door and apprehend him, which was done, but by some means he escaped and came to me. I trust I have for a time secured to him his domestic rights. At Buckingham and Boston, James Harris has six children, two of whom are incurably diseased, and requiring one person's constant attention; and Ann Barnswell had two children and an aged and impotent mother with two or three others. The moment their release was effected, they were served with notices to quit, or to remain only on condition of paying an exorbitant rent, though occupying the same houses with their apprenticed children, and relieving the estate from the necessity of supporting and nursing their sick and disabled families. The same system has been pursued at Garland Hall and Serge Island, and *I have reason to believe, it is as extensively and as insidiously carried on, in every part of the island."*

SECTION XII.

THE MARRIAGES OF APPRENTICES.

It may surprise one, who reading the Abolition Act literally, finds that, subject to the conditions which it imposes, the apprenticed laborer is in all other respects, "to all intents and purposes free," to be informed that this high sounding prerogative of freedom, purchased by the British nation for twenty millions sterling, does not enable him to contract marriage, without the written permission of his owner, or his owner's attorney or overseer. We have in our possession several original "permissions" to apprentices to be married. We have also been favored with the perusal of a correspondence relating to a marriage, which was contracted at the Baptist Mission Station at Yallahs, in the parish of St. David, during our stay there. The parties, two apprentices on Coley Estate, had wished to be married at church, and applied to their Special Magistrate, E. B. Lyon, to write to the rector of the parish, S. H. Cooke, and request him to publish the banns. The rector refused to publish the banns, and wrote a note to the overseer of Coley, in which he described the conduct of Special Justice Lyon, "As an impertinent interference with the management of the estate." It must be observed, that the said apprentices had lived together unmarried for several years, but the interests of religion and morality appear to be of secondary importance in the eyes of the rector of St. David's, to those involved in the management of a sugar estate. The Special Magistrate and the rector both wrote to the attorney of the estate, JAMES Mc WILLIAM, on the subject; who, in reply, assures the former, that his application to the rector to publish the banns, "*is certainly a most gratuitous and unprecedented interference with the internal regulations of the property, and quite unwarrantable.*" The Special Magistrate then appealed to the Governor, who directed his secretary to reply, "that there is no law to restrict the marriages of apprenticed laborers in any greater degree, than the marriage of free persons; and that His Majesty's Attorney General is of opinion, that the Rev. S. H. Cooke was, in the cases alluded to by you, bound to publish the banns." Notwithstanding this declaration of the rights of the apprentices, the estate's attorney and the rector successfully defied the authority of the Governor and Attorney General, and of the law itself; and the poor apprentices were compelled to contract a marriage which the law does not recognise as legal, at a dissenting place of worship.

The same correspondence discloses another case of two apprentices residing on different estates, who were anxious to marry, but could obtain permission from only one of their overseers; the other refusing his consent. We have an autograph letter of another estate's attorney refusing to permit an apprentice under his control to contract marriage.

SECTION XIII.

A. L. PALMER.

Dr. PALMER was appointed a Special Magistrate by Lord SLIGO, soon after the commencement of the Apprenticeship. When Sir LIONEL SMITH assumed the Government, he had been for a short time in charge of a district, in St. Thomas in the Vale, in which the apprentices had been mercilessly coerced by his predecessors. His impartial administration occasioned violent opposition on the part of the planters, and on the arrival of a new Governor, was the signal for a simultaneous attempt to procure his removal, by representing the parish as in a state of insubordination. Dr. PALMER suggested to Sir LIONEL SMITH, to issue a Commission of Inquiry into his conduct, and thus give his accusers an opportunity of establishing their charges, and to afford himself the means of vindicating his administration of the law. The Governor appointed the special magistrates and two *local* magistrates a Commission for that object, two latter being *planters* in a neighbouring parish. The proceedings of the Commission were characterised by extreme unfairness towards Dr. PALMER, and at its conclusion a report was drawn up and signed by the Commissioners, upon which he was immediately suspended by the Governor from his office. The report is in itself a complete justification of his conduct, and is an instructive illustration of the manner in which the planters and the Government interpret and carry into effect the *Abolition* Law. Every paragraph of the report might be quoted by Dr. PALMER in triumphant vindication of his impartial conduct as Special Magistrate. We quote the most important parts of it:—

" In the first place we consider the parish of St. Thomas in the Vale was in a quiet and orderly state, when Special Justice PALMER took charge of his district in July last. Secondly, that certain questions of law arose between the managers and the Special Magistrate, such as ' The right of the husband (in the Tulloch case) to visit his wife.' ' The eight hour system.' ' The want of time for going to work.' ' The want of cooks,' &c. ' The taking away of the hoes on Palm estate from the apprentices in their own time, and other supposed grievances,—all ending in opposite views, and inducing the magistrate to state his view of the law, in place of conciliating and restoring confidence.' "

APPENDIX.

We have explained on previous occasions what meaning the planters attach to the terms *order* and *quiet*, and their opposites, *disturbance* and *insubordination*. Before Dr. PALMER went into the parish, the apprentices endured the violation of all their legal rights in silence, despairing of redress from any appeal to the magistrate. On the arrival of Dr. PALMER their " *supposed grievances*" were brought before him, and the Commissioners themselves have enumerated a list of what they term " questions of law," sufficient to show how that law had been previously administered. That they were oppressions of the gravest kind will be evident to the reader of the preceding pages, particularly of the 13th chapter.

We would, however, call particular attention to the *supposed grievance* of taking away the agricultural tools from the apprentices on Palm estate. The apprentices have no food allowed them from the estates; they support themselves by cultivating provision grounds in their own time. To deprive them, therefore, of their hoes, is to deprive them of food. Such a measure, so far from being " a question of law," or a " supposed grievance," is the very extreme of malignant persecution. Such cases being brought before Dr. PALMER, could he do otherwise than state his view of the law? By what other mode could he redress wrongs and oppressions, but by pointing out the legal boundary within which violence and outrage should be confined? In the opinion of the Commissioners, however, he ought *to have conciliated and restored confidence*. The interpretation of these ambiguous expressions is contained in the succeeding paragraph:—" It is impossible that any reciprocal good feeling can exist between the masters and apprentices, when a *mutual understanding does not exist with the Special Magistrate, and those placed in authority over the laborers*," i. e. between the magistrates and overseers." This mutual understanding, when it does exist, is based upon the sacrifice of the rights of the apprentices. It is a maxim in the colony, that the irresponsible powers of the overseers must be upheld at all sacrifices of law or right. But the Commissioners supply the best commentary on their own proceedings and views in the concluding paragraph of their report:—" Having been called upon to report, and give an opinion on the administration of the law by the Special Justices of St. Thomas' in the Vale, we must observe, *that we consider Special Justice Palmer has administered the Abolition Law in the spirit of the English Abolition Act;* that, in his administration of the law, he has adapted it rather to the comprehension of freemen, than to the understanding of apprenticed laborers; and that the present state of St. Thomas in the Vale is to be attributed to such a mode of administration of the Abolition Law."

The Governor, on receiving this report, immediately suspended Dr. PALMER, " for his perverse conduct in the administration of the Law," or, as the Commissioners express it, for administering the law in the spirit of the English Abolition Act. Lord GLENELG has confirmed the Governor's decision, and directed Dr. PALMER's dismissal, and has thereby proclaimed to every planter and every Special magistrate in the West Indies, that the Abolition Law is not to be administered in the spirit of the Imperial Act. In this proceeding, the Colonial Office have made, for the first time, a distinct avowal of the policy on which they have been acting from the commencement of the apprenticeship; and it only remains to ask; if the Imperial Act is not to be administered in its spirit, which means according to the rules of an honest interpretation, for what object did the nation pay the ransom of £20,000,000 sterling? What have the negros, the objects of its benevolence and justice, gained but the exchange of a name, the privation of some of the necessaries of life, and new and more galling chains and punishments.

xcii.   APPENDIX.

SECTION XIV.

SCALE OF "THE INDULGENCES OF SLAVERY," AND THEIR EQUIVALENT IN EXTRA LABOR.

"Memorandum of extra allowances formerly granted to Slaves, say to a gang of 100, with a comparative view of labor, which ought to be returned if continued to Apprentices and Free Children under six years of age."

	£	s.	d.		£	s.	d.
To 34 barrels of herrings	56	13	4	By the hire of 34 able people for 52 half days (half Fridays,) or 26 whole days each	73	0	0
100 gallons of rum at 3s.	15	0	0	The hire of 20 second class, at 10d.	20	6	8
10 cwt. of sugar at 30s.	15	0	0	The hire of 12 in the grass gang, 5d.	6	5	0
Extra allowance of osnaburghs to 12 head people, domestics, &c. 720 yards, at 10d.	3	0	0	The hire of 13 able people for mill and boiling house, from four o'clock, A. M. till eight, P. M., 7 extra hours a day for five months, or 20 weeks of five days, equal to 700 hours, or 77½ days of nine hours, at 1s. 8d.	84	0	0
Half dozen head people's hats	4	0	0				
25 yards of check	1	12	0				
4 great coats or coatees	5	0	0				
100 caps	7	5	0				
1 tierce of fine salt	2	10	0	Hire of three dry trash carriers, and one child cleaning the mill bed, for the same time, at 10d.	13	0	0
1 puncheon of oatmeal	12	0	0				
2 dozen of port wine	3	15	0				

APPENDIX.   xciii.

	£	s.	d.
Medical attendance on 12 infants, supposed number, under six years of age, at 5s.	3	0	0
Clothing for ditto	7	13	4
231 working days of a nurse sitting down in field attending ditto, at 1s. 8d.	19	5	0
Probability of sickness of infants, equal to one for 100 days, and mother attending, at 1s. 8d.	8	6	8
Two hogsheads of fish, one at crop over, and one at Christmas	27	0	0
Hot liquor from coppers, and canes from mill, equal at least to one-third of a hogshead of sugar	8	0	0
Balance in favor of the negro	2	8	8
	£199	0	4

Besides the privilege of keeping goats, asses, horses, and horned cattle, and selling provisions. Boilermen and distillers who work continuously to be paid extra.

APPENDIX.

This scale was drawn up by a planting attorney, in the district of Manchineal, in the parish of St. Thomas in the East, for the purpose of obtaining without payment, the half-Fridays and extra time of the negros during crop. It is a document, which speaks for itself. It is an index to that fraudulent system, which has been so generally pursued towards the apprentices. The extra allowances, as they are called, which the negros receive, and some which they never receive, all of which are legally due to the apprentices, according to the letter and spirit of the Imperial Act, are placed as a set-off against an amount of time, which was given by the same Act to the negros, to be enjoyed as their own for their own benefit. The late Special Magistrate of the district sanctioned *agreements* on the basis of this scale, on several, if not on all, the estates in his district. The arrangement was in every instance a compulsory one; the extra allowances being of no equivalent value to the extra labor required, and which is rated in the scale, at from one third to one half the amount at which the services of negros are valued, when they desire to purchase their manumission. Many of the extra allowances also, it will be observed, are not distributed to those who perform the work, for which they are assumed to be equivalent, but according to the capricious and arbitrary arrangement which prevailed in slavery. Unjust, however, as the scale is in itself, and unjustly as it has been forced upon the negros, its terms have not been fulfilled by the planters; nor though the negros are coerced to perform their part of it, do they possess any means of ensuring the observance of the stipulation on the part of their taskmasters. The weekly distribution of herrings, which forms the principal item, has been sometimes discontinued for several months on estates, where negros were subjected to this scale.

The concluding remark, respecting the " privilege" of selling provisions, is worthy of especial notice. It would have been a fit addition to have enumerated the consumption of air and water as " privileges," which the planters accorded their apprentices of their own free bounty.

ERRATA.

Page 22, *ninth line* from the top, *for* "the members," *read* their members.

" 71, *nineteenth* ditto, *for* "indulged," *read* indulgent.

" 111, 19th and 20th ditto, *for* "droghero," *read* drogers.

" 123, 27th ditto, *for* "men," *read* man.

" 132, 32nd and 33rd, ditto, *for* "a once humane resident proprietor," *read* humane resident proprietors.

" 133, dele foot note, see Appendix E. Sec. VI.

" 215, 21st line from the top, *for* "wáve," *read* waive.

" 220, 28th ditto, *for* "workhouses," *read* workshops.

" 247, 5th line of the foot note, *for* "magistrates," *read* magistrate.

" 284, 34th line from the top, *for* "tanners," *read* tannin.

" 293, 1st line, *for* "she," *read* the.

" 330, 30th line from the top, *for* "at our," *read* of our.

" 339, 1st line, *for* "Friday night," *read* Friday nights.

P 18, 20, 25

86

142 - C g thorewood

use of treadmill —

gangs chained together. — use of

the iron collar.

253-6

258